GAINES & COLEMAN

# POST-LICENSING EDUCATION
## FOR REAL ESTATE SALES ASSOCIATES

SIXTH EDITION

EDWARD J. O'DONNELL

**Dearborn**™
Real Estate Education

This publication is designed to provide accurate and authoritative information in regard to the subject matter covered. It is sold with the understanding that the publisher is not engaged in rendering legal, accounting, or other professional service. If legal advice or other expert assistance is required, the services of a competent professional person should be sought.

**President:** Roy Lipner
**Vice-President of Product Development and Publishing:** Evan Butterfield
**Associate Publisher:** Louise Benzer
**Development Editor:** Tony Peregrin
**Managing Editor, Production:** Daniel Frey
**Art and Design Manager:** Lucy Jenkins

© 1990, 1993, 1996, 1999, 2002, 2005 by Dearborn Financial Publishing, Inc.®

Published by Dearborn™ Real Estate Education
a division of Dearborn Financial Publishing, Inc.®
30 South Wacker Drive
Chicago, IL 60606-7481
312-836-4400
www.dearbornRE.com

Printed in the United States of America.

06  07  10  9  8  7  6  5  4  3

**Library of Congress Cataloging-in-Publication Data**

O'Donnell, Edward J. (Edward James), 1939-
    Post-licensing education for real estate sales associates / Edward J. O'Donnell—6th ed.
      p. cm.
    Rev. ed. of: Post-Licensing education for real estate salespersons. 5th ed. c2002.
    Includes index.
    ISBN 0-7931-9325-7
    1. Real estate business—Florida. 2. Real property—Florida.
3. Real estate agents—Licenses—Florida. 4. Real estate business—
Florida—Examinations, questions, etc. 5. Real property—Florida—
Examinations, questions, etc.   I. O'Donnell, Edward J. (Edward James), 1939-
Post-licensing education for real estate salespersons.   II. Title.

HD266.F6G35  2004
333.33'09759—dc22

                         2004025082

# C O N T E N T S

# ACKNOWLEDGMENTS

The authors wish to express their appreciation to the following persons who were willing to provide their professional advice and the assistance necessary for the completion of this edition.

The authors are indebted to other Dearborn authors identified in this book, to the publisher's professional staff, and especially to the editor of this edition, Tony Peregrin. His suggestions and prodding were done in a most agreeable way and helped make this a better book.

Special thanks go to those individuals who thoughtfully and thoroughly reviewed this edition of the text:

John Anderson, Bob Hogue School of Real Estate; Mary Basler, Basler's Academy of Real Estate, Inc.; Jack R. Bennett, DREI, Gold Coast School of Real Estate; Richard T. Fryer, ABR, Institute of Florida Real Estate Careers, Inc.; and Andy Gray, Andy Gray Schools of Real Estate, Inc. Particular thanks go to Sharon O'Donnell for her creative ideas.

We also would like to acknowledge those who reviewed previous editions of this book:

John F. Phillips, Ph.D., Curtis H. Wild, Donald L. Ross, John L. Greer, James Sweetin, Mary E. Sweetin, Anthony L. Griffon, Ron Guiberson, Linda Crawford, Audrey Van Vliet, Ronald O. Boatright, Terrance M. Fitzpatrick, Lawrence D. Greer, Robert L. Hogue, Michael Rieder, Roger L. Satterfield, Donald E. Tennant, and Audrey M. Conti.

# INTRODUCTION

Florida real estate sales associates must complete the 45-hour post-licensing education course before their first license renewal, on subjects approved by the Florida Real Estate Commission. This book is approved by the Commission for use in meeting the post-licensing education requirement for sales associates.

This textbook will give new licensees the opportunity to build on the principles and practices learned in the prelicensing course and to present new, hands-on training in many important subject areas.

Because many licensees work in residential real estate, the topics covered in this course book focus primarily on that part of the real estate industry. Many of the principles and practices described in this book also apply to the commercial and investment sectors.

Learning objectives are listed at the beginning of each chapter to help the student focus on the most important points. Discussion questions are provided throughout each chapter to help the student acquire a more complete understanding of the material. A quiz has been included at the end of each chapter for additional review of the material.

The book is divided into five sections arranged in the logical sequence of real estate activities: law and planning, listing and marketing properties, selling real property, obtaining financing and closing the transaction, and working with investors.

Section I updates the licensee on the many complex and important laws that regulate the licensee's daily activities. A chapter on business planning helps the new licensee get organized.

Section II focuses on building a strong listing portfolio, including prospecting, pricing the property, making the listing presentation, and getting the listing agreement signed.

Section III shows the licensee how to work with buyers effectively, from the initial contact with a buyer to analysis of the buyer's needs and ability to purchase to showing the property. A detailed section on sales and option contracts is included, as well as a chapter on writing and presenting the offer.

Section IV concentrates on obtaining financing and closing the sale. The coverage starts with an evaluation of current lending practices and programs, and continues with a step-by-step discussion of how a loan is processed after a contract is written. Another chapter gives the new practitioner a step-by-step guide to getting the contract to closing. Responsibilities of each cooperating sales associate are covered in detail. The section ends with complete coverage of closing statements.

Section V is an overview of investment in real estate, covering advantages and disadvantages of each property type. The student will have an opportunity to practice financial analysis techniques. The final chapter covers the management of investment property.

We have attempted to make this text as thorough and practical as possible and included many new features that we hope you find helpful.

A **"Forms-To-Go"** section is in the back of the book with symbols like the one on the left to show you when a form is available. The section has FREC registration forms, brokerage relationship disclosures, and other forms you might find useful in your daily practice.

**WEB LINKS**

**Web links** are indicated throughout the book with an icon like the one shown on the left, so you can use the Internet to find more resource material.

At the end of this book are six items of interest:

1.  Appendix of Resources, which lists books and articles appropriate for further study in each subject area;
2.  Practice Final Exam of 100 multiple-choice questions similar to those in the end-of-course exam;
3.  Glossary of key terms identified in the chapters, with definitions;
4.  Index;
5.  Forms-To-Go Section to provide the student with useful forms for real estate practice; and
6.  Course Feedback Form, to be completed once the course has been taken.

While it is difficult for one book to meet all of the needs of every real estate sales associate entering the profession in Florida, it is the intention of the authors that this book provide a bridge from basic classroom knowledge to deeper understanding and practical hands-on experience in real estate.

Please complete the Course Feedback Form with your specific reactions and suggestions once you have completed the course and submit it so that the authors may improve the book for those who follow you.

We wish you well.

*Edward J. O'Donnell*

*George Gaines, Jr.*

*David S. Coleman*

# LAYING THE FOUNDATION FOR A SUCCESSFUL CAREER

The section will familiarize licensees with the important license law changes relating to the broker's relationships with customers. It describes the disclosure forms that licensees must give to clients and customers with whom they work and lists the situations when the disclosure requirements do not apply.

State and federal laws that affect real estate are also described to help the licensee stay current on important laws such as fair housing, property condition disclosure, federal income taxes, and lead-based paint disclosures.

In Chapter 2, the student will learn the basics of developing a business plan, setting goals, and time management. ∎

# LEGAL ISSUES AND RISK MANAGEMENT

## LEARNING OBJECTIVES

Upon completion of this chapter, *you should be able to*

1. describe the required education for the first renewal and the required education for subsequent renewals;

2. describe the differences between fraudulent misrepresentation and negligent misrepresentation;

3. list at least six questions that should be asked in a property condition disclosure form;

4. list the differences between the duties of single agent brokers, transaction brokers, and brokers with no brokerage relationship;

5. distinguish between the terms *principal* and *customer;*

6. list the different disclosure forms a licensee must give to buyers and sellers of residential property and understand the uses of each; and

7. describe the legal requirements for including the personal name of a licensee in an advertisement.

## OVERVIEW

This chapter is intended to update new real estate licensees on laws and trends in the real estate industry so they can serve their customers professionally. This course must be completed before the first renewal or before applying for a broker license. The first section of this chapter describes how to renew a real estate license. The second section is designed to help licensees avoid charges of misrepresentation. A discussion of brokerage relationships describes the duties and disclosures required of licensees in their dealings with customers. The final section of the chapter is a review and update of important laws. ■

# RENEWING YOUR FLORIDA REAL ESTATE LICENSE

The Department of Business and Professional Regulation is required to send a renewal notice to the last known address of the licensee at least 60 days before the expiration date. Licensees who do not receive a renewal notice should ensure that the Department has their current address on file. If not, they should send a change of address to the Department using Form DBPR 0080-1. A licensee may also use the Department's Web site at *www.myfloridalicense.com* to change address and to renew his or her license.

After the first renewal, the license will expire on the same date every two years. If a licensee fails to renew the license, the license will become *involuntarily inactive,* and the licensee may not perform real estate services.

Licensees should send the renewal notice and a check to the Department before the renewal date, or renew online with a credit card. The renewal request must be postmarked on or before the renewal date to avoid a $45 late renewal fee. The late fee does not apply to the first renewal, as the initial license will become void if not renewed by the renewal date.

## Required Education for Renewing the Initial License

The initial real estate license expires on the first of two dates after 18 months have elapsed following issue: March 31 or September 30.

A sales associate must successfully complete a 45-hour sales associate post-licensing course before the first renewal. A new broker must complete the 60-hour broker post-license course before the first renewal. If the licensee does not successfully complete the post-license course, the license becomes void. A sales associate wanting to continue in real estate would have to take the prelicense course again and pass the state exam. If a broker does not complete the required post-license course, the broker's license will become void. The broker may, however, take a 14-hour continuing education course and apply for sales associate status. If the licensee wishes to become a broker again, he must successfully complete the broker prelicense course and pass the state exam.

Students failing the post-licensing education end-of-course examination prescribed by the Florida Real Estate Commission (FREC) must wait at least 30 days from the date of the original examination and pass a different end-of-course examination. A student may retake the prescribed end-of-course examination only one time, and the exam must be taken within one year of the original end-of-course examination. Otherwise, students failing the Commission-prescribed end-of-course examination must repeat the course before retaking a different form of the examination.

A licensee who has received a four-year degree in real estate from an accredited institution of higher education is exempt from the post-license education requirements.

## Required Education for Subsequent Renewals

Before all subsequent renewals, a licensee must complete a FREC-approved 14-hour continuing education course.

The licensee should not send proof of the required education with the renewal application but must retain the original grade report for at least two years following the end of the renewal period. If audited by the DBPR, the licensee must furnish the original grade report. Licensees who are unable to provide the grade report if audited are subject to disciplinary action.

# MISREPRESENTATION AND CONDITION DISCLOSURE

While the legal definition is much broader, the common definition of **misrepresentation** is the act of a licensee who, either intentionally or unintentionally, fails to disclose a **material fact** or makes a **false or misleading statement** that is justifiably relied on by another, resulting in damage. Intentional misrepresentation is actionable as *fraud*. Unintentional misrepresentation is *negligence*.

Buyers sometimes claim misrepresentation by the listing brokers. All licensees, regardless of their brokerage relationship, have the duty of **disclosure,** that is, the duty to disclose material facts affecting the value of residential property. Buyers frequently ask brokers to describe a property and to make representations about the condition of the property or other facts associated with the sale. A licensee may never conceal material defects about a house.

To win a fraudulent misrepresentation case against a broker, the plaintiff must prove

- the broker made an error in giving information, oral or written, to the buyer or failed to disclose a material fact to the buyer
- the broker knew the statement was not accurate or the information should have been disclosed
- the buyer reasonably relied on such statement, and
- the buyer was damaged as a result

The buyer is entitled to relief if the representation was a material inducement to the contract. The broker's duty stems from the seller's duty not to misrepresent.

In establishing liability or in applying remedies, it does not make a difference whether the misrepresentation was fraudulent (intentional) or negligent (unintentional). The most common remedies available to the offended party include monetary damages, rescission of the contract, forfeiture of the broker's commission, and disciplinary action by the FREC.

## Careless or Negligent Statements

Brokers must consider carefully statements made to buyers and sellers. Because a broker is considered a real estate expert, the consumer may rely on what the broker says, even when the broker does not act as the buyer's agent. Some statements licensees should never make include the following:

- "No need to get a title search. I sold this same property last year, and there was no title problem."
- "Don't worry, the seller told me by phone I could sign the contract for her."
- "I won't be able to present your offer until the seller decides on the offer submitted yesterday."
- "Don't worry about the due-on-sale clause. The lender will never find out about the sale."

## Avoiding Misrepresentation

A real estate licensee can take several practical steps to decrease the risk of misrepresentation claims:

1. Have the seller complete a **property condition disclosure** form, such as the one shown in the Forms-To-Go Appendix, and discuss any potential problem areas.
2. Inform the seller of the legal duty to disclose material facts that affect the value of residential property and are not readily observable.
3. With respect to condominiums, find out about the following common problem areas
   - House rules regarding children, pets, and waterbeds
   - Location of lockers and parking stalls

1    ■ Existence of special assessments (for what and how much)
2    ■ Maintenance fee(s) (what is included, proposed increases)
3   4. Ask about factors external to the property that might influence its value and affect a
4      person's decision to buy, for example
5      ■ Abutting and nearby uses (present and proposed), for example, a rock band next door
6      ■ Highway expansion, rerouting of a bus line
7   5. Do not make statements concerning matters about which you do not have firsthand
8      knowledge or that are not based on expert opinion or advice. Have a list of
9      government agencies from which you can get information. Suggest that the buyer
10     check things out, too, by giving the buyer the telephone numbers and Web site
11     addresses of the appropriate government agency. It is best that important technical
12     information come directly to the buyer from the government agency.
13  6. Do not participate with the seller in nondisclosure of required information. If the
14     seller refuses to disclose material defects, decline the listing. Taking a listing of this
15     nature is not worth damage claims, loss of reputation, and loss of license.
16  7. Avoid exaggeration. If you wish to venture a "quick" opinion about things you are not
17     certain about, make sure the buyer understands that it is only a guess, and be certain
18     the buyer does not rely on it in making a decision.
19  8. Disclose pertinent information in writing, such as in a property condition disclosure
20     form from the sellers. The buyers should sign the disclosure indicating that they have
21     received it. A confirmation letter would confirm earlier discussions in which you
22     pointed out a leaky roof or the need to consult with a soil engineer, and would affirm
23     that neither you nor the seller makes any warranty as to the condition of the roof or
24     the foundation. Keep copies of these documents in the transaction file.

## Home Inspection

One of the most effective risk-management tools available to licensees is a home inspection.
The inspection is intended to disclose defects in a building that buyers, sellers, and real estate
licensees have missed. It is better to identify problems before the closing so the parties can
negotiate a settlement. If a material defect is discovered after closing, the buyer may sue the
licensee rather than the seller, who may now live in a distant city.

Florida does not regulate or license home inspectors. To become a home inspector, a person need only call himself one. Home inspectors rarely guarantee their work, and most have a
disclaimer limiting damages to the amount of their fee.

The licensee should encourage the buyer to select his or her own inspector; otherwise, the
buyer may infer collusion between the sales associate and the inspector if the inspector misses
an important defect. Many excellent home inspectors are members of the American Society
of Home Inspectors.

**WEB LINK**

American Society of Home Inspectors: www.ashi.com

## Other Laws Affecting Disclosure

**Death in a property.**  For years, residential licensees were unclear about what disclosures were
required when a murder, suicide, or death occurred in a house. A law change in 2003 removed
the duty of a seller or a licensee to disclose such incidents.

*The fact that a property was, or was at any time suspected to have been, the site of a homicide,*
*suicide, or death is not a material fact that must be disclosed in a real estate transaction. A cause*
*of action shall not arise against an owner of real property, his or her agent, an agent of a*

*transferee of real property, or a person licensed under Chapter 475 for the failure to disclose to the transferee that the property was or was suspected to have been the site of a homicide, suicide, or death or that an occupant of the property was infected with human immunodeficiency virus or diagnosed with acquired immune deficiency syndrome. [689.25(1)(b), F.S.]*

## THE REAL ESTATE LICENSE LAW

Students should be familiar with the Florida real estate license law and stay current on important changes to the law. This section covers brokerage relationships in detail and reviews and updates licensees on other requirements of the law.

## AUTHORIZED BROKERAGE RELATIONSHIPS

A real estate licensee may work with potential buyers and sellers

- as a transaction broker (this relationship is presumed under state law unless the licensee enters into a different relationship with the customer)
- as a single agent
- with no brokerage relationship
- as a designated sales associate (but only in a nonresidential transaction)

Florida law prohibits **dual agency,** because a licensee cannot be an advocate for both parties in a transaction.

If a single-agency relationship is established with a residential seller, all licensees in that brokerage firm have single-agent duties to that seller. It is not legal for another sales associate in the firm to represent a buyer when selling that property, nor can that sales associate be a transaction broker. It would, however, be legal for the sales associate to work with the buyer in a no-brokerage-relationship role.

If a broker has a single-agent relationship with a principal, the broker may change ("transition") to a transaction broker relationship. The licensee must make the appropriate disclosure of duties to the buyer or seller. The principal must give written consent before the change. A **customer** is not required to enter a brokerage relationship with any real estate licensee. [475.278(1)]

## DISCLOSURE REQUIREMENTS FOR RESIDENTIAL PROPERTY TRANSACTIONS

A licensee in a residential sales transaction must give a brokerage relationship notice to potential buyers or sellers before or at the time of entering into a listing agreement or before the showing of property, whichever occurs first. A *residential sale* is defined as

- property with four units or fewer
- unimproved residential property intended for use of four units or fewer, or
- agricultural property of ten acres or fewer

The four types of required brokerage notices include the following:

1. **No Brokerage Relationship Notice**
2. **Single Agent Notice**
3. **Transaction Broker Notice**
4. **Consent to Transition to Transaction Broker Notice**

Brokers must keep copies of the disclosure notices for all residential transactions that result in a written sales contract for at least five years.

### Property Transactions That Do *Not* Require Disclosure Notices

A licensee need not give a brokerage relationship notice when

- the licensee knows that a single agent or a transaction broker already represents the potential seller or buyer
- an owner is selling new residential units built by the owner and the circumstances or setting should reasonably inform the potential buyer that the owner's employee or single agent is acting on behalf of the owner, whether because of the location of the sales office or because of office signage or placards or identification badges worn by the owner's employee or single agent
- selling nonresidential property
- renting or leasing real property, unless the buyer has an option to purchase all or a portion of the property improved with four or fewer residential units
- holding a bona fide "open house" or model home showing that does not involve eliciting confidential information; the execution of a contractual offer or an agreement for representation; or negotiations concerning price, terms, or conditions of a potential sale
- engaging in unanticipated casual conversations with a seller or buyer that do not involve eliciting confidential information; the execution of a contractual offer or agreement for representation; or negotiations concerning price, terms, or conditions of a potential sale
- responding to general factual questions from a potential buyer or seller concerning properties that have been advertised for sale
- the licensee's communications with a potential buyer or seller are limited to providing general factual information, oral or written, about the qualifications, background, and services of the licensee or the licensee's brokerage firm
- auctioning, appraising, and disposing of any interest in business enterprises or business opportunities, except for property with four or fewer residential units

## TRANSACTION BROKER RELATIONSHIP

All licensees are presumed to be working as transaction brokers unless they have entered into another brokerage relationship with a customer. A **transaction broker** provides limited representation to a buyer, a seller, or both in a real estate transaction, but does not represent either in a fiduciary capacity. The licensee "works for the contract" without being an advocate for either party. The customer is not responsible for the acts of the transaction broker.

### Transaction Broker Duties

A transaction broker owes the following duties to the customer:

1. Dealing honestly and fairly.
2. Accounting for all funds.
3. Using skill, care, and diligence in the transaction.
4. Disclosing all known facts that materially affect the value of residential real property and are not readily observable to the buyer.
5. Presenting all offers and counteroffers in a timely manner, unless a party has previously directed the licensee otherwise in writing.
6. Limited confidentiality, unless waived in writing by a party. The transaction broker may *not* reveal to either party
   - that the seller might accept a price less than the asking or list price
   - that the buyer might pay a price greater than the price submitted in a written offer
   - the motivation of any party for selling or buying property

■ that a seller or buyer will agree to financing terms other than those offered, and

■ any other information requested by a party to remain confidential

7. Any additional duties that are entered into by this or a separate agreement.

## Transaction Broker Notice

The Transaction Broker Notice must be given to a customer before or at the time of entering into a listing agreement, agreement for representation, or showing a property, whichever occurs first. The notice itemizes the legal duties of the licensee and informs the customer that his or her representation is limited, allowing the licensee to facilitate a transaction.

The customer should sign the Transaction Broker Notice. If a customer refuses to sign it, the licensee may still work as a transaction broker for that customer, but should note on the form that the customer declined to sign. The Transaction Broker Notice is shown in the Forms-To-Go Appendix.

## SINGLE AGENT RELATIONSHIP

A **single agent** represents either the buyer or seller, but not both, in the same transaction. The **principal** relies on the single agent to give skilled and knowledgeable advice and to help negotiate the best terms in dealings with the customer. Because only single **agency** creates a **fiduciary relationship,** only single agents may call their customers *principals*. The principal is responsible for the acts of his single agent.

## Single Agent Duties

A single **agent** owes nine specific duties to a buyer or seller:

1. Dealing honestly and fairly
2. Loyalty
3. Confidentiality
4. Obedience
5. Full disclosure
6. Accounting for all funds
7. Skill, care, and diligence in the transaction
8. Presenting all offers and counteroffers in a timely manner, unless a party has previously directed the licensee otherwise in writing
9. Disclosing all known facts that materially affect the value of residential real property and are not readily observable

## Single Agent Notice

The *Single Agent Notice* must be given before, or at the time of, entering into a listing agreement or an agreement for representation or before the showing of property, whichever occurs first. It may be a separate and distinct disclosure document or part of another document, but it is most often made part of a listing agreement or a **buyer brokerage agreement.**

The notice should be signed. If a principal who wants the single agent form of representation refuses to sign a Single Agent Notice, the licensee may still work as a single agent for that person but should note on the licensee's copy that the principal declined to sign. The Single Agent Notice is shown in the Forms-To-Go Appendix.

## Role of Sales Associates

Sales associates are agents of, and act for, the employing brokers. If a seller's broker has a listing, that broker and all the sales associates in that firm represent the seller.

## Transitioning from Single Agent

When a single agent for one party begins working with the party on the other side of the transaction, the single agent must be either a nonrepresentative with the other party or transition to transaction broker. In that case, he or she may not disclose to the other party any confidential information learned while he was a single agent.

> **EXAMPLE:**  Broker James listed the Smiths' house as their single agent. Sally, a licensee in Broker James' office, is working as the single agent for a buyer, Mr. Farley. Mr. Farley becomes interested in the Smiths' house. Because the broker cannot represent both parties (dual agency), the broker obtains the informed written consent of both parties for him to transition to transaction broker status.

## Consent to Transition to Transaction Broker Notice

The *Consent to Transition to Transaction Broker Notice* allows a single agent to change his or her brokerage relationship to that of a transaction broker. The principal must sign this notice before the single agent becomes a transaction broker. The Consent to Transition to Transaction Broker Notice is shown in the Forms-To-Go Appendix.

# NO BROKERAGE RELATIONSHIP

Licensees working with no brokerage relationship to the customer owe the following duties:

1.  Dealing honestly and fairly
2.  Disclosing all known facts that materially affect the value of the residential real property that are not readily observable to the buyer, and
3.  Accounting for all funds entrusted to the licensee

A single agent for one party in a transaction may decide to work with the other party as a nonrepresentative. If a broker does not have a brokerage relationship with a customer and is a single agent for the other party, the customer is at a disadvantage. It is the duty of the single agent to work diligently for his principal and to get the best price and terms for the principal.

The duties of a licensee who has no brokerage relationship with a buyer or seller must be fully described and disclosed in writing to the buyer or seller. The *No Brokerage Relationship Notice* must be given to prospective buyers and sellers of residential property before showing a property. The notice need not be signed. The No Brokerage Relationship Notice is shown in the Forms-To-Go Appendix.

---

### DISCUSSION EXERCISE 1.1

**Nonrepresentation.**  Broker Helen lists the Smith's home as a single agent. Later, Helen shows it to Mr. Jones, a prospective buyer, and gives him a No Brokerage Relationship Notice.

While Helen is writing his offer for the property, Mr. Jones says, "I'll pay the asking price of $200,000 if I have to, but I would like to start the negotiations at $185,000."

When Helen presents the offer, she must tell the Smiths that Jones has said he will pay up to the listed price. Failure to make this disclosure would expose her to disciplinary action and civil liability for violation of her fiduciary duties.

---

## THE DESIGNATED SALES ASSOCIATE

A broker may legally appoint one sales associate in the firm to act as the agent for the buyer (or lessee) and another sales associate in the firm to act as the agent for the seller (or lessor). This status may be used only in a nonresidential transaction. In this status, each **designated sales associate** is an advocate for the party he or she represents in the transaction and can actively help in the negotiations. To meet the requirements of the law, buyers and sellers must have personal assets of at least $1 million, must sign disclosures that their assets meet the requirement, and must request this representation status. The licensees must give the parties a *Single Agent Notice* and a *Designated Sales Associate Notice*. The Designated Sales Associate Notice is shown in the Forms-To-Go Appendix.

---

**DISCUSSION EXERCISE 1.2**

**Designated Sales Associate.** FatBurgers, Inc., is searching for five store locations in Pompano. It engages Mary Stevens of Pompano Commerce Realty as single agent because of her knowledge and expertise in the Pompano fast-food field. Jack Wilson, of the same firm, represents the seller of one of the potential sites.

FatBurgers, Inc., wants Mary to be its single agent, so the broker appoints Mary as a single agent for FatBurgers, Inc., and Jack as single agent for the seller. Mary and Jack are now designated sales associates.

---

## SELECTED LAWS REGULATING REAL ESTATE PRACTICE

Chapter 475, F.S., and Chapter 61J2 of the Florida Administrative Code, the rules of the FREC, are changed as the need arises. Licensees may stay current on the law by using the Division of Real Estate's Web site.

**WEB LINK**

Division of Real Estate: www.state.fl.us/dbpr/re/dre.shtml.

---

### Broker Applicants

A person who applies for a broker's license must hold

- an active real estate sales associate's license for at least 12 months during the preceding five years in the office of one or more real estate brokers licensed in this state or any other state, territory, or jurisdiction of the United States or in any foreign national jurisdiction
- a current and valid real estate sales associate's license for at least 12 months during the preceding five years in the employ of a government agency for a salary and performing the duties authorized for real estate licensees, or
- a current and valid real estate broker's license for at least 12 months during the preceding five years in any other state, territory, or jurisdiction of the United States or in any foreign national jurisdiction

A person who has been licensed as a real estate sales associate in Florida may not be licensed as a real estate broker unless, in addition to the other requirements of law, she or he has completed the sales associate post-license course if it was required when the initial license was obtained.

1   ## Mutual Recognition Agreements

2   The Commission has reached **mutual recognition agreements** with ten states: Alabama,
3   Arkansas, Colorado, Georgia, Indiana, Kentucky, Mississippi, Nebraska, Oklahoma, and
4   Tennessee. Florida has ongoing negotiation with other states as well. The applicant may not
5   be a Florida resident when applying for mutual recognition. Applicants holding a real estate
6   license in one of these states may become a Florida licensee by passing a 40-question exam on
7   Florida Real Estate Law. Thirty correct answers (75 percent) are passing. Any Florida licensee
8   may become licensed in one of those states by the same method.

9       Nonresident licensees, whether or not they have qualified under mutual recognition,
10  must successfully complete the same post-licensing and continuing education required for
11  Florida resident licensees.

12  ## Licensee's Personal Name in Advertising

13  If a licensee wants his or her personal name to appear in a brokerage firm's ad, the licensee's
14  last name must be included at least once in the ad. The brokerage firm's name must be
15  included to avoid charges of "blind" advertising. For example, Joseph J. Perkins, a sales associ-
16  ate, could place an advertisement with "call Joe for more information," provided the ad
17  includes the brokerage firm's name and Joe's last name somewhere in the ad. [61J2-10.025(2)]

18  ## Antitrust Legislation

19  Brokers risk their assets and careers by attempting to get other brokers to charge a standard
20  commission. *Antitrust* laws prohibit any action by a party to fix prices or inhibit competition
21  by using unfair practices. Some of the prohibited actions include

22  ■   conspiracy to set prices
23  ■   splitting up competitive market areas
24  ■   conspiring to boycott cut-rate brokers or otherwise interfering with their business, and
25  ■   requiring a minimum commission before allowing listings to be circulated in any
26      service, such as through a multiple-listing service (MLS)

---

### DISCUSSION EXERCISE 1.3

**Boycotting.** Gloria, President of Big Tree Realty, Inc., had a luncheon meeting with Samuel, President of Statewide Residential Brokers, Inc. The subject of the meeting was Southern Discount Realty and the increased market share it had achieved since it announced its new discount fee structure. Big Tree and Statewide had previously had a 47 percent market share between them, but their combined share was now 39 percent.

They agreed to tell their sales associates not to show Southern Discount Realty listings to their buyers. Also, they agreed to call several other brokers in the area to do the same.

"A broker simply cannot give good service by charging that little. It's unprofessional," Gloria said.

If you were a sales associate for Statewide Realty and your sales manager suggested that you boycott Southern Discount listings, what would your response be?

---

27  ## Florida Growth Management Act (Chapter 163, F.S.)

28  Florida's Growth Management Act requires that every city and county in Florida prepare a
29  comprehensive plan of land use, together with controls that implement the plan. The com-

prehensive plan affects nearly every parcel of undeveloped land and many buildings that need renovation or enlargement. **Concurrency** is one of the significant requirements of the act. It requires that a minimum level of infrastructure be present before development can take place. **Infrastructure** includes such things as transportation systems, schools, and utilities.

Licensees must become knowledgeable about the comprehensive plans in their areas so that they can act competently with sellers and buyers. A licensee takes on substantial liability when representing that a site can be used for a specific purpose. Properties outside the urban services area are more difficult to subdivide, and the number of homes per acre is limited. This has affected the ability of licensees to market property for development. Most licensees, even after investigating the possible uses of an undeveloped commercial parcel, insert a land-use contingency clause into the contract for purchase. In this way, the buyer has the right to cancel the contract for property that cannot be used as represented.

Many cities and counties in Florida now require land-use disclosures before a purchaser signs a contract. Such disclosures may cover items such as

- restrictive covenants for the neighborhood
- the buyer's responsibility to investigate whether the anticipated land use conforms to comprehensive plan, zoning, building codes, and so on, and
- whether streets and drainage are publicly maintained or are the homeowner's responsibility

## The Florida Building Energy-Efficiency Rating Act (Chapter 553.990, F.S.)

The *Florida Building Energy-Efficiency Rating Accessibility Implementation Act* creates an energy-efficiency rating and provides for disclosure of the rating system for residential and commercial buildings. Disclosure must be made affirming that such a rating system exists, and a pamphlet explaining the system must be given to buyers. Pamphlets may be obtained from the Department of Community Affairs. A rating need not be given. A sample rating form is shown in Figure 1.1.

## Radon Gas Protection Act (Chapter 404.056, F.S.)

Some authorities say that **radon gas** is the second most common source of lung cancer in the United States. Radon is produced by uranium in the soil that decays and creates a gas. While radon gas is all around us, it is not usually a problem because of very low concentrations in the atmosphere. When uranium decays under a home the gas seeps into the home through foundation cracks and plumbing lines. Improved building techniques and insulation intended to provide energy-efficient homes have the unintended side effect of trapping the gas inside the home.

Testing is the only way to learn if radon levels are a health hazard. The EPA recommends intervention if testing shows radon level at four *picocuries* per liter of air. This would be a concentration approximately ten times that of outdoor air. Exposure to radon inside the home can be reduced to an acceptable level by sealing foundation cracks and other openings.

The radon levels in a building can also be reduced by mitigation systems. Such systems use PVC pipes installed through the slab with a fan that draws air from beneath the building and vents it above the roofline. Such systems may cost from $1,000 to $3,500. The electric cost for running the fan is only about five dollars per month.

**F I G U R E   1.1**   ■   **Sample Rating Form**

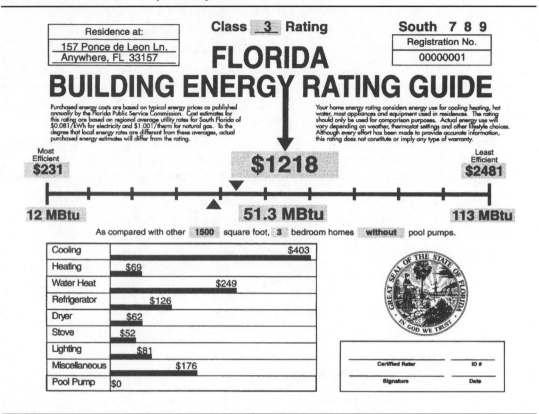

1  Florida law requires disclosure of the characteristics of the gas but does not require an inspec-
2  tion. The wording must be on every sale contract and on every lease contract for more than 45
3  days and is part of the Comprehensive Buyer's Disclosures seen in the Forms-To-Go Appendix.

**WEB LINK**

4  *A Citizen's Guide to Radon,* 2d ed. (U.S. EPA): www.epa.gov/iedweb00/radon/pubs/citguide.html

## Federal Residential Lead-Based Paint Hazard Reduction Act

6  Because of the danger of neurological damage, the *Residential Lead-Based Paint Hazard Reduc-*
7  *tion Act* requires that disclosure be made to purchasers of residential buildings constructed
8  before 1978. The law requires that the seller, landlord, or licensee provide the following
9  before the contract is signed:

10  ■  A lead hazard information pamphlet
11  ■  Information about the presence of any known lead-based paint or lead-based paint hazard
12  ■  A ten-day period to conduct an inspection

13  The lead warning statement shown in the Forms-To-Go Appendix must be attached to the
14  contract.

**WEB LINK**

15  U.S. Department of Environmental Protection: National Lead Information Clearinghouse:
16  www.epa.gov/lead/
17  U.S. Department of Housing and Urban Development: Office of Healthy Homes and Lead Hazard Control:
18  http://www.hud.gov/lea/leahome.html

## Comprehensive Environmental Response, Compensation, and Liability Act of 1980 (CERCLA)

The Comprehensive Environmental Response, Compensation, and Liability Act of 1980 imposes substantial liability on owners of real property that has been contaminated with toxic or hazardous substances. The liability also extends to other parties in a transaction, such as attorneys, developers, lenders, and real estate brokers. The liability in the act is joint and several, which means that all present or former property owners may be forced to pay (joint) or only one owner may be required to pay (several).

A purchaser who wishes to avoid liability under the statute must do intensive research, usually in the form of an environmental audit. The audit is expensive and time-consuming. The statute allows the purchaser to defend against any later action by claiming **innocent purchaser status,** provided that the purchaser exercised due diligence to investigate the property. Licensees should be particularly careful when listing or selling sites such as former gas stations or dry cleaning establishments. Residential properties built on former farmland have been contaminated by pesticide use (Dioxin, DDT) or old farm gas tanks that have leaked. Other problem areas for residential licensees are old, leaking heating oil tanks buried in the ground.

## The National Do-Not-Call Registry

In June 2003, the Federal Communications Commission (FCC), exercising its authority under the Telephone Consumer Protection Act (TCPA), established a national Do-Not-Call Registry. The registry is a list of phone numbers of consumers who do not want to be contacted by commercial telemarketers. It is managed by the Federal Trade Commission (FTC), the nation's consumer protection agency, and is enforced by the FTC, the FCC, and state officials.

The Do-Not-Call rules cover the sale of goods or services by telephone. Political organizations, charities, telephone surveyors, or companies with which a consumer has an existing business relationship are exempt from the Do-Not-Call rules.

A company may call a consumer, even if that consumer is on the registry, for

- 18 months after that consumer's last purchase, delivery, or payment, even if the consumer's number is on the registry, or
- three months after that consumer makes an inquiry or submits an application to the company

If the consumer asks the company not to call again, the company must honor the request.

## Accessing the Do-Not-Call Registry

Only sellers, telemarketers, and other service providers may have access to the registry. The Do-Not-Call registry may not be used for any purpose other than preventing telemarketing calls to the telephone numbers on the registry. The only consumer information available from the registry is telephone numbers. The numbers are sorted and available by area code. Companies will be able to access as many area codes as desired (and paid for), by selecting, for example, all area codes within a certain state.

Telemarketers must pay for consumer data in any area code before they or their telemarketer calls any consumer within that area code, even those consumers whose telephone numbers are not on the registry. The only exceptions are for sellers that call only consumers with which they have an existing business relationship or written agreement to call and that do not access the Do-Not-Call registry for any other purpose.

A company that is a seller or telemarketer could be liable for placing any telemarketing calls (even to numbers NOT on the Do-Not-Call registry) unless the seller has paid the required fee for access to the registry. Violators may be subject to fines of up to $11,000 for each call placed.

If a seller or telemarketer can show that, as part of its routine business practice, it meets all the requirements of the following conditions, it will not be subject to civil penalties or sanctions for mistakenly calling a consumer who has asked for no more calls or for calling a person on the Do-Not-Call registry. To successfully avoid penalties ("safe harbor"), the seller or telemarketer must demonstrate that

- it has written procedures to comply with the Do-Not-Call requirements
- it trains its personnel in those procedures
- it monitors and enforces compliance with these procedures
- it maintains a company-specific list of telephone numbers that it may not call
- it accesses the national registry no more than three months before calling any consumer and maintains records documenting this process, and
- any call made in violation of the Do-Not-Call rules was the result of an error

The best source of information about complying with the Do-Not-Call Registry rules is the FTC's Web site. It includes business information about the registry.

**WEB LINK**

FTC: www.ftc.gov/donotcall

## Florida's Do-Not-Call Law

The Do-Not-Call registry has not affected Florida's Do-Not-Call law. Florida intends to continue enforcing this law and accepts new consumer telephone numbers. The national registry supersedes portions of the Florida law that are less strict. Florida telemarketers would have to consult both lists to ensure that a consumer is not on *either* list before placing a sales call. The Florida law allows licensees to contact for-sale-by-owners to solicit a listing, and this is still permissible *only if the owner is not in the national Do-Not-Call registry.*

## Effect of Do-Not-Call Lists on Real Estate Licensees

Licensees must comply with both the national and Florida Do-Not-Call laws.

If a person is on the national Do-Not-Call registry, it would be a violation to call a person on the list for the purposes of getting a listing or prospecting for a buyer. However, a recent interpretation by a Federal Trade Commissioner at a National Association of REALTORS® convention says licensees can call for-sale-by-owners if they have a buyer who wants to buy the property.

If a person is on the Florida Do-Not-Call list, but *not* on the national registry, it is permissible for a licensee to call past customers or a for-sale-by-owner to prospect for business. The Florida law allows licensees to contact for-sale-by-owners to solicit a listing, and this is still permissible *only if the owner is not in the national Do-Not-Call registry.*

**WEB LINK**

National Do-Not-Call Registry: www.donotcall.gov

# INCOME TAX REGULATIONS AFFECTING RESIDENTIAL REAL PROPERTY

Real estate licensees are not expected to be income tax experts, but they should be knowledgeable about basic provisions of the Internal Revenue Code (IRC) as they relate to real estate transactions. Licensees always should advise consumers to seek professional tax advice. An important benefit to homeowners is that interest and property taxes are deductible if the taxpayer itemizes. Additionally, all or part of the gain on sale of the property is exempt from taxes.

A taxpayer currently may exclude up to $250,000 ($500,000 for a married couple filing jointly) of gain on the sale of a personal residence if the taxpayer owned and occupied the residence for at least two of the previous five years. If the taxpayer held the home less than two years, a prorated portion of the exclusion may apply. The number of times a homeowner may use this exclusion is unlimited, except that the exclusion can be used only once every two years. While the change is extremely advantageous to most families because it allows them to earn large profits on their residences tax free, owners of more expensive homes may find it to be a mixed bag.

**EXAMPLE:** The Wilsons bought their home in 1992 for $50,000. In 1992, they added a deck and pool for $25,000. They lived in the home until they sold it for $300,000 in March of this year. Selling costs were $20,000. They would calculate their taxes as follows:

| | | |
|---|---|---|
| Selling price | | $300,000 |
| Less selling expenses | | − $ 20,000 |
| Equals net selling price | | $280,000 |
| Basis | | |
| Original cost | $50,000 | |
| Plus improvements | + $25,000 | |
| Equals cost basis | | $ 75,000 |
| Gain on sale ($280,000 − $75,000) | | $205,000 |
| Less exclusion on sale of residence | | − $500,000 |
| **Taxable capital gain** | | **$0** |

## Lower Capital Gains Tax Rates on Investment Property

The rates for long-term (holding period more than 12 months) capital gains have been reduced from 20 percent to a maximum of 15 percent (5 percent for persons in the 10 percent ordinary income tax rate). When investment property is sold, any depreciation taken must be "recaptured" and is taxed at 25 percent.

# HOMEOWNERS' ASSOCIATION DISCLOSURE (CH. 689, F.S.)

Some homebuyers in Florida have been surprised shortly after the purchase when they discovered that they must pay dues to a **community association.** If owners are required to be members in a community association, the developers or owners of the parcel must disclose before a buyer signs a purchase contract

- that the property owner must be a member of the community association
- that recorded covenants govern the use and occupancy of the property
- that the property owner is obligated to pay an assessment to the association and the failure to pay the assessment could result in a lien being placed on the property
- any land use or recreation fees and the amount of the obligation. This section does not apply to any condominium, cooperative, or time-share association

1   Any contract or agreement for sale must refer to and incorporate the disclosure summary
2   and shall include, in prominent language, a statement that the potential buyer should not
3   sign the contract or agreement before having received and read the disclosure summary
4   required by this section.

5   Each contract entered into for the sale of property governed by covenants subject to dis-
6   closure required by this section must contain in conspicuous type a clause that states:

7   IF THE DISCLOSURE SUMMARY REQUIRED BY SECTION 689.26, FLORIDA
8   STATUTES, HAS NOT BEEN PROVIDED TO THE PROSPECTIVE PURCHASER
9   BEFORE EXECUTING THIS CONTRACT FOR SALE, THIS CONTRACT IS
10  VOIDABLE BY BUYER BY DELIVERING TO SELLER OR SELLER'S AGENT
11  WRITTEN NOTICE OF THE BUYER'S INTENTION TO CANCEL WITHIN 3
12  DAYS AFTER RECEIPT OF THE DISCLOSURE SUMMARY OR PRIOR TO
13  CLOSING, WHICHEVER OCCURS FIRST. ANY PURPORTED WAIVER OF THIS
14  VOIDABILITY RIGHT HAS NO EFFECT. BUYER'S RIGHT TO VOID THIS
15  CONTRACT SHALL TERMINATE AT CLOSING.

16  A contract that does not conform to the requirements of this subsection is voidable at the
17  option of the purchaser within three days, or prior to closing, whichever comes first.

18  This section does not apply to any association regulated as Condominiums (Chapter
19  718), Cooperatives (Chapter 719), Vacation and Time-Sharing (Chapter 721), or Mobile
20  Home Park Lots (Chapter 723), or to a subdivider registered under the Land Sales Act
21  (Chapter 498). It also does not apply if disclosure regarding the association is otherwise made
22  in connection with the requirements of those chapters.

## 23   QUICK REFERENCE CHART FOR REQUIRED DISCLOSURES

24  Figure 1.2 shows the numerous required disclosures. It is a quick reference guide intended to
25  help licensees understand some of the many requirements but should not be considered all-
26  inclusive.

**F I G U R E   1.2  ■   Florida Real Estate Disclosure Chart**

| Subject | Disclosure Trigger | To | Disclosure Requirement |
|---|---|---|---|
| Brokerage relationship disclosures | | | Review this chapter for disclosure requirements |
| Property condition disclosure | When listing property / At time of showing property | Seller / Buyer | Any material defects that affect the property's value |
| Radon gas | Contracts for purchase or lease | Buyer or tenant | Statement as to the nature of the gas and how to get more information |
| Lead-based paint | Contracts for purchase or lease | Buyer or tenant | Lead hazard information pamphlet; disclosure of any known hazards; ten-day inspection and cancellation privilege |
| Federal Reserve's Regulation Z | When advertising financial terms on real property, a trigger item is included in ad | Readers of ads | Full disclosure of all material factors in financing, including price, down payment, monthly payment, finance costs, and annual percentage rate of interest |

**F I G U R E   1.2  ■  Florida Real Estate Disclosure Chart (continued)**

| Subject | Disclosure Trigger | To | Disclosure Requirement |
|---|---|---|---|
| Wood-destroying organisms report | Closing of a real estate transaction that includes commercial or residential buildings | Buyer | Wood-destroying organisms report signed by a licensed pest inspector, made within 30 days before closing date |
| Roof inspection ordinance—some jurisdictions | Closing of a real estate transaction | Buyer | Disclosure of condition of roof covering, decking, and framing, usually made within 30 days before closing |
| Land use disclaimer—some jurisdictions, but not statewide | Contract for purchase | Buyer | Restrictive covenants for the neighborhood; buyer's responsibility to investigate whether the anticipated land use conforms to comprehensive plan, zoning, building codes, etc.; public or private street and drainage maintenance |
| Landlord and Tenant Act | Within 30 days of signing lease | Tenant | Where deposit is being held; whether it is in an interest-bearing account and the interest rate, if any |
| Condominium Act—recreation lease | Contract to purchase | Buyer | Whether a recreational lease exists; when membership in a recreation facilities club is required; description of the facilities and the charges |
| Condominium Act—purchase cancellation | Contract to purchase | Buyer | 15-day cancellation privilege when buying from a developer; 3-day cancellation privilege when buying a resale unit |
| Time-Share Act—purchase cancellation | Contract to purchase | Buyer | All material aspects of the property; rights and obligations of buyer and seller; ten-day cancellation privilege; notification that purchase is a leisure time activity, not an appreciating investment |
| Time-Share Act—unit assessments | Contract to purchase | Buyer | Annual assessment for common expenses |
| Florida Building Energy-Efficiency Act | Contract to purchase | Buyer | Energy-efficiency rating system description and how to get the building rated |
| Florida Uniform Land Sales Practices Act | Contract to purchase a property in subdivided lands with 50 or more lots | Buyer | Seven-day cancellation privilege; notification of financial exposure if purchased with a contract for deed |

## SUMMARY

When a licensee renews a license for the first time, the licensee must complete a post-license course, or the license will be void. After the first renewal, a licensee must complete 14 hours of continuing education before renewing. If a licensee fails to complete the required education, the licensee may be disciplined.

Florida has mutual recognition of education with ten states. This allows nonresidents to become Florida licensees by passing a 40-question exam on the Florida license law. Florida licensees may become licensed in one of the mutual recognition states in the same manner.

There are three brokerage relationships available to licensees who sell residential property:

- Single agent brokers represent either the buyer or the seller, but not both, in a transaction. Only single agent brokers may call their customers *principals*. Principals are responsible for the acts of their single agent. The broker must give a Single Agent Notice before showing property or before entering a representation agreement. The notice should be signed, but if the principal declines to sign the notice, the licensee may note the fact on the form and work with the principal.
- Transaction brokers provide limited representation but do not have a fiduciary relationship with the customer. The customer is not responsible for the acts of the transaction broker. A transaction broker must give a Transaction Broker Notice before showing property or before entering an agreement for limited representation. The notice should be signed, but if the customer declines to sign the notice, the licensee may note the fact on the form and work with the customer. A single agent may enter into a transaction broker relationship by having the principal sign a Consent to Transition to Transaction Broker Notice.
- Brokers who will not represent the customer as a single agent or a transaction broker must give the customer a No Brokerage Relationship Notice before showing property. The notice need not be signed.

Brokers in nonresidential transactions may work with a customer in one of the ways shown above but need not give a brokerage relationship notice. Nonresidential brokers may appoint one sales associate in the firm to represent the seller and one sales associate to represent the buyer. They are called *designated sales associates* and act as single agents for their principal. The buyer and seller must each have at least $1 million in assets and agree to the relationship. A Designated Sales Associate Notice and a Single Agent Notice must be given to each party. The law specifically forbids dual agency.

Florida regulation of real estate practices has been strengthened considerably by passage of many consumer protection laws. Licensees who fail to maintain their professional education risk violation of new laws. In some cases, the violation occurs because licensees were unaware that the law existed.

In real estate transactions, licensees must be careful to disclose fully any material facts that affect the property's value. A licensee must avoid making statements that could result in a claim of misrepresentation. The licensee must take steps, such as using a property condition disclosure statement and inspecting the property, to ensure the buyer has full knowledge of defects.

The licensee must be familiar with important federal laws including income tax regulations affecting real estate, environmental protection, and lead-based paint.

Important Florida laws and disclosure requirements that licensees must observe include comprehensive plans and concurrency, homeowners' association disclosures, energy-efficiency disclosures, and radon gas disclosures.

The professional real estate practitioner should keep a checklist of required disclosures for every type of property. By observing the law and disclosing the required information, licensees enhance their reputation for fair and honest dealing, and the consumer is informed and protected.

# KEY TERMS

agency

agent

buyer brokerage agreement

community association

concurrency

Consent to Transition to Transaction Broker Notice

customer

designated sales associate

disclosure

dual agent

false or misleading statement

fiduciary relationship

infrastructure

innocent purchaser status

material fact

misrepresentation

mutual recognition agreement

No Brokerage Relationship Notice

principal

property condition disclosure

radon gas

single agent

Single Agent Notice

transaction broker

Transaction Broker Notice

# PRACTICE EXAM

1. Before showing homes to a customer she has just met, a transaction broker must give the customer a:
   a. buyer broker agreement.
   b. No Brokerage Relationship Notice.
   c. No Brokerage Relationship Notice and a Transaction Broker Notice.
   d. Transaction Broker Notice.

2. A *principal* is legally represented by a:
   a. single agent.
   b. dual agent.
   c. transaction broker.
   d. nonrepresentative.

3. Which statement to a prospective buyer is NOT likely to increase a licensee's liability?
   a. "The title to the property is clear; I checked the courthouse yesterday."
   b. "I used to be in construction, so I can tell you that the roof is in perfect condition."
   c. "You should be able to get information from the School Board about which school your child would attend if you purchase this home."
   d. "You don't need a home inspection because the house is only five years old."

4. A licensee is legally required to disclose to a prospective homebuyer that:
   a. there was a recent murder in the house.
   b. the roof occasionally leaks.
   c. the occupant of the property is infected with human immunodeficiency virus.
   d. the former owner was killed when he fell from the roof.

5. A broker may not legally work with a buyer or seller as a:
   a. transaction broker.
   b. single agent.
   c. dual agent.
   d. nonrepresentative.

6. A principal is responsible for the acts of her:
   a. transaction broker.
   b. dual agent.
   c. single agent.
   d. nonrepresentative.

7. A student failed her sales associate post-licensing course for the second time. What are her options if she wishes to maintain her license?
   a. She must wait 30 days and pass a different end-of-course exam.
   b. She must take the 63-hour prelicense course for sales associates and pass the course exam and the state exam.
   c. She must retake at least 45 hours of the sales associate prelicense course and pass a course exam.
   d. She must retake the course and pass a different end-of-course exam.

8. Licensees who live in a state that has a mutual recognition agreement with Florida may become a Florida licensee by passing:
   a. the sales associate course and the 100-question state exam.
   b. the sales associate course and the 40-question state exam on Florida law.
   c. the sales associate course only.
   d. the 40-question state exam on Florida law.

9. Licensed sales associates working at the seller's single agent brokerage firm:
   a. may represent either the seller or the buyer in a transaction.
   b. are legally bound to represent the seller.
   c. may have another principal in the transaction.
   d. may be transaction brokers for the buyer to ensure limited confidentiality.

10. If Jill sells commercial property exclusively, she:
    a. need not give the customer a No Brokerage Relationship Notice before showing property.
    b. may be a single agent, a transaction broker, a designated sales associate, or have no brokerage relationship with the customer.
    c. must give the customer a No Brokerage Relationship Notice before showing property.
    d. Both a and b

11. What is *NOT* a requirement for applying for a Florida broker license?
    a. At least one year's experience as a sales associate in any jurisdiction
    b. Minimum education of at least an associate's degree from a community college or university
    c. Successful completion of the sales associate post-license course
    d. Successful completion of the broker prelicense course

12. A broker must disclose known facts that materially affect the value of residential property when she is a:
    a. licensee with no official brokerage relationship.
    b. single agent.
    c. transaction broker.
    d. All of the above

13. A single agent for the seller has no brokerage relationship with a buyer. The buyer agrees to pay up to the listed price, if necessary, but first wants to submit an offer 10 percent below that price. The broker should:
    a. tell the seller, "The buyer said he will pay up to the listed price."
    b. refuse to disclose the statement because of the broker's duty of limited confidentiality.
    c. suggest that the seller counteroffer, if desired.
    d. tell the seller, "The buyer is qualified."

14. For how many years must a broker retain required brokerage relationship disclosures?
    a. One
    b. Three
    c. Four
    d. Five

15. John and Bill are sales associates working for Southland Commercial brokers. The broker of Southland Commercial Brokers, Inc., allows sales associate John to act as a single agent for the buyer and sales associate Bill to act as a single agent for the seller. Both the buyer and the seller have assets of more than $1 million and each agrees to this form of representation. The situation describes a:
    a.  transaction broker relationship.
    b.  designated sales associate.
    c.  single agency.
    d.  dual agency.

16. Broker Sherrill is working with Loretta, who wishes to purchase a vacant site in Orange Park. Loretta is told that concurrency requirements may delay her building plans, and she asks Sherrill about the meaning of the word. Sherrill's response should be:
    a.  "It is a requirement that you get a building permit and an environmental audit at the same time."
    b.  "You must provide a development of regional impact statement before building."
    c.  "You must disclose whether the building plans cover any recreational leases."
    d.  "There could be a lack of infrastructure in place that would put a moratorium on construction until the situation is remedied."

17. Henry has a capital gain of $197,000 on the sale of his home, which he owned for three years. The sales price was $425,000. Sales costs were $7,000, qualified fix-up costs were $1,000, and moving costs were $2,000. How much must Henry pay in capital gains taxes on this sale if his normal tax rate is 25 percent?
    a.  $197,000
    b.  $98,500
    c.  $39,400
    d.  $0

18. New concern about the presence of radon gas is the result of the increase in:
    a.  radon levels at large factories.
    b.  the number of energy-efficient buildings.
    c.  the depletion of the ozone layer.
    d.  Freon in air-conditioning systems.

19. There is special significance for licensees who sell homes built before 1978. That has to do with:
    a.  coastal management zones.
    b.  lead-based paint disclosures.
    c.  Americans with Disabilities Act properties.
    d.  the end of freely assumable FHA loans.

20. To claim innocent purchaser status under the hazardous substance statutes, a purchaser should:
    a.  refuse to purchase former gas stations.
    b.  pay for and obtain an extensive environmental audit.
    c.  show that the seller did not reveal any problems.
    d.  ask the real estate agent for a property warranty.

# 2

# BUSINESS PLANNING AND TIME MANAGEMENT

## LEARNING OBJECTIVES

Upon completion of this chapter, *you should be able to*

1. explain why a real estate sales associate needs additional knowledge and experience to become more professional;

2. list three types of communication skills that the professional real estate sales associate must master;

3. list the three types of knowledge a real estate sales associate needs and distinguish the differences between each type;

4. list the five requirements for effective goal setting; and

5. list at least ten services that an unlicensed personal assistant can perform.

# ACHIEVING PROFESSIONALISM

Customers of real estate licensees expect them to be knowledgeable, organized, and effective in their duties. The Florida Real Estate Commission (FREC) has established the requirement for post-licensing education to help new sales associates become proficient in the day-to-day practice of real estate.

Professionalism is not easily achieved. Professional knowledge and behavior result from additional study and hard work and go beyond minimum legal requirements.

The sales associate who provides honesty, service, diligence, and knowledge tends to be more successful than the stereotypical "hard sell" sales associate who "closes" with manipulative techniques. This chapter deals with the basic qualities that better serve clients and customers:

- Professional ethics
- Communication skills
- Professional education
- Goal setting
- Time management

# PROFESSIONAL ETHICS

A distinct difference exists between what is *ethical* and what is *legal*. License laws set a minimum standard of professional behavior, while codes of ethics set the higher standard of what is honest and fair to all parties involved in a real estate transaction.

Even the appearance of impropriety may cause customers to avoid doing business with a sales associate and his or her brokerage firm. The expression "perception is reality" is true; such shortcomings are very damaging to a real estate career.

The National Association of REALTORS® (NAR) has standardized a code of **professional ethics,** so that all members are aware of and follow their professional responsibilities. NAR's Code of Ethics is extremely influential, not only for REALTORS® but for other licensees, because ethical codes often later become license laws. The code may be the best available guideline for ethical behavior, whether or not a licensee is a member of NAR.

# COMMUNICATION SKILLS

Communication is the core of the real estate brokerage business. A licensee may be knowledgeable, competent, and ethical, yet because of a lack of communication skills, be unable to help customers successfully. The three types of communication skills necessary are:

1. Verbal communication skills
2. Written communication skills
3. Nonverbal communication skills

## Verbal Communication Skills

Talking to buyers, sellers, appraisers, surveyors, and other licensees enables the professional to share information, ask questions, and better understand the needs of others. The professional must be able to express information completely, honestly, and clearly. The individual who fails to master **verbal communication skills** may be misunderstood, appearing incompetent or even dishonest.

Community colleges and universities offer communication and public speaking classes to the public. One inexpensive way to learn to speak effectively is by joining a Toastmasters Club, a nonprofit service organization devoted to enhancing verbal communication skills. Many real estate licensees point to their years in Toastmasters as a key factor in their success.

**WEB LINK**

Toastmasters International: http://www.toastmasters.com

When licensees prepare for oral presentations, they should know exactly what they are going to say and organize the presentations logically.

Word choice is important. For instance, the statement "We can finish the deal by the end of the month" would sound better as "We should be able to close the transaction by the end of the month."

**Jargon** is a word or an expression related to a specialized vocation that a layperson might not understand. Licensees should avoid using jargon. For example, the term *floor duty* describes the period during which a sales associate is entitled to take all customer calls. While it's a well-known expression in real estate circles, it is not as familiar to consumers. A customer who calls the office for information on a listed property who is told "Just a minute, I'll let you talk to the associate on the floor" may wonder whether there has been an accident or just a lack of chairs. By avoiding jargon, a real estate professional helps clients and customers better understand the information he or she is trying to relate.

## Written Communication Skills

Letters, e-mail, flyers, and other forms of written communication are often the first impression licensees make on members of the public. Bad grammar and misspellings may reflect poorly on the licensee and the brokerage firm. Written communications skills are even more important for writing a contract provision. An ambiguous clause may result in a lost sale, a lawsuit, and disciplinary action by the FREC.

---

### DISCUSSION EXERCISE 2.1

Les shows a town home to a married couple who are interested in purchasing it despite the fact that the property has been poorly maintained. The seller has told Les that he would be willing to make reasonable repairs if the buyers include them in the sales contract. So Les writes the following special clause in the contract:

"Seller agrees to remodel the town home and put everything into first-class condition."
Based on this clause, what will the buyer expect?
What will the seller want to do?
Is there a possibility for miscommunication here?
How should this clause have been written?

---

**Written communication skills** may be enhanced by taking courses at community colleges, by reading books to improve writing skills, or by purchasing a book of ready-made real estate letters, such as *Power Real Estate Letters,* by William H. Pivar. A dictionary, a spell-checker, and a grammar checker on a software program are minimum requirements for achieving better written communication.

## Nonverbal Communication Skills

**Nonverbal communication,** often called **body language,** can be very important in sales. The real estate sales associate who understands body language will be better able to read the attitudes of customers and develop body language that can make a customer comfortable and establish rapport. Often, nonverbal communication can be far more revealing than what a person says. Some obvious body language styles include those described in Figure 2.1.

**F I G U R E   2.1   ■   Body Language Indicators**

| Body Language | Probably Means... | Comments |
|---|---|---|
| Pyramiding fingertips—the classic "banker" look | I'm superior to you, and I'm making some judgments about you | Don't do this when talking to a customer |
| Pyramiding, leaning back in the chair with hands joined behind the head—the "boss" | I'm superior to you; you have less status here | Don't do this when talking to a customer |
| Arms folded across the chest | Closed, defensive | Bad sign; you'll get nowhere in this presentation until you get the listener loosened up |
| Legs crossed at the knee away from the listener with body facing to the side | Closed, defensive | Bad sign; you'll get nowhere in this presentation until you get the listener loosened up |
| Customer looking away (no eye contact) during a sales presentation | Closed, often unfriendly | Bad sign; unlikely to buy until you can establish rapport |
| Palms toward the person just before speaking | Stop talking; I have more important things to say | Don't do this when talking to a customer |
| Stroking the chin (mostly males); fingertips to the neck (mostly females) | Sign of seriously considering the proposal | Get ready to write the offer |
| Scratching the head | Thinking; may be about to make a decision | Ask to help with any questions the customer may have |
| Staring at the ceiling | Thinking; trying to remember a fact | Ask to help with any questions the customer may have |
| Leaning forward into sales presentation | Interested, attentive | Good sign; you're doing something right |
| Customer frowning during sales presentation | May indicate the customer disagrees or does not understand some point | Trouble; try to ask a question to find out what's happening here |
| Hands hiding mouth while person is talking | Sometimes a habit of persons who are not speaking honestly | Probably OK, but some information may be incorrect |
| Hands on hips, head bowed, staring at you | Aggressive stance; challenge | This could mean trouble |

A real estate sales associate who wants to be more effective might consider using some of the following body language:

- Your handshake should be firm, but not too hard.
- Usually, direct eye contact when you are talking or listening is good. Staring without blinking or looking away occasionally may be disconcerting to the listener. Persons from certain cultures may perceive constant direct eye contact as disrespectful.
- Don't cross anything. Arms and legs should be open and relaxed.
- Lean forward into the conversation to display your interest. If you lean backward, especially if hands are joined behind the head, it may be perceived as a sign of superiority or aloofness.

**WEB LINK**

Center for Nonverbal Studies. This is a site rich in observations of nonverbal communication: http://members.aol.com/nonverbal2/index.htm.

---

### DISCUSSION EXERCISE 2.2

Larry is making a listing presentation to Jack, a for-sale-by-owner. He notices Jack has faced to the side, folded his arms over his chest, and looked in another direction.

What feedback is Jack giving Larry about his presentation?

## PROFESSIONAL EDUCATION

Licensees enhance their professionalism through continuing education. The law requires continuing education before renewal of a license, but many professionals take more courses than are required by the law. National organizations award professional designations to graduates of their educational programs. The designations make consumers aware of those persons who have exceeded the legally required continuing education.

Other types of education, when combined with formal instruction, also enhance a licensee's competence. In *Real Estate Brokerage: A Success Guide,* by Cyr, Sobeck, and McAdams, the authors describe three types of knowledge sales associates need:

1. Technical knowledge
2. Marketing knowledge
3. Product knowledge

### Technical Knowledge

**Technical knowledge** provides the tools of the business, such as completing contracts properly, knowing sellers' and buyers' costs, and understanding the comparative market analysis process.

This course includes technical knowledge in the following areas:

- State and federal laws
- Preparing a comparative market analysis
- Preparing a listing contract
- Qualifying a buyer
- Understanding financing plans
- Preparing a sales contract
- Reviewing closing statements
- Analyzing real estate investments

1 Sales associates should not work in the field without the appropriate technical knowl-
2 edge. For example, sales associates will feel quite incompetent if they cannot fill out the cost
3 disclosure statement or contract form. One of the purposes of this course is to provide the new
4 licensee with the technical knowledge to become competent and confident with consumers.
5 Technical knowledge also includes knowledge about state and federal laws, such as fair-housing
6 and antitrust laws.

---

### DISCUSSION EXERCISE 2.3

Traci has been in the real estate business for about a month and is working with her first buyer
customers, referred to her by a close friend. She shows them a home listed by another sales
associate in her office. The buyers immediately start to talk about where to place their furniture. "We think this is the one," they tell Traci.

It is Saturday afternoon, and Traci is unable to contact the broker to answer some questions about how to complete the required forms. Nervously, she tells the buyers, "You know, I
hate to see you rush into anything. There are some other houses out there you might like better. I can show them to you tomorrow, if you like. That'll give you time to think about it all,
too!"

What is Traci's main objective at this moment?

How could Traci have been better prepared for this situation?

---

## Marketing Knowledge

8 Learning how to sell real estate comes from **marketing knowledge.** It encompasses the knowl-
9 edge of psychology and the ability to assess a consumer's specific housing needs. This course
10 includes marketing knowledge in some of the following areas:

11 ■ Business planning (section on self-marketing)
12 ■ Prospecting for listings
13 ■ Making an effective listing presentation
14 ■ Prospecting for buyers
15 ■ Showing and selling the property

16 Many sales training books and tapes are available commercially. Institutes and societies of the
17 National Association of REALTORS® as well as local Boards of REALTORS® offer sales train-
18 ing classes. Many brokerage firms and franchise companies hold regular sales training courses
19 for sales personnel. Marketing knowledge is an important tool and a major part of the service
20 consumers expect when buying and selling real estate.

## Product Knowledge

22 Customers expect their real estate sales associates to know the market. They want the benefits
23 of that product knowledge in marketing a property or finding the right property for purchase.
24 A new practitioner should work hard to get that knowledge as quickly as possible to best serve
25 the consumer. This course cannot help you acquire **product knowledge.**

26 How does one gain product knowledge? By seeing property. Outstanding trainers say the
27 most important step a new licensee can take is to become familiar with the marketplace,
28 which means looking at properties. Some firms recommend their new sales associates take at
29 least two weeks to see as many listings as possible. They suggest maintaining that product
30 knowledge by regularly scheduling time to look at property.

# SETTING GOALS, BUSINESS PLANNING, AND TIME MANAGEMENT

Setting realistic goals is extremely important in real estate sales. Because real estate sales associates are usually independent contractors, they receive little supervision. Without a clear set of goals and a strong plan, the licensee may lose focus and direction. Goals should be written, measurable, attainable, and flexible and should contain deadlines. Once goals have been set, a business plan should show how to achieve the goals. Time management is an important part of that plan.

A distinction can be made between goals, plans, and time management. For example, an automobile trip from Orlando to St. Louis requires all three

1. The goal is St. Louis.
2. The plan is the road map on which is drawn the route and mileage.
3. **Time management** consists of the daily objectives: When do we leave, when do we stop for food, and how far should we go today?

Goal setting should begin with a long-term view: What accomplishments does a person want to achieve in his lifetime? Once this long-term view is established, the next step is to work back to the present, using smaller increments of time. By working from the long term to the short term, it becomes clear what a licensee must do this year, this week, and today to achieve the long-term goal.

When setting these goals, the professional should always include personal and family objectives. An example of professional goal setting follows. (See Figure 2.2.)

A licensee's five-year goals are

- earning the following professional education designations: CRS and CRB;
- obtaining a broker's license;
- owning a brokerage firm with 15 associates; and
- acquiring $150,000 in additional net worth;

Once the licensee establishes her one-year goal, she converts it into monthly and weekly goals—short-term tasks.

A new sales associate must remember that setting income goals is different in real estate sales from what it would be in a salaried position. Because of the independent contractor relationship, the broker does not pay the normal employee's share of Social Security and Medicare taxes and does not pay for health insurance or other benefits. Also, the sales associate will have expenses like Board of REALTORS® dues, license fees, education, office supplies, and advertising. To be safe, the sales associate should estimate those costs at 35 percent. So if the sales associate plans to earn $31,200 in the first year, the gross income goal should be $48,000 ($31,200 ÷ .65).

### FIGURE 2.2 ■ Sample Long-Range Plan

| Year 5 | CRS designation | Own brokerage firm | $150,000 net worth |
| --- | --- | --- | --- |
| Year 3 | Finished 2 courses | Open office | $90,000 net worth |
| Year 1 | Finished first course | Pass course and state exam | Must save at least $30,000 this year |
| Month 1 | Check class schedule | Check class schedule | Must save at least $2,500 this month |

## FIGURE 2.3 ■ Goals Worksheet

| | |
|---|---:|
| 1. During the next 12 months, I want to earn | $48,000 |
| 2. That works out to be monthly earnings of (Line 1 ÷ 12) | $4,000 |
| 3. Probably 60% of my earnings should come from listings sold (Line 2 × .60) | $2,400 |
| 4. Probably 40% of my earnings should come from sales made (Line 2 × .40) | $1,600 |

**Achieving my listing income:**

| | |
|---|---:|
| 5. In my market area, the average listing commission amount is (Figure used here, should be changed to fit your market.) | $1,800 |
| 6. So I must have the following number of listings sold (Line 3 ÷ Line 5) | 1.5 |
| 7. If only 75% of my listings sell, I have to get this many listings (Line 6 ÷ .75) | 2 |
| 8. It may take this many listing appointments to get a listing (Get this number from your broker.) | 5 |
| 9. So I need to go on this many listing appointments (Line 7 × Line 8) | 10 |
| 10. It may take this many calls to get an appointment (Get this number from your broker.) | 15 |
| 11. So I have to make this many calls per month (Line 9 × Line 10) | 150 |
| 12. Which means I must make this many calls per week (Line 11 ÷ 4.3 weeks per month) | 35 |

**Achieving my sales income:**

| | |
|---|---:|
| 13. In my market area, the average sales commission is (Figure used here should be changed to fit your market.) | $1,800 |
| 14. So I've got to make this many sales per month (Line 4 ÷ Line 13) | 0.9 |
| 15. It takes about this many showings to make a sale (Get this number from your broker.) | 20 |
| 16. So I must show this many properties per month (Line 14 × Line 15) | 18 |

Source: *30-Day Track to Success* by Edward J. O'Donnell, O'Donnell Publishing, Tallahassee, 2003.

Use the worksheet shown in Figure 2.3 to see what you must do today to achieve a $48,000 income. If the assumptions shown are appropriate for your market area, it is simple to project how you can accomplish the goal. This example focuses on income goals, but the same exercise could be completed for other goals.

A blank worksheet for *your* personal goals is included in the Forms-To-Go Appendix.

When the licensee is aware of what she must do today to achieve her long-term goals, she writes out the goals in contract form. It can be a private contract or a "public" document, with copies delivered to the broker and a mentor. Giving a copy to another person usually strengthens a commitment to succeed in the goals. A sample goals contract might look like the one in Figure 2.4.

The licensee then posts the goals where they are visible. "Out of sight, out of mind" is true where goals are concerned.

**F I G U R E  2.4  ■  Goals Contract**

I, _____, have determined my career and financial goals voluntarily, independently, and without coercion. I now formally commit to the following:

During the next 12 months, I will earn (from Line 1)                                                    $48,000

I will obtain at least this number of listings per month (from Line 7)                                    2

I will go on this number of listing appointments weekly (Line 9 ÷ 4.3)                                   2.3

I will make this many listing calls weekly (from Line 12)                                                 35

I will make this many sales each month (from Line 14)                                                    0.9

I will show this many properties each week (Line 16 ÷ 4.3)                                                 4

If I begin to fall behind, I request that my broker remind me of this commitment and prod me to stay on schedule so that I can achieve my goals.


Date  _____       My signature  _____


Date  _____       My broker's signature _____


Date  _____       My mentor's signature _____

Source: *30-Day Track to Success* by Edward J. O'Donnell, O'Donnell Publishing, Tallahassee, 2003.

## Daily Goals and Time Management

*Time management* goes hand in hand with goal setting. Goals don't work without a schedule. Besides being measurable and attainable, a deadline must be set for achieving the goals. For example, the goal of "making as many calls as possible to prospective sellers" is attainable, but immeasurable because no time deadline has been established. The statement "I will make five calls to prospective sellers by 6 P.M. today" is clear, measurable, and more likely to accomplish the goal.

The licensee should make a **"to-do" list** before each workday starts. The licensee should keep the list nearby and check off each item as it is completed. This provides a sense of accomplishment and motivation to continue. Some helpful points to remember about the list:

- Transfer unfinished tasks from the previous day.
- Include those daily tasks from the goals worksheet that are necessary to achieve long-term goals.
- **Prioritize** items on the list.
- Put the least pleasant items at the beginning of the list ("Eat the frog first"). Completing the tough tasks results in the ability to get on with achieving important goals.
- Establish times for completing each task. Even if they need to be adjusted later, you have established a basic guideline to follow.
- Make notes for items to include on tomorrow's list.

**FIGURE 2.5 ■ Sample Daily Activity Log**                                                    Date:_____

| **A** Direct $ | Hours [Goal] | Hours [Actual] | Comments |
|---|---|---|---|
| Prospecting for sellers | 1 | 1 | Pretty good. Got a lead for a listing. |
| Prospecting for buyers | 1 | 0 | Just couldn't get to this. |
| Make appointments with buyers or sellers | | | |
| Showing homes | | | |
| Presenting offers | | | |
| Making listing presentation | | | |
| Other activities that will directly produce $: | | | |
| Calling friends for referrals | 1 | 1 | Jane said she has a good friend who needs to sell a house. Maybe I'll call her tomorrow. |
| **TOTAL** | 3 | 2 | I need to do better at this. |
| **B** Office and Administrative | | | |
| Prepare CMAs | | | |
| Write ads | .5 | 0 | |
| Attend office meetings | 1 | 1 | |
| Look at properties | 2 | 1 | Just didn't have time to see more. |
| Attend education meeting | | | |
| Other administrative activities: | | | |
| Prepare announcement and mail out | 1 | 0 | I'll try to do this tomorrow. |
| **TOTAL** | 4.5 | 2 | |
| **C** Wasted Time | | | |
| Stopped to shop at Dillard's | 0 | 1 | Had a sale; shouldn't have, but... |
| Friend stopped by office | 0 | 1 | She had a day off and wanted to talk. Should have arranged to see her at lunch. |
| **TOTAL** | ___ | 2 | Makes me mad at myself. |
| **?** Personal | | | |
| Scheduled time off | | | |
| Other: (Describe): | | | |
| Renew driver's license | .5 | 1.5 | Went to tax collector's office, traffic snarled. Should have just mailed it. |
| **TOTAL** | .5 | 1.5 | |
| **GRAND TOTAL HOURS** | **8.5** | **7.5** | |

**Time Management Hints.** A licensee can do many things to help manage his or her time more effectively:

- Schedule time off for family, recreation, exercise, and relaxation. Failing to plan for these items can result in guilt feelings, discontent, poor health, or burnout.
- Make a time log of all activities in 15-minute segments for about two weeks. This will show where time is wasted and may give clues for being a more effective time manager. Your time can be rated as A, B, or C with respect to productivity. A time is most productive because it represents time actually spent with customers. B time is necessary work that can sometimes be handled by a personal assistant. C time is wasted time. Doubling your income may require only moving more of your workday to A time, not working twice as many total hours. See Figure 2.5 for a sample daily activity log. A blank worksheet is included in the Forms-To-Go Appendix.

- Qualify sellers and buyers based on their financial ability to complete a transaction, as well as on their motivation. Working with unqualified buyers and sellers is both a disservice to the consumers and a nonproductive use of time.
- Be on time for appointments. Being late is a quick way to lose the confidence of customers. Plan for contingencies such as rush-hour traffic, last-minute phone calls, and weather-related inconveniences.
- Understand how much each hour of your day is worth. For example, if you earn $48,000 per year and work 290 days per year, nine hours per day, you work 2,610 hours, and the hourly rate is approximately $18.40.
- Make cost-effective decisions. If you make $18.40 per hour, hiring a personal assistant for $10 per hour is more cost-effective than doing your own mail-outs and clerical work. Going home to wash the car Monday afternoon may cost you $18.40 versus $9.95 at a car wash.
- Utilize technology to increase productivity.

## Power Prospecting

Setting high income goals requires a commitment to prospect. The three keys to prospecting success are

1. Numbers
2. Consistency
3. Organization

**Numbers.**  The difference between making a living and becoming a superstar is numbers. Figure 2.6 shows the real estate sales process. Notice the first activity is "prospecting." Following these tips will help you become a successful prospector:

- Follow all laws when prospecting, paying particular attention to the federal Do-Not-Call list.
- A cross-reference directory can give you information on area residents and businesses. Cross-reference directories are arranged by street addresses and numerically by phone number. Listings arranged by street addresses allow you to find all the residents and businesses on a particular street in sequence. Listings arranged by phone number allow you to find all the numbers and names for a particular area code and exchange. The product is available in print or on CD. An annual subscription (costing from $150 to $400, depending on the location) will give current information, and can filter out phone numbers that appear on the national Do-Not-Call list.

**WEB LINK**

Hill-Donnelly Corp., sells cross-reference directories for many market areas: http://www.hill-donnelly.com

- Use a prospecting tool like The Daily 100 Power Prospecting Points Chart. (See Figure 2.7.) Note that this chart awards more weight to activities that are more likely to result in a listing or a sale. For example, sending a mailing to for-sale-by-owners is worth one point, but visiting in person gives five points because it is a more productive activity.
- Stay out of the office as much as possible. The only people you'll see there are other sales associates.
- Avoid time-wasting activities like idle conversation, poor organization and planning, and uncontrolled interruptions. If you're worth $18.40 per hour, four hours per week of idle conversation with associates in the office costs you nearly $75!

**F I G U R E   2.6  ■   The Real Estate Listing and Selling Process**

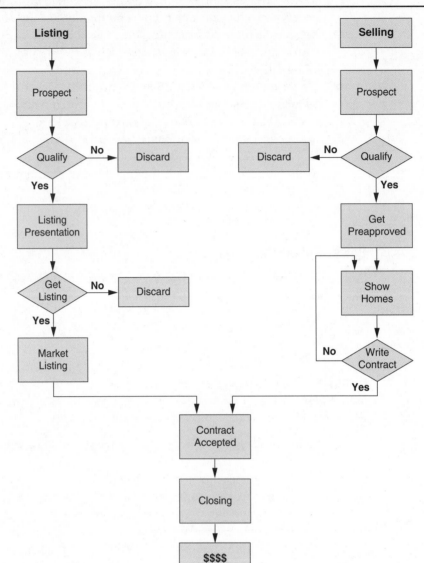

1    It's all about prospecting. If a sales associate can just reduce wasted hours and hours spent
2    on administrative "support" functions and shift them to A-level activities, income should
3    show a dramatic rise.

4    For example, if a sales associate decides to make a commitment to do power prospecting,
5    and is able to increase contacts, the increase in income should show a geometric increase.
6    Figures 2.8 and 2.9 show what can happen to the income stream in seven months if a person
7    goes from little or no prospecting to power prospecting. The figures shown won't magically
8    work for every sales associate, but depend on the following assumptions:

9    1. The sales associate is articulate, likes people, and is disciplined.
10    2. The sales associate has finished training and knows how to
11       a.  prepare a CMA
12       b.  make an effective listing presentation
13       c.  show properties
14       d.  ask closing questions
15       e.  ask for the order

**FIGURE 2.7** ■ **The Daily 100 Power Prospecting Points Chart—How to Survive and Make Money Selling Real Estate**

Directions: Complete any combination of the activities listed below. If you consistently "earn" at least 100 Daily Power Prospecting points, your personal income will increase dramatically!

Name:_____ Week Beginning:_____ Goal for Wk:$_____

| Suggested Activity | Points | Mon. | Tue. | Wed. | Thu. | Fri. | Sat. | Sun. | Total |
|---|---|---|---|---|---|---|---|---|---|
| **Listings:** | | | | | | | | | |
| FSBO (For Sale by Owner)—Mail | 1 | | | | | | | | |
| FSBO—Phone | 2 | | | | | | | | |
| FSBO—Visit | 5 | | | | | | | | |
| Expired Listing—Mail | 1 | | | | | | | | |
| Expired Listing—Phone | 2 | | | | | | | | |
| Expired Listing—Visit | 5 | | | | | | | | |
| Notice of Listing—Mail | 1 | | | | | | | | |
| Notice of Listing—Phone | 2 | | | | | | | | |
| Notice of Sale—Mail | 1 | | | | | | | | |
| Notice of Sale—Phone | 2 | | | | | | | | |
| FRBO (For Rent by Owner)—Mail | 1 | | | | | | | | |
| FRBO—Phone | 2 | | | | | | | | |
| Cold Call Completed | 2 | | | | | | | | |
| Follow up on Listing Prospect | 2 | | | | | | | | |
| Listing Presentation Made | 10 | | | | | | | | |
| Listing Taken | 20 | | | | | | | | |
| Servicing Listing by Mail | 2 | | | | | | | | |
| Servicing Listing by Phone | 3 | | | | | | | | |
| Servicing Listing by Visit | 5 | | | | | | | | |
| Listing Price Change | 5 | | | | | | | | |
| Listing Term Extended | 5 | | | | | | | | |
| Contract on Listing Presented | 10 | | | | | | | | |
| Listing Sold | 20 | | | | | | | | |
| **Sales:** | | | | | | | | | |
| Office Caravan (per home seen) | 3 | | | | | | | | |
| Previewing Listings | 3 | | | | | | | | |
| Prospecting Calls to Renters | 2 | | | | | | | | |
| Open House | 10 | | | | | | | | |
| Name and Phone from Ad Call | 5 | | | | | | | | |
| Follow up on Buying Prospect | 2 | | | | | | | | |
| Property Shown to Buyer | 5 | | | | | | | | |
| Contract Written | 10 | | | | | | | | |
| Contract Accepted | 20 | | | | | | | | |
| Sales Servicing Call | 3 | | | | | | | | |
| Referral Requested from Buyer | 2 | | | | | | | | |
| Referral Sent to Another City | 5 | | | | | | | | |
| Closing Attended | 10 | | | | | | | | |
| **Other:** | | | | | | | | | |
| Attend Office Meeting | 10 | | | | | | | | |
| Attend MLS Marketing Session | 10 | | | | | | | | |
| Attend Education Meeting (hr) | 10 | | | | | | | | |
| Past Customer Contacted | 3 | | | | | | | | |
| Phone Friend about Real Estate | 3 | | | | | | | | |
| Lunch with a Prospect | 5 | | | | | | | | |
| Attend Civic Club Meeting | 5 | | | | | | | | |
| Thank-You Card Mailed | 3 | | | | | | | | |
| Personal Referral Received | 5 | | | | | | | | |
| Newsletter Mailed | 2 | | | | | | | | |
| Other Productive Activities | ? | | | | | | | | |
| **Total Points** | | | | | | | | | |

Source: *30-Day Track to Success* by Edward J. O'Donnell, O'Donnell Publishing, Tallahassee, 2003.

**F I G U R E   2.8**   ■   **John's Power Prospecting Program**

|  | Month 1 | Month 2 | Month 3 | Month 4 | Month 5 | Month 6 | Month 7 |
|---|---|---|---|---|---|---|---|
| **Points on Daily 100** | **700** | **1,000** | **1,200** | **1,400** | **2,000** | **2,200** | **2,500** |
| Following month business results |  |  |  |  |  |  |  |
|    Listings taken | 1 | 1 | 1 | 2 | 2 | 2 | 3 |
|    Sales made | 0 | 0 | 1 | 1 | 2 | 2 | 3 |
| Listings sold | 0 | 1 | 1 | 2 | 2 | 3 | 4 |
| Total transactions | 1 | 2 | 3 | 5 | 6 | 7 | 10 |
| Commissions: ($150,000 price with a 1.5% commission to sales assoc.) | $0 | $2,250 | $4,500 | $6,750 | $9,000 | $11,250 | $15,750 |

For example, John is a sales associate who has been "drifting" through his startup-training program. After he completes the program, he decides to work smarter and increase his prospecting time. The first month he works 20 days and gets 700 points (35 per day). He continues to work the program, becomes more focused, and is finally able to achieve a 2,500-point month. His business increases dramatically. He finally understands that "prospecting is the name of the game." While some licensees may be skeptical of the income levels shown in Figure 2.8, power prospectors know the numbers *work*. Figure 2.9 is a graphic illustration of the results of the power prospecting program.

**F I G U R E   2.9**   ■   **Income-to-Effort Ratios Using the Daily 100**

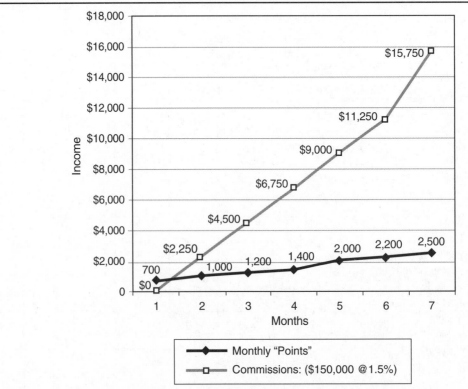

## Time Management and the Use of a Personal Assistant.

***Licensed Personal Assistants.*** Licensed personal assistants are very valuable and can provide all real estate services for the customers of the employing licensee, including showing and listing properties, calling prospects, and providing access to a listed property. A licensed personal assistant must be registered under the employing broker and may be paid for brokerage activities only by the broker. A sales associate may pay the licensed personal assistant for nonselling activities, but may not compensate a personal assistant for performance of brokerage activities that require a license.

***Unlicensed Personal Assistants.*** Many licensees now employ unlicensed assistants to help complete routine office activities, such as mass mailings, writing ads, and preparing comparative market analyses. Sales associates who employ such assistants and their brokers must ensure that the assistant does not perform any activities that violate the law. A list of activities that may be performed by unlicensed personal assistants is shown in Figure 2.10.

An unlicensed individual may *not* negotiate or agree to any commission split or referral fee on behalf of a licensee.

Unlicensed personal assistants, because they are paid by salary and may not be paid commissions, are under the control of their licensee employers. They may not be classified as independent contractors. The employers must withhold and pay FICA and income taxes and file withholding tax reports on a timely basis. Penalties for noncompliance can be substantial. Licensed personal assistants may be paid by commission, but commissions may be paid only by the broker. If the licensed assistant is paid a salary or assigned specific working hours or told how to do the work, she would be an employee rather than an independent contractor.

**F I G U R E  2.10 ■  Unlicensed Personal Assistant Activities**

1. Answer and forward telephone calls.
2. Fill out and submit listings and changes to any multiple-listing service.
3. Follow up on loan commitments.
4. Assemble documents for closing.
5. Secure public information documents from courthouse, utility district, etc.
6. Make keys for company listings.
7. Write ads for approval of licensee and supervising broker, place advertising in newspapers, and so forth.
8. Receive, record, and deposit earnest money, security deposits, and advance rents.
9. Type contract forms for approval by licensee and supervising broker.
10. Monitor licenses and personnel files.
11. Compute commission checks.
12. Place signs on property.
13. Order items of repair as directed by the licensee.
14. Prepare flyers and promotional information for approval by licensee and supervising broker.
15. Act as a courier service to deliver documents, pick up keys.
16. Place routine telephone calls on late rent payments.
17. Schedule appointments for licensees to show *listed* property.
18. Be at an open house
    a. for security purposes.
    b. to hand out materials (brochures).
    c. to respond to questions that may be answered with objective information from preprinted information.
19. Answer verbal questions concerning a listing if the answer to the question may be obtained from preprinted information, and is objective in nature, and if no subjective comments are made.
20. Gather information for a comparative market analysis (CMA).
21. Gather information for an appraisal.
22. Hand out objective, written information on a listing or rental.
23. Drive a customer or client to a listing or rental.
24. Give a key to a prospect at the licensee's office and nowhere else.

1    A licensee also should be aware of the liability of having employees. An accident on the
2  job could make the licensee's employer liable, as could an employee who injures another per-
3  son while running errands for the licensee.

---

**DISCUSSION EXERCISE 2.4**

Do a role-playing session, assigning parts to Sharon, John, and the broker.

**Sharon:** (*Excited*) I did it! I got that FSBO over on Killearney Way! Now I have another show-ing appointment. I *love* this business.

Gotta go! See you later!

**John:** (*Dejected, shaking head*) How does she keep doing it? She seems to get one appointment after another. I'm still slogging along trying to finish up my daily plan. I've got eight more things to do!

**Broker:** (*Sympathetically*) Tell me what you have done today, John.

**John:** Well, I had to make copies of the plat book pages for my farm area, make up a list of all the people on Scenic Drive, take my clothes to the cleaners, shop for a financial calculator, go to the title insurance company to get a rate card, and get my car washed. I did all that.

**Broker:** What is still on the to-do-list?

**John:** I still need to find some listings for the guy who called on my floor duty yesterday and tell him about some property. I've got to get back in touch with the buyer I showed property to last week to set up another appointment. Oh! And I need to get a market report back to my wife's friends who said they're interested in selling their house. I also got a response to the notice of sale cards I mailed last week. I need to call those people back. They said they might consider selling. And the tenants on Jackson Bluff Road think they may be ready to buy. I need to call them and set up a time.

There's just not enough time in the day!

Can you help John evaluate his time management skills so he can be as productive as Sharon?

---

## SUMMARY

Licensees who meet only the minimum education requirements of the license law cannot be called professionals in the true sense of the word. To be perceived as a professional, a real estate sales associate will

- acquire verbal, written, and nonverbal communication skills to share information clearly in order to reduce the chance of misunderstandings and misrepresentation
- acquire technical knowledge, marketing knowledge, and product knowledge
- set goals that are written, measurable, attainable, flexible, and that establish deadlines (Setting goals allows new licensees to achieve those business and personal objectives that provide the ability to grow professionally and provide better customer service. Time management allows sales associates to meet commitments and maximize their efforts to provide good service.), and
- practice effective time management

## KEY TERMS

| | | |
|---|---|---|
| body language | prioritize | time management |
| jargon | product knowledge | "to-do" list |
| marketing knowledge | professional ethics | verbal communication skills |
| nonverbal communication | technical knowledge | written communication skills |

# PRACTICE EXAM

1.  Jacqueline is a new agent with Seashore Realty. She hires an unlicensed personal assistant for $7 per hour. The unlicensed assistant can *NOT*:
    a.   write ads for approval by the licensee and her supervising broker and place classified advertising.
    b.   place signs on properties.
    c.   show a buyer several listed properties (inside and out), provide complete information, and help the buyer write the offer.
    d.   gather information for a CMA.

2.  When a sales associate pyramids his fingers during a discussion, a customer is likely to perceive that the sales associate:
    a.   is listening carefully.
    b.   is closed and defensive.
    c.   is not speaking honestly.
    d.   has a superiority complex.

3.  Within five years, Cindy wants to have $50,000 in cash in the bank. She is just starting out in real estate and has just enough cash available for her living expenses. Without considering interest on the funds, how much cash should Cindy have by the end of year three to be on target to reach her goal?
    a.   $35,000
    b.   $32,000
    c.   $30,000
    d.   $24,000

4.  A sales associate, to make the best impression, would *NOT*:
    a.   keep his arms open and relaxed.
    b.   cross his arms across his chest.
    c.   have a firm handshake.
    d.   lean forward into the conversation.

5.  You can improve your written communication skills by:
    a.   attending a community college course on writing.
    b.   joining Toastmasters.
    c.   reading books on the subject.
    d.   doing both a and c.

6.  Jonathon calls Jones Realty to speak with Arthur about a property he wants to see. Arthur's secretary tells him, "Arthur is on the caravan." Puzzled, Jonathon hangs up with thoughts of the desert. This is an example of:
    a.   Jonathon's lack of communication skills.
    b.   jargon.
    c.   nonverbal communication.
    d.   a common term that buyers and sellers of real estate should understand.

7.  Jan is in the office when she gets a call from a property owner who wants to list her home. Jan is uncertain about how to do a CMA and how to complete the necessary forms. Based on this information, Jan lacks:
    a.   technical knowledge.
    b.   product knowledge.
    c.   marketing knowledge.
    d.   communication skills.

8. What is *NOT* true about an unlicensed personal assistant?
   a. The employing licensee may be financially liable for accidents involving the personal assistant.
   b. The employing licensee may be responsible for violations of the license law or FREC rules.
   c. The licensee's employing broker may be financially responsible for acts of the personal assistant, as well as for violations of the license law or FREC rules.
   d. Assistants rarely help increase the income of the sales associate enough to cover the assistant's compensation.

9. Setting and meeting goals does *NOT* involve:
   a. starting with short-range increments.
   b. starting with long-term goals, then breaking them down into short-term objectives.
   c. writing them down.
   d. giving a copy to a mentor to help strengthen commitment.

10. Tim's goal is to make $58,000 in gross collected commissions next year. He feels that his listings should contribute about 50 percent of the required income. The average commission per transaction in his office is $1,200, and about two-thirds of his listings are expected to sell. He gets about three listings in five listing presentations. Approximately how many presentations must he make monthly to stay on target?
    a. Two
    b. Three
    c. Five
    d. Ten

11. Larry's goal is "to make as much money as I can next year." What is true about his goal?
    a. As long as he works toward the goal, it is effective.
    b. It is not measurable.
    c. It is not attainable.
    d. It should be combined with a time management plan that says "I'll work until I get tired most days."

12. An effective method of finding out where time is wasted in a daily schedule is to:
    a. keep good goal sheets.
    b. make a time log of activities.
    c. ask your spouse.
    d. measure the distance from appointment to appointment.

13. According to the text, sales associates should make a log of daily activities and:
    a. try to move most activities into Section B (Office and Administrative).
    b. attempt to move hours spent on Section A (Direct $) to Personal Time.
    c. spend more time on Section A (Direct $).
    d. reduce personal time to 0 hours.

14. Sara, a new sales associate, needs to earn $40,000 in her first year. If expenses like Social Security, Medicare, and operating expenses average 35 percent of gross income, what should Sara's goal be for gross income received from real estate commissions?
    a. $14,000
    b. $29,630
    c. $56,615
    d. $61,538

15. Guilt feelings, discontent, or burnout is likely to result from:
    a. wasting time in the office.
    b. working too hard.
    c. failing to schedule time off for family, recreation, and exercise.
    d. not staying focused on business.

16. Which prospecting activity would more likely result in a licensee getting a listing?
    a. Visiting a for-sale-by-owner
    b. Mailing to a for-sale-by-owner
    c. Telephoning a for-sale-by-owner
    d. Mailing to a person whose home is not for sale

17. John works nine hours every day but Sunday. Last year he made $68,000. What is his gross hourly rate, assuming he worked 50 weeks?
    a. $34.00
    b. $25.19
    c. $22.35
    d. $17.92

18. When making a "to-do" list for the day, a sales associate should *NOT*:
    a. establish times for completing each task.
    b. save the least pleasant tasks for after lunch.
    c. transfer unfinished tasks from the previous day.
    d. make notes to include on tomorrow's list.

19. A customer who observes a sales associate covering his mouth while giving a listing presentation most likely would perceive that the sales associate:
    a. has chapped lips.
    b. feels superior.
    c. is closed and defensive.
    d. may not be speaking honestly.

20. A productive sales associate should *NOT*:
    a. stay out of the office as much as possible.
    b. employ a personal assistant.
    c. work with unqualified buyers.
    d. prioritize his or her time.

## APPLY WHAT YOU'VE LEARNED!

The authors suggest the following actions to reinforce the material in *Section I—Laying the Foundation for a Successful Career:*

❑ Write a concise description of each brokerage relationship disclosure form that you could use to explain the form to customers.

❑ List the customer contacts you have had in the previous two weeks. If you acted as a transaction broker, did you tend to favor one party over another?

❑ Write a short list of each of the fiduciary responsibilities required of a single agent. Analyze each carefully, then select the responsibility you believe is most likely to be violated in the real world. Explain why.

❑ Write a script that you could use with a seller for introducing and explaining the property condition disclosure statement.

❑ Select a federal law in this section. Go to the Internet and find a site that includes the statutes. Print the statutes, then read the law, highlighting the important parts.

❑ Using the "Daily 100" chart, begin recording your success in making contacts with as many potential customers as possible. Involve your broker in the program and ask his or her help in staying on track.

❑ List your personal characteristics that you believe will be of most value to you in your real estate career, then refine the list by showing which activities will best use those strengths.

❑ List your personal characteristics that you believe need improvement to enhance your career. Make one action plan focusing on ways to achieve those improvements and another focusing on ways to reduce the impact of those personal characteristics that are hard to change.

❑ At the next meeting of your Board of REALTORS®, don't hesitate to give an opinion on the subject under discussion or to market your listing during the marketing time.

❑ Prepare a to-do list for tomorrow, arranged by priority.

❑ Set a goal of getting one new listing within the next seven days, and write out an action plan to achieve the goal.

❑ Prepare a short-term goal that includes the number of customer contacts you intend to make each day for the next ten days.

# OBTAINING LISTINGS THAT SELL

This section of the text leads the new associate through the activities with the most important goal in real estate—obtaining salable listings. Listings generate sales leads. Those persons with a large inventory of salable listings will make the highest income, because listers are the only sales associates who can get paid on both sides of the transaction.

Chapter 3 shows how to build a strong prospecting program to generate a substantial listing inventory. Power prospecting is hard work that separates the highly successful professional from the making-a-living licensees.

Chapter 4 shows how to make that listing salable by pricing it to sell.

Chapter 5 shows how to turn the hard work of prospecting into signed listing agreements through effective listing presentations.

Chapter 6 describes the listing contract, showing licensees how to explain the agreement to the sellers. ■

# 3

# PROSPECTING FOR LISTINGS

1  **LEARNING OBJECTIVES**

2  Upon completion of this chapter, *you should be able to*

3  **1.** List the five principal sources of listings;

4  **2.** Describe at least three types of properties a licensee should not attempt to list;

5  **3.** Explain why a listing commission seems much higher than the stated percentage to the seller;

6  **4.** List at least three circumstances under which an FSBO might be ready to list right away;

7  **5.** Describe the three transactions that can be generated from a call to a for-rent-by-owner;

8  **6.** State the principal reason that listings expire; and

9  **7.** List the five categories in a leads database.

# PROSPECTING OBJECTIVES

The main objective when prospecting for listings is to get an appointment to make a listing presentation. Because listings are the lifeblood of the real estate business, sales associates must know how to find sellers who need their professional services. In this chapter, the new sales associate will learn the most productive sources of listings and how to effectively approach the sellers and obtain an appointment to make a listing presentation.

The most important sources of listings for a *new* sales associate are

- for-sale-by-owners (FSBO)
- for-rent-by-owners (FRBO)
- expired listing
- farm
- canvass

Canvassing includes cold calls, knocking on doors, and direct mail. Other sources for listings are your centers of influence, personal contacts, notices of listings, and sales to neighbors and out-of-town owners. Notice that the discussion began with sources of listings for *new* sales associates. In two, three, or four years, the new sales associate who uses these sources will have the most powerful listing source of all: previous customers.

No matter which method a sales associate uses to locate prospective listings, he must prepare for listing appointments carefully. The comparative market analysis, CMA, is necessary to help price the listing. The sales associate also must understand what costs the seller can be expected to pay, how to complete and explain the listing agreement, and how to market and service the listing.

## YOU DON'T WANT THEM ALL

When prospecting for listings, qualify the properties and prioritize your efforts. Be picky. Your time is limited, and there are only so many listings you can work to get. The amount of effort required for prospecting and making a listing presentation is the same for a good listing as for a poor one. Don't spend time working to get a listing

- if the seller is not motivated.
- if the seller suggests you break the law by nondisclosure or discriminatory practices.
- in a market area you don't service, such as in an adjoining community.
- outside of your preferred price ranges.
- if the property condition is so bad you would be embarrassed to show it.
- if the owners are so rude or demanding you don't want to work with them.

The secret is to prioritize your efforts and focus only on those listings that will sell within a reasonable time with reasonable effort on your part.

# FOR-SALE-BY-OWNER

The only potential prospect we know *for sure* who wants to sell his house is the **for-sale-by-owner.** It is surprising that so few new sales associates use this outstanding source of listings in their daily plan. The myths many sales associates quote to avoid prospecting the FSBO market include:

- It takes more organizational skills to make the prospecting pay off.
- Sometimes FSBOs are not courteous to licensees who phone or visit (but remember, you can phone only if the owner is not on the national Do-Not-Call registry).
- They won't agree to add the commission to their price.
- It takes significant selling skills to get a listing from an FSBO.
- FSBO houses are overpriced already.

Sales associates who master the FSBO market by adapting to its unique characteristics are able to significantly increase their listing inventories.

## FSBO Characteristics

First, anyone in sales can be much more effective with a healthy supply of *empathy*. Empathy is the sensitivity to the thoughts and feelings of others. To be able to persuade an owner to list, the licensee must first understand the mindset of that owner.

## WHY FSBOs ARE FSBOs

If you were an owner of a property, try to think why you might consider selling it yourself rather than listing it. Assume your home is worth $200,000. A broker's commission of 6 percent would result in your paying $12,000, a pretty substantial amount. But if you further assume you bought the home two years ago for $185,000, with a 10 percent down payment, your equity is approximately $35,000.

*Calculation:* $200,000 minus the original mortgage of $166,500 (.90 × $185,000) less some principal paid back.

Now, you see, the $12,000 is *much* greater than 6 percent. It's actually closer to 34 percent of the equity, perhaps explaining why a seller might want to try it alone. It also explains why you will need a good presentation to show them why they need you.

Those of us who have sold a car directly, rather than trading it in, usually did it to make more money from the sale. Whether that savings occurs is not the point; the fact is we did it for that purpose.

It's fair to assume that of all the FSBOs out there, at least 90 percent are trying to sell without a broker in order to save the commission. It's also likely that only a certain set of circumstances will change that mindset. The FSBO may be ready to list if he or she:

1. is moving out of town right away
2. is concerned about personal security
3. is baffled by the home-selling process
4. is not available during normal hours to show the home

1    5.  does not like negotiating with people, or
2    6.  is convinced that a buyer will reduce the price offered by *at least* the amount of the
3        commission

4    The sales associate who has made a positive contact with the sellers when those circum-
5    stances exist is most likely to get the listing. While item 1 on the list above is based on exter-
6    nal conditions, the licensee may be able to change the sellers' minds on the others during the
7    listing presentation (covered in Chapter 5).

8        The low interest rates we have seen in recent years have turned buyers' markets into sell-
9    ers' markets in nearly every area of Florida. Because demand has been greater than the avail-
10   able supply, prices have appreciated significantly, and FSBOs have been more successful in
11   selling their homes. But it would be a mistake to think they don't need a real estate profes-
12   sional to get the best price with the least inconvenience.

## Finding and Tracking the FSBOs

14   An important part of the FSBO prospecting process is finding and tracking FSBOs. Most sell-
15   ers use a yard sign, classified ad, or a note on a community bulletin board.

16       Most sales associates locate FSBOs in the classified ads. The licensee may assume that all
17   ads that don't have the name of a brokerage firm are FSBOs. A broker's ad without the firm
18   name is a *blind ad*, a violation of Chapter 475.

19       Warnocks By Owner, Inc., provides a daily e-mail service to subscribers in most cities for
20   about $40 monthly, showing all new FSBOs advertised in the local newspapers that day. It
21   includes the owner's name, phone number (with Do-Not-Call list status), address, and other
22   advertised information. See Figure 3.1 for a sample of e-mail data. Subscribers can also view
23   complete data on Warnock's Web site and search FSBOs by city area or price range.

**WEB LINK**

24   www.wbyowner.com

25       A list of all FSBOs coming on the market for the previous week or month is also available
26   with the service, so it becomes easier to track time on the market.

### F I G U R E  3.1  ■  For-Sale-by-Owner E-Mail Service

From: Warnock's By Owner [mailto:support@wbyowner.com]
Sent: Thursday, May 13, 2004 3:29 AM
To: AliceNewby@Hendricksrealty.com
Subject: May 13 2004 - FSBO Information

(1 of 2)
FL: Tallahassee (All) Source: TAL Newspapers A
First Advertised: 05/13/2004
850-555-0001       Do Not Call Registry

Sam Seller

5555 Main Rd., Tallahassee, FL 323104635
HOME in TALLAHASSEE     $525,000
Bd: 3   Ba: 4///   Style:   Ga:
Sq Ft: 3645   Year Built:   Lot Size:

1     Because not all FSBOs advertise in the newspaper, the licensee can find those properties
2 by driving through neighborhoods and asking friends and family to call when they see a sign
3 or notice on a bulletin board.

4     If you don't use an FSBO service such as the one shown, you should organize the FSBOs
5 by phone number. Even though this is the age of technology, many sales associates keep index
6 cards with the phone number prominently placed in the upper right corner of the card. You
7 then sort the cards by the number. When going through the paper, look for the number, then
8 compare it with the cards. If it's not there, this is a new property. See Figure 3.2 for an exam-
9 ple of the file card system. To find the owners' information, use a cross-reference directory as
10 described on page 35 in Chapter 2.

11     It's easier to sort the ads if the records are on your computer. A spreadsheet or a database
12 program like Access makes it easier. Even your word processor makes it simple to sort using
13 the "table" function. (See the sample of table function in Figure 3.3.) Contact programs like
14 *Top Producer* or *Act!* are specifically designed for this purpose, have many more functions, and
15 are more user-friendly.

**F I G U R E  3.2  ■  FSBO Index Card**

---

W. H. Lister (305) 555-4369
0123 Street Way
Miami, 33165

Contacts:

| 4/15 | Phoned, said he did not want to list now. |
| 4/20 | Stopped by and gave him sample contracts. "Thanks!" |
| 4/25 | He got my "thanks" card. Called to ask me if I could give him an opinion of value. |
| 4/26 | Went over my CMA with him at the house. |
| 4/27 | He called me to come over and list his house at $220,000. |

---

**F I G U R E  3.3  ■  Sample Table for FSBO Information Sorted by Phone Number**

| Phone | Name / Address | Price | Contacts |
|---|---|---|---|
| (305) 555-2527 | J. B. House<br>1111 Another St.<br>Miami, 33185 | $175,000 | 4/12 Phoned. Made listing appointment.<br>4/13 Got listing at $175,000. |
| (305) 555-2421<br><DO NOT CALL LIST!> | Mary Mover<br>2222 Avenue<br>Miami, 33134 | $215,000 | 4/16 Stopped by. Told me she wasn't interested, but took sample contract. |
| (305) 555-4369 | W. H. Lister<br>0123 Street Way<br>Miami, 33165 | $220,000 | 4/15 Phoned, said he did not want to list now.<br>4/20 Stopped by and gave him sample contracts. "Thanks!"<br>4/25 He got my "thanks" card. Called to ask me if I could give him an opinion of value.<br>4/26 Went over my CMA with him at the house.<br>4/27 He called me to come over and list his house at $220,000. |

## FSBO Prospecting Techniques

Licensees who work the FSBO market must be persistent, organized, and disciplined ("POD"). The first approach to an FSBO can be done by

- direct mail
- telephone, or
- visit

Direct mail is a low-risk exercise that is likely to have a fairly low reward ratio. Direct mail is **passive prospecting** and should always be followed by a phone call or a visit. When used in conjunction with one of the other methods, it can be an effective way to prospect. The objective of sending direct mail is to introduce yourself to the seller. See the Forms-To-Go Appendix for a sample FSBO letter.

Before telephoning an FSBO, be certain to reread the section covering the national Do-Not-Call registry in Chapter 1. The liability for a violation of the law is quite substantial. If an FSBO's phone number is on the list, make a note in all data like <DO NOT CALL LIST>. (See Figure 3.3.)

The objective for the call is to get an appointment to give a listing presentation. See Figure 3.4, FSBO Telephone Calling Guide.

The most effective way to get a listing is by visiting the house. Many licensees don't like to do this because of the risk of rejection. When you see an FSBO sign, just stop the car and walk to the door. You can also set up the visits by geographic area, using your FSBO data cards. Asking questions is the best approach. The objective for the visit is to get an appointment to give the sellers a listing presentation. (See Figure 3.5.)

## At the FSBO's Front Door

Questions that may help you build rapport with the sellers include

1. How much are you asking for the home?
2. How long has it been for sale?
3. Are you moving out of town?
4. Have you had any offers?
5. If I brought a buyer to you, would you pay commission?
6. Do you have a sales contract?
7. Would you like to see a market report on your neighborhood?

Don't forget, sellers are also buyers. You have to find out what they intend to buy, and where, when this house is sold. If the seller tells you they are moving to another city, you have an opportunity to send a referral to a broker in that area. Referral commissions can be a significant part of your annual income if you always get the information about where people are moving.

### F I G U R E  3.4  ■  FSBO Telephone Calling Guide

1. Check the Do-Not-Call registry before calling.
2. Introduce yourself, your company, and say why you're calling.
3. Ask to visit the home at a specific time.
4. If the seller declines, you could ask if the seller would agree to pay a commission if you bring a buyer.
5. If the seller agrees to pay a commission, get an appointment to see the home.
6. If the seller doesn't agree, ask if he'd sell if the buyer agreed to pay the commission.
7. If the seller says no, ask if you can call again in the future.

**F I G U R E   3.5  ■   So, You've Got an FSBO Appointment?**

If an owner accepts your request to visit, set the appointment for a time when both parties will be home and available to talk. Ask that the sellers have several items ready for you, if possible:

- a copy of the paperwork when they purchased, especially the deed and title insurance documents;
- their homeowners' insurance policy;
- acopy of the property survey, if available; and
- an extra set of front door keys.

Why do you need these items now?

1. Because they will be helpful when you list the home
2. Because when you get there and find all these items neatly stacked on the table, it's your signal that they are ready to list their home

## FOR-RENT-BY-OWNER

The most common way to find many **for-rent-by-owners** (FRBOs) is by reading the classifieds in the newspaper or other classified publication. Owners trying to rent a house are good prospects for either a listing, a sale, or property management.

**FRBO as Listing Prospect.**   Those who own rental homes experience difficulties such as vacancies, uncollectible rent, evictions, and damage to the property. When the home is currently for rent, the sales associate must understand that some or all of those problems may have occurred very recently.

**FRBO as Buying Prospect.**   Sometimes investors have factored such problems into their business plan, understanding the characteristics of rental property. Those investors frequently plan to continue investing in rental property.

**FRBO as Property Management Prospect.**   Persons who have their property for rent may be weary of the time and effort involved in managing their own property. They may have had difficulty showing the property because of other commitments, and sometimes rental prospects are "no-shows." Your call may come at the right moment and may turn into an opportunity for management. If your company does not have a property management department, ask your broker to send a referral to a local company that will pay a referral fee for the business.

### FRBO Prospecting Techniques

The first approach to an FRBO can be made by

- direct mail
- telephone, or
- visit

Because the phone number in the ad is that of the owner's home, not the rental, it's difficult to learn where the rental property is located. The first contact can be direct mail followed by a phone call. Before telephoning an FRBO, be certain to check the national Do-Not-Call registry. (See Figure 3.6.)

The objective for this call is to get an appointment to give a listing presentation. Remember, the advertised phone number matches the owner's address, not the rental property. See Figure 3.7 for an illustration of the possible business that can be generated from a call to an FRBO.

Another mailing, a phone call, or a visit should always follow direct mail. When used in connection with one of the other methods it can be an effective way to prospect. The objective of sending direct mail is to get a call from the seller.

**F I G U R E  3.6  ■    FRBO Telephone Calling Guide**

1. Check the Do-Not-Call registry before calling.
2. Introduce yourself, your company, and say why you're calling.
3. Ask if the owner has considered selling rather than renting.
    a.  If the answer is yes, suggest you do a market report, and get an appointment.
    b.  If the answer is no, go to the next step.
4. Ask if the owner might consider buying other income property.
    a.  If the answer is yes, get an appointment to discuss other properties.
    b.  If the answer is no, go to the next step.
5. Ask if the owner has considered hiring a professional property manager.
    a.  If the answer is yes, get an appointment for your company's property manager.
    b.  If the answer is no, thank the owner for his or her time and say goodbye.

**F I G U R E  3.7  ■    Business Options from FRBO Call**

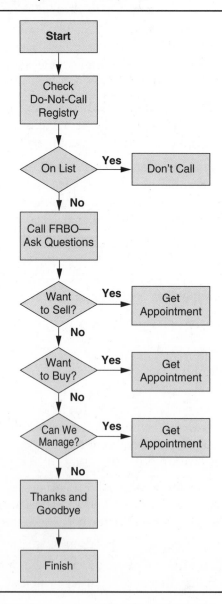

Because the owner does not live at the rental property, visiting is probably the least effective method.

## EXPIRED LISTINGS

### Why Listings Expire

Some listings don't sell during the listing period for a variety of reasons, including

- market conditions (oversupply of homes available for sale)
- property condition
- listing period too short
- uncooperative owner or tenant
- overpriced, or
- poor marketing effort

Except for the uncooperative owner or tenant, the major reason listings expire *is almost always price*. If there is an oversupply of homes, the price should have been reduced. If the property condition is poor, it was overpriced. A short listing period calls for a low price.

### Finding Expired Listings

Listings expire from the multiple-listing service (MLS) every day. They are shown in the change-of-status section where you can also find sales and price changes. Without the MLS, it is more difficult to work this market. An excellent way to find expired listings is to get a recommendation from sales associates who have a listing about to expire when the owner won't relist. You can either pay a referral fee or have a cooperative arrangement to send your sellers to them at the end of a listing period.

### How to Approach Owners of Expired Listings

The owner whose property did not sell may be disillusioned with brokers and nonreceptive to your approach. To effectively work expired listings, you must have empathy. The seller whose home was on the market for six months and didn't sell might

- wonder why he or she bought a home that no one else likes
- feel the broker did little or nothing to market the property
- believe the home was overpriced during the listing period

Once you understand how the owner might feel, you will be better able to tailor your approach to the situation.

Licensees can prospect for expired listings using the same methods used with FSBOs or FRBOs, by

- direct mail
- telephone, or
- visit

Direct mail may be too late because owners who want to sell often list with another broker immediately after the listing expires. A visit may not be as time-effective as first telephoning, but visiting the owner is more likely to result in getting the listing. When the owner answers the door, you might ask the questions in the telephone calling guide in Figure 3.8. Your objective is to be invited inside to view the home, getting an opportunity for a listing presentation.

**F I G U R E  3.8  ■  Expired Listing Telephone Calling Guide**

1. Check the Do-Not-Call registry before calling.
2. Introduce yourself, your company, and say why you're calling.
3. Tell the seller the listing has expired and ask if he or she still wants to sell.
   a. If the answer is yes, get an appointment.
   b. If the answer is no, ask if the seller would like to know why the house didn't sell. Get an appointment, and make a CMA study.
   c. If the answer is no, say thanks and place another call.

# FARMING

Think of farming as the cultivation of listings, much like establishing an orange grove. You can't get rich planting one tree. The more trees you plant, the greater the harvest. The grove takes a lot of work for some time without any apparent return. But when the grove begins to produce, it can shower you with fruit for years to come. And as the trees grow larger, the size of the harvest increases and can make you rich.

The listing **farm** requires lots of hard work to get established and for a time may have no apparent return. Many listing farmers abandon the grove just before it produces. If you decide to farm an area, you must make a commitment to continue for at least three years.

## What's the Payoff?

Farming is a disciplined approach to prospecting. It is intended to expand a sales associate's sphere of influence, thus increasing listings and sales. Joyce Caughman's book, *Real Estate Prospecting,* 2nd ed. (Dearborn Real Estate Education, 1994), describes how farming should produce 20 percent of the listings in the farm area in the second year, 50 percent in the third year, and up to 75 percent of the listings after that.

Assume that owners in your farm area move once every six years and your farm has 800 houses. That means 133 homes will be listed this year ($800 \div 6$). If you're in the third year of your farm and get 50 percent of those listings, you'll get 67 listings, or 5½ each month. Assuming further that the average sales price is $200,000, ⅔ of your listings sell, and your share is 1.5 percent, your listing commissions alone would be over $134,000 ($200,000 $\times$ 67 $\times$ ⅔ $\times$ .015).

## How Many Homes Should Be in a Farm?

Because the farm may take six months before generating listings, a sales associate must also prospect using other methods. A new licensee should start a farm with no more than 200 homes but should select an area that allows for expansion of the farm. Many successful sales associates ultimately develop farms with 800 to 1,000 homes in several neighborhoods.

## How to Choose the Farm Area

You must carefully select your listing farm. It should have the following characteristics:

- Middle to upper price range
- High turnover
- Increasing property values
- Not currently being farmed by any other sales associate

The steps to take are:

1. Select at least six potential farm neighborhoods. Check the MLS or the tax appraiser's office for all sales during the previous year.
2. Of those sales, review the listing office and sales associate so you can see if one person is getting a large market share. This would indicate that person is farming the area.
3. Get the total number of homes in the area by looking at the subdivision plat map.
4. Divide the number of sales by the number of homes in the neighborhood to get the turnover index.
5. Select the neighborhood that is not currently being farmed that has the highest turnover index.

Figure 3.9 is an example of the evaluation process. Blackwater Farms and Green Valley are currently being farmed, so it's not worthwhile to try to compete if other good areas are available. Orangewood has a 25 percent turnover ratio, and the home prices are in the $200,000 range. Orangewood is our choice.

## Make Contacts Now, Organize over Time

Some sales associates spend too much time preparing to farm and too little time making contacts. While it's nice to have a map wall, a database of information about each homeowner, or prepared mailings for the next six months, that can be done later. It's tempting to "play office" rather than take the risk of talking with prospective sellers.

One task that you should do up front, however, is to prepare a comparative market analysis (CMA) for the neighborhood, showing listings and sales for at least three years. This will help you discuss prices and also to know what prospective sellers paid when they purchased. Preparation of a CMA is discussed in Chapter 4.

## Making Contacts in Your Farm Area

Contacts in your farm area should be a combination of direct mail, telephone, and a visit. Remember, direct mail is passive prospecting that works well as long as personal contact is part of the farming program. A color newsletter with your name and company logo is inexpensive and can result in more business. You can also send a letter of introduction, a postcard, or any other mailing piece that keeps your name in front of the owners. Notice of listings and sales in the farm area can be one of the most effective and cost-efficient mailings but should be followed up with a phone call or a visit. (See Figure 3.10.)

Calling persons in a farm area can be effective, but there should be a good reason for the call. Some of those reasons include telling about a new listing, a sale, or that you will be holding an open house.

### FIGURE 3.9 ■ Farm Area Evaluation

| Neighborhood | Currently Farmed? | Home Prices | Sales Last Year | Homes in Neighborhood | Turnover Index |
|---|---|---|---|---|---|
| Rustling Woods | No | $175,000 | 88 | 521 | 17% |
| Blackwater Farms | Yes | $200,000 | 86 | 416 | 21% |
| Dolphin Downs | No | $150,000 | 145 | 740 | 20% |
| Glass Springs | No | $250,000 | 52 | 345 | 15% |
| Orangewood | No | $200,000 | 172 | 685 | 25% |
| Green Valley | Yes | $250,000 | 68 | 534 | 13% |

**F I G U R E   3.10  ■   Notice of Sale Card**

# We've done it again!

We have just participated in the sale of your neighbor's home located at

## 724 Oak Street.

Your neighborhood is very attractive and much in demand by buyers.
You might be pleasantly surprised when you learn the market value
of your home. I'd be glad to furnish information to you about
prices and marketability.

*Please call me right away if you might be considering selling your home.*

*Hilda Cummings, Sales Associate*
*(312) 555-4300 • Floyd Realty, Inc.*

The best way to cultivate your farm is by visiting owners in the neighborhood. Saturdays are wonderful visit days. A drive through the neighborhood will allow you to stop and meet people out walking or doing yard work. A cold canned drink is a good "ice-breaker."

Of course, just knocking on doors is one of the best activities. Give the homeowner a gift such as a calendar or yardstick with your name (and company name) imprinted. The owners will remember you when it's time to sell their homes.

You should make at least one contact each month with everyone in your farm area. If you work 25 days each month and farm 500 homes, you must make at least 20 contacts each day. Rotating between mailings, phone, and visits may reduce your workload. After you become fairly well known, you can increase the mail contacts and reduce the personal contacts.

## CANVASSING

Canvassing is prospecting by mail, telephone, and in person, not necessarily in your farm. All **power prospecting** programs include canvassing. The Daily 100 prospecting chart in Chapter 2 is a good reminder list.

Every sales associate who aspires to attaining top producer status understands the power of canvassing. While this is the last prospecting tool mentioned as a listing source, it is likely the most important. Canvassing is the process of contacting prospective customers by mail, telephone, or in person.

## BECOMING A LISTING SUPERSTAR

This section is designed for sales associates who are not satisfied with the median net income but who want to be in the 90th percentile and above. The average licensee does some prospecting in small numbers and the results are modest. The superstar prospects to a huge base of leads and harvests huge rewards. You should go back to your goals worksheet and "kick it up a notch!" Make the worksheet show you want gross income of $200,000.

## Your Leads Database

First, set up a software database. There are many databases available, including MS Outlook, Palm Pilot software, and Top Producer. One of the first steps is to organize your potential leads into five database categories:

1. Close friends and family
2. Friends
3. Customers
4. Acquaintances
5. **Targeted strangers**

You need the different categories because your prospecting methods depend on your relationship.

There is another category of persons called "others," who won't be put in our database. They make up the general population, strangers whom we don't consider prospects.

## Close Friends and Family

This category will be very small, probably having no more than 30 to 50 names. Close friends and members of your family will do business with you and send you referrals, but you may need to ask. The term *close friend* suggests a very strong, usually long-term relationship with mutual trust, care, and respect. Sometimes even close friends are reluctant to do business with friends for fear that the relationship could be affected. Your friends must be convinced of your professionalism and dedication. You must let them know that when you do business you will wear your "professional hat." The contacts within this group are natural and frequent, and all requests for business should be low key.

## Friends and Past Customers

These are people we know reasonably well but who are not close friends. Perhaps we have had lunch together or worked on a committee together. We should be working hard to move more people to this list from the list of acquaintances and targeted strangers. The size of this category will grow with the number of years you are in real estate. This group is a significant source of new business and referrals. Work it diligently! Each person on the list should hear from you by mail or phone at least twice monthly.

## Acquaintances

These are people we've met or spoken to by phone but don't yet know well. We will develop this group into a powerhouse of direct and referral business. One of the major objectives of our prospecting efforts is to move as many targeted strangers to this category as possible. We should have a combination of contacts with this group using mail and telephone at least twice monthly.

## Targeted Strangers

This list contains persons we don't know who are qualified by income, occupation, or residence address. This is by far the largest group in your database. The names might come from mailing list companies based on income levels, or from cross-reference directories, or from lists of doctors, attorneys, accountants, and business owners. This list should be very large, starting with at least 5,000 names and addresses. In the beginning you should send a direct mail piece (it could be a postcard or newsletter) at least six times annually. Leads that are gen-

1   erated must be followed up immediately. If you generate one transaction for every 100 names
2   (a modest goal), you will have an additional 50 transactions this year. If your average commis-
3   sion is $2,000 per sale, your income has increased by $100,000.

## 4    What Will It Cost?

5   Postcards can be designed online through companies like VistaPrint.com using one of hun-
6   dreds of templates. Five thousand glossy finish postcards, printed front and back cost about
7   $400 plus shipping. You can upload your photo and company logo. Send a different postcard
8   each month. Your software will make label printing easy. Let's check the numbers:

| | | |
|---|---|---|
| Estimated gross income: | | $100,000 |
| Less prospecting costs: | | |
| Postcards – $399 (for 5,000) for 12 months (12 × $399) | $ 4,788 | |
| Estimated mailing costs | $ 612 | |
| Postage (60,000 cards × .23) | $13,800 | |
| Labor 6 hrs. × $8/hr. × 12 mo. | $ 576 | |
| Total Costs | | $ 19,776 |
| **Net income generated** | | **$80,224** |

## 9    Making Contacts

10   Some important points to remember when you are prospecting:

11   **1. Success is in the numbers.** Be confident that this process will result in much higher
12   income levels. You will discover that there is a strong correlation between your prospecting
13   and the number of transactions you make. (See Figure 2.9 in Chapter 2.) When you discover
14   what your personal ratios are, it's easy to better control your income levels by your daily pros-
15   pecting. If you get $3,000 extra income, on average, from every 100 contacts you make, you
16   should assume that by making 1,000 additional contacts (20 per week) you can increase your
17   income by $30,000.

18   **2. Be consistent.** Set the same time every day to make your contacts. Stick to the schedule,
19   but if a closing or appointment is unavoidably scheduled, make sure the time is rescheduled
20   for later in the day. It's like a diet; you might get off track, but success will come only if you get
21   back to the plan.

22   **3. Call at your best time of day.** Some of us are great in the morning. Others are a little
23   grumpy and should set their prospecting time later. Just be sure you have a high energy level.
24   Because showing and listing appointments are usually set for afternoons or evenings, morning
25   may be the best time for a prospecting routine.

26   **4. Make the first call!** The rest will be easier. Think of the athletic slogan "Just do it!" The
27   hardest call is the first call. Just think one call at a time.

28   **5. You'll get better.** As you make your daily calls, your contact skills will get better and your
29   enthusiasm levels will increase.

30   **6. Remember the goal.** Before you make your calls, visualize what you want to happen as a
31   result of the call. Put a sign above the phone that says, "Get an appointment!" Another sign
32   might read "Get a referral!"

## 33    Saturate and Remind

34   When you put a new entry into your "acquaintances" category, your strategy should be to
35   "saturate and remind."

1     If you watch television, you have undoubtedly seen one or more companies start a major
2 media campaign with saturation broadcasting. A three-hour sports program, for example,
3 might have as many as ten 30-second commercials in the first two hours. For the next hour,
4 the commercial is often abbreviated to 15 seconds, but we know it well enough so that the
5 short ad is as effective as the longer one. This is saturate and remind.

6     When you meet a new qualified prospect by phone or in person, that person is now put in
7 the saturate mode, with at least a weekly contact for six weeks. Now they know who you are
8 and what you do. If your contacts have been skillful, they also like you, will do business with
9 you, and will send you referrals.

10     After the saturation period, you can reduce the number of contacts to twice monthly, and
11 you'll have a steady source of business.

## SUMMARY

The main objective of a licensee when prospecting is to get an appointment. The most important sources of listings for new sales associates are for-sale-by-owners, for-rent-by-owners, expired listings, farms, and canvassing.

Licensees should be selective about which listings to try to obtain and avoid listing property if the seller is not motivated or wants you to break the law. Also avoid listings out of your market area or in poor condition.

Most FSBOs try to sell direct in order to save the commission. Licensees who work the FSBO market must be persistent, organized, and disciplined (POD). Most FSBOs advertise in the classifieds. Organize the FSBOs by telephone number. The most effective way to get a listing from an FSBO is to pay a visit.

A sales associate who prospects for-rent-by-owners has a chance of three types of transactions: the FRBO might list the house, buy another house, or ask the licensee to manage the property.

Farming is a prospecting activity with long-term results. Persons who farm an area for several years may get up to 75 percent of the listings in a given neighborhood. The farm should be in a large area, but the associate should start with no more than 200 houses. The farm should be in a high-turnover neighborhood that is not currently being farmed.

Canvassing is the process of contacting prospective customers by mail, telephone, or in person. Licensees who want to engage in power prospecting must establish a leads database containing close friends and family, friends and past customers, acquaintances, and targeted strangers. Friends, past customers, and acquaintances should be contacted in some way at least twice monthly. New persons in the acquaintances category should have a contact program called *saturate and remind*, meaning weekly contacts for at least six weeks, then twice monthly.

## K E Y   T E R M S

| | |
|---|---|
| **farm** | **passive prospecting** |
| **for-rent-by-owner** | **power prospecting** |
| **for-sale-by-owner** | **targeted stranger** |

# P R A C T I C E   E X A M

1. Which is *NOT* a prospecting source to find listings?
   a. For-sale-by-owners
   b. Expired listings
   c. Buyer seminars
   d. Farming

2. According to the text, the most powerful listing source of all is:
   a. referrals from previous customers.
   b. for-sale-by-owners.
   c. farming.
   d. expired listings.

3. A sales associate who has limited time should *NOT* try to get a listing where the:
   a. seller is motivated.
   b. property is in good condition.
   c. sellers don't need to sell.
   d. property is in the licensee's market area.

4. A sales associate is trying to list an FSBO house valued at $250,000 with a $220,000 mortgage. The seller says, "Your commission is too high!" The sales associate says, "But our listing commission is only 6 percent!" What is the commission as a percent of the seller's equity?
   a. 6
   b. 10
   c. 25
   d. 50

5. It is more likely that a seller will list if he or she:
   a. does not need to move right away.
   b. is available during normal hours to show the home.
   c. does not like meeting and negotiating with people.
   d. understands the home-selling process.

6. Lower interest rates tend to create:
   a. sellers' markets.
   b. buyers' markets.
   c. lower home prices.
   d. higher mortgage payments.

7. Finding new FSBOs in the classifieds is easier if the prospect cards are arranged by:
   a. addresses.
   b. sellers' names.
   c. telephone numbers.
   d. city area.

8. What type of prospecting is direct mail?
   a. High risk
   b. Passive
   c. Stand-alone
   d. Wasted

9.   What must be consulted before making telephone canvassing calls?
     a.   The broker
     b.   The national Do-Not-Call registry
     c.   The national No-Spam directory
     d.   Local ordinances

10.  What is the most effective way to get an FSBO listing?
     a.   Visit
     b.   Telephone
     c.   Direct mail
     d.   Canvass

11.  What is *NOT* a type of income transaction that can reasonably result from contacting a for-rent-by-owner (FRBO)?
     a.   Sale
     b.   Listing
     c.   Management contract
     d.   Appraisal

12.  When using direct mail as a prospecting tool for FSBOs, the mailing:
     a.   should stand alone as the principal activity.
     b.   should be followed with a phone call or a visit.
     c.   has been shown to be wasted time and effort.
     d.   will generate many calls in response.

13.  When prospecting for for-rent-by-owners, probably the *LEAST* effective contact method is:
     a.   direct mail.
     b.   telephoning.
     c.   visiting.
     d.   direct mail with a follow-up call.

14.  The principal reason a listing expires is:
     a.   market conditions.
     b.   uncooperative owner.
     c.   property condition.
     d.   price.

15.  The best source for finding expired listings is through:
     a.   classified ads.
     b.   multiple-listing service.
     c.   a sign on the property.
     d.   friends and family.

16.  Direct mail is not usually a good idea for prospecting expired listings because:
     a.   by the time it gets there, a motivated seller has already listed.
     b.   no one reads mail.
     c.   it's too expensive.
     d.   it's against Federal Trade Commission rules.

17.  The principal drawback of a farm is:
   a.  farms have proven to be time-wasters.
   b.  you may have to work for a long period before any returns are realized.
   c.  ordinances that prevent such activities.
   d.  too many sales associates are competing with you.

18.  A listing farm should *NOT* have the following characteristic:
   a.  highly desirable area with low turnover.
   b.  middle to upper price range.
   c.  increasing property values.
   d.  not currently being farmed.

19.  A neighborhood has 480 homes. Last year, 69 homes were listed and 60 were sold. What is the turnover rate?
   a.  14%
   b.  12.5%
   c.  8.3%
   d.  7.2%

20.  The largest number of names in your database will be in what category?
   a.  Friends
   b.  Acquaintances
   c.  Targeted strangers
   d.  Close friends and family

# 4

# PRICING THE PROPERTY TO SELL

1 **LEARNING OBJECTIVES**

2 Upon completion of this chapter, *you should be able to*

3 **1.** explain the types of appraisals a real estate licensee may provide for a fee;

4 **2.** explain the difference between an appraisal and an opinion of value;

5 **3.** list four conditions that must be met in order to fairly use a comparable sale;

6 **4.** list the three categories of properties shown in a CMA;

7 **5.** list at least three sources of information used in compiling a CMA; and

8 **6.** explain the adjustment process and direction of the adjustment.

9 **OVERVIEW**

10 A duty owed to customers by single agents and transaction brokers is the duty of skill, care, and diligence.
11 Assisting a seller in setting a realistic listing price or helping a buyer understand the market and assisting in
12 setting a realistic offering price are two of the most important services a sales associate can offer.

13     Because all real estate activity is related to value, a valid estimate of property value has a significant effect on
14 marketing a listing.

15     One term—*market value*—is the most important value in a real estate transaction. The market value of real
16 estate is the most probable price a property should bring in an arm's-length transaction occurring in a competitive
17 and open market.

18     Real estate licensees use the **appraisal** process to produce opinions of value, comparative market analyses
19 (CMAs), and non-federally related appraisals.

20     Licensees must be familiar with the valuation of real property. While most licensees do not prepare formal real
21 estate appraisals, they will go through the appraisal process to some degree during the listing of properties.
22 Licensees must have a good working knowledge of the market in which they operate to be able to use evaluation
23 methods competently. ■

# OPINION OF VALUE VERSUS CERTIFIED APPRAISAL

Real estate licensees may not refer to themselves as appraisers unless they are licensed or are certified appraisers. All active licensees may be paid for providing appraisals or appraisal services as long as they do not represent themselves or their reports as being certified. The appraisal may not be used in a **federally related transaction.** However, the lack of state certification as an appraiser does not prevent a real estate licensee from appraising a property for compensation in a non-federally related transaction. An appraisal must be professionally, competently completed and comply with the **Uniform Standards of Professional Appraisal Practice (USPAP).** Failure to do so leaves the licensee open to civil liability and disciplinary action. A licensee involved in the listing or sale of a property should not prepare an appraisal for that property.

A licensee may give an **"opinion of value"** when making a prospective sale or taking a listing. This opinion of value may not be referred to as an *appraisal* or a *certified appraisal,* because the licensee has a personal interest in the transaction. This chapter focuses primarily on preparing opinions of value.

## Basic Principles of Value

Many economic principles influence the value of real property. They are interrelated, and their relative importance varies, depending on local conditions. The following principles are important to licensees attempting to estimate market value:

- Substitution
- Highest and best use
- Law of supply and demand
- Conformity
- Contribution
- Law of increasing and diminishing returns
- Competition
- Change
- Anticipation

**Substitution.** This is probably the most important factor in pricing residential property in a neighborhood with an active market. The value of a given parcel of real property is determined by using the principle of substitution. The maximum worth of the real estate is influenced by the cost of acquiring a substitute or comparable property.

---

### DISCUSSION EXERCISE 4.1

You have prepared a CMA for Savannah Cooley. Your opinion of value, based on sales of comparable homes, falls in a range between $192,000 and $203,000. Cooley needs $215,000 from the sale of her home to pay a number of obligations and requests that you list it at that price. Give four persuasive arguments for listing her property at market value.

---

**Highest and Best Use.** Of all the factors that influence market value, the primary consideration is the highest and best use of the real estate. A property's highest and best use is its most profitable legally and physically permitted use—that is, the use that provides the highest present value.

**Law of Supply and Demand.** As it does with any marketable commodity, the law of supply and demand affects real estate. Property values rise as demand increases or supply decreases. For example, when interest rates declined recently, demand for property increased significantly, resulting in dramatic increases in prices throughout most of Florida.

**Conformity.** In neighborhoods of single-family houses, buildings normally should follow the principle of conformity; that is, they should be similar in design, construction, and age to other buildings in the neighborhood to realize their maximum value. An elaborate mansion on a large lot with a spacious lawn is worth more in a neighborhood of similar homes than it would be in a neighborhood of more modest homes on smaller lots. Subdivision restrictive covenants are designed to promote the principle of conformity to maintain and enhance values.

**Contribution.** Any improvement to a property, whether to vacant land or a building, is worth only what it adds to the property's market value. An improvement's contribution to the value of the entire property may be greater or smaller than its cost. A licensee's opinion should be governed by a feature's contribution to value, not its actual cost.

---

**DISCUSSION EXERCISE 4.2**

You have prepared a CMA for Phyllis, who lives in Scenic Heights, an area of $100,000 homes. Phyllis reviews the recent sales and sees that her house has a large swimming pool, a feature that is not present in the homes in the report. She produces the invoices for the cost of her pool, which total $25,000, and suggests a $125,000 list price. You believe that pools in the neighborhood add about $6,000 to the properties' list prices.

   Do a role-playing exercise, with another person taking Phyllis' part, and discuss the principles involved.

---

**Law of Increasing and Diminishing Returns.** Improvements to land and structures reach a point at which they have no positive effect on property values. As long as money spent on such improvements produces a proportionate increase in income or value, the law of increasing returns is in effect. When additional improvements bring no corresponding increase in income or value, one can observe the law of diminishing returns.

   Smaller homes in a neighborhood of larger homes may experience increasing returns by improvement. Homes that are the same size or larger than surrounding homes should not be improved significantly until the owners have considered the economics of their decisions.

---

**DISCUSSION EXERCISE 4.3**

Sandy Brantly purchased a two-bedroom home in Betton Hills for $200,000. She builds an extra bedroom and bath and finds that the value has increased by much more than the cost of the improvements. She continues improving the property by adding two more bedrooms and a large family room with a fireplace. Sandy decides to sell, and she calls you to list the property. Your CMA shows that the value increase was much less than the construction cost. Sandy disagrees with your findings.

   Do a role-playing exercise, with another person playing the part of Sandy, while you explain to her why the value may not have increased as much as the cost of improvements.

---

**Competition.** All residential properties are susceptible to competition, some more than others. The only house for sale in a nice, well-maintained neighborhood has a better chance of selling at or near market value than if several houses on the same street were for sale.

**Change.** All property is influenced by the principle of change. No physical or economic condition remains constant. Licensees must be aware of market forces when preparing opinions of value.

**Anticipation.** Most buyers purchase real estate with the expectation that its value will increase—and they have been rewarded when the anticipation proves correct. In inflationary times, the anticipation of higher prices creates a multitude of buyers, driving prices higher than can be supported for long periods. In Florida, the prices for oceanfront properties have increased dramatically.

But when the market begins to top out, the anticipation of a price recession can cause investors to dump property on the market, forcing prices lower. Anticipation also is important to prices of property in times of decreasing interest rates, when builders rush to fill the expected demand. Licensees must be aware of the importance of anticipation when valuing property for sale.

## COMPARATIVE MARKET ANALYSIS

Most licensees use a **comparative market analysis (CMA)** for arriving at an opinion of value. A CMA is a process of gathering and analyzing the **property characteristics** of homes currently for sale, homes recently sold, and homes listed that did not sell. It may range in form from a simple list of recent sales with no adjustments to a detailed adjustment grid. Whether taking a simple or a complex approach, a licensee needs to ensure that she has met all of the conditions for selecting comparables.

### Gathering CMA Data

First, the sales associate must have knowledge of the **subject property.** If it is a standard floor plan subdivision home, it may be possible to complete a market analysis without a property inspection. However, if the seller has made many improvements or if the home has other amenities not typical of the market, it may be difficult to make adjustments during the CMA's presentation phase. The truly professional approach is to inspect the property before completing the CMA.

Once the property inspection has been completed, the licensee should select the best properties for comparison. Three categories of comparison help sellers and buyers better understand the market:

1. Properties that have sold
2. Properties that are now on the market
3. Property listings that have expired

The CMA will be a good indication of value only when comparables exist in a reasonably active market and where sufficient, reliable market sales information is available.

A **comparable property** should meet four conditions before it is used in a CMA:

1. It should be similar to the subject property
2. If this is a sale, it should have sold recently—within the past year
3. It should be located in the same market area as the subject property
4. It should have changed owners as a result of an arm's-length transaction

Reviewing actual sales prices of comparable properties helps buyers and sellers see what buyers actually pay in the marketplace. Comparable sales data are important when new financing is necessary because an appraiser relies on these data to estimate market value. Many sales are contingent on financing the purchase price, so it is of no value to overprice a property only to lose the sale when the lender and buyer receive the appraisal report.

Reviewing the prices of comparable properties now on the market shows the seller what owners of properties with similar characteristics are asking. These are the properties that will compete with the seller's. The principle of substitution means that a buyer will select the property with the best price, all other things being equal. A seller who wishes to position the property in the most effective price window values it just above recent sales and just below competing properties. A properly priced listing should experience a reasonably quick sale at the optimum price.

The listing prices of properties that do not sell tell a great deal about the resistance level of buyers to overpriced listings. In almost every case, the expired listing has been priced too high for the amenities offered.

The best sources for gathering CMA information include:

- multiple-listing service (MLS) records
- company files
- public records
- other licensees, and
- data service companies

MLS records are the most convenient and comprehensive method of getting listings and sales information. MLS computer records can be searched by address and subdivision for ease in finding comparable sales. The information can be retrieved for sold, current, or expired property listings.

Company files are limited in scope but may be more complete as to property descriptions and financing used in purchases.

The public records include information recorded in the clerk's office and information on file with the tax appraiser. Except for verification of sales data and identities of the parties, the information from the clerk's office is not as important as the information available at the tax appraiser's office. While the information from the property appraiser's records is sometimes outdated, the records are still a useful source of data. Because the "sold" section of the CMA should include for-sale-by-owner properties, the appraiser's office is often the best information source for such sales.

Licensees often know of properties that have just closed. The information given should be verified and added to the report to include current sales.

Data service companies compile property sales data and sell the information to interested parties. This information does not give complete property descriptions and is best used as a checklist to ensure that all sales have been considered.

## Selecting Comparable Properties

A licensee preparing a CMA has two choices when selecting properties to compare. The first is to report every sale and every listing in the neighborhood, together with features and prices. The other is to analyze only the properties that are comparable.

Reporting all properties gives the seller an overview of the entire neighborhood market. Some sellers believe a list is incomplete if they know of a neighbor's home that sold recently that is not on the list; therefore, a complete list may make sellers more comfortable. However, problems sometimes arise with this all-inclusive list. Properties that are not comparable may mislead a seller concerning values. Properties that should not be used as comparables when making CMA adjustments include those that have significant differences in construction quality or size. Properties sold to relatives may be suspect as to fair value of the price and should be excluded from consideration.

**FIGURE 4.1 ■ Sample Property Characteristics***

| | |
|---|---|
| Location | Number of bedrooms |
| Size and shape of lot | Number of bathrooms |
| Landscaping | Kitchen characteristics |
| Style | Condition of exterior |
| Construction quality | Condition of interior |
| Design | Garage |
| Age | Other improvements |
| Square feet of gross living area | General condition |
| Number of rooms | |

*These are selected examples only; more or fewer characteristics may be applicable.

Listing only three or four comparable properties makes a clearer presentation for a seller and reduces the chance for confusion about values. This is the approach appraisers use.

Perhaps the best approach for the licensee is to prepare a comprehensive list of all properties that have sold, are listed currently, or have expired and then select the most comparable properties from that list for analysis. This method satisfies the needs of completeness and clarity. The characteristics for comparison are described below.

## Common Elements of Comparison

Clearly, the accuracy of the comparable sales approach relies on the elements of comparison selected for adjustment. The elements listed on the CMA chart in Figure 4.1 are some of the most common and significant factors that affect value in standard residential appraisals. In any given analysis, it may be necessary to include other adjustments. The easiest way to fill out the CMA is to list all of the details of the subject property, then evaluate each comparable with the data that have been gathered.

**Location.** What are the three most important determinants of property value? The old expression "location, location, location" is the best answer. Location is so important that only in very unusual circumstances would a licensee use a property outside the subject's neighborhood as a comparable sale. In such a case, the comparable should come from a similar neighborhood. Even within the same neighborhood, locations can result in significant variances. A property across the street from a park is more valuable than one across the street from a commercial area.

---

**DISCUSSION EXERCISE 4.4**

Sara Bilina wants a for-sale-by-owner to list with her, but the FSBO says that the commission added to his price would make the property overpriced. Sara really wants the listing, so she finds several homes the same size as the FSBO's property and prepares a CMA. However, the comparables she uses are located in another, more upscale neighborhood. The owner looks at the CMA and lists with Sara.

    Has Sara prepared an acceptable CMA? Why or why not?

    Has Sara violated any ethical or legal code? Why or why not?

---

**Size and Shape of Lot.** Irregularities can make portions of a site unusable for building, impair privacy, or restrict on-site parking, which could require major adjustments. Street frontage and total square footage are other important considerations.

1  **Landscaping.**  Trees, plantings, and other types of landscaping should be evaluated as to matu-
2  rity, quantity, and quality.

3  **Construction Quality.**  If construction quality of a comparable is not equivalent to that of the
4  subject property, a major adjustment must be made. It is possible that the difference in quality
5  might disqualify the property as a comparable.

6  **Style.**  Generally, the style of a house follows the rule of conformity (a house should not be
7  the only one of its type in the neighborhood). An important aspect of style is the number of
8  floors of the residence. A one-story ranch house probably could be compared to a split-level,
9  with some adjustment made. A three-story house is not comparable to a one-story ranch
10  house, however.

11  **Design.**  Design must be viewed from both functional and aesthetic standpoints. Functional
12  aspects include the existing traffic patterns in a house, placement of doors and windows,
13  room-to-room relationships, and the usefulness of rooms. Aesthetic aspects focus on how
14  pleasant and attractive an interior appears to an observer.

15  **Age.**  Because most subdivisions are built within a relatively short period of time, there may
16  not be significant age differences among comparables. A brand-new home is likely valued by
17  the builder according to actual costs, overhead, and profit. While overall upkeep is important,
18  the home's age may alert the licensee to outmoded design and fixtures or to needed repairs.

19  **Square Feet of Gross Living Area.**  This is one of the most common areas for making adjust-
20  ments because size differences among homes can be calculated easily. If licensees make adjust-
21  ments for square footage, they also must be careful when adjusting for number of rooms or
22  bedrooms because this could lead to double counting. Adjustments for gross living area can be
23  misleading if all properties are not comparable. For instance, a small house normally sells for
24  more per square foot than a large house in the same area. A one-story house has a higher cost
25  per square foot than a two-story house. Be sure that all properties used are comparable to the
26  subject property. Appraisers normally do not count any floor area that is below grade as gross
27  living area; so do not use such properties unless the subject also has below-grade area.

---

### DISCUSSION EXERCISE 4.5

Silas Dean is trying to set a price for a 1,500-square-foot home in Green Hills. He finds the
following comparable sales:

| Price | Square Feet | Price per Square Foot |
|-------|-------------|------------------------|
| $49,500 | 980 | $50.51 |
| 51,000 | 1,025 | 49.76 |
| 50,000 | 1,000 | 50.00 |
| 61,500 | 1,500 | 41.00 |

The average price per square foot for these properties is $47.82. Sam Williamson, who
owns the home, asks, "What is it worth?" Dean replies, "Houses sell for $47.82 per square foot
in this neighborhood. Based on that, your property should sell for about $71,700." Williamson
agrees and lists at $71,500.

Do you agree with Dean's analysis? If not, why not?

---

28  **Measuring Practice.**  Measurement of a house is extremely important. An error could cause
29  problems in pricing the property if the home's square footage is given to buyers. Calculate the
30  square footage of gross living area of the house shown on the following page:

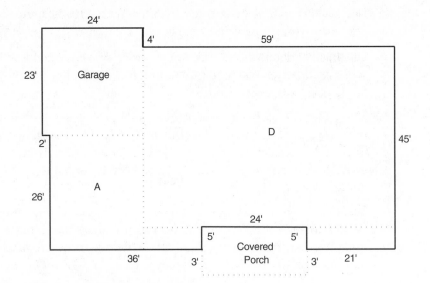

You have done a market report for the Meadows at Woodrun subdivision. Your analysis of property value, based on several 1,200-square-foot homes, indicates that homes sell at prices averaging $50 per square foot. When talking by phone with a prospective seller, you quote that figure after setting the listing appointment. When you arrive at the property with your listing information in hand, the seller proudly shows you the 500-square-foot two-car garage that has been converted into a heated and cooled family room. He indicates that the price at which you should list the home is $85,000, based on 1,700 square feet times your $50-per-square-foot figure. Role-play this situation, and explain why it may be difficult to market this home at $85,000. Also discuss some methods of arriving at a more realistic price.

**Number of Rooms.** The total number of rooms in a house does not include the foyer or bathrooms and generally does not include basement rooms. Don't double count when adjusting for square feet and number of bedrooms.

**Number of Bedrooms.** A major adjustment is needed if the subject property has two bedrooms and the comparables have at least three, or vice versa. Don't double count when adjusting for square feet.

**Number of Baths.** Full baths (lavatory, toilet, and tub, with or without shower), three-quarter baths (lavatory, toilet, and shower), and half baths (lavatory and toilet) comprise this category. Modern plumbing is assumed, so an adjustment must be made for out-of-date fixtures if different from the subject property.

**Kitchen.** Licensees should focus on certain key factors

- Location
- Counter space and storage
- Service triangle
- Appliances

The location of the kitchen is an important factor, based on its convenience to dining areas and accessibility for unloading groceries. The market will not accept a kitchen with inadequate counter and storage space. The service triangle is calculated by drawing straight lines connecting refrigerator, range, and sink. Most consumer polls show that the total length of the three lines should be greater than 12 feet but should not exceed 22 feet. Appliances represent a sizable portion of the home's cost, and their age and condition are important.

**Other Space.** Unfinished attic, porch, utility room, Florida room, or any other room not part of the primary house area is included in this category.

**Condition of Exterior.** An adjustment should be made for any needed repair work.

**Condition of Interior.** An adjustment should be made for needed repairs. Luxurious finishing such as real wood paneling, adds to a home's value.

**Garage.** If the subject does not have one, any garage on a comparable property requires an adjustment. Garages on the subject and comparable properties must be compared for type of construction and size.

**Other Improvements.** An adjustment should be made for differences between the subject property and the comparable. Landscaping, driveways, trees, and pools should be adjusted based on their contribution to value.

## Adjusting for Differences

Ideally, the licensee wants to find comparable sales that are identical in characteristics to the subject property. In the real world, this doesn't always happen. While the CMA is not meant to be an appraisal, it is necessary to make **adjustments** for some of the differences discussed above. A major difference between the subject property and comparable property, such as a pool, could make an opinion of value very misleading if no adjustment is made for the pool. Many licensees recognize the difficulty in doing a CMA because when they look at a sold property, they see it as it is *today*, not how it looked when it went under contract. The important consideration in adjusting the comparable sale is how it looked at the time of sale.

> **EXAMPLE:** Whitney Cooley, a licensed sales associate, is preparing a CMA for Brian Edwards' three-bedroom, two-bath home in Eastgate. One of the comparable properties with the same floor plan sold recently for $73,000. The only difference between the properties is that the comparable property has a swimming pool. Whitney has done CMAs in Eastgate before and estimates that a pool contributes about $4,000 to value. The subject property doesn't have a pool, so Whitney makes a minus adjustment of $4,000 to the comparable's sales price. This indicates a value of $69,000 for the subject.
>
> How did Whitney determine that a pool contributes $4,000 to value in that neighborhood? The matched pair technique helped her make the estimate. She examined two recent sales in which the only difference was the fact that one property had a pool. The property with the pool sold for $4,000 more than the home without the pool. Because the pool was the only difference, the $4,000 must be attributable to that amenity. It would be better to make the comparison with several matched pairs to support the conclusion, but the technique is valid. The cost to build the pool is not added, just the value buyers and sellers place on the pool.

Adjustments are always made to the comparable property, never to the subject. Adjustments are subtracted from the comparable property if the comparable is bigger or better. Adjustments are added if the comparable is smaller or less desirable. An easy way to remember is "CIA, CBS":

- If the Comparable is Inferior, Add
- If the Comparable is Better, Subtract

Adjustments should be made for sold properties, listed properties, and expired properties; then each category should be reconciled.

## Reconciliation

**Reconciliation** is the resolution of several adjusted values on CMAs into a single estimate of value. While an appraiser is expected to report a single-market value amount, a licensee making an opinion of value may prefer to report a range of values, from lowest to highest adjusted value of the comparables. Presenting a range rather than a single estimate of value allows a seller to price the property somewhat higher than the sold properties would indicate. The seller should understand that the home will likely sell at some price other than the list price and should consider all offers within the range of values.

Reconciliation enables the licensee to set the range differently. The first step is to estimate the value for each section of the report (sold properties, listed properties, and expired listings). Reconciliation is not simply the averaging of these values. The process requires the licensee to examine carefully the similarity of each comparable property to the subject property. If one comparable is nearly identical to the subject, including all relevant **transactional characteristics,** the sales price of that comparable might be the subject's estimated market value. When the comparables vary in their degree of similarity to the subject, the comparable property judged most similar is assigned the greatest weight in the reconciliation process.

The estimates for each section should be rounded. The range would then be calculated from the reconciled value of sold properties and the reconciled value of properties listed currently.

Another method for setting a range of values is to reconcile the sold properties to a value estimate, then check to see what properties sell for as a percentage of list price, then divide the value estimate by that amount. The two values comprise the range high and low.

---

### DISCUSSION EXERCISE 4.7

You have just completed a CMA for Tim Palmer's home at 1112 Bristol Court. The reconciled market value of his home is $127,500. MLS statistics indicate that homes sell at approximately 95 percent of list price.

What is the range of value you quote to Tim?

---

## A Visual Aid to the CMA

"A picture is worth a thousand words" is a timeworn expression because it is true. Sellers who review CMAs with licensees often have difficulty visualizing the comparable properties. The licensee who provides visual data can make a clearer presentation, which may result in more realistic pricing. Owners who are motivated to sell do not set out to overprice their properties. Overpricing is usually the result of an inadequate understanding of the market, and that responsibility belongs to the listing sales associate.

Valuable visual aids include plat maps of the subdivision and pictures of the comparable properties. The plat map should be color-coded to show which properties were sold, which properties are now for sale, and which listings have expired. (See Figure 4.2.) Photos can be clipped from an MLS book, printed from the MLS computer system, or taken with a digital camera. The licensee who wants the listing should not fail to include a photo of the seller's home, also. The seller will appreciate your personal touch and the extra photo for her scrapbook. Leaving a family home of some years can be a sentimental experience, and the seller will remember a licensee who is sensitive to those feelings.

**F I G U R E  4.2  ■  Plat Map of Neighborhood**

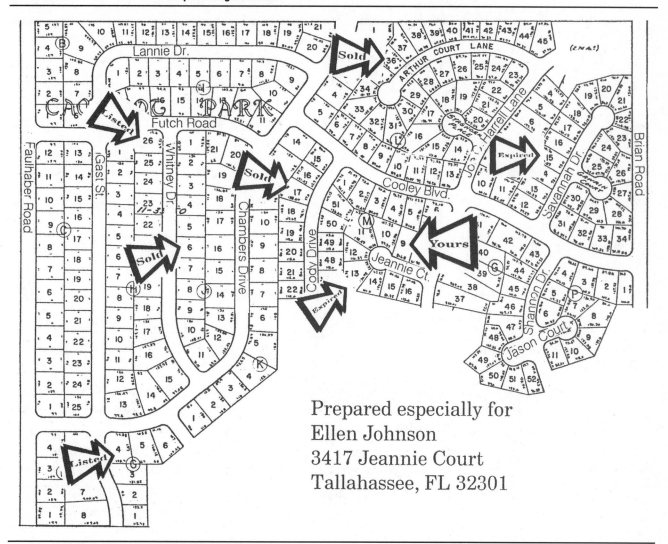

Prepared especially for
Ellen Johnson
3417 Jeannie Court
Tallahassee, FL 32301

C A S E   S T U D Y

## COMPARATIVE MARKET ANALYSIS

**Getting information from the owner.** You have just received a request from John Halliburton to discuss listing his family's home. Mr. Halliburton gives you some basic information:

- The full name of all persons on the deed
  *John Halliburton and Susan C. Halliburton, HW*
- The property address
  *4316 Landtowne Drive, Orlando*
- The owner's home and office phone number
  *(407) 555-3557; (407) 555-3917*
- The number of bedrooms and baths in the home
  *Four bedrooms, two baths*

■ A description of extras in the home
*1,920 square feet of gross living area, two-car garage*

■ A convenient time for an appointment. This is the time to decide whether to do a pre-presentation inspection of the property (two appointments required: one to inspect the property, one to present the CMA).

*You decide to have one appointment at 6:20 this evening and will inspect the property at that time.*

**Gathering information from the online tax rolls through the MLS system.**  The tax rolls for Orange County show the following information for the property

| | |
|---|---|
| Legal description: | Lot 14, Block H, Landover Hills, Unit 2 - Orange County |
| Property tax appraisal: | $149,300 |
| Annual taxes: | $2,986.45 |
| Year built: | 1989 |
| Base area: | 1,920 square feet (later verified by physical measurement) |
| Total area: | 2,420 square feet (includes 2-car garage) |
| Last sale: | 1996 |
| Last sale price: | $128,000 |
| Mortgage: | Sun Title Bank |

A search of the tax records shows seven sales in the subdivision within the previous year, ranging from $168,000 to $174,800. Six of the seven sales were reported in the MLS. The sales are shown in the first section of the CMA in Figure 4.3.

There are four properties currently for sale in the MLS, shown in the second section of the CMA, and three listings have expired within the last 12 months, shown in the third section.

**Analysis of amounts contributed by amenities.**  Over a period of time, in reviewing data on sold properties, we can estimate what a pool, a garage, an extra bedroom, or a fireplace contributes to value. The matched pair technique would compare similar houses with and without a particular feature. The difference in price would tend to show what the feature contributes in value.

For purposes of this CMA, we shall assume that sold properties in the neighborhood have shown the following value contributions over time:

■ The contribution of a pool is $7,000.
■ The contribution of a fireplace is $1,800.
■ The contribution of an extra garage stall (2 cars, rather than 1) is $2,800.
■ The contribution of extra square footage differences is $50/sq. ft.
■ The contribution of a screened porch is $2,000.

The CMA has been filled in with the exception of the adjustments shown above. Please compare the subject property with the comparable properties and make adjustments to the comparable properties. Then complete the analysis and estimate the marketing range for the property. Presenting this CMA to the sellers will be discussed in Chapter 5.

**F I G U R E  4.3  ■  Comparative Market Analysis**

**Comparative Market Analysis**

Prepared by: _____

Date: _____

Prepared for: _____
Property Address: _____
Features: _____

### Properties sold within the previous 12 months

| Property Address | Sales Price | List Price | Days on Mkt. | Living Area | Features | Estimated Adjustment | Adjusted Sales Price | Comments |
|---|---|---|---|---|---|---|---|---|
| 1816 Hibiscus | 172,800 | 180,000 | 120 | 1,820 | Pool, FP, Screen Porch | | | |
| 2412 Nasturtium | 169,900 | 177,900 | 71 | 1,920 | FP | | | |
| 1763 Camellia | 173,500 | 182,000 | 45 | 1,900 | Pool | | | |
| 1421 Azalea | 168,900 | 175,000 | 52 | 2,000 | Screen Porch | | | |
| 1640 Clover | 171,200 | 179,500 | 61 | 2,000 | 1 Car Garage | | | |
| 2210 Hibiscus | 168,000 | 175,900 | 32 | 1,900 | | | | |
| 1240 Camelia | 174,800 | 182,500 | 70 | 1,920 | Screen Porch, FP | | | |

Percent sales price/list price _____ %

### Properties currently on the market

| Property Address | List Price | Days on Mkt. | Living Area | Features | Estimated Adjustment | As Adjusted | Comments |
|---|---|---|---|---|---|---|---|
| 1818 Azalea | 191,000 | 75 | 2,100 | Pool | | | |
| 1740 Hibiscus | 178,800 | 120 | 1,900 | FP | | | |
| 2210 Clover | 185,000 | 38 | 1,820 | Screen Porch, Pool | | | |
| 1604 Magnolia | 177,000 | 45 | 1,920 | Screen Porch | | | |

### Properties which were listed but failed to sell during the previous 12 months

| Property Address | List Price | Days on Mkt. | Living Area | Features | Estimated Adjustment | As Adjusted | Comments |
|---|---|---|---|---|---|---|---|
| 2212 Camelia | 192,800 | 180 | 1,900 | Pool, FP, Screen Porch | | | |
| 1812 Hibiscus | 185,500 | 240 | 2,000 | Screen Porch | | | |
| 2211 Azalae | 186,600 | 140 | 1,800 | FP | | | |

Median $ _____

The suggested marketing range is $ _____ to $ _____

This information is believed to be accurate, but is not warranted.
This is an opinion of value and should not be considered an appraisal.

### CMAs Using Comparable Sales and Listings (No Adjustments)

Licensees commonly use this method in pricing property. It involves listing properties for sale now, properties sold in the previous year, and expired listings, without adjustments. Its simplicity is appealing to licensees and sellers alike because it provides an overview of the market. However, if properties on the chart are not comparable and the subject property is priced from an average of sales prices or square-foot calculations, the pricing method can be misleading.

---

**DISCUSSION EXERCISE 4.8**

In this role-playing session, assume the CMA has been explained but the seller is attempting to set an unreasonably high listing price. Discuss as many persuasive points as possible to encourage the seller to price the property in the range suggested.

---

### Computer-Generated CMAs

As computers have become more important in every phase of the real estate business, software programs have been written that make impressive presentations to buyers and sellers. Many of these programs are formatted to print out an entire listing presentation to the seller, tailored to his specific needs. In many cases, the time required is less than that of handwriting the old CMA grids. Most of the programs are designed to interface directly with the MLS system program and download the necessary data. This saves the licensee time because she does not have to type the information. Most programs provide raw sales data without adjustment, although the sales associate, by selecting only comparable properties, can come quite close to market value.

## SUMMARY

A real estate licensee may prepare an appraisal in a transaction that is not federally related. F.S. 475 requires that the appraisal be done in conformity with the Uniform Standards of Professional Appraisal Practice. Normally, when listing or selling property, licensees prepare a comparative market analysis and give their opinion of value. Many important principles of value exist, including highest and best use, substitution, supply and demand, contribution, and conformity.

The comparable sales approach to estimating value is the most appropriate method appraisers use to value homes and vacant sites. The comparative market analysis is the method most licensees use to prepare an opinion of value. The three sections of a CMA are properties that have sold recently, properties for sale now, and properties that did not sell during the listing periods. Data for the CMA are gathered primarily from the MLS and county property appraiser's records. Only comparable properties should be used in the analysis. A range of values is provided to the seller because it is more meaningful than a single value.

## KEY TERMS

adjustments

appraisal

comparable property

comparative market analysis (CMA)

federally related transaction

opinion of value

property characteristic

reconciliation

subject property

transactional characteristic

Uniform Standards of Professional Appraisal Practice (USPAP)

# PRACTICE EXAM

1.  An appraisal of real property is a(n):
    a.  accurate determination of its value.
    b.  process of arriving at its value.
    c.  estimate of its value.
    d.  reconciled statement of just value.

2.  Of all the factors shown below that influence market value, the most important is the:
    a.  principle of substitution.
    b.  highest and best use.
    c.  law of increasing and diminishing returns.
    d.  principle of conformity.

3.  The Joneses live in a 2,100-square-foot home. Home sizes in the area range from 1,200 square feet to 2,100 square feet. Sales Associate Sam found seven comparable sales from different sized homes. He calculated the sales price per square foot for each home, averaged all the prices, and applied it to the square feet in the subject home. In preparing the CMA, Sam:
    a.  has prepared the CMA properly.
    b.  should have asked the Joneses how they wanted him to do it so they could get the best price for their home.
    c.  has violated Chapter 475 because he did not follow the USPAP.
    d.  should have used only the sales prices of similar size homes.

4.  The most profitable legally and physically permitted use of real property is called its:
    a.  market value.
    b.  appraised value.
    c.  location.
    d.  highest and best use.

5.  A comparative market analysis would be *LEAST* effective when trying to establish value for a:
    a.  residential property.
    b.  duplex.
    c.  public school property.
    d.  vacant property.

6.  Which is designed to promote the principle of conformity to maintain and enhance value in a subdivision?
    a.  Restrictive covenants
    b.  Zoning codes
    c.  Comprehensive plans
    d.  Land use codes

7.  When Mr. Wilson added a family room to his house, which was already too large for the area, he did not see the value increase as much as the cost of the addition. What principle was demonstrated?
    a.  Highest and best use of the land
    b.  Increase in value at least equal to the cost of construction
    c.  Law of increasing returns
    d.  Law of diminishing returns

8.  When listing a property in the ordinary course of business, any active real estate licensee in Florida is authorized to prepare an:
    a.  opinion of value.
    b.  appraisal report.
    c.  appraisal assignment report.
    d.  analysis assignment report.

9.  A mansion in a neighborhood of smaller, more average homes would violate the principle of:
    a.  change.
    b.  conformity.
    c.  competition.
    d.  contribution.

10.  In a neighborhood of three-bedroom, two-bath homes, an owner added a second bathroom at a cost of $1,600. An appraiser adjusted the value of the home upward by $2,000 due to the improvement. This is an example of the principle of:
    a.  change.
    b.  conformity.
    c.  competition.
    d.  contribution.

11.  Traci is preparing a CMA for property located in Arbor Hills. She finds three homes that sold recently: a four-bedroom home with a pool that sold for $90,000; a three-bedroom home with no pool that sold for $81,000; and a three-bedroom home with a pool that sold for $85,000. Based solely on the above information, what does a swimming pool contribute to value in Arbor Hills?
    a.  $9,000
    b.  $5,000
    c.  $4,000
    d.  $0

12.  The ideal kitchen service triangle should be from:
    a.  9 to 25 feet.
    b.  12 to 22 feet.
    c.  120 square feet.
    d.  12 by 24 feet.

13.  The comparable sales approach to value is based primarily on what principle of valuation?
    a.  Conformity
    b.  Substitution
    c.  Supply and demand
    d.  Highest and best use

14.  Which one of the following is NOT important in comparing properties using the comparable sales approach?
    a.  Date of sale
    b.  Size of house
    c.  Original cost of improvements
    d.  General condition and appearance

15. You are preparing a CMA and want to be certain that it reflects comparable sales of properties sold directly by owners. The best place to find the information is in:
    a.  either the clerk's office or the tax appraiser's office.
    b.  city hall.
    c.  the MLS records.
    d.  the tax collector's office.

16. When the term *recently* is used to describe a comparable sale, it is generally understood to mean that the property sold within the past how many months?
    a.  12
    b.  8–15
    c.  12–18
    d.  18

17. Which is NOT a condition that a licensee must meet when selecting comparable properties using the comparable sales approach to value?
    a.  Similar
    b.  Sold recently
    c.  Same market area
    d.  Same floor plan

18. When preparing a CMA, John evaluated three sales in the neighborhood, as shown below. Each comparable sale had only one adjustment. Based solely on the figures shown, on which comparable sale should John place the most reliance?

|  | Sale A | Sale B | Sale C |
|---|---|---|---|
| Sale price | $167,000 | $168,000 | $157,000 |
| Adjustments | –$ 14,000 | –$ 14,000 | –$ 2,000 |
| As adjusted | $153,000 | $154,000 | $155,000 |

    a.  Sale A
    b.  Sale B
    c.  Sale C
    d.  All comparables should be treated equally and averaged.

19. You are estimating the value of a vacant lot zoned for single-family residence use. One year ago, a comparable lot sold for $25,000. Your analysis of market conditions and property characteristics produced the following needed adjustments: subject lot, $2,000 inferior; subject site location, $3,000 superior. These adjustments result in an estimated market value for the subject lot of:
    a.  $26,000.
    b.  $23,000.
    c.  $24,000.
    d.  $27,000.

20. A home has dimensions of 35 feet by 57 feet that include a 24-foot by 22-foot garage and a 200-square-foot screen porch. How many square feet of gross living area does the home have?
    a.  1,267
    b.  1,467
    c.  1,995
    d.  2,354

# CHAPTER 5

# MAKING THE LISTING PRESENTATION

1 **LEARNING OBJECTIVES**

2 Upon completion of this chapter, *you should be able to*

3 **1.** list at least four requirements for a proper listing presentation;

4 **2.** list the five major steps in a listing presentation;

5 **3.** describe the steps in explaining a CMA;

6 **4.** list two visual aids for a CMA presentation;

7 **5.** list the three major sections in a Sellers' Net Proceeds Form;

8 **6.** list at least eight costs that a seller may be expected to pay at closing;

9 **7.** explain why insurance and escrow amounts usually are not included in the Seller's Net Proceeds
10 Form;

11 **8.** explain the reasons for rounding all figures used in the Seller's Net Proceeds Form;

12 **9.** prepare a Seller's Net Proceeds Form; and

13 **10.** describe the problems an FSBO may face when selling his or her house.

14 **OVERVIEW**

15 When a licensee is able to deliver an effective listing presentation, the "close" rate for listing appointments
16 will be much higher. Prospecting is a numbers game. It may take up to 50 calls to get one listing
17 appointment. What a shame it would be to have all that effort rendered worthless by failing to prepare
18 carefully before sitting down with the sellers. ■

# REQUIREMENTS FOR THE PRESENTATION

This presentation is a "sit down at the dining room table" discussion when both husband and wife are present. It will be successful *only* if you

1. know all the parties who need to sign your listing are available
2. are fully prepared to list the property, which means you must have all the forms ready for signature when the parties agree to list
3. know this presentation thoroughly
4. know about the house you are trying to list. Use the information from the tax appraiser's office, the plat books, or from your own personal inspection
5. have prepared a Comparative Market Analysis. The report will help you to show the sellers a fair value for their house and to protect you from the "overpriced listing," which will cost you time, aggravation, and unhappy customers
6. have your information organized in a businesslike fashion and your mind organized as well
7. are properly dressed and professional in appearance and manner
8. are on time for the appointment

# THE FIVE MAJOR SEGMENTS OF THE PRESENTATION

A listing presentation consists of five major segments:

1. Building rapport with the sellers
2. Explaining the pricing process (going over the CMA)
3. Showing the sellers how much they might receive from the sale (the Seller's Net Proceeds Form)
4. Discussing the importance of listing the property with you
5. Ask for the listing

# BUILDING RAPPORT WITH THE SELLERS

1. Greet the sellers at the door with a smile, and be yourself. Thank them for the opportunity to visit their home, and after some initial small talk, begin taking control of the interview.
2. If you haven't already made a preliminary visit to the property, ask the sellers to give you a tour. Have a note pad to record your observations for each room. Ask questions about the house while on the tour. If you see any features that indicate the sellers' hobbies, awards, or family photos, try to acknowledge them. Show the owners that you've done your homework by confirming some of the information you've gotten from the tax appraiser.
3. Inspect the property boundaries; make notes of exterior features, then ask the sellers to help you measure the exterior of the house. Confirm that total with the information you have from the tax appraiser.
4. After returning indoors, arrange to have all parties sit at a dining or kitchen table. Suggest that the TV be turned down (or off) so that you can hear them well.
5. Find out why they are selling. If they are moving to a new town, find out how they feel (not think) about the move. Is it scary? Has he or she met the new boss? How do they feel about the new job? Let them know you care about them as individuals.

## Explaining the Pricing Process

The presentation should provide information the sellers need to fully understand the listing process. Agents who give a value without first going over the CMA may lose the opportunity for realistic pricing if the sellers are surprised and offended at the value. A proper presentation should proceed in the following sequence:

1. Help the sellers understand the current market conditions. You can get this information from MLS statistics or from your broker. Give statistics for the overall market. The CMA will help show the neighborhood statistics. For example, tell the sellers the
   a. Number of houses currently listed;
   b. Number of homes sold last month;
   c. Month's supply of homes on the market (divide listed homes by sales).
2. Give the sellers your analysis of the market:
   a. Is it a buyers' or a sellers' market?
   b. Are prices rising or falling?
   c. What is likely to happen if interest rates rise (or fall)?
3. Explain the importance of pricing the property within the selling range.
4. Inform the sellers that the purpose of the CMA is to determine the best list price for the property.
5. Explain the report and how you researched the material in it. If your conclusions of market value are less than the sellers' desired price, you may have a problem. Do not state your conclusions at this time. Wait to see what the sellers conclude from the comparable sales. (Often sellers will quickly realize that their price is too high and, if motivated to sell, will agree to reduce the price.)
6. Explain how each section of the CMA is important in the decision-making process by giving the sellers an overview of the following:
   a. Sold listings prove what selling prices have been and what bank appraisals might show.
   b. Homes now for sale illustrate the importance of competitive pricing.
   c. Expired listings demonstrate the futility of pricing property at an unrealistically high price.
7. Review individual properties on the report while referring to visual aids such as a subdivision map and photos.
8. Ask the sellers for questions or comments.
9. Give the sellers time to arrive at a range of values independently.
10. If the sellers want to price the property too high, discuss the reasons why that approach is unproductive.
11. When a realistic listing price has been agreed upon, complete the Seller's Net Proceeds Form.

### C A S E   S T U D Y

## PRESENTATION OF A CMA

**Assumptions.** Use the CMA from Chapter 4.

You visited the house yesterday when Mrs. Halliburton was home to measure it, evaluate its features, and take some digital photos for the presentation this evening. This allowed you to prepare a CMA with confidence that there would be no surprises.

*Cast:* **Sales Associate:** Alice Newby
　　　　**Sellers:** John Halliburton, Susan Halliburton

**Sales Associate:** Mr. and Mrs. Halliburton, thanks for inviting me into your home. Helping you get the most dollars for your home in a reasonable time is one of my most important responsibilities in my real estate practice. One of the ways I can really be helpful is by carefully preparing a market report. It's called a *Comparative Market Analysis*. Have you seen one of these before? [Hand them a copy of the CMA.]

**John:** No, we haven't. But this is our first home.

**Sales Associate:** OK, it will take us a few minutes to go over it, but it's well worth the time. The decisions we make based on this analysis are going to be very important to you as we go forward.

You can see I've put your names and addresses here at the top. You can see that the report is broken into three main sections [pointing]: Here are the sales in your neighborhood for the last 12 months. The sold properties section will tell us what homes appraisers can use and will give us an idea of the value for a homebuyer's bank appraisal. The section on properties that are now listed shows your competitors. And here are the properties that failed to sell, usually because they were overpriced. All of these properties are going to help us to decide at what price we should offer your home. Here's a map of the neighborhood so you can see where each of these homes is located. Do you have any questions so far?

**Susan:** Well, I don't see one of our neighbor's homes on your list, and I know he sold his house last May. The address is 4425 Landtowne Drive.

**Sales Associate:** Right. Let me see [looks at another list of every sale in the area]. Yes, you're right. Here it is on this list [shows list]. As you can see, his house had only 1,500 square feet, while yours has more than 1,900. I didn't use it in our pricing guide because it's just not comparable, don't you agree?

**Susan:** Yes, I see.

**Sales Associate:** On each of the homes included on our list, I've made some adjustments based on major differences from your house. For example, the house at 1640 Clover has only a one-car garage, and yours has a two-car garage. The price difference for that feature is about $2,800, so your house should sell for about $2,800 more.

**John:** OK, that makes sense.

**Sales Associate:** You can see that in the first section, sold properties, the median sales price of properties—and what yours will probably appraise for—is about $167,500. In the second section, your competition has a median listed price of $177,500. Now our best chance at a sale within reasonable time frames is to price your home somewhere above the sold properties and below the competing properties. Does that make sense?

**John:** Sure does.

**Sales Associate:** Here are the properties that were overpriced and stayed on the market a long time. They didn't sell. You can see they had a median price of $183,000. We want to avoid being in this group, don't you agree? [Shows them the pyramid (like the one in Figure 5.1).] Let me show you the Pricing Pyramid. As you can see, if you price the home at the median of the sold homes in your area, you'll attract the most buyers. If you price at what the other homes are listed for, you'll get some activity, but not as much. And if you price it too high, you won't see many buyers at all. The more buyers we can get to look, the better the chance of a sale.

**John:** Yes, we'd like to get it sold within the next few months.

**Sales Associate:** Great. Based on what you've seen here, what price do you think would be the best listing price for us to put it on the market?

FIGURE 5.1 ■ **The Pricing Pyramid**

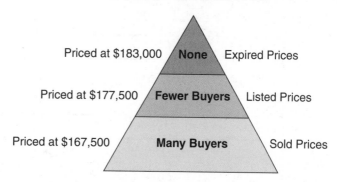

The Number of Potential Buyers Is
Related to Your Home's Price

Priced at $183,000  **None**  Expired Prices

Priced at $177,500  **Fewer Buyers**  Listed Prices

Priced at $167,500  **Many Buyers**  Sold Prices

This chart helps sellers to visualize the effect pricing
may have on the activity level the house will experience.
The lower the price, the more buyers will be attracted.

**Susan:** Well, I think we've got to be somewhere in between the sold ones and the listed ones. Do you think we could list it at the higher end, like $177,500?

**Sales Associate:** What do you think, John?

**John:** I'd like to get as much as possible, Susan, but two of the homes for sale now are at $175,000. I think maybe $174,500 might get it sold faster.

**Susan:** Yes, that's true. I'm cool with $174,500.

**Sales Associate:** I wholeheartedly agree. Could we schedule your home for our office inspection next Monday, or will the following week give you more time to get it ready? (This is the first time you ask for the order.)

**Susan:** Well, we may not be quite ready to do anything yet. Can we think about it and let you know?

**Sales Associate:** Absolutely. Maybe it would be helpful if I showed you what you are likely to clear from the sale after paying off the mortgage and all your expenses. Would that be helpful?

**John:** Sure would.

---

**DISCUSSION EXERCISE 5.1**

Using the CMA report in Figure 4.2, role-play the complete presentation of a CMA without referring to the script above. The instructor might assign several persons to present the different sections of the material. Assign a classmate to represent a "reasonably motivated" seller who is kind to the agent.

---

## ESTIMATING THE SELLER'S PROCEEDS

A seller generally is reluctant to enter into a listing agreement until she understands what expenses she must pay at closing. The **net proceeds** after paying off the mortgage and expenses of a sale are of primary interest to the seller and are often a factor in setting a list price. It is extremely imr

**FIGURE 5.2 ■ Seller's Net Proceeds Form**

Seller's Name: _____

Property Address: _____

| | | |
|---|---|---|
| **Selling Price** | $ | $ |
| **Less:** 1st Mortgage<br>2nd Mortgage<br>Other | | |
| **Seller's Equity** | $ | $ |
| **Less: Expenses** | | |
| Doc Stamps on Deed | | |
| Termite Inspection and Treatment | | |
| Title Insurance | | |
| Homeowner's Warranty | | |
| Buyer's Closing Costs<br>Buyer's Origination Fee<br>Buyer's Discount Points | | |
| Repairs and Replacements | | |
| Seller's Attorney Fee | | |
| Brokerage Fee | | |
| Other Miscellaneous Costs | | |
| Other | | |
| **Total Expenses** | $ | $ |
| **Less: Prorations** | | |
| Property Taxes | | |
| Interest | | |
| Homeowner's Dues | | |
| Rents and Deposits | | |
| **Total Prorations** | $ | $ |
| **Net Proceeds to Seller** | $ | $ |

These figures are estimates and intended only as a guide. They will vary at closing because of prorations, the mortgage balance, and unforeseen costs. An exact itemization will be provided to you at closing. Please read this and all other documents relating to this sale carefully. If you require further explanation, please consult an attorney.

Date: _____     Prepared by: _____

Seller: _____     Seller: _____

1   tant that a licensee use skill, care, and diligence in estimating the seller's proceeds from the sale.
2   The following is a discussion of the **Seller's Net Proceeds Form** (see Figure 5.2).

# Seller's Net Proceeds Form

A section for the seller's name and the property address should be completed. The left side of the form itemizes income and expenses related to the sale. Two columns are provided for calculations:

- *When listing the property.* The licensee might use column 1 when calculating an estimate based on a recommended price; the licensee would use column 2 if the seller wanted to know how much a different list price would net
- *When giving the seller a range of values.* The sales associate could provide for the seller a high-end list price and a low-end list price
- *At the time of listing.* Column 1 could be used for showing the net proceeds if customary seller's expenses were paid; column 2 could be used if the seller were asked to pay the buyer's loan closing costs. This is much like a best-case, worst-case scenario
- *For estimates given at the time of listing.* Column 1 is for listing proceeds; column 2 could be used when an offer is submitted
- *At the time an offer is submitted.* Column 1 shows the seller's net if the offer was accepted; column 2 shows the seller's net if a counteroffer was accepted

**Seller's Equity Section.** The seller's **equity** section consists of the sales price, less mortgage balances and other encumbrances. Special assessment liens and construction liens would be shown in the space provided for other encumbrances. All items should be rounded because this is an estimate. An exact mortgage balance is unnecessary because of the closing date's uncertainty. Uneven dollars and cents amounts should not be included. Exact amounts imply an accuracy that does not exist in the estimate.

**Expenses Section.** Any expenses that the seller might be required to pay should be listed. It is better to overestimate than to underestimate the expenses. A seller will not be unhappy if he receives more at the time of closing than he had expected, but he likely will be upset if expenses have been underestimated. Even though the bottom of the form provides a disclaimer, the licensee must be careful to avoid errors. Some expenses that should be discussed follow:

- Documentary stamps on deed are $.70 per $100 or fraction thereof of the sales price. The seller normally pays the cost of these stamps.
- Termite inspection (treatment and repairs) could be a substantial expense to the seller but is not known at the time of listing or contract. A conservative approach would be to show the cost of both in this section. A licensee should stay current on the costs of inspection and treatment in her market area. In many areas, the inspection is the buyer's expense.
- When making the seller's statement, the licensee would include the typical charge a seller might be expected to pay for title insurance and related costs based on local practice.
- Homeowner's warranty costs often are associated with the seller's need to assure the buyer that the home is in good condition and will be warranted against many defects by an independent home warranty company. Depending on the company, these costs may range from $300 to $500.
- Buyer's closing costs, the origination fee, and discount points can be very substantial expenses to the seller if the seller agrees to pay them. When taking a listing, a sales associate should include these items if the custom in the market area dictates. When preparing this estimate at the time of contract, the sales associate should take extra care if the seller will pay the buyer's costs. The licensee should use the lender's good-faith estimate, with a maximum amount agreed to in the contract. Leaving this open-ended in a contract can be problem if the discount points or other costs increase between the time of acceptance and the time of closing.

- Repairs and replacements usually are those that a lender might require. They also could be the result of wood-destroying organisms or nonfunctioning appliances. The licensee should use a cushion for such contingencies.
- The seller's attorney fee is an expense left to the seller to decide. The licensee should list the normal closing review fee for the seller in his market area.
- The brokerage fee is the commission the brokerage firm charges.
- Other miscellaneous costs include items like express mail fees for mortgage payoffs and recording mortgage satisfactions. The licensee should include a cushion here, to allow for contingencies. A seller on a tight budget cannot afford unpleasant surprises. This line also could be used to round uneven expense amounts into even amounts. For example, if the expenses were $8,945.60, the miscellaneous costs could be estimated at $54.40, resulting in total estimated expenses of $9,000.

**Prorations Section.** This section, if not carefully estimated, could result in an unpleasant surprise for the seller, because most prorations are debits (charges) to the seller. Because the closing date is not certain, it is not necessary to do exact prorations; approximations are satisfactory if amounts are rounded higher. The statement offers no provision for insurance prorations or proceeds from a lender's escrow account. Insurance should *not* be prorated; the buyer should purchase her own policy, and the seller should get a cancellation refund. Because the insurance refund and escrow refund from loans paid off are not received at closing, the net proceeds statement does not include these items. (If the mortgage is to be assumed, the prorations could be offset by the amounts held in escrow, as the buyer will be expected to reimburse the seller for those amounts.)

- Property taxes should be estimated for the year if tax information is not available. An assumed closing date is used to estimate prorations. If the closing were anticipated for June 28, for example, the licensee would show a charge to the seller for half the year's taxes.
- Interest prorations can be difficult to calculate. The amount depends on the time of month for the closing. Most interest is paid in arrears, but not all loans have that feature. The safest policy (if the loan is current) is to show a charge for a full month's interest.
- Homeowner's dues can be substantial in some areas, particularly with condominiums and other properties having substantial common maintenance areas. The dues may be paid in advance but often are paid in arrears. The homeowner should be questioned about the status of the dues.
- Rents and deposits can be major charges to the seller of an income property. If the seller has collected rent in advance, the buyer is entitled to the rent for the part of the month after the closing. The buyer also should be paid the security deposits.

**Net Proceeds to Seller.** The net proceeds equal the seller's equity less expenses and prorations. The amount of the seller's proceeds should be rounded to the next lowest $100.

## Exercise: Estimating Net Proceeds to Seller

Estimating the seller's net proceeds properly is extremely important. This exercise should be completed carefully using the Seller's Net Proceeds Form in Figure 5.2. Round up on expenses, prorations, and mortgages, and do not use cents. The final estimate should be rounded to the lowest hundred, using the following information:

| | | |
|---|---|---|
| 1 | Seller's name | Cindy Lewis |
| 2 | Property address | 1947 Oldfield Circle |
| 3 | Prepared by | Janice Brown |
| 4 | Estimated closing date | August 26 |
| 5 | Sales price | $93,800.00 |
| 6 | Existing first mortgage (8.5%) | 47,425.67 - ~~000~~ 336 |
| 7 | Home equity loan (11%) | 14,659.42 135 |
| 8 | Brokerage fee | 7% |
| 9 | Termite inspection and treatment | 400.00 |
| 10 | Buyer's title insurance | 650.00 |
| 11 | Repairs and replacements | 450.00 |
| 12 | Seller's attorney fee | 350.00 |
| 13 | Homeowner's warranty | 375.00 |
| 14 | Discount points | 2,100.00 |
| 15 | Annual taxes | 1,325.00 |
| 16 | Interest | ? |
| 17 | Annual homeowner's dues | 150.00 |

---

**DISCUSSION EXERCISE 5.2**

Using the Seller's Net Proceeds Form prepared in the above exercise, role-play the presentation of the form to the seller. The instructor might assign several persons to present the different sections of the material. Assign a reasonably motivated seller who is kind to the agent. The licensee should ask a closing question when showing the net proceeds from the sale.

---

18 ## Ask for the Order

19 Show the sellers the net amount to be received and ask, "Can you live with this figure?" If the
20 answer is "Yes," follow up with, "Do you have any objections to my making the property avail-
21 able to all the REALTORS® in the city through the multiple-listing service?" If the answer is
22 "OK," ask for the current mortgage information, and proceed to fill out the listing forms. You
23 have obtained the listing!

24 If the answer is "We are not ready to list at this time," say "I understand," then go to the
25 next step.

26 ## DISCUSS THE REASONS MOST FSBOs DON'T SELL THEIR HOMES

27 ### The Problem of Showing the Property

28 1. Explain that the sign in front of the home invites any passersby to come to the front
29 door and ask to be let inside. Normally, a resident of a home would never allow the
30 person access, but it's now more difficult to say "No." Talk for a moment about the
31 family security and that you'll escort all buyers after they are qualified.
32 2. Remind the owners that a buyer cannot know everything about their property by
33 simply looking at the front of the house. This is a very important point, especially if
34 the home has only average curb appeal but the inside is far nicer than average.
35 Without knowing about the good features, a buyer might drive right by. You should
36 explain that when you show the home, you will escort them inside, the only place
37 they can truly evaluate this home.

3.  You can remind the sellers that if they are not home all day and on the evenings and weekends to show the home, the buyer may not call back. Every time they go shopping or to work, their property is "off the market." Explain that when they list with you, the property will be on the market 24 hours a day, because they can reach a licensee who will have the information the buyer wants.

## The Problem of Financing

Because the buyers will likely need new financing on the property, you could explain that they may want assistance in deciding where to go for a home mortgage and may not understand the process. Because of that reason, many buyers ask for the help of a real estate professional.

## The Problem of Verbal Negotiations

Discuss with the sellers the disadvantage of direct negotiations with a buyer. Many buyers buy direct because their negotiation skills give them an advantage. Buyers will ask questions about the reason for selling and about how much lower the sellers might go. If the sellers remain firm, explain that the buyers may leave. But the sellers should also know that if they give a buyer a lower figure, that buyer may later try to negotiate even lower.

The sellers should be told that when a buyer wants to make an offer, the licensee will put it in writing and ask for a good-faith deposit so that if the price offered by the buyer is acceptable, all the sellers need to do is sign it.

## The Problem of Writing a Purchase Contract

You can ask sellers whether they have a contract form and whether they feel comfortable filling it in for the buyers to sign. If the sellers have a contract form and think they can fill it in, let them know about the education process most licensees undergo so they can write one that will not end up in court.

If the sellers say they have an attorney to write the contract, suggest that it's important for the attorney to be qualified in real estate practice. You might also raise the question of how quickly a good, but busy, attorney could get a contract written when a buyer is ready to buy.

## The Major Problem: Saving the Commission

In this last part of your discussion, you want to get the sellers' agreement that they are willing to try to overcome these obstacles in order to save the commission. When they agree, you must answer their objection to listing with you by letting them see their efforts won't save a commission. Ask the sellers why they believe a buyer would be willing to take the time and make the effort to buy a house directly from a seller when the buyer could get much more help from a licensee. Then explain to them that the reason is that the buyer is also buying direct solely to save the commission and that it won't be possible for both parties to save the full commission. In the unlikely event that both seller and buyer complete the transaction without help from a licensee, why couldn't both parties save the full commission?

## Ask for the Order

A closing question like "Can you see how most persons who try to sell their homes turn to a real estate professional?" might generate a positive answer. You can then ask if they'd like you to try to get the home into the MLS as soon as possible, or bring your office staff over on Monday morning to see it, or whether they would like you to hold an open house next Sunday. If their response is positive, you can begin filling out listing paperwork.

In many cases, the sellers won't be ready to list with your company. You should ask for the reason, and if they want to think about it, you should tell them why, when they decide to list the property, the listing person should be you.

**Show the Seller Why the REALTOR® Should Be You.** Tell the sellers about you and your brokerage firm, for example, that

- your office is in a high traffic location
- your training program makes all your associates more professional and successful
- your office listing caravans generate more sales
- you will put the home into MLS
- you will be advertising the home
- you will be holding open houses
- your office is a member of an out-of-town referral agency
- you offer a warranty program; then describe how that will help to sell the property
- you will call them each week to tell them of your progress
- you will give them your special "Seven-Step Service" program

## SEVEN-STEP SERVICE

A seller wants to know what the brokerage firm will do to earn the commission, and a chart similar to the one shown in Figure 5.3 may be helpful. While the chart itself is rather sparse, for easy understanding, the sales associate might tell the seller about each step in more detail. After you have finished your presentation, you should clearly and directly ask for the order. "Mr. and Mrs. Halliburton, may I help you sell your property?"

If the answer is no, you should review every point of the presentation point-by-point, then ask for the order again. In many cases, the presentation will result in a listing. If for any reason you do not get a listing, arrange to visit again in three days. You may never get the listing, but it won't be because you gave up too soon.

## SUMMARY

Making an effective listing presentation will result in a much higher close rate for listing appointments. Several conditions must be met in order to succeed:

- All parties on the deed must be present
- All forms must be ready for the sellers' signature
- The licensee must know each step of the presentation
- The licensee must have complete information about the property to be listed
- A comparative market analysis must be prepared
- The licensee must be organized, have a professional appearance, and be on time

**FIGURE 5.3 ■ Seven-Step Service Chart**

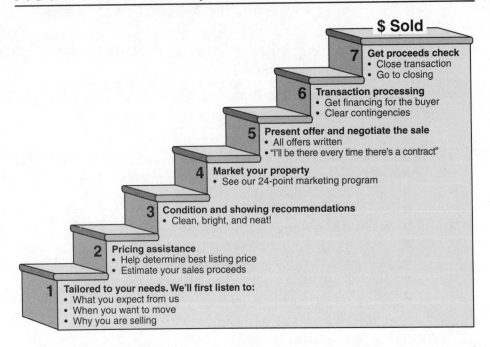

**$ Sold**

7 **Get proceeds check**
   • Close transaction
   • Go to closing

6 **Transaction processing**
   • Get financing for the buyer
   • Clear contingencies

5 **Present offer and negotiate the sale**
   • All offers written
   • "I'll be there every time there's a contract"

4 **Market your property**
   • See our 24-point marketing program

3 **Condition and showing recommendations**
   • Clean, bright, and neat!

2 **Pricing assistance**
   • Help determine best listing price
   • Estimate your sales proceeds

1 **Tailored to your needs. We'll first listen to:**
   • What you expect from us
   • When you want to move
   • Why you are selling

[The material in the listing presentation section is from *30-Day Track to Success,* © 1984, 1996, and 2002 by Edward J. O'Donnell.]

The five major parts of a listing presentation are

1. Building rapport with the sellers
2. Explaining the pricing process
3. Explaining the Seller's Net Proceeds Form
4. Discussing the importance of listing with your brokerage firm
5. Asking for the listing

A seller usually is more interested in the net proceeds from the sale of his property than the home's actual sales price. The Seller's Net Proceeds Form—the financial disclosure to the seller—consists of three major sections. The seller's equity section provides the sales price less mortgage balances, with the difference being the seller's equity. The expenses section shows expenses the seller must pay at closing. The prorations section includes taxes, interest, rents, and homeowner's dues.

## KEY TERMS

equity

listing presentation

net proceeds

Seller's Net Proceeds Form

# PRACTICE EXAM

1.  When presenting a CMA, a licensee should *NOT*:
    a.  discuss current market conditions for the overall market, only for the sellers' neighborhood.
    b.  recommend a price for the property before going over the data in the CMA.
    c.  give the seller a range of values rather than a single value.
    d.  ask for the order after the explanation.

2.  Where is the best place in the house to make the listing presentation?
    a.  Living room sofa
    b.  On the deck outside
    c.  At the dining room table
    d.  In front of the TV

3.  The reason for eliminating cents and rounding to the nearest $100 on the Seller's Net Proceeds Form is to:
    a.  avoid giving the impression that the figures will be exactly as shown at closing.
    b.  make the statement easier to understand.
    c.  provide a cushion in the estimate.
    d.  All of the above

4.  The components of the seller's equity section of the Seller's Net Proceeds Form include:
    a.  seller's equity, expenses, and seller's net proceeds.
    b.  sales price, prorations, and expenses.
    c.  seller's equity, prorations, and seller's net proceeds.
    d.  sales price, mortgages, and seller's equity.

5.  What is the proper order for a complete listing presentation?
    a.  CMA, sellers' net, building rapport with the sellers, reasons for listing with your brokerage firm, ask for the order
    b.  Ask for the order, CMA, sellers' net, building rapport with the sellers, reasons for listing with your brokerage firm
    c.  Building rapport with the sellers, ask for the order, CMA, sellers' net, reasons for listing with your brokerage firm
    d.  Building rapport with the sellers, CMA, sellers' net, reasons for listing with your brokerage firm, ask for the order

6.  When explaining the current market conditions to the seller, one piece of information that would *NOT* normally be included is the:
    a.  aggregate square footage of all listed homes.
    b.  number of houses currently listed.
    c.  month's supply of homes on the market.
    d.  number of homes sold last month.

7.  Which part of the CMA would indicate overpriced listings?
    a.  Sold houses
    b.  Houses currently for sale
    c.  Expired listings
    d.  Withdrawn listings

8.  The preferable approach to setting the listing price is to:
    a.  list at the price the seller wants.
    b.  go over the CMA carefully and to help the seller to arrive at an appropriate range of values.
    c.  tell the seller the maximum price at which you will list the house at the beginning of the meeting.
    d.  find out what the seller needs from the sale and add your commission.

**Use the following information to answer questions 9 through 12.**

Broker Sharon is compiling a Seller's Net Proceeds Form for Ellen Johnson. The figures she gathers are as follows:

| | |
|---|---|
| Brokerage fee | 7% |
| Title insurance | $ 780.00 |
| Termite inspection and treatment | 300.00 |
| Sales price | 127,500.00 |
| Existing first mortgage @ 10% | 98,601.60 |
| Documentary stamps on deed | ? |
| Property taxes for the year | 1,745.60 |
| Interest proration (paid in arrears) | ? |
| Closing date | June 30 |

9.  What is the seller's equity, rounded to the nearest $100?
    a.  $29,000
    b.  $28,900
    c.  $20,000
    d.  $16,300

10. What are the total expenses, rounded to the next highest $100?
    a.  $10,100
    b.  $10,800
    c.  $10,900
    d.  $11,800

11. What are the total prorations, rounded to the nearest $100? Will the prorations be added or subtracted from the equity?
    a.  $2,600 added
    b.  $900 subtracted
    c.  $1,300 subtracted
    d.  $1,700 subtracted

12. What are the seller's net proceeds, rounded to the nearest $100?
    a.  $14,500
    b.  $15,400
    c.  $16,300
    d.  $17,100

13. Patti is making a listing presentation to an FSBO. She completes the CMA and gets the sellers to accept the net amount on the Seller's Net Proceeds Form. She should be able to take the listing now primarily because:
    a.  she has completed all steps of the listing presentation.
    b.  the commission is included on the Seller's Net Proceeds Form, and the sellers have agreed to the amounts shown.
    c.  the FSBOs should know they would not be able to sell the property themselves.
    d.  she has not gone over the reasons the sellers should list with her firm.

14. The reason it is not practical for a licensee to determine the exact prorations on the Seller's Net Proceeds Form when taking a listing is that:
    a. it takes too long.
    b. a mistake will likely lose the listing.
    c. most sellers refuse to list when they see the prorations.
    d. the exact closing date is unknown.

15. When preparing the interest proration on a Seller's Net Proceeds Form, the best policy is to:
    a. enter zero on the line, with a note that it can't be determined at this time.
    b. enter a full month of interest.
    c. enter one-half month of interest.
    d. enter two months of interest.

16. Which is *NOT* one of the three major problems in showing the property an FSBO should be told to expect?
    a. The risk to personal safety because of letting all prospective buyers into the house
    b. The fact that most new buyers will need financing
    c. Difficulty in getting prospective buyers inside if the exterior of the house is not particularly attractive
    d. The house is off the market when the seller is away from home

17. The reason most FSBOs won't be able to save the commission is that:
    a. they may not understand how to help the buyer get financing.
    b. they may show the house to an unqualified buyer.
    c. the prospective buyer is buying direct to save the same commission.
    d. the seller may not know how to write a binding contract.

18. The final step in the listing presentation is:
    a. explaining to the sellers why they should list with your brokerage firm.
    b. asking for the order.
    c. delivering the CMA.
    d. putting the listing into the MLS.

19. If a seller wants to list the property before you have completed the listing presentation, you should:
    a. politely request a little more time to cover the presentation.
    b. suggest he may wish to think about it overnight, and leave the paperwork for him to sign later.
    c. ignore the interruption and continue with your presentation.
    d. take the listing.

20. On the Seller's Net Proceeds Form, which proration should *NOT* be included?
    a. Property taxes
    b. Insurance
    c. Interest
    d. Rents, if this is a rental property

# CHAPTER

# 6

# LISTING CONTRACTS

1 **LEARNING OBJECTIVES**

2 Upon completion of this chapter, *you should be able to*

3 **1.** explain the wording that could be used to protect both seller and broker from commission disputes
4 caused by a buyer who improperly tries to leave the broker out of the transaction in an open listing;

5 **2.** state the legally required elements in a listing contract;

6 **3.** explain the distinguishing characteristics of each of the following types of listings: open, exclusive
7 agency, and exclusive-right-of-sale;

8 **4.** discuss the purpose of an owner's warranty in a listing contract;

9 **5.** discuss the purpose of the latent defects disclosure in the process of listing real property for sale;

10 **6.** explain the steps required to complete a residential profile sheet;

11 **7.** complete the residential profile sheet;

12 **8.** complete a listing contract;

13 **9.** explain each paragraph of the listing agreement that applies to your market area; and

14 **10.** design a listing servicing program for your personal listings.

15 **OVERVIEW**

16 A listing contract is an agreement between a real estate broker and a property owner. The listing
17 contract specifies the duties of both the broker and the owner in the sale of the owner's real property.
18 Without listing contracts, there would be little or no inventory to sell, exchange, lease, rent, or
19 auction. In Florida, a listing contract may be written, oral, or implied. Every written listing agreement
20 must include a definite expiration date, a description of the property, the price and terms, the fee or
21 commission, and the principal's signature. A legible, signed, true, and correct copy of the listing
22 agreement must be given to the principal(s) within 24 hours of obtaining the written listing agreement.
23 Also, a written listing contract may not contain a self-renewing or an automatic renewal provision. If it

contains such a provision, the agreement is void. It is important to understand that a listing agreement is a personal services (employment) contract that requires that the broker perform one or more professional services to fulfill the agreement. The broker may seek assistance from other licensees, but the primary responsibility remains with the listing broker. The listing contract is a broker's employment contract, and all listings should be in writing. If litigation should result from some misunderstanding, default, or breach, it is much easier to resolve by showing the terms of a written contract than by obtaining testimony to prove the terms or conditions of an oral listing. Because the statute of frauds does not cover listing contracts, oral listing contracts are enforceable with the proper amount of evidence and testimony. ■

## TYPES OF LISTING CONTRACTS

In this chapter, three types of listing contracts are identified. The exclusive-right-of-sale listing contract is emphasized because of its predominance in residential property transactions.

### Open Listing

An **open listing** is a contract in which an owner reserves the right to employ any number of brokers. Brokers may work simultaneously, but the first broker who produces a ready, willing, and able buyer at the terms accepted by the seller is the only one who earns a commission. If the owner himself sells the property without the aid of any of the brokers, he is not obligated to pay any commission; but if a broker can prove she was the procuring cause of the transaction, she may be entitled to a commission. While most residential brokers will not accept open listings, commercial and agricultural property brokers sometimes work with sellers with this type of listing.

Any listing contract normally creates an open listing unless the contract is worded in a manner that specifically provides for a different type of listing. While open listings may be either oral or implied, a contract does not exist until terms are negotiated. For example, a for-sale-by-owner sign that indicates "brokers protected" or in some other way invites offers from brokers does not create a listing contract.

Either or all parties may terminate an open listing at will, and in the absence of formal notification, an open listing may terminate after a reasonable time. The owner principal is not obligated to notify any of the brokers that the property has been sold.

### Exclusive-Agency Listing (Exclusive Listing)

The **exclusive-agency listing** is the preferred listing agreement of an owner who has selected one particular broker as his or her exclusive agent, for a specified period of time, to sell real property according to the owner's stated terms. In an exclusive-agency listing, the owner appoints the broker but reserves the right to sell the property without paying a commission to the broker if the broker has not introduced or identified the buyer. If the broker performs by selling the property before the owner can do so, the broker is entitled to a commission. Exclusive-agency residential listings are less common than exclusive-right-of-sale listings.

A common problem with exclusive-agency and open listings is the exposure to lawsuits for procuring cause between the broker and the seller.

> **DISCUSSION EXERCISE 6.1**
>
> Arthur Cody lists Donald Wilson's home under an exclusive-agency listing agreement. Arthur shows the property to William Farkas. William notices that the seller has a sign on the property saying For Sale By Owner—555-1145. Arthur drops William off and writes a letter to Donald, registering William as a prospect. Immediately after Arthur drops him off, William calls Donald directly. Donald does not know that Arthur has shown the property and agrees to a reduced price since no commission is involved. Donald and William enter into a contract for sale. It is only after the contract is signed that Donald gets Arthur's prospect registration letter. When the sale closes, Arthur brings suit for commission as the procuring cause of the sale.
>
> Role-play the court argument: Arthur, arguing for a commission on the sale, and Donald, explaining why no commission is due.

In the discussion exercise above, Donald, whom we assume to be an honest person, was sued because of the buyer's actions, not his own. How can a broker prevent this type of misunderstanding? Registration is not enough, because the notification may come after the parties have entered into a contract. A better method to help the seller receive fair disclosure is for the sales associate to recommend that the seller require the following words in all contracts the seller believes to be the procuring cause of the sale:

*"This property is listed with a broker under an agreement that the broker will be paid a commission for procuring a buyer for the property. Buyer warrants to seller that he or she was not shown or made aware of this property by any real estate broker or sales associate. Buyer agrees that if a broker claiming a commission provides information to the contrary, buyer will reimburse seller for commissions due to said real estate broker as well as legal fees."*

A buyer who has seen the property with a broker will refuse to sign such a statement, putting the seller on notice that the buyer is trying to save the commission by excluding the broker.

Two other problems can arise from an exclusive-agency agreement. First, a broker is reluctant to show property to a buyer if the owner's phone number is displayed prominently on a sign in front of the property. The sign invites the buyer to exclude the broker to get a better price. If the broker takes the listing under an exclusive agency, the broker should get the owner's agreement to remove the sign.

Another problem the broker faces is the possibility of the owner's advertising a lower price (broker's price less commission). The broker likely will lose the buyer if the buyer sees the owner's ad. The broker and the owner should quote the same price.

## Exclusive-Right-of-Sale Listing

The **exclusive-right-of-sale listing** is the most advantageous listing from the broker's viewpoint and the most common type of listing. The listing is given to a selected broker, who then becomes the exclusive broker for the sale of the property. The broker is due a commission regardless of who sells the property. That is, if the owner sells the property during the contract period, the broker still earns a commission. Also, if the owner sells the property within a designated time period after the listing contract has expired to a buyer originally introduced to the property by the broker, the owner usually is liable for a sales commission to the broker.

1    To be enforceable, this type of listing contract should be in writing and include valuable
2    consideration. Only exclusive-right-of-sale and exclusive-agency listings may be entered into
3    the MLS by the listing brokers.

## Warranties by the Owner

5    If the listing broker is a single agent for the seller, both the broker and the seller have obliga-
6    tions under the listing agreement. The principal has legal obligations to the broker, including
7    performance of all promises made in the contract, as well as the obligation to engage in hon-
8    est, straightforward dealing. The actions and misrepresentations of a seller can become a lia-
9    bility to the agent. For example, if a seller tells a sales associate that the plumbing pipes are
10   copper and the sales associate passes along that information to a buyer without qualification,
11   both the seller and the brokerage firm may be liable for damages if the buyer later discovers
12   the plumbing pipes are polybutylene. Litigation may result in damages assessed against both
13   the seller and the broker.

## Latent Defects Disclosure

15   To reduce the liability, most listing contracts in Florida contain a **warranty of owner** clause.
16   The clause has a promise that the "seller will warrant the accuracy of information set forth
17   herein and on the data sheets, exhibits, and addenda attached hereto and will indemnify and
18   hold harmless the licensee in the transaction or anyone relying on the owner's representa-
19   tions." The changing attitude of the courts today can be seen in the relatively new practice of
20   attaching **latent defects addenda** to listing contracts. The owner and the broker are liable for
21   failing to disclose known defects that materially affect the value of residential property. The
22   disclosure is simply an attempt to create a degree of protection for the broker against potential
23   liability resulting from oversight or the owner's dishonesty. It is closely related to the property
24   condition disclosure described earlier.

## C A S E   S T U D Y

# PREPARATION OF THE RESIDENTIAL PROFILE SHEET

On December 13, 20AA, John K. and Elizabeth J. Scott conclude a contractual agreement
with you, a licensed real estate sales associate. You have a six-month exclusive right to sell
their home, which has been granted homestead tax exemption and is owned as an estate by
the entireties. The house is an all-electric, three-bedroom, two-bath, single-story structure,
with an efficient traffic pattern. The master bath has an oversized, Roman-style bathtub. The
house is brick veneer over concrete block with a Spanish tile roof. Insulation used in the attic
space has an R-23 rating. The house is five years old, but a new heat-pump-type air-condi-
tioner and heater was installed in November 20AA.

The entire neighborhood is zoned R-1A and consists of quality homes on quiet, tree-lined
streets, with city and county utilities and telephone and power lines underground. City bus
service is two blocks away, and elementary, junior high, and high schools are all within six
blocks of the property.

While different areas of the state use different listing forms, **profile sheets,** and exclusive-
right-of-sale listing contracts, they all require the same basic information. The listing form
used in your area should be substituted for the one in this chapter. (See Figure 6.1.) If none
is available, complete the sample residential profile sheet and listing contract in this text to

develop the skill needed to gather important information. Use the following case study to fill out the residential profile sheet.

The Scotts have decided that $71,500 is a fair selling price. The county has assessed the 110′ × 150′ lot at $15,000, and the dwelling at $55,600. The Scotts briefly considered an offer of a year's lease at $600 per month but decided to sell instead. The property, located at 1234 Sunny Circle, Sunshine City, is legally described as Lot 21, Block C, Cool Canal Subdivision, Sunshine City, as recorded in Plat Book 39, Page 543, Lottery County, Florida.

The lot is completely landscaped and well maintained. The house consists of a 14′ × 24′ great room, 14′ × 18′ master bedroom, 10′ × 14′ den, 14′ × 14′ second bedroom, and 12′ × 14′ third bedroom. The dining area between the 10′ × 10′ kitchen and the great room is 12′ × 12′. A utility room, a foyer, a pantry, a hall, two baths, and four large closets bring the total air-conditioned and heated living area to 1,776 square feet. An unusually large garage of 720 square feet brings the total square footage under roof to 2,496.

The Scotts have paid the property taxes for 20AA. Because John must report to his new job in another state by April 1, 20BB, at the latest, he will pay the new owner the 20BB taxes, which will be prorated at the closing. The city, county, and school board tax rate for the subdivision was 29 mills for 20AA, including all bond and tax levies.

The Scotts have just refinanced and now hold a 10½ percent, 30-year conventional mortgage in the amount of $55,000 with the Secured Profit Savings Association. Their monthly payment for principal and interest is $503.11. A comprehensive homeowner's hazard and liability policy with a face value of $56,500, purchased at a cost of $264 for one year, is due to expire at midnight, October 18, 20BB.

All floors except the kitchen and bathrooms have custom carpets, and every window is equipped with custom-made draperies. The Scotts are willing to leave all carpets and draperies. The kitchen is all electric, and the electric water heater is a 60-gallon, quick-recovery unit. The kitchen appliances include a large, beverage-center-type refrigerator, a built-in food processor; a microwave oven; an electric oven over range; a disposal; a dishwasher; and a trash compactor. The Scotts have decided to leave all of the appliances except the refrigerator.

The Scotts have stipulated that their home is to be shown by appointment only and have provided you with their telephone number (655-3210). They have indicated a willingness to take back a second mortgage or a contract for deed, but they will not agree to any financing that results in a cost to them. Your employer, Super Real Estate, Inc. (555-6543), and the Scotts have agreed on a 7½ percent sales commission on the gross sales price. The Scotts have agreed to give possession no later than the actual date of closing. If the Scotts withdraw the listing, the fee will be 1 percent. You agree to put the listing into the MLS within three working days. In case the Scotts want to lease the property, your fee is 10 percent. The Scotts authorize you to put a **lockbox** on the home.

# PREPARATION OF AN EXCLUSIVE-RIGHT-OF-SALE LISTING CONTRACT

Once she has gathered and entered the property information on the profile sheet, the licensee should prepare the listing agreement. The sales associate should complete as much of the paperwork as possible before the listing appointment. Because the task can be done in a controlled environment without distractions, it is more likely to be correct. The advance preparation also results in a more efficient process once the sales associate is with the seller.

A listing contract is shown in Figure 6.2. Fill in the information on this form or on one used in your area, as appropriate.

F I G U R E   6.1   ■   **Residential Profile Sheet**

# TALLAHASSEE BOARD OF REALTORS

## Residential-Condo/Townhouse-Mobile Homes/Modular Homes

LISTING INPUT SHEET

The Information Requested In This Section must be Provided

PROPERTY ADDRESS

OFFICE NAME                                        #                LISTING NUMBER

AGENT NAME
AGENT HOME PHONE
LIST Office Number                                 #                FIRST ISSUE NUMBER

RS=1
CT=6
MH=7

All Key words Required

TYP  STN          STR                              LAG              LO
RS - Residential   Street Number   Street Name     List Agent Number   List Office Number
CT - Condo/Townhouse
MH - Mobile Homes/
Modular Homes

UNT  LOT           AR                              CIT
unit  Lot          Area (Major)                    City Name

YRB                BLK    TXN    MB                 SUB
Year Built (ex: 1991)   Block   Tax Item Number (NO Dashes)   Y/N   Subdivision Name (as per Legal Description in Tax Rolls)
                              Metes & Bounds

LRM                SQF    LTS
Living /Great Rm Dimensions   Square Feet   Lot Dimensions

BR    BR1          FAM    DRM    KIT            BR4
Number Bedrm   Master Bedrm Dimensions   Family Room Dimensions   Dining Room Dimensions   Kitchen Dimensions   Bedroom #4 Dimensions
                                     BR2    BR3
                                     Bedroom #2 Dimensions   Bedroom #3 Dimensions

OTR                BAT    FBT    HBT    POL    LP          TAX
Other Rm (Dimension/Descrip.)   Total No. Baths   No.Full Baths   No.Half Baths   Pool   List Price   Taxes/Annual
                                                    Y/N

AS1  Y/N  ASM1     M1P    M1D    M1L    M1R
First Mortgage   1st Mtg Amt. Assumable   1st Mtg Payment   1st Mtg Desc. PI,PIT, PITI   1st Mortgage Lender   1st Mtg Interest Rate
Assumable

AS2  Y/N  ASM2     M2P    M2D    M2L    M2R
2nd Mortgage   2nd Mtg Amt Assumable   2nd Mtg Payment   2nd Mtg  Desc. PI,PIT, PITI   2nd Mortgage Lender   2nd Mtg Interest Rate
Assumable                                          Avail for Purch=A
                                                   None-N
SPA  Y/N           INS    WRR    HFE            DWP
Special Assessments   Insurance/Annual   Warranty   Home Owner Fee/Annual   Down Payment
                              Seller = S
                              Contractor = C
                                                             SAC              or  BBC
OWN                XD     OWP                                 Sub Agency          Buyer Brokerage
Owner Name   Expiration Date   Owner Phone                    Commission          Commission

LD   /    /
List Date

**F I G U R E   6.1   ■   Residential Profile Sheet (continued)**

WHEN SOLD, CHANGE REMARKS TO REFLECT TERMS AND OTHER SALES INFORMATION

RE1  Remarks Line 1
RE2  Remarks Line 2
RE3  Remarks Line 3
RE4  Remarks Line 4
DIR  Directions

All Coded Info. is Searchable & MUST be entered in Alpha Order
* Denotes Required Fields

**\*BKD - Book Desc.**
A - New Construction — NEW CONST
B - ReSale — RESALE

**\*CAT - Category**
A - Single Family — SNGL FAM
B - Single Family & Acreage — SNGL FAM+ACR
C - Coastal Property — COASTAL PROP
D - Office - Residential — OFFICE-RES

**\*CON - Construction**
A - Brick/Brick Veneer 2 Sides or Less — BRK-2
B - Brick/Brick Veneer 3 Sides — BRK-3
C - Brick/Brick Veneer 4 Sides — BRK-4
D - Frame — FRA
E - Redwood/Cedar/Cypress — RW/CED
F - Stucco — STUC
G - Concrete Block — CONC
H - Manuf. Siding — M. SID
I - Vinyl Siding — V. SID
J - Aluminum Siding — A. SID
K - Masonite — MASON
L - Asbestos Siding — ASB
M - Log — LOG
N - Stone — STONE
O - Other — OTH

**\*COO - Cooling**
A - Central — CENT
B - Heat Pump — HPMP
C - Electric — ELEC
D - Natural Gas — GAS
E - Window/Wall — WW
F - Solar — SOL
G - Ceiling Fans — C-FAN
H - Attic Fans — A-FAN
I - None — NONE

**\*LAD - Living Area Description**
A - Eat-in-Kitchen — EAT-IN-K
B - Separate Kitchen — SEP-KIT
C - Separate Dining Rm — SEP-DIN
D - Kit/Din Rm/Liv Rm — KT/DR/LR
e - Kit/Family Rm — KT/FR
F - Living Rm/Dining Rm — LR/DR
G - Family Rm/Dining Rm — FR/DR
H - Great Room — GRT RM
I - Family Room — FAM RM
J - Galley Kitchen — GALLEY
K - Kitchen w/Bar — KTW/BAR

**EQP - Equipment**
A - Range — RNG
B - Refrig/Icemaker — REF-I
C - Refrigerator — REF
D - Dishwasher — DSHW
E - Disposal — DISP
F - Microwave — MICRO
G - Garage Door Opener — GAR-O
H - Security System — SECSYS
I - Smoke Detector — SM-D
J - Deadbolt — BOLT
K - Trash Compactor — TR-COMP
L - Washer — WASH
M - Dryer — DRY
N - Intercom — INTERCOM
O - Central Vacuum — C-VAC
P - TV Antenna — TV-A
Q - Satellite Dish — S-DISH
R - Gas Grill — GAS GRL
S - Sprinkler Sys-Lawn — SPR SYS
T - None — NONE

**LT - Listing Type**
A - Exclusive Right of Sale — ERS
B - Exclusive Right of Sale w/Named Exemption — ERS-E
C - Exclusive Agency — EA

**\*FEE - Fee Includes**
A - Road Maint. — RD MAINT
B - Common Area — COM AREA
C - Water/Sewer — WTR/SWR
D - Exterior Maint. — EXT MAINT
E - Insurance — INS
F - Trash/Garbage — TRSH/GRBG
G - Pool — POOL
H - Street Lights — ST LITE
I - Cable TV — CABLE-TV
J - Tennis Membership — TENNIS
K - Other — OTH
L - None — NONE

**\*FLO - Flooring**
A - Slab — SLAB
B - Off Grade — OF-GD
C - Hardwood — HARDWD
D - Parquet — PARQ
E - Carpet — CARPET
F - Some Carpet — S-CRPT
G - Ceramic/Clay — C-TILE
H - Vinyl Tile — V-TILE
I - Vinyl — VINYL
J - Terrazo — TRZO

# FIGURE 6.1 ■ Residential Profile Sheet (continued)

**\* Denoted Required Fields**

**Coded Information**
All Coded Information is Searchable
Must Enter in Alpha Order

`1/6/7`

**\*FMF - Existing First Mortgage Financing**

| | |
|---|---|
| A - Non-Assumable | NO-ASM |
| B - Assumable-Non Qualify | ASM-NQ |
| C - Assumable-Qualify | ASM-Q |
| D - Conventional | CONV |
| E - FHA | FHA |
| F - VA | VA |
| G - Wrap | WRAP |
| H - Private | PRIV |
| I - GPM | GPM |
| J - ARM | ARM |
| K - Assume Current Rate | ASM CUR |
| L - Assume Escalating | ASM ESC |
| M - None | NONE |
| N - Other | OTH |

**FRT - Frontage**

| | |
|---|---|
| A - Golf Course | GOLF |
| B - Pond | POND |
| C - Canal | CANAL |
| D - Gulf | GULF |
| E - Bay | BAY |
| F - River | RIVER |
| G - Stream/Creek | STRM/C |
| H - Spring | SPRING |
| I - Government Forest | GOV-F |
| J - Lake | LAKE |
| K - Greenbelt | GREENB |
| L - Park | PARK |

**GAR - Garage**

| | |
|---|---|
| A - 1 Car Carport | 1-CPT |
| B - 2 Car Carport | 2-CPT |
| C - 3+Car Carport | 3+CPT |
| D - 1 Car Garage | 1-GAR |
| E - 2 Car Garage | 2-GAR |
| F - 3+Car Garage | 3+GAR |
| G - Driveway Only | DRV |

**HEA - Heating**

| | |
|---|---|
| A - Central | CENT |
| B - Heat Pump | HPMP |
| C - Electric | ELEC |
| D - Natural Gas | GAS |
| E - Propane Gas | PROP |
| F - Oil | OIL |
| G - Solar | SOL |

**PTY - Pool Type**

| | |
|---|---|
| A - Inground Pool | IG POOL |
| B - Above Ground Pool | AG POOL |
| C - Concrete | CONC |
| D - Vinyl Liner | VINYL LNR |
| E - Screened Pool | SC POOL |
| F - Pool Equipment | POOL EQPT |

**\*ROA - Road Frontage Type**

| | |
|---|---|
| A - Gov.Maint. | GOV MNT |
| B - Other Maint. | OTH MNT |
| C - Paved | PAVD |
| D - Unpaved | UNPVD |
| E - Curb & Gutters | CB&GT |
| F - Street Lights | ST LITE |
| G - Sidewalks | SD WLKS |
| H - Other Access | OTH-ACC |

**DRV - Driveway**

| | |
|---|---|
| A - Concrete | CONC |
| B - Gravel/Dirt | GRVL |
| C - Asphalt | ASPLT |
| D - Exposed Aggregate | EXPAGG |
| E - Circle Drive | CRC DRV |
| F - Unpaved Maint | UNPVD |
| G - Assoc. Maint | ASSN MNT |
| H - Other | OTH |

**\*SHO - Showing Instructions**

| | |
|---|---|
| A - Vacant | VAC |
| B - Owner Occupied | OC-OW |
| C - Tenant Occupied | OC-TN |
| D - Lock Box | LB |
| E - Appointment Only | AP |
| F - Call Occupant | OO |
| G - Call Manager | CM |
| H - Call Listing Office | CL |
| I - Key in Listing Office | KL |
| J - Caution!! Guard Dog | G-DOG |
| K - Caution!! Pets | PETS |
| L - Leave Card | LC |
| M - Day Sleeper | DAY SLPR |
| N - Under Construction Renovation | UN CONST |
| O - Proposed Construction | PROPOSE |

**STY - Style**

| | |
|---|---|
| A - Traditional | TRAD |
| B - Ranch | RNCH |
| C - Contemporary | CONTEMP |
| D - Colonial | COLONIAL |
| E - Spanish | SPAN |
| F - 2 Story | 2STY |
| G - Split Level | SPLIT |
| H - Raised Ranch | RAISE |
| I - Split Foyer | SPLIT F |
| J - Victorian | VICT |
| K - Cape Cod | CAPE |
| L - 1 Story | 1STY |
| M - 2 Story Br Down | 2STY BR D |
| N - 2 Story Br Up | ALL BR-UP |

**\*TRM - Terms (Potential Financing)**

| | |
|---|---|
| A - Owner | OWN |
| B - Wraparound | WRAP |
| C - Second | 2ND |
| D - FHA | FHA |
| E - VA | VA |
| F - Conventional | CONV |
| G - Contract for Deed | DEED |
| H - Lease/Purchase | LEA/PUR |
| I - Exchange | EXCH |
| J - Private | PRIV |
| K - Subordination | SUBOR |
| L - ARM | ARM |
| M - GPM | GPM |
| N - FHMA | FHMA |
| O - Federal Land Bank | FLB |
| P - Cash | CASH |
| Q - Assumable-N/Q | ASM-NQ |
| R - Assumable -Qualify | ASM-Q |
| S - Call LAG for Terms | C-LAG |
| T - Other | OTH |

**\*WHT - Water Heater**

| | |
|---|---|
| A - Gas | GAS |
| B - Electric | ELEC |
| C - Solar | SOLAR |
| D - 2+ Heaters | 2+HTR |
| E - 40 or Less Gallons | -40 GAL |
| F - 40 or More Gallons | +40 GAL |
| G - Other | OTH |

**F I G U R E 6.1 ■ Residential Profile Sheet (continued)**

**H - Wood Burning Stove** WOOD
**I - Space/Wall** SP/WA
**J - None** NONE

**MSC - Miscellaneous Items Included**

A - Some Items Excluded — EXCLUD
B - Wood Burning Fireplace — W-FRPL
C - Other Fireplace — O-FRPL
D - Deck — DECK
E - Patio — PATIO
F - Fenced — FENCE
G - Privacy Fence — PRIV FEN
H - Cathedral Ceiling — CATH CEL
I - Window Treatments — WND TRT
J - Some wind Treatments — S-WIND T
K - Hot Tub — H-TUB
L - Whirlpool — WHRLPL
M - Garden Tub — GDN TUB
N - Shower Stall — SHW STALL
O - Sauna — SAUNA
P - Cable TV — CABLE
Q - Wallpaper — WALLPAP
R - Wet Bar — WETBAR
S - Storage Shed — SHED
T - Gazebo — GAZBO
U - Barbeque Pit — BBQ
V - Stables — STBL
W - Tennis Court — TENNIS
X - 1-5 Acres — 1-5 AC
Y - 5+ Acres — 5 + AC

**ORM - Other Rooms**

A - Family Room — FAM RM
B - Utility Room Inside — UT RM IN
C - Utility Room Outside — UT RM OT
D - Garage Enclosed — GAR-ENC
E - Master Br-Apart — M BR-AP
F - Master Br-Suite — M BR-SU
G - Bedroom-Down — BR-DWN
H - Walk-in Closet — W/CLOS
I - Study/Office — ST/OFC
J - Breakfast Room — BRKFST
K - Pantry — PTRY
L - Recreation Room — REC RM
M - Foyer — FOYR
N - Guest Apartment — G-APT
O - Screened Porch — S-PORCH
P - Workshop — WRK SHP
Q - Greenhouse — GREEN HS
R - Atrium/Solarium — ATRM/SLRM

**SMF - Existing Second Mortgage Financing**

A - Non-Assumable — NO-ASM
B - Assumable-Non-Qualify — ASM-NQ
C - Assumable-Quality — ASM-Q
D - Assm Current Rate — ASM CUR
E - Assumable Escalating — ASM-ESC
F - Private — PRIV
G - Conventional — CONV
H - Wraparound — WRAP
I - ARM — ARM
J - Other — OTH

**SPE - Special Exemption**

A - No Homestead — NOH
B - Homestead — HOM
C - Other Exemptions — OTH
D - Tax on Lot Only — TXLT
E - Partial Homestead — PART

**DFC-Distance from Capitol**

A - Less than 3 Miles — LESS 3 MI
B - 3-5 Miles — 3-5 MI
C - 6 - 10 Miles — 6-10 MI
D - 11 - 15 Miles — 11-15 MI
E - 16 - 20 Miles — 16-20 MI
F - 21 - 25 Miles — 21-25 MI
G - 25 + Miles — 25+MI

**MAJOR AREA**

1 Northeast Quardant
2 Northwest Quadrant
3 Southeast Quadrant
4 Southwest Quadrant
5 Jefferson County
6 Franklin County
7 Gadsden County
8 Wakulla County
20 Other Areas

**\*WND - Windows**

A - Single Hung — SNGL HUNG
B - Double Hung — DBL HUNG
C - Insulated — INSUL
D - Sliding Glass — SLID GLAS
E - Wood Sash — WOOD SASH
F - Jalousie — JALS
G - Casement — CASE
H - Bay Window — BAY WNDW
I - Skylight — SKYLITE
J - Storm Window — STRM WNDW
K - Stained Glass — STAINED
L - Garden Window — GDN WNDW
M - Aluminum Awning — ALUM AWN
N - Vinyl Clad — VINYL CLD
O - Picture Window — PICT WNDW
P - Clerestory — CLERE
Q - Other — OTH

**\*WTR - Water**

A - City — CITY
B - Talquin — TALQ
C - Well Installed — WELL-I
D - Private System — PRIV
E - Community — COMM
F - Other — OTH

**PHO - Photo**

A - Photo Needed — TAKE PHO
B - Photo Submitted — PHO SUB
C - Sketch Submitted — SKT SUB
D - No Photo Required — NO PHO
E - Out of Area — OUT
F - Photo Taken — PHO TAKN
G - Photo Retake — PHO RETK
H - Addn'l Photo/Call Agt — ADL PHO

**FLP - Floor Plan**

A - One Story — 1-STRY
B - Two Story — 2-STRY
C - Ground Floor Unit — GRD FLR
D - Upstairs Unit — UP UNT
E - End Unit — END UNT
F - Interior Unit — INT UNT

**APD**

Additional Photo Description
( Only if Choice H is Selected from PHO )

**F I G U R E   6.2   ■   Exclusive Right of Sale Listing Agreement**

---

## Exclusive Right of Sale Listing Agreement
FLORIDA ASSOCIATION OF REALTORS®

This Exclusive Right of Sale Listing Agreement ("Agreement") is between

_____ ("**Seller**") and

_____ ("**Broker**").

**1. AUTHORITY TO SELL PROPERTY: Seller** gives **Broker** the EXCLUSIVE RIGHT TO SELL the real and personal property (collectively "Property") described below, at the price and terms described below, beginning the _____ day of _____, _____, and terminating at 11:59 p.m. the _____ day of _____, _____ ("Termination Date"). Upon full execution of a contract for sale and purchase of the Property, all rights and obligations of this Agreement will automatically extend through the date of the actual closing of the sales contract. **Seller** and **Broker** acknowledge that this Agreement does not guarantee a sale. This Property will be offered to any person without regard to race, color, religion, sex, handicap, familial status, national origin or any other factor protected by federal, state or local law. **Seller** certifies and represents that he/she/it is legally entitled to convey the Property and all improvements.

**2. DESCRIPTION OF PROPERTY:**
  **(a)** Real Property Street Address: _____

_____

  Legal Description: _____

_____ ❏ See Attachment _____

  **(b)** Personal Property, including appliances: _____

_____ ❏ See Attachment _____

  **(c)** Occupancy: Property ❏ is ❏ is not currently occupied by a tenant. If occupied, the lease term expires _____.

**3. PRICE AND TERMS:** The property is offered for sale on the following terms, or on other terms acceptable to **Seller**:
  **(a)** Price: _____
  **(b) Financing Terms:** ❏ Cash ❏ Conventional ❏ VA ❏ FHA ❏ Other _____
  ❏ **Seller** Financing: **Seller** will hold a purchase money mortgage in the amount of $_____ with the following terms: _____
  ❏ Assumption of Existing Mortgage: Buyer may assume existing mortgage for $_____ plus an assumption fee of $_____. The mortgage is for a term of _____ years beginning in _____, at an interest rate of _____% ❏ fixed ❏ variable (describe) _____.
  Lender approval of assumption ❏ is required ❏ is not required ❏ unknown. Notice to **Seller**: You may remain liable for an assumed mortgage for a number of years after the Property is sold. Check with your lender to determine the extent of your liability. **Seller** will ensure that all mortgage payments and required escrow deposits are current at the time of closing and will convey the escrow deposit to the buyer at closing.
  **(c) Seller Expenses: Seller** will pay mortgage discount or other closing costs not to exceed _____% of the purchase price; and any other expenses **Seller** agrees to pay in connection with a transaction.

**4. BROKER OBLIGATIONS AND AUTHORITY: Broker** agrees to make diligent and continued efforts to sell the Property until a sales contract is pending on the Property. **Seller** authorizes **Broker** to:
  **(a)** Advertise the Property as **Broker** deems advisable in newspapers, publications, computer networks, including the Internet and other media; place appropriate transaction signs on the Property, including "For Sale" signs and "Sold" signs (once **Seller** signs a sales contract); and use **Seller's** name in connection with marketing or advertising the Property;
  **(b)** Obtain information relating to the present mortgage(s) on the Property.
  **(c)** Place the property in a multiple listing service(s) (MLS). **Seller** authorizes **Broker** to report to the MLS/Association of Realtors® this listing information and price, terms and financing information on any resulting sale. **Seller** authorizes **Broker**, the MLS and/or Association of Realtors® to use, license or sell the active listing and sold data.
  **(d)** Provide objective comparative market analysis information to potential buyers; and
  **(e)** (Check if applicable) ❏ Use a lock box system to show and access the Property. A lock box does not ensure the Property's security; **Seller** is advised to secure or remove valuables. **Seller** agrees that the lock box is for **Seller's** benefit and releases **Broker**, persons working through **Broker** and **Broker's** local Realtor Board/Association from all liability and responsibility in connection with any loss that occurs. ❏ Withhold verbal offers. ❏ Withhold all offers once **Seller** accepts a sales contract for the Property.
  **(f)** Act as a transaction broker.

**5. SELLER OBLIGATIONS:** In consideration of **Broker's** obligations, **Seller** agrees to:
  **(a)** Cooperate with **Broker** in carrying out the purpose of this Agreement, including referring immediately to **Broker** all inquiries regarding the Property's transfer, whether by purchase or any other means of transfer.
  **(b)** Provide **Broker** with keys to the Property and make the Property available for **Broker** to show during reasonable times.

**F I G U R E   6.2  ■  Exclusive Right of Sale Listing Agreement (continued)**

(c) Inform **Broker** prior to leasing, mortgaging or otherwise encumbering the Property.

(d) To indemnify **Broker** and hold **Broker** harmless from losses, damages, costs and expenses of any nature, including attorney's fees, and from liability to any person, that **Broker** incurs because of (1) **Seller's** negligence, representations, misrepresentations, actions or inactions, (2) the use of a lock box, (3) the existence of undisclosed material facts about the Property, or (4) a court or arbitration decision that a broker who was not compensated in connection with a transaction is entitled to compensation from **Broker**. This clause will survive **Broker's** performance and the transfer of title.

(e) To perform any act reasonably necessary to comply with FIRPTA (Internal Revenue Code Section 1445).

(f) Make all legally required disclosures, including all facts that materially affect the Property's value and are not readily observable or known by the buyer. **Seller** represents there are no material facts (building code violations, pending code citations, unobservable defects, etc.) other than the following: _____

_____

**Seller** will immediately inform **Broker** of any material facts that arise after signing this Agreement.

(g) Consult appropriate professionals for related legal, tax, property condition, environmental, foreign reporting requirements and other specialized advice.

**6. COMPENSATION: Seller** will compensate **Broker** as specified below for procuring a buyer who is ready, willing and able to purchase the Property or any interest in the Property on the terms of this Agreement or on any other terms acceptable to **Seller**. **Seller** will pay **Broker** as follows (plus applicable sales tax):

(a) _____% of the total purchase price OR $_____, no later than the date of closing specified in the sales contract. However, closing is not a prerequisite for **Broker's** fee being earned.

(b) _____ ($ or %) of the consideration paid for an option, at the time an option is created. If the option is exercised, **Seller** will pay **Broker** the paragraph 6(a) fee, less the amount **Broker** received under this subparagraph.

(c) _____ ($ or %) of gross lease value as a leasing fee, on the date **Seller** enters into a lease or agreement to lease, whichever is soonest. This fee is not due if the Property is or becomes the subject of a contract granting an exclusive right to lease the Property.

(d) **Broker's** fee is due in the following circumstances: (1) If any interest in the Property is transferred, whether by sale, lease, exchange, governmental action, bankruptcy or any other means of transfer, regardless of whether the buyer is secured by **Broker**, **Seller** or any other person. (2) If **Seller** refuses or fails to sign an offer at the price and terms stated in this Agreement, defaults on an executed sales contract or agrees with a buyer to cancel an executed sales contract. (3) If, within _____ days after Termination Date ("Protection Period"), **Seller** transfers or contracts to transfer the Property or any interest in the Property to any prospects with whom **Seller**, **Broker** or any real estate licensee communicated regarding the Property prior to Termination Date. However, no fee will be due **Broker** if the Property is relisted after Termination Date and sold through another broker.

(e) Retained Deposits: As consideration for **Broker's** services, **Broker** is entitled to receive _____% of all deposits that **Seller** retains as liquidated damages for a buyer's default in a transaction, not to exceed the paragraph 6(a) fee.

**7. COOPERATION AND COMPENSATION WITH OTHER BROKERS. Broker's** office policy is to cooperate with all other brokers except when not in **Seller's** best interest: ❏ and to offer compensation in the amount of _____% of the purchase price or $_____ to **Buyer's** agents, who represent the interest of the buyers, and not the interest of **Seller** in a transaction; ❏ and to offer compensation in the amount of _____% of the purchase price or $_____ to a broker who has no brokerage relationship with the **Buyer** or **Seller**; ❏ and to offer compensation in the amount of _____% of the purchase price or $_____ to Transaction brokers for the **Buyer**; ❏ None of the above (if this is checked, the Property cannot be placed in the MLS.)

**8. BROKERAGE RELATIONSHIP:**

IMPORTANT NOTICE

**FLORIDA LAW REQUIRES THAT REAL ESTATE LICENSEES PROVIDE THIS NOTICE TO POTENTIAL SELLERS AND BUYERS OF REAL ESTATE.**

You should not assume that any real estate broker or sales associate represents you unless you agree to engage a real estate licensee in an authorized brokerage relationship, either as a single agent or as a transaction broker. You are advised not to disclose any information you want to be held in confidence until you make a decision on representation.

TRANSACTION BROKER NOTICE

**FLORIDA LAW REQUIRES THAT REAL ESTATE LICENSEES OPERATING AS TRANSACTION BROKERS DISCLOSE TO BUYERS AND SELLERS THEIR ROLE AND DUTIES IN PROVIDING A LIMITED FORM OF REPRESENTATION.**

As a transaction broker, _____ and its associates, provides to you a limited form of representation that includes the following duties:

1. Dealing honestly and fairly;
2. Accounting for all funds;
3. Using skill, care, and diligence in the transaction;
4. Disclosing all known facts that materially affect the value of residential real property and are not readily observable to the buyer;
5. Presenting all offers and counteroffers in a timely manner, unless a party has previously directed the licensee otherwise in writing;
6. Limited confidentiality, unless waived in writing by a party. This limited confidentiality will prevent disclosure that the seller will accept a price less than the asking or listed price, that the buyer will pay a price greater than the price submitted in a written offer, of the motivation of any party for selling or buying property, that a seller or buyer will agree to financing terms other than those offered, or of any other information requested by a party to remain confidential; and
7. Any additional duties that are entered into by this or by separate written agreement.

**F I G U R E   6.2  ■   Exclusive Right of Sale Listing Agreement (continued)**

Limited representation means that a buyer or seller is not responsible for the acts of the licensee. Additionally, parties are giving up their rights to the undivided loyalty of the licensee. This aspect of limited representation allows a licensee to facilitate a real estate transaction by assisting both the buyer and the seller, but a licensee will not work to represent one party to the detriment of the other party when acting as a transaction broker to both parties.

_____    _____    _____
Date                                         Signature                                     Signature

**9. CONDITIONAL TERMINATION:** At **Seller's** request, **Broker** may agree to conditionally terminate this Agreement. If **Broker** agrees to conditional termination, **Seller** must sign a withdrawal agreement, reimburse **Broker** for all direct expenses incurred in marketing the Property and pay a cancellation fee of $_____ plus applicable sales tax. **Broker** may void the conditional termination and **Seller** will pay the fee stated in paragraph 6(a) less the cancellation fee if **Seller** transfers or contracts to transfer the Property or any interest in the Property during the time period from the date of conditional termination to Termination Date and Protection Period, if applicable.

**10. DISPUTE RESOLUTION:** This Agreement will be construed under Florida law. All controversies, claims and other matters in question between the parties arising out of or relating to this Agreement or the breach thereof will be settled by first attempting mediation under the rules of the American Arbitration Association or other mediator agreed upon by the parties. If litigation arises out of this Agreement, the prevailing party will be entitled to recover reasonable attorney's fees and costs, unless the parties agree that disputes will be settled by arbitration as follows: **Arbitration:** By initialing in the space provided, **Seller** (____) (____), Listing Associate (____) and Listing Broker (____) agree that disputes not resolved by mediation will be settled by neutral binding arbitration in the county in which the Property is located in accordance with the rules of the American Arbitration Association or other arbitrator agreed upon by the parties. Each party to any arbitration or litigation (including appeals and interpleaders) will pay its own fees, costs and expenses, including attorney's fees, and will equally split the arbitrators' fees and administrative fees of arbitration.

**11. MISCELLANEOUS:** This Agreement is binding on **Broker's** and **Seller's** heirs, personal representatives, administrators, successors and assigns. **Broker** may assign this Agreement to another listing office. Signatures, initials and modifications communicated by facsimile will be considered as originals. The term "buyer" as used in this Agreement includes buyers, tenants, exchangors, optionees and other categories of potential or actual transferees.

**12. ADDITIONAL TERMS:** _____
_____
_____
_____
_____
_____
_____
_____
_____
_____
_____
_____
_____
_____
_____
_____
_____
_____
_____

Date: _____    **Seller:** _____    Tax ID No: _____
Telephone #'s: Home_____ Work_____ Cell_____ Fax:_____
Address:_____ E-mail: _____
Date: _____    **Seller:** _____    Tax ID No: _____
Telephone #'s: Home_____ Work_____ Cell_____ Fax:_____
Address:_____ E-mail: _____
Date: _____    **Authorized Listing Associate or Broker:** _____
Brokerage Firm Name: _____    Telephone: _____
Address: _____

| Copy returned to **Seller** on the _____ day of _____, _____ by: ❑ personal delivery ❑ mail ❑ facsimile. |

The real estate licensee is expected to be knowledgeable about the listing contract and able to explain the provisions clearly and completely. Sellers lose confidence in a sales associate who stumbles through an explanation of the agreement or who doesn't know the meaning of a clause.

The Florida Association of REALTORS® distributes the sample shown. If you use a different form, the clauses in your listing agreement probably are very similar. The numbered paragraphs below correspond to the 11 paragraphs in the agreement.

***Parties.*** The parties are the owner(s) of the property and the brokerage firm, not the sales associate. All persons owning an interest in the property should be included here. The licensee should check the seller's deed to ensure that all persons on the deed sign the listing. Corporations, partnerships, trusts, and estates require special treatment. See the broker or an attorney for advice.

1. ***Authority to Sell Property.*** This paragraph gives the broker an exclusive right to sell the property. The listing term also is shown here. Many brokerage firms have policies for the listing term, depending on the type of property. A typical residential period is six months. The licensee should examine that policy carefully, however, in light of the best marketing period. For instance, in many areas of Florida, the best sales period is from May through August. If that is the case, a six-month listing taken on January 2 expires July 2, with two months remaining in the best selling period. A far better approach is a minimum of six months, provided all listings remain active at least through August 31. A contract written during the listing period extends the listing until the closing. The seller agrees to offer the property without unlawful discrimination. The seller warrants that he can convey the property legally.

2. ***Description of Property***
   (a) The property address is entered here. The legal description should be taken from the public records or from the owner's deed, if available. If it is a metes-and-bounds description, it should be attached. A description taken from the tax records or from former listing information is not satisfactory, as these sources are not always reliable.
   (b) *Personal Property.* Fixtures as well as other personal property must be listed here. Often a seller agrees to leave a refrigerator, drapes, or a washer/dryer; however, the licensee should discuss with the seller the possibility of holding back the offer of these items, using them as negotiating tools when an offer is made. (For example, "The seller says that if you can increase your offer by $1,000, she will give you her washer-dryer.")
   
   *Not included as part of the agreement.* The licensee should ask the seller an important question: "Is any item attached to the property that you *do not want to be included with the sale?*" The agreement does not provide a section for this exclusion, but the licensee should be certain to include any such items on an addendum. If possible, the fixture should be removed before the home is shown.
   (c) *Occupancy.* This section covers the seller's representation about occupancy rights by another party. If a third party is in possession of the property, the buyer's rights are subject to those of the tenant.

3. ***Price and Terms***
   (a) *Price.* Here the licensee records the price at which the property will be offered.
   (b) *Financing Terms.* The terms are important to the seller and the listing broker, particularly in the way the property is marketed. If the seller agrees to seller financing, the terms of such financing are stated here. If there is an existing mortgage on the property, the seller is asked whether it can be assumed with or without lender approval. The seller is warned about liability in case of an assumption. The seller also agrees that the loan is current in case of assumption.

(c) *Seller Expenses.* This section limits the amount the seller agrees to pay for discount points and other closing costs as a percentage of the sales price. The licensee should take care to ensure that the amount shown here is enough to pay typical costs of sale, including a commission. Of course, the seller could agree to pay more when signing a contract for sale. The licensee should disclose anticipated seller's costs on the Seller's Net Proceeds Form before presenting the listing agreement and each time an offer is presented to the seller.

4.  **Broker Obligations and Authority.**  The broker makes promises in this section (the consideration that makes this a bilateral contract) that include working diligently to sell the property. The seller authorizes the broker to take the following steps:

(a) Advertise the property as the broker deems advisable, place an appropriate sign on the property, and use the seller's name in marketing the property.

(b) Obtain information about the mortgage (usually a signed request from the seller for a status letter).

(c) Place the property in the MLS. Some brokers hold a listing out for an extended period of time, during which the broker attempts to sell the property himself. If the licensee is a single agent, this could be considered as subordinating the principal's interests to the broker's personal interests, a clear violation of fiduciary duties.

(d) Provide a CMA to potential buyers.

(e) Place a lockbox on the property if the seller specifically authorizes it. The seller is asked to relieve the broker, staff, and Board of REALTORS® from liability due to loss. The seller may request that the broker withhold verbal offers and *all* offers once the seller accepts a contract.

(f) Act as a transaction broker.

5.  **Seller Obligations.** The seller agrees to:

(a) cooperate with the broker to obtain a sale and refer all inquiries to the broker;

(b) give keys to the broker and make property available for showing during reasonable times;

(c) inform the broker before leasing or mortgaging the property;

(d) hold the broker harmless because of (1) the seller's negligence or misrepresentations, (2) losses from the use of a lockbox, (3) the existence of undisclosed facts about the property, or (4) arbitration or lawsuits against the broker by another broker (This serves as a warranty that the seller's statements to the broker are true and that indemnifies the broker against representations made by the seller that the broker passes on to a buyer. The warranty against seller misrepresentations is commonly called the *warranty of owner clause.*);

(e) comply with the Foreign Investment in Real Property Tax Act (FIRPTA) require-ments in case the seller is a foreign national (This could require that the buyer withhold 10 percent of the sales proceeds and forward the funds to the IRS.);

(f) make legally required disclosures affecting the property's value (This section requires due diligence by the licensee, who must question the seller on all aspects of the property. Obviously, comments the seller makes in this section should be disclosed to prospective buyers.); and

(g) consult with qualified professionals for legal, tax, and other matters, the intent of which is to reduce the licensee's liability.

6.  **Compensation.** This is an agreement to find a purchaser who is ready, willing, and able to buy, either at the list price or any other price agreeable to the seller. It is not dependent on a closing (as in a listing "to effect a sale").

(a) This paragraph sets the commission as a percentage of the price or as a dollar amount. The commission is due no later than closing but may be due whether or not a closing occurs.

(b) In case the seller and a buyer agree to an option contract, this paragraph sets the commission as a percentage of the option amount or as a dollar amount. The commission is due at the time the option is created. The total commission, less the commission received from the option, is due when the option is exercised.

(c) In case a lease agreement is created, this paragraph sets the commission as a percentage of the price or as a dollar amount. The commission is due when the seller enters into an agreement to lease. An exception occurs if the seller employs another broker under an exclusive-right-to-lease agreement.

(d) *Broker's Fee.* This paragraph describes when the broker's fee is due:

    (1) if any interest in the property is transferred, whether by sale, lease, exchange, government action (e.g., eminent domain), or bankruptcy, no matter who finds the buyer;

    (2) if the seller refuses to sign an offer at full price and terms, defaults on a contract, or agrees with a buyer to cancel an executed sales contract; or

    (3) if, after the listing's expiration, a prospect who learned about the property through a broker buys the property within the protection period. An exception occurs if another broker has subsequently listed the property.

(e) *Retained Deposits.* This paragraph entitles the broker to a specified percentage of all deposits that the seller retains as liquidated damages for a buyer's default. The amount cannot exceed the total commission as shown in paragraph 6(a).

7. ***Cooperation and Compensation with Other Brokers.*** This section states that the broker's policy is to cooperate with all other brokers except when it would not be in the seller's best interests. It authorizes the listing broker to offer commission splits with other brokers. The seller checks her approval for splits with (1) buyers' agents, (2) nonrepresentatives, (3) transaction brokers, or (4) none of the above. If the seller checks "none of the above," the listing broker may not put the listing into the MLS, because the MLS requires an offer of compensation to a cooperating broker.

8. ***Brokerage Relationship.*** As described in Chapter 1, brokers may work with buyers or sellers as nonrepresentatives, single agents, or transaction brokers. The listing contract includes the disclosure forms for single agent or transaction broker. The seller should sign the forms, or, if the seller declines to do so, the licensee should so indicate on the listing contract form. If the broker is starting as a single agent and may become a transaction broker, the transition notice *must* be signed.

9. ***Conditional Termination.*** If the seller decides not to sell the property, the broker may agree to terminate the contract. The seller must sign a withdrawal agreement, then pay the broker's direct expenses and a specified cancellation fee. If the seller contracts to transfer the property during the protection period, the broker may cancel the termination and collect the balance of the commission due.

10. ***Dispute Resolution.*** This paragraph requires that conflicts be submitted to a mediator agreed to by the parties. If the mediation is not successful, and unless the parties agree in advance to arbitration, either party may sue. The prevailing party is entitled to recover attorney's fees and costs.

11. ***Arbitration.*** This section allows the parties (seller, listing associate, and listing broker) to agree to settle disputes by binding arbitration in the county where the property is located. The parties agree to split the costs equally. The inclusion of the listing associate in the contract is curious, since the listing agreement is between the seller and the broker, and only the broker is authorized to take action for a commission. If the intent was to protect the broker from the sales associate's later claims for a commission if arbitration was unsuccessful, that might be better handled in the employment agreement. The agreement suggests that the costs will be split among the three parties.

12. ***Miscellaneous.*** The agreement may be assigned to another listing office, which is a departure from the former practice. Fax communications are enforceable.

13. *Information and Signature Section.* This section provides space for additional terms and personal information, including tax ID numbers as well as signature lines. Note that the listing sales associate may be authorized to sign the listing for the broker. This facilitates giving the seller a copy of the agreement immediately, satisfying the 24-hour requirement. The box at the bottom of the contract indicates when the seller's copy was legally delivered.

## Explaining the Agreement to the Seller

The presentation of the listing agreement to the seller needs to be thorough to ensure that the seller fully understands. Sales associates sometimes take a casual approach to explaining the listing agreement or offer no explanation at all to the seller. A sales associate may say, "Don't worry, it's the standard agreement. Sign here." Or the sales associate might try an explanation even though he doesn't understand the agreement himself. This misleads the seller and is not acceptable. The licensee's job is to give the seller an understanding of the important provisions the agreement contains.

New sales associates should understand the agreement totally and explain each paragraph clearly. If a seller asks, "What happens during the listing period if I decide I want to lease the property to a tenant?" the sales associate should answer, "If you'll look at paragraph 6(c), you'll see that the property can be leased. You agree to pay my company a fee of _____ percent, but the fee does not include management."

The professional sales associate explains the listing agreement in language that the seller understands easily. Role-playing is an excellent method of learning this skill. When the role-playing results in wording that sounds appropriate, the sales associate should write it down so she can then refer to the written explanation during the listing appointment.

The following scenario might result from a licensee's role-playing exercise:

"Mr. Jones, this is the standard agreement all brokers use for homes listed in the MLS system. Let's go over it together, paragraph by paragraph.

"This top section shows your name as the seller and _____ Realty as the broker. Do I have your names spelled correctly?

"Section 1 shows that you give my company the authority to sell your property starting today and ending on _____. You understand that I can't *guarantee* a sale of the property. I must offer property without violating any fair housing laws. And you agree that you can legally sell the property.

"Section 2 shows that the address of the property is _____. And the legal description of the property taken from your deed is shown here."

The sales associate continues to explain sections 3 through 11 of the listing contract in a similar manner. She refers to the checklist in Figure 6.4 to be certain she has completed all the necessary documents and taken all the necessary actions in regard to the listing.

---

### DISCUSSION EXERCISE 6.2

Using the listing agreement for your market area, paraphrase the legal words in everyday language that will help a seller understand the agreement better. In a group situation, each person should be assigned a paragraph. The person then explains the paragraph to the group in lay language, and the group provides constructive criticism. Because each person would explain each paragraph differently, every sales associate should prepare his own written text for use in presentations.

**F I G U R E   6.3   ■   Getting Signatures on Listing Documents**

Mr. and Mrs. Jackson, I've prepared this letter to your mortgage company to send us the current balance and payoff amount. We'll use this when we have your house sold. They'll send it to me, and I'll give a copy to you for your records. They require your approval, so I'll need your signatures right here, please. [When they sign the form, put it back in your stack.]

Now, we agreed to market the property at $_____. Based on that, you remember we went over the statement showing your expenses of the sale and what you would receive as proceeds. Here's a copy for your records, and I need you to OK this form for our records. [After they sign the form, put it back in your stack.]

OK, you completed the disclosure statement that we'll give to buyers when they are interested in the home. This will protect you from later claims that you held back important information. I need your signatures here please. [After they sign the form, put it back in your stack.]

Great. We've gone over the agreement for us to market your home. I need your OK right here. [After they sign the form, put it back in your stack.]

I appreciate your confidence, and I'll start the marketing of your home right away. I'm going to try to get back to the office and prepare information to put the property into MLS. Before I leave, do you have any questions?

## Closing for the Listing

All necessary forms should be completed by this time. The best approach would be to have the seller sign all forms at the same time rather than sign each as they are presented. A sample discussion of the conversation is shown in Figure 6.3.

## Marketing the Listing

The seller employs the listing broker to market the property. Many sellers believe that the licensee has not done her job unless the listing broker actually sells the listing. The licensee should discuss this misconception with the seller during the listing presentation. The seller should understand that if the licensee does her job properly, the house will sell through the licensee's marketing efforts—both to potential buyers and to other licensees, who will show the property to their buyers.

The broker has been hired to get the best price in the shortest time and with the least inconvenience to the seller. This requires the licensee to market the property in ways other than just showing it herself. Some of these activities include

- disseminating the property information to all agents in the company
- putting the sign on the property
- putting an MLS lockbox on the property (if approved by the seller and available in the market area)
- arranging for all company sales associates to inspect the listing on caravan day
- getting the information into the MLS service as soon as possible (It is unethical and self-serving to withhold the information from other brokers and sales associates while the agent attempts to sell the property herself.);
- announcing the listing at company sales meetings and at Board of REALTORS® marketing meetings
- preparing a brochure to place in the home for prospective buyers and cooperating licensees
- scheduling an open house if appropriate for the listing
- writing at least three good ads to generate potential buyers
- putting listing on Web sites (personal page, company page, and other advertiser's pages)
- using e-mail auto responders to get immediate feedback for customers who ask for information from a Web site

**F I G U R E   6.4   ■   Listing Procedure Checklist**

Complete Brokerage Relationship Disclosures in accordance with Chapter 475, F.S. This form should accompany all listings.

Property Address: _____

Listing Associate: _____

**Listing Packet Contents** (bold print indicates seller's signature is required):
- ❏ Comparative Market Analysis
- ❏ Brokerage Relationship Disclosures
- ❏ **EXCLUSIVE-RIGHT-OF-SALE AGREEMENT**
- ❏ MLS Profile Sheet
- ❏ **MORTGAGE STATUS REQUEST**
- ❏ **PROPERTY CONDITION DISCLOSURE STATEMENT**
- ❏ **HOME WARRANTY AGREEMENT**
- ❏ **SELLER'S NET PROCEEDS FORM**
- ❏ Survey, if available
- ❏ Copy of mortgage and note
- ❏ Copy of deed restrictions
- ❏ Title Insurance Policy
- ❏ Key to property
- ❏ Floor plan, if available
- ❏ Copy of seller or buyer referral sent out
- ❏ Three ads
- ❏ Sign installation form
- ❏ Lockbox installation form
- ❏ Client contact sheet
- ❏ Copy of computer printout

**Office Action:**
- ❏ Get office manager's approval on listing forms.
- ❏ Enter listing data into computer.
- ❏ Put copy of printout into Floor Duty Book.
- ❏ Distribute copies of printout to all sales associates.
- ❏ Turn in listing packet to secretary.

**Follow-up Action:**
- ❏ Return all original documents to seller.
- ❏ Send seller copy of the MLS listing book photo and information.
- ❏ Contact seller weekly.
- ❏ Send seller copy of mortgage status letter when received.
- ❏ Send copies of all ads to seller.

- ■ preparing mail-outs to send to potential buyers
- ■ preparing a property brochure for potential buyers and other sales associates
- ■ telling 20 neighbors about the listing by mail
- ■ calling the neighbors to ask for help in finding buyers
- ■ holding a REALTORS® luncheon at the property to increase activity, and
- ■ reviewing sales and listing activity in the neighborhood. Update the CMA at least once a month

A detailed marketing program such as this could be the basis for a "Satisfaction Guarantee" or "Steps to a Successful Sale" listing presentation.

---

**DISCUSSION EXERCISE 6.3**

In small groups, prepare a 30-point marketing plan for a brochure you use in your listing presentation. Brainstorm to come up with different marketing ideas.

---

## Servicing the Listing

**Servicing the listing** often is more important than acquiring it. "I never hear from him!" is probably the complaint sellers make most often about their sales associates. If a seller does not hear from his listing sales associate, the seller perceives that she is not doing her job.

---

**DISCUSSION EXERCISE 6.4**

You are a real estate sales associate who is quite busy and disorganized. You have had a listing for six months that is about to expire, and you wish to renew it. Despite your best intentions, you have failed to contact your clients, Harold and Deidra, for more than two months. As the time progressed, it became even harder for you to make the call. You set an appointment to visit the home at 7:30 P.M. Because you are caught in traffic, you are 20 minutes late when you walk up to the house. You are surprised to see that a competitor has listed the property next door. Even worse, it has a "contract pending" sign attached. Harold answers the door, nods his head seriously, and says, "Well, stranger. Long time no see!"

Role-play this situation. Try your best to reestablish the trust and rapport you had at the beginning of the listing period. It may be instructive enough that you will never allow this situation to happen in your career.

---

Those professional licensees who are successful consistently do not accomplish this on the strength of salesmanship alone. The licensees are successful because they provide service to their clients and customers. Often, a family's home is the largest asset it will ever have, so a sales associate never must take the marketing of the home lightly. Failure to maintain regular contact with a seller is a detriment to a sales associate's future success.

Several methods ensure that a sales associate will contact each seller at least once a week:

- The sales associate selects one evening each week, such as Thursday night, to service listings.
- The sales associate contacts every seller, in person, by phone, or if personal contact is not successful, by mail or e-mail. If she calls and the seller does not answer, the sales associate writes a card immediately to let them know the seller was called.
- The sales associate clips every ad from every paper and homes magazine, then pastes it on a note card and mails it with a note that says, "Thought you'd like to see a recent ad on your home. Regards, Sally."
- The sales associate asks every seller to call her immediately if another licensee shows the property. The licensee then follows up to help achieve a sale.
- The sales associate calls every seller after talking to a cooperating broker and gives feedback about a visit to the home.

Often sales associates lose touch with sellers because they don't know what to talk about and feel that they sound like broken records because they say the same things over and over. Each sales associate should prepare a Listing Servicing Schedule, which provides a basic format for the servicing of every listing. A sample form is shown in Figure 6.5.

**F I G U R E  6.5  ■  Listing Servicing Schedule**

Property Address_____ H Phone: _____ W Phone: _____

Sellers' Names _____ Children: _____

**First Day:**

❏   Verify tax information and legal description.

❏   Send out mortgage status request.

❏   Write three ads.

❏   Place listing on Web page.

❏   Send thank-you card to seller.

❏   Enter listing information in computer.

❏   Put copies of listing information in floor book.

❏   Distribute copies of listing information to all sales associates.

❏   Put sign and lockbox on property.

**Second Day:**

❏   Mail out notice of listing cards to at least 20 neighbors.

❏   Call or e-mail seller to tell of above steps.

**End of First Week:**

❏   Send letter to seller signed by broker.

**Day after Caravan:**

❏   Collect caravan comment sheets.

❏   Visit with seller to evaluate results of caravan and comments.

**Second Week:**

❏   Clip ads of property. Send to seller in postcard format.

❏   Check MLS information on computer, verify information, then e-mail to seller.

❏   Call seller to tell of progress. Ask seller to call when house is shown.

**Third Week:**

❏   Clip ads of property. Send to seller in postcard format.

❏   Run MLS computer check for new listings and listings under contract, then e-mail information to seller.

❏   Call or e-mail seller to find out who has seen home.

❏   Check with sales associates who have shown home; give feedback to seller.

**Fourth Week:**

❏   Clip ads of property. Send to seller in postcard format.

❏   Run MLS computer check for new listings and listings under contract, then e-mail information to seller.

❏   Call or e-mail seller to find out about who has seen home.

❏   Check with sales associates who have shown home; give feedback to seller.

**Fifth Week:**

❏   Clip ads of property. Send to seller in postcard format.

❏   Run MLS computer check for new listings and listings under contract, then e-mail information to seller.

❏   Visit seller in the home, and go over CMA. Get price reduction if appropriate.

❏   Walk through property again. Point out areas needing attention.

**F I G U R E  6.5** ■  **Listing Servicing Schedule (continued)**

**Sixth Week:**

❑  Clip ads of property. Send to seller in postcard format.

❑  Run MLS computer check for new listings and listings under contract, then e-mail information to seller.

❑  Call or e-mail seller to find out who has seen home.

❑  Check with sales associates who have shown home; give feedback to seller.

❑  Schedule open house for the property, if appropriate.

❑  Send notice of open house to at least 20 neighbors.

**Seventh Week:**

❑  Run open house, and leave a note for seller on results. Call later.

❑  Clip ads of property. Send to seller in postcard format.

❑  Run MLS computer check for new listings and listings under contract, then e-mail information to seller.

❑  Call or e-mail seller to find out who has seen home.

❑  Check with sales associates who have shown home; give feedback to seller.

❑  Send out notice of listing to additional 20 homes in neighborhood.

**Eighth Week:**

❑  Clip ads of property. Send to seller in postcard format.

❑  Run MLS computer check for new listings and listings under contract, then e-mail information to seller.

❑  Call or e-mail seller to find out who has seen home.

❑  Check with sales associates who have shown home; give feedback to seller.

**Ninth Week:**

❑  Clip ads of property. Send to seller in postcard format.

❑  Run MLS computer check for new listings and listings under contract; then e-mail information to seller.

❑  Call or e-mail seller to find out who has seen home.

❑  Check with sales associates who have shown home; give feedback to seller.

❑  Do another CMA. Visit with seller, and get price reduction and extension.

❑  Schedule luncheon for sales agents.

**Tenth Week:**

❑  Clip ads of property. Send to seller in postcard format.

❑  Run MLS computer check for new listings and listings under contract, then e-mail information to seller.

❑  Call or e-mail seller to find out who has seen home.

❑  Check with sales associates who have shown home; give feedback to seller.

**Continue this pattern until listing has been sold.**

## WHEN LISTINGS DON'T SELL

Occasionally, sales associates feel that they are wasting their time listing property. "I make more money working with buyers. I have ten listings and haven't earned a dime!"

Sales associates who feel that way may need to evaluate their listing inventory using the Listing Quality Report in Figure 6.6.

Notice that the bottom part of the listing evaluation indicates that the sales associate who thinks he or she has five listings has the equivalent of only 1.65 listings (adding the percentages of chance of sale). The associate may boast of a listing volume of $1,160,700 (aver-

FIGURE  6.6  ■  Listing Quality Report

|  | 123 Main St. | | 412 First St. | | 821 Jones St. | |
| --- | :---: | :---: | :---: | :---: | :---: | :---: |
|  | Yes | No | Yes | No | Yes | No |
| Listed at recommend CMA price? |  | ✓ |  | ✓ |  | ✓ |
| House in good condition? | ✓ |  |  | ✓ |  | ✓ |
| Seller motivated? | ✓ |  | ✓ |  |  | ✓ |
| Yard sign? | ✓ |  | ✓ |  | ✓ |  |
| Easy showing access? (Lockbox, etc.) | ✓ |  | ✓ |  | ✓ |  |
| Good curb appeal? |  | ✓ | ✓ |  |  | ✓ |
| Recommend price reduction | $10,000 | | $15,000 | | $17,500 | |

| A. Address | B. Time Left | C. List Price | D. Chance of Sale During Term | E. Quality Volume [CxD] | F. Recommended Price Change |
| --- | --- | --- | :---: | --- | --- |
| 123 Main St. | 3 months | $ 205,000 | 25% | $ 51,250 | $10,000 |
| 412 Monroe St. | 1 month | $ 178,200 | 10% | $ 17,820 | $15,000 |
| 821 Jones St. | 2 months | $ 312,500 | 40% | $125,000 | $17,500 |
| 1250 Sipa Rd. | 4 months | $ 285,000 | 60% | $171,000 | $10,000 |
| 116 Third St. | 5 months | $ 180,000 | 30% | $ 54,000 | $10,000 |
| TOTAL | Avg 3 mo. | $1,160,700 | 1.65 listings | $419,070 | $62,500 |

age of $232,140) but really has the equivalent of only $419,070 (average of $83,814) when considering the chance of sale.

Overpriced listings result in frustration for the sales associate and resentment by the owner, who may become more demanding and tell friends of the lack of effort on the part of the sales associate. Sometimes, if the seller will not price the property appropriately, it may be best for the sales associate to give the listing back to the seller. A comment such as "We value our relationship with you and don't want you to feel we are not being productive. I feel you may be mad at us later on if we didn't give you the opportunity to talk with other agencies."

If the sales associate internalizes this evaluation and mentally reviews it when taking a listing, it is more likely that only salable listings would be taken thereafter.

# K E Y   T E R M S

| | |
| --- | --- |
| exclusive-agency listing | open listing |
| exclusive-right-of-sale listing | profile sheet |
| latent defects addenda | servicing the listing |
| lockbox | warranty of owner |

## SUMMARY

Three major types of listing agreements are open listings, exclusive-agency listings, and exclusive-right-of-sale listings. An owner's warranty in a listing indemnifies the broker from false statements the owner makes to the broker. A latent defects addendum to a contract holds the owner accountable for failing to disclose existing defects to the property that are known or should have been known.

Licensees should review carefully and understand thoroughly the listing contracts they use. A licensee should be able to explain clearly to a seller the important provisions of a listing agreement.

A licensee must market property with skill, care, and diligence. A major part of the licensee's professional duties, in addition to listing and selling, is servicing listings and keeping in touch with sellers on a regular basis.

# PRACTICE EXAM

1.  If an owner reserves the right to sell the property himself, but allows many brokers to work simultaneously, he has given the brokers:
    a.  exclusive agency listings.
    b.  no listings.
    c.  exclusive-right-to-sell listings.
    d.  open listings.

2.  An open listing is created by:
    a.  written document only.
    b.  a sign that says "brokers protected."
    c.  negotiation.
    d.  a broker putting a sign on property.

3.  Broker Jim just listed a house for six months. The listing will automatically renew for an additional three months unless canceled in writing by either party. This type of agreement:
    a.  is advantageous to the seller and is endorsed by the National Association of REALTORS®.
    b.  is a violation of the license law.
    c.  is permissible provided full disclosure is made to the seller of its self-renewing provision.
    d.  may be used only by single agents and is not available to transaction brokers.

4.  What clause in a listing contract contains a promise by the owner certifying that all of the information related to the property is true and accurate?
    a.  Property owner's
    b.  Property condition
    c.  Warranty of owner
    d.  Owner's certification

5.  What addendum to a listing contract states that the owner has a duty to disclose any facts materially affecting the property's value?
    a.  Caveat emptor
    b.  Latent defects
    c.  Special clauses
    d.  Hold harmless

6.  What type of listing is used when an owner selects one brokerage firm to sell his property but reserves the right to sell the property personally and not pay a commission?
    a.  Exclusive-right-of-sale
    b.  Exclusive-agency
    c.  Open
    d.  Option contract

7.  A seller refuses to allow the listing broker to split commissions with buyers' brokers, transaction brokers, or nonrepresentation brokers. Based on this information, which of the following statements is correct?
    a.  The seller's viewpoints are perfectly acceptable and understandable; the broker may take the listing and enter it in the MLS.
    b.  The broker may not take the listing under these circumstances.
    c.  The broker may take the listing but may not enter it in the MLS.
    d.  The listing may be placed into MLS only if it is an exclusive right of sale.

8.  Seller Diane tells Sales Associate Todd that she intends to take the ceiling fan when she moves, so he should be sure the listing information shows that it is not part of the sale. In this case, Todd should do which of the following?
    a.  Tell Diane that the ceiling fan is a fixture and must stay with the property.
    b.  Tell Diane, "Let's wait and see if it's mentioned in the purchase contract; if it is not specifically itemized, you can take it."
    c.  Strongly urge Diane to leave the fan.
    d.  Tell Diane to remove the fan before the property is shown.

9.  The legal description entered into the listing agreement and into MLS:
    a.  should be taken from the owners' deed or the public records.
    b.  is usually omitted in listing and sales contracts.
    c.  should be either the lot and block number or the seller's mailing address.
    d.  is not a significant piece of information for listing or sales contracts.

10. If sellers, when listing the property, offer to leave a washer/dryer combination, the sales associate should:
    a.  warn them of the sales tax liability.
    b.  tell them not to leave it.
    c.  suggest it not be included until an offer is received.
    d.  disregard the offer without discussing it with the sellers.

11. The section of the FAR listing agreement titled "Cooperation and Compensation with Other Brokers," indicates that:
    a.  the broker need not cooperate with other brokers.
    b.  the broker's policy is to cooperate with other brokers except when it would not be in the seller's best interests.
    c.  the broker pays the cooperating broker at least 50 percent of the total listing commission.
    d.  the broker may not cooperate with any other broker without prior written approval.

12. The FAR listing agreement has a dispute resolution clause that:
    a.  requires the parties to seek redress in a court of law.
    b.  allows only the broker and the seller to settle disputes by binding arbitration.
    c.  allows the broker, the sales associate, and the seller to settle disputes by binding arbitration.
    d.  requires the parties to seek resolution at a hearing before the Florida Real Estate Commission.

13. Broker John lists a large town home in Pebble Creek. How long does John have to give the seller a signed copy of the agreement?
    a. It must be done before John leaves the seller's presence.
    b. Within 48 hours
    c. Within 7 days
    d. Within 24 hours

14. Broker Sandy Brantly is talking with Robert about listing his home. If Robert says that he is ready to list but has two people he wants to exclude from the listing for three weeks, what should Sandy do?
    a. Wait three weeks, then come and get the listing.
    b. Have Robert sign an open listing.
    c. Have Robert sign an exclusive-right-of-sale listing.
    d. Have Robert sign an exclusive-right-of-sale listing with an addendum that excludes the two prospective buyers.

15. The two biggest problems faced by a licensee who has taken an exclusive-agency listing are:
    a. a dishonest seller and a dishonest broker.
    b. other brokers and other sales associates.
    c. an owner's sign on the property and the owner advertising a different price.
    d. a buyer going to another broker and the other broker failing to disclose his brokerage relationship.

16. The maximum period between a listing sales associate's calls to the seller should be how many days?
    a. 1
    b. 7
    c. 10
    d. 14

17. An open listing:
    a. may be terminated at will.
    b. must be written to be enforceable.
    c. may be given to only one broker at a time.
    d. requires the owner to notify the broker if the property is sold.

18. On June 18, Broker Susan listed the Smith's house for six months. On August 16, the Smiths terminated the listing, paying Susan a cancellation fee of $250. In September, the Smiths listed their house with Cobble Realty. They accepted a contract in October, which closed on November 28. Based on the conditional termination clause of the FAR listing agreement, the Smiths:
    a. are liable to Broker Susan for the full commission.
    b. have acted in violation of state law.
    c. have terminated the original listing and need pay only Cobble Realty.
    d. may owe Broker Susan up to 1 percent of the sales price of the home.

19. The parties to a listing agreement are the:
    a. seller and buyer.
    b. seller and sales associate.
    c. sales associate and broker.
    d. seller and broker.

20. Susan lists property with Jack Smith, a multimillion-dollar producer. Jack's agreement calls for him to enter the listing into the MLS within three working days. On the second day, Jack shows the property to Sally Shuler, who loves it. She is leaving town the next day, she tells him, but will be back in one week to purchase it if it is still on the market. Jack wants to double his commission by selling his own listing, so he withholds the information from the MLS for ten days. Based on this information, Jack:
    a. is following a legal, time-honored tradition in real estate by working to sell his own listing.
    b. is liable to the seller for violating fiduciary duties required by the listing agreement.
    c. will not be disciplined by FREC if he does in fact sell the property.
    d. is likely to be more successful in real estate.

## APPLY WHAT YOU'VE LEARNED

The authors suggest the following actions to reinforce the material in *Section II—Obtaining Listings That Sell:*

❏ Set up your Power Prospecting database. Start with your close friends and family, then list all the friends and past customers you can think of. After that, try to think of anyone even vaguely familiar that you have met and get the names down. You can get the addresses and contact information later.

❏ If you own a home, estimate its current value, then prepare a CMA. If you do not own your home, do this exercise for a friend. Does the CMA support the value you guessed?

❏ Based on the CMA you did on your or your friend's house, prepare a Seller's Net Proceeds Statement.

❏ Complete a listing agreement for your home, along with other forms required by your broker. Ask your broker to review them.

❏ Prepare an MLS computer input form describing the features of your house. Be certain it is complete.

❏ Write three practice ads to market your home.

❏ Pick a neighborhood in your city with homes priced from $100,000 to $150,000. Find as many sales as possible for the previous 12 months. Using the matched pair technique, identify the dollar contribution from

    ❏ a swimming pool,

    ❏ an extra bedroom,

    ❏ an enclosed garage, and

    ❏ a corner lot.

❏ Using the same analysis, calculate the percentage difference between listing price and selling price.

❏ Using MLS data, divide the number of houses on the market by the number of house sales last week to find how many weeks' supply of homes are on the market. Do this at least once a month. It's an excellent indicator of market activity.

❏ Write a script for the explanation of a CMA to a prospective seller. Record your presentation on audiotape to hear how it sounds. Edit as necessary until it sounds just right.

❏ Record your explanation of the listing agreement used in your office. Edit your remarks until you are satisfied.

# SELLING REAL PROPERTY

A sales associate must understand the buyer's needs and financial abilities. Licensees should understand how to find buyers and live up to the buyers' expectations. Buyers expect licensees to have broad knowledge about properties on the market and market values. They also want to know how much they can afford to pay for a house, based on their income.

The sales associate must be able to estimate the buyer's costs so that the buyer who contracts for a property is aware of the cash requirements expected at closing.

Knowledge of contracts is extremely important to sales associates. Not only do licensees need to know how to prepare purchase agreements, they must be able to explain the basic terms of the agreements so that buyers and sellers are aware of their rights and responsibilities.

Once a licensee shows the right property, the licensee must be ready to write the offer. This chapter has a case study on writing and presenting the offer that will help the new licensee understand the process of presenting offers and negotiation counteroffers. ■

# 7

# WORKING WITH BUYERS

## LEARNING OBJECTIVES

Upon completion of this chapter, *you should be able to*

1. explain four different ways to enhance your product knowledge;

2. list at least five sources of buyers;

3. give at least three methods to show a buyer why an appointment with you will benefit him or her;

4. list two important reasons for qualifying a buyer;

5. explain how prioritizing buyers benefits both the buyers and the sales associate;

6. qualify a buyer using the Fannie Mae/Freddie Mac housing expense ratio and the total obligations ratio;

7. calculate the total monthly payment (PITI) on a mortgage loan;

8. qualify a buyer using the do-it-yourself prequalification form;

9. list two benefits in having a buyer prequalify at a mortgage lender's office;

10. list the steps between setting up an initial appointment with a buyer and writing a contract for purchase; and

11. explain why you would show a limited number of homes to a potential buyer in one day.

## OVERVIEW

Working with buyers is an important function of the professional real estate sales associate. Buyers are interested in working with knowledgeable, caring sales associates and generally are reluctant to make appointments without evaluating the sales associate's skills. A sales associate must be adept at handling telephone inquiries, must know the inventory, and must stay current with available financing plans. Above all, the sales associate must understand and observe the laws with respect to required disclosures and fair housing. ■

# BUYER BROKERAGE AGREEMENT

While licensees nearly always require a written agreement from sellers, they often work with buyers on an "open listing" basis. A licensee may give the customer valuable information on the market and other ideas on purchasing a home but may end up working for nothing. Many successful licensees are requesting that buyers also enter into a written **buyer brokerage agreement** for representation by the licensee, either as a single agent or as a transaction broker.

Some prospective buyers will be reluctant to sign such an agreement because they may be required to pay a commission. They may not be aware that the agreement calls for the broker to offset the commission from monies received from a seller if the property is listed with a cooperating broker. A buyer who understands the benefits will be more likely to sign the agreement. When the buyer agrees to pay a commission, the broker can show the buyer unlisted property (FSBOs, properties being foreclosed, real estate owned by banks, etc.). Buyers would not see such properties without a commission agreement.

The real estate licensee should understand the Exclusive Buyer Brokerage Agreement (Figure 7.1) and be able to explain its provisions clearly and concisely. The numbered paragraphs below correspond with the 14 sections of the agreement.

1. **Parties:** The parties are the buyer and the broker. This paragraph also defines the terms of "acquisition" to be purchase, option, exchange, lease, or other acquisition or ownership or equity interest in real property.

2. **Term:** This paragraph sets forth the dates the agreement will be effective. Notice that if there is a contract pending on the expiration date of the agreement, the agreement is extended until the contract is closed or terminated.

3. **Property:** This section shows the
   a. *Type of property:* for example, residential, agricultural, office, etc.
   b. *Location* would normally be used to describe a city or county, or another geographic area.
   c. *Price range* would set the minimum and maximum limits the broker should use in selecting properties to show. This section also discloses that the buyer may have already been preapproved for a mortgage.
   d. *Preferred terms and conditions* sets out the buyers' preferences, such as owner financing, small down payment, lease-purchase, and so forth.

4. **Broker's Obligations:**
   a. *Broker assistance:* The broker agrees to cooperate with seller's brokers to complete a transaction. It also states that even if the broker is paid a commission split from the seller's broker, the broker's duties to the buyer are not reduced.
   b. *Other buyers:* This section discloses to the buyer that the broker may work with another buyer interested in the same property but must maintain confidentiality as to the terms of any offers.
   c. *Fair housing:* Broker states he or she will not participate in unlawful discrimination.
   d. *Service providers:* Broker shall not be responsible for acts of a third party recommended by the broker, such as a home inspector or title insurance company.

5. **Buyer's Obligations:** In this section, the buyer agrees to tell sellers or other brokers he is working under contract with a broker, to conduct all negotiations through the broker, to give the broker personal financial information and allow the broker to run a credit check, to hold the broker harmless for any damages, and to consult an appropriate professional for tax, legal, and other services.

**F I G U R E  7.1  ■  Exclusive Buyer Brokerage Agreement**

---

**Exclusive Buyer Brokerage Agreement**
FLORIDA ASSOCIATION OF REALTORS®

1. **PARTIES:** _____ ("**Buyer**") grants

_____ ("**Broker**")

*Real Estate Broker          /          Office*

the exclusive right to work with and assist **Buyer** in locating and negotiating the acquisition of suitable real property as described below. The term "acquire" or "acquisition" includes any purchase, option, exchange, lease or other acquisition of an ownership or equity interest in real property.

2. **TERM:** This Agreement will begin on the _____ day of _____, _____ and will terminate at 11:59 p.m. on the _____ day of _____, _____ ("Termination Date"). However, if **Buyer** enters into an agreement to acquire property that is pending on the Termination Date, this Agreement will continue in effect until that transaction has closed or otherwise terminated.

3. **PROPERTY: Buyer** is interested in acquiring real property as follows or as otherwise acceptable to **Buyer** ("Property"):

   (a)  Type of property: _____

   (b)  Location: _____

   (c)  Price range: $_____ to $_____.

   ❏ **Buyer** has been ❏ pre-qualified ❏ pre-approved by _____

   for (amount and terms, if any) _____

   (d)  Preferred terms and conditions: _____

   _____

   _____

   _____

   _____

4. **BROKER'S OBLIGATIONS:**
   **(a) Broker Assistance. Broker** will
      * use **Broker's** professional knowledge and skills;
      * assist **Buyer** in determining **Buyer's** financial capability and financing options;
      * discuss property requirements and assist **Buyer** in locating and viewing suitable properties;
      * assist **Buyer** to contract for property, monitor deadlines and close any resulting transaction;
      * cooperate with real estate licensees working with the seller, if any, to effect a transaction. **Buyer** understands that even if **Broker** is compensated by a seller or a real estate licensee who is working with a seller, such compensation does not compromise **Broker's** duties to **Buyer**.
   **(b) Other Buyers. Buyer** understands that **Broker** may work with other prospective buyers who want to acquire the same property as **Buyer**. If **Broker** submits offers by competing buyers, **Broker** will notify **Buyer** that a competing offer has been made, but will not disclose any of the offer's material terms or conditions. **Buyer** agrees that **Broker** may make competing buyers aware of the existence of any offer **Buyer** makes, so long as **Broker** does not reveal any material terms or conditions of the offer without **Buyer's** prior written consent.
   **(c) Fair Housing. Broker** adheres to the principles expressed in the Fair Housing Act and will not participate in any act that unlawfully discriminates on the basis of race, color, religion, sex, handicap, familial status, country of national origin or any other category protected under federal, state or local law.
   **(d) Service Providers. Broker** does not warrant or guarantee products or services provided by any third party whom **Broker**, at **Buyer's** request, refers or recommends to **Buyer** in connection with property acquisition.

**F I G U R E   7.1  ■   Exclusive Buyer Brokerage Agreement (continued)**

5. **BUYER'S OBLIGATIONS: Buyer** agrees to cooperate with **Broker** in accomplishing the objectives of this Agreement, including: **(a)** Conducting all negotiations and efforts to locate suitable property only through **Broker** and referring to **Broker** all inquiries of any kind from real estate licensees, property owners or any other source. If **Buyer** contacts or is contacted by a seller or a real estate licensee who is working with a seller or views a property unaccompanied by **Broker, Buyer** will, at first opportunity, advise the seller or real estate licensee that **Buyer** is working with and represented exclusively by **Broker**. **(b)** Providing **Broker** with accurate personal and financial information requested by **Broker** in connection with ensuring **Buyer's** ability to acquire property. **Buyer** authorizes **Broker** to run a credit check to verify **Buyer's** credit information. **(c)** Being available to meet with **Broker** at reasonable times for consultations and to view properties. **(d)** Indemnifying and holding **Broker** harmless from and against all losses, damages, costs and expenses of any kind, including attorney's fees, and from liability to any person, that **Broker** incurs because of acting on **Buyer's** behalf. **(e)** Not asking or expecting to restrict the acquisition of a property according to race, color, religion, sex, handicap, familial status, country of national origin or any other category protected under federal, state or local law. **(f)** Consulting an appropriate professional for legal, tax, environmental, engineering, foreign reporting requirements and other specialized advice.

6. **RETAINER:** Upon final execution of this Agreement, **Buyer** will pay to **Broker** a non-refundable retainer fee of $_____ for **Broker's** services ("Retainer"). This fee is not refundable and ❑ will ❑ will not be credited to **Buyer** if compensation is earned by **Broker** as specified in this Agreement.

7. **COMPENSATION: Broker's** compensation is earned when, during the term of this Agreement or any renewal or extension, **Buyer** or any person acting for or on behalf of **Buyer** contracts to acquire real property as specified in this Agreement. **Buyer** will be responsible for paying **Broker** the amount specified below plus any applicable taxes but will be credited with any amount which **Broker** receives from a seller or a real estate licensee who is working with a seller.
  **(a) Purchase or exchange:** $_____ or _____% (select only one) of the total purchase price or other consideration for the acquired property, to be paid at closing.
  **(b) Lease:** $_____ or _____% (select only one) of the gross lease value, to be paid when **Buyer** enters into the lease. If **Buyer** enters into a lease-purchase agreement, the amount of the leasing fee which **Broker** receives will be credited toward the amount due **Broker** for the purchase.
  **(c) Option: Broker** will be paid $_____ or _____% of the option amount (select only one), to be paid when **Buyer** enters into the option agreement. If **Buyer** enters into a lease with option to purchase, **Broker** will be compensated for both the lease and the option. If **Buyer** subsequently exercises the option, the amounts received by **Broker** for the lease and option will be credited toward the amount due **Broker** for the purchase.
  **(d) Other: Broker** will be compensated for all other types of acquisitions as if such acquisition were a purchase or exchange.
  **(e) Buyer Default: Buyer** will pay **Broker's** compensation immediately upon **Buyer's** default on any contract to acquire property.

8. **PROTECTION PERIOD: Buyer** will pay **Broker's** compensation if, within_____days after Termination Date, **Buyer** contracts to acquire any property which was called to **Buyer's** attention by **Broker** or any other person or found by **Buyer** during the term of this Agreement. **Buyer's** obligation to pay **Broker's** fee ceases upon **Buyer** entering into a good faith exclusive buyer brokerage agreement with another broker after Termination Date.

9. **EARLY TERMINATION: Buyer** may terminate this Agreement at any time by written notice to **Broker** but will remain responsible for paying **Broker's** compensation if, from the early termination date to Termination Date plus Protection Period, if applicable, **Buyer** contracts to acquire any property which, prior to the early termination date, was found by **Buyer** or called to **Buyer's** attention by **Broker** or any other person. **Broker** may terminate this Agreement at any time by written notice to **Buyer**, in which event **Buyer** will be released from all further obligations under this Agreement.

10. **DISPUTE RESOLUTION:** Any unresolveable dispute between **Buyer** and **Broker** will be mediated. If a settlement is not reached in mediation, the matter will be submitted to binding arbitration in accordance with the rules of the American Arbitration Association or other mutually agreeable arbitrator.

11. **ASSIGNMENT; PERSONS BOUND: Broker** may assign this Agreement to another broker. This Agreement will bind and inure to **Broker's** and **Buyer's** heirs, personal representatives, successors and assigns.

## FIGURE 7.1 ■ Exclusive Buyer Brokerage Agreement (continued)

**12. BROKERAGE RELATIONSHIP: Buyer** authorizes **Broker** to operate as (check which is applicable):
❑ single agent of **Buyer.**
❑ transaction broker.
❑ single agent of **Buyer** with consent to transition into a transaction broker.
❑ nonrepresentative of **Buyer.**

**13. SPECIAL CLAUSES:** _____

_____

_____

_____

_____

_____

**14. ACKNOWLEDGMENT; MODIFICATIONS: Buyer** has read this Agreement and understands its contents. This Agreement cannot be changed except by written agreement signed by both parties.

Date: _____  **Buyer:** _____  Tax ID No: __ __ __ - __ __ - __ __ __ __

Address: _____

Zip: _____  Telephone: _____  Facsimile: _____

Date: _____  **Buyer:** _____  Tax ID No: __ __ __ - __ __ - __ __ __ __

Address: _____

Zip: _____  Telephone: _____  Facsimile: _____

Date: _____  **Real Estate Associate:** _____

Date: _____  **Real Estate Broker:** _____

EBBA-4  Rev. 10/98  ©1998 Florida Association of REALTORS® All Rights Reserved  **Page 2 of 2**

6. **Retainer:** Many licensees ask prospective buyers for a nonrefundable retainer at the time this contract is signed. It has an option for the retainer to be credited to the total compensation.

7. **Compensation:** This obligates the buyer to pay a commission to the broker, offset by any commissions the broker may receive from a seller or a broker working with the seller. The broker is entitled to his or her commission if the customer purchases, leases, or options the property. The commission may be stated as a percentage of the sale, lease, or option, or it can be a fixed fee. The broker is also entitled to a commission if the buyer defaults on any contract.

8. **Protection Period:** If the broker has shown property to the buyer and the buyer purchases the property within the agreement period, the buyer will owe the commission unless the buyer has entered into a buyer brokerage agreement with another broker after the termination date.

9.  **Early Termination:** The buyer may terminate the agreement, but if the buyer buys property the buyer learned about during the contract term, the buyer owes the commission. The broker may terminate the agreement at any time by giving written notice.

10. **Dispute Resolution:** Disputes must be mediated first. If mediation is not successful, the parties must agree to submit the dispute to binding arbitration.

11. **Assignment; Persons Bound:** The broker is allowed to assign the agreement to another broker.

12. **Brokerage Relationship:** This section has several checkboxes for the parties to indicate what type of broker relationship they will have. *Note:* The fact that a box is checked does not discharge the broker from giving the buyer the prescribed brokerage relationship notice before showing a property or entering into this agreement.

13. **Special Clauses:** This gives the parties additional space to add other provisions to the agreement.

14. **Acknowledgment; Modifications:** Indicates the buyer has read and understands the agreement. There are spaces for signatures of the buyer(s), sales associate, and broker.

## PRODUCT KNOWLEDGE

A buyer usually benefits from working with a licensee, regardless of the brokerage relationship, because of the licensee's product knowledge. It is hard work to acquire the extensive product knowledge that buyers expect. To become proficient, the sales associate should accomplish the following goals:

- Spend a majority of the first few weeks in real estate looking at property.
- See at least 30 new properties each week.
- Keep a record of listings she has viewed by using one of the client follow-up programs mentioned in Chapter 4 or even by using index cards grouped by price range and outstanding features. The sales associate may use the cards like flash cards to remember five good listings in each price range or five with pools or five fixer-uppers. With practice, the sales associate can remember more listings than five.
- Constantly practice matching neighborhoods with price ranges or house sizes.
- Prepare a "Five-Star Home List" showing the best-buys-on-the-market sheet for each price range (for instance, $175,000 to $200,000). See a sample "Five-Star Homes" listing in Figure 7.2.

**F I G U R E  7.2  ■  Five-Star Homes**

**FIVE-STAR Homes**
**(BEST BUYS ON THE MARKET)**
**Price Range: $175,000–$200,000**

| Price | Address | MLS # | Comments |
|-------|---------|-------|----------|
| $176,900 | 116 Belmont Rd. | 15432 | Great deck, vaulted ceiling |
| $179,500 | 1272 Scenic Rd. | 16523 | Brick, large oak in front |
| $185,000 | 784 Wilson Ave. | 16132 | Wood frame colonial |
| $185,000 | 1216 Kara Dr. | 15478 | Huge back yard with hot tub |
| $188,500 | 8754 Skate Dr. | 15843 | Heavily wooded, secluded |
| $199,900 | 124 E. Call St. | 16021 | Downtown, arched doorways |

If a buyer calls to ask for an address of one of the sales associate's listings, the sales associate should provide the information to the caller and, if needed, use "my five favorite homes on the market in your price range" to get an appointment with the buyer.

---

**DISCUSSION EXERCISE 7.1**

If you actively sell residential properties, try to name from memory the location for at least three single-story, four-bedroom listings. Try to name the location for four listed homes with swimming pools.

---

## FINDING BUYERS

Some good sources of buyers include

- calls resulting from advertising
- calls resulting from signs
- past customers and clients
- friends and family
- open house visitors
- canvassing prospects, and
- buyer seminar attendees

---

**DISCUSSION EXERCISE 7.2**

Carol is on floor duty when she receives a call from a buyer who says, "I'm looking for a four-bedroom home with a pool, northeast, but it's got to have a large workshop. Do you have anything like that listed in the $150,000 range?"

"No, I don't have any listings like that," she says, "but I can show you another company's listing that may be just right for you. I saw it last week. It's very spacious, in an elegant setting with a great view. I believe it's priced at $148,500. I'm available to show it to you this afternoon at 4:30, or I have another time available at 6:15. Which is better for you?"

Is Carol likely to get an appointment to show the property? Why or why not? Is there something she said that you would say differently?

---

### Calls Resulting from Advertising

Advertisement calls are an extremely important source of buyers. A buyer calls for more information to determine whether a house is right for him. A buyer seldom calls to make an appointment with a sales associate, but the sales associate's objective is *always to get the appointment with the buyer.* The sales associate must remember two important points when answering buyer advertisement calls:

1. It is difficult for the sales associate to talk intelligently about properties that she has not seen. For this reason, the sales associate *should see every company listing* before answering calls on ads or signs.
2. The sales associate should review all company advertising in newspapers and homes magazines. The licensee should clip each ad and paste it on a separate piece of notebook paper or index card. A **fallback list,** sometimes called a *switch list* or *pivot list,* should be prepared for each ad. A fallback list comprises three to five properties that are similar to the property being advertised. The list can consist of the sales associate's personal listings, the brokerage firm's listings, or other brokers' listings. If a caller isn't satisfied after learning more about the property in question, the sales

**F I G U R E   7.3  ■   Fallback List**

| "FALLBACK LIST" FOR 3415 MONITOR LANE | | | |
|---|---|---|---|
| Address | MLS # | Price | Comments |
| 1546 Merrimac Dr. | 16546 | $89,500 | Large workshop, lots of trees, 2 streets over |
| 1247 Thresher Ln. | 16478 | $94,500 | 20′ × 30′ deck, screened pool area, spotless |
| 1687 Woodgate Way | 16521 | $95,000 | 2 stories, 4 bedrooms, close to town |
| 1856 Hoffman Dr. | 16493 | $85,000 | Huge oak in front, lots of azaleas, big kitchen |
| 1260 Dunston Ct. | 16470 | $92,500 | Quiet street off Meridian, very clean, bright |

associate can refer to the fallback list of other properties that might be suitable. The fallback list becomes invaluable in getting the appointment and helping the buyer find the right property. A sample fallback list is shown in Figure 7.3.

### DISCUSSION EXERCISE 7.3

Do a role-playing exercise, with a class member calling on an ad for 3415 Monitor Lane. Try to get an appointment using one of the methods discussed.

Often, a caller wants a property's address but is unwilling to give her name or phone number. "I just want to ride by to see whether I like it," the caller says. The sales associate will not get the appointment unless the caller feels she will benefit by meeting with the sales associate. The best-buys sheet and the fallback list may come in handy to get the appointment. Most buyers would feel that the sales associate had market information that would make it worthwhile to make an appointment.

Another way to suggest to the caller that meeting with the sales associate would benefit the caller is to explain that many listings are not advertised. A lot of the best properties are sold almost immediately by sales associates who watch carefully for new listings for their clients or customers. Many buyers want to know that someone constantly watches the market for the right properties for them. "Would you like to have first opportunity to see these prime properties?" is the question that can get the appointment.

When a caller is adamant about wanting an address but will not make an appointment, some sales associates do not give the address because they will lose the call. It is not worthwhile, however, to generate ill will with the consumer. Perhaps a better approach is to be helpful in every way. Ask how many property ads the caller has circled in the newspaper or homes magazine. Tell the caller you will give him an address and information on each listing advertisement, even though other real estate companies hold the listings. You should have a copy of the classified ad section and a homes magazine handy. Follow along with the caller, mark each ad, and set a time that you can get together. Prepare a list with addresses, prices, square footage, and other property features. The attraction to the buyer? One call gets it all because the consumer sees a benefit to meeting with the licensee. The attraction to the sales associate? The buyer places no calls to the competition, and an appointment has been set.

Once an appointment is made, it is time to evaluate the buyer's needs and financial capabilities. This is called **qualifying** the buyer.

Often the first visit with the buyer is simply a get-acquainted visit, meant for making required disclosures and for qualifying. After this is completed, a second appointment is set to show properties.

## Calls Resulting from Signs

Another source of buyers is calls on property signs. Callers on real estate ads generally want the properties' addresses. Callers on signs generally want the prices because they already know the locations. A sales associate should handle a sign call like an ad call, with the exception of the information provided.

## Past Customers and Clients

One of the best sources of buyers is past customers and clients because they already have enjoyed the benefits of the sales associate's services. Agency representation may be a problem, however. If the sales associate listed a client's property in a prior relationship, the person may feel that the same agency relationship exists in the purchase of a new home. The sales associate must give the buyer the appropriate brokerage relationship disclosures.

## Friends and Family

Among the sales associate's first sources of buyers when he starts in real estate are friends and family. The agent should write to everyone he knows and stay in contact for news of potential customers. When working with a friend or family member, the sales associate must evaluate the loyalty issue to decide whether being a single agent for the buyer is more appropriate than being a transaction broker.

## Open House Visitors

Holding open houses is a good way to find prospective buyers. The primary objective of an open house is *not* to make the seller happy (a sale makes the seller happy) but to get buyer prospects. If the buyer purchases the home on display, so much the better. The sales associate should prepare a brochure for the home with the sales associate's name and picture prominently placed.

Usually, open house visitors are just looking. The sales associate should tell them that they are welcome to walk through the home but that she wants to point out a few features that are not readily apparent. If this home is not right for the visitors, the licensee should have ready her list of the five best homes in the price range as well as a fallback list, then set an appointment to talk.

## Canvassing Prospects

**Canvassing** is an excellent method of finding buyers and is discussed in detail in Chapter 3. The same canvassing call can be a source of either buyers or sellers. The sales associate might ask, "Do you know someone who may be getting ready to buy or sell real estate?" Often the answer is yes, and the sales associate can set an appointment. Remember, you may not call anyone on the national Do-Not-Call registry.

## Buyer Seminar Attendees

Many sales associates and brokers consider buyer seminars to be outstanding prospecting tools and offer them to the public to attract large numbers of buyers at one time. Some real estate companies have impressive materials and workbooks for attendees of the classes, which run over two or three evenings. Often attendees pay a nominal fee to cover the cost of books. Most seminars entitle an attendee to schedule a one-hour consultation with the seminar leader about a specific real estate problem or need. This can benefit both the consumer and the licensee if a business relationship results. Remember that the appropriate brokerage relationship disclosures must be made.

## Qualifying the Buyer

It is a waste of time to show properties the buyer does not like or cannot afford. So, before showing properties, the sales associate must get the answers to two important questions: 1.) What are the buyers' housing objectives? 2.) What can the buyer afford to pay?

## What Are the Buyers' Housing Objectives?

Some of the information the sales associate should get from the buyers includes

- What features do they want in the home?
- How quickly do they need to move?
- Must the buyers sell their current home?
- If they're leasing now, when does the lease expire?
- Have the buyers already spoken to a lender and been preapproved?
- Is there a specific area they want?

**Desired Features.** The sales associate should ask the buyers what features the home *must have* and what features would be *nice to have*. The *must have* could be features like a particular area of town, four bedrooms, and a two-car garage. The *nice to have* might be features like high ceilings, heat pump, or a wood deck.

**Urgency Level.** The sales associate also needs to know the buyer's urgency level. Each buyer should be classified based on urgency and motivation to purchase (see Figure 7.4). A person needing to move within the next 30 days, for example, is a Priority 1 buyer, needing immediate attention. A person who doesn't have an immediate need, but who should not be ignored, is classified as Priority 2. A buyer who either will not or cannot purchase immediately is Priority 3 and should be contacted regularly for showings. If a buyer relocating to the city is in town just for the weekend to purchase a home, the sales associate knows this is a Priority 1 buyer. After financial qualifying shows the buyer to be capable of making a purchase, the sales associate might say, "It sounds like your situation needs my full attention. If you approve, I'll clear my calendar so we can find the right home for you." A buyer whose present lease expires in six months has less urgency to purchase now and is classified as Priority 3.

**Current Housing Situation.** If the buyers currently own a home that must be sold, one of the first actions should be to look at their home and make a listing presentation. After their home is listed, the best way to motivate the buyers-sellers to price their present home competitively

### F I G U R E  7.4  ■  Prioritizing Your Buyers

| Buyer's Situation | Priority Level |
| --- | --- |
| Needs to move within 30 days or in town for the weekend to find a house | 1 |
| Wants to buy a house within the next three to six months | 2 |
| Can't buy right now but is just starting to look; perhaps on a lease expiring next year | 3 |

is to show homes they might want to purchase during that listing period. When they see the right home, they will be prepared to sell their own quickly.

If the buyers are currently leasing, the licensee must determine when the lease expires. That will help in prioritizing the buyer.

**Buyer's Family Helping in the Decision.**  The sales associate must also find out whether someone other than the buyers will be involved in making the final purchasing decision. If the buyers' uncle will evaluate the final choice, the sales associate should try to get the uncle to see each property along with the buyers. Why? The uncle may have a better grasp of the market and of property values and may help the buyers reach a decision sooner.

**Best Times to See Property.**  The licensee must find out what times are most convenient for the buyers to look at properties. Are they available during the day? Can they come immediately to see a property if the right one comes on the market? Or does their job situation require that they see property only in the evenings after work or on weekends?

## Describing the Process to the Buyer

At the first meeting with the buyer, the sales associate should provide, in addition to the agency disclosure form, a clear picture of the entire process, from the time of this first meeting right up until the day the buyer moves into his new home. The buyer who understands the process is less likely to become uneasy or reluctant to purchase when he finds the right property. The buyer should be given a copy of the purchase agreement, and the sales associate should explain important provisions in the agreement. A buyer's cost disclosure should be prepared for the home the buyer desires. This also helps in the financial qualifying process.

## Financial Qualification

Financial qualification is crucial to a successful sale. If the buyer contracts for a home and applies for a loan that is later denied, the seller, buyer, and sales associate have wasted time and effort. In addition, loan application fees ranging from $250 to $500, depending on the lender, could be lost. Licensees should explain both issues to their customers to help them understand the importance of financial qualifying.

Financial qualification is designed to determine how much money the buyer can borrow for the purchase of property. The sales associate has two ways to qualify a buyer financially:

1.  Have a financial institution to prequalify (or, better, preapprove) the buyer.
2.  Use a Do-It-Yourself Prequalification form.

**Lender Prequalifying versus Preapproval.**  Having a lender prequalify or preapprove the buyer is the best approach and should be used whenever possible, but certainly before the buyer actually contracts for property. **Prequalification** is a lender's evaluation based on answers to questions given by the prospective buyer. Preapproval is given only after the buyer has been interviewed and the buyer's credit report has been reviewed and the income verified.

A lender's preapproval letter makes the buyer's offer much stronger in the eyes of a seller and will result in more contracts.

**Do-It-Yourself Prequalification Form.**  The prequalification form (see example, Figure 7.5) gives the licensee an opportunity to explain each entry on the form and thereby dispel some of the uneasiness that the potential borrower typically feels. This method should be used only when a buyer wants to see homes immediately after meeting with a sales associate and a lender's representative cannot be found for a prequalification interview.

**F I G U R E   7.5  ■  Do-It-Yourself Prequalification Form (for Conventional Mortgage Loans)**

| | | |
|---|---|---|
| Purchase price | $115,000.00 | (A) |
| Desired mortgage amount | $ 92,000.00 | (B) |
| Term of mortgage | 30 years | |
| Mortgage rate | 7.0% | |
| Loan-to-value ratio: (B) ÷ (A) = | 80.0% | (C) |
| GROSS MONTHLY INCOME | $ 3,000.00 | (D) |
| Mortgage principal and interest payment:<br>(Payment factor: 6.6530) × (B) ÷ 1,000 = | $    612.08 | |
| Annual real estate taxes ÷ 12 = | + 110.21 | |
| Homeowner's insurance premium ÷ 12 = | + 50.00 | |
| MONTHLY HOUSING EXPENSE | $    772.29 | (E) |
| Car payments | + 250.00 | |
| Alimony or child support payments | + 225.00 | |
| Credit card or charge account payments | + 50.00 | |
| Other loan payments | + | |
| FIXED MONTHLY OBLIGATIONS | $  1,297.29 | (F) |

HOUSING RATIO (E) ÷ (D) = 25.7%

DEBT RATIO (F) ÷ (D) = 43.2%

Source: Thomas C. Steinmetz, *The Mortgage Kit*, 4th ed. (Chicago: Dearborn Financial Publishing, Inc.®, 1998), 33.

Most lenders adhere to the Fannie Mae/Freddie Mac standards in reviewing loan applicants. Those agencies recommend the maximum housing expense ratio (front) of 28 percent and the maximum total obligations ratio (back) of 36 percent for qualifying potential buyers for first mortgage (conforming) loans. The Federal Housing Administration's (FHA's) maximum housing expense ratio is 29 percent, and the maximum total obligations ratio is 41 percent. These figures are guidelines only. Many portfolio lenders will vary from these guidelines, so a prospective buyer who does not meet the guidelines may still be able to talk with a lender that will make the loan.

The common reason buyers don't qualify under the Fannie Mae/Freddie Mac standards is usually the back ratio: total obligations. If that's too high, perhaps a creative lender can still help by increasing the qualifying income or suggesting prepaying some installment debt to less than 10 months so that it's no longer counted. A very high credit score could also help get the loan. Other compensating factors include

- having a good record of promotions and raises
- having little or no installment debt if housing expense ratio is too high
- making a down payment greater than 20 percent
- having saved money while making rent payments higher than the mortgage payments of the new mortgage, and
- having a job with great benefits, such as a company car, free health plan, and high company contributions to a 401(k) plan

**F I G U R E   7.6** ■ **Do-It-Yourself Prequalification Form (for Conventional Mortgage Loans)**

Purchase price _____ (A)

Desired mortgage amount _____ (B)

Term of mortgage _____

Mortgage rate _____

Loan-to-value ratio: (B) ÷ (A) _____ (C)

GROSS MONTHLY INCOME _____ (D)

Mortgage principal and interest payment: _____
(Payment factor for a _____%, _____-year loan: _____) × (B) ÷ 1,000

Annual Real Estate Taxes ÷ 12 _____

Homeowner's insurance premium ÷ 12 _____

Mortgage insurance: (B) × .00025 (if (C) is more than .80) _____

MONTHLY HOUSING EXPENSE _____ (E)

Car payments _____

Alimony and child support payments _____

Credit card and charge account payments _____

Other loan payments _____

FIXED MONTHLY OBLIGATIONS _____ (F)

HOUSING RATIO (E) ÷ (D) = % _____

DEBT RATIO (F) ÷ (D) = % _____

Source: Thomas C. Steinmetz, *The Mortgage Kit,* 4th ed. (Chicago: Dearborn Financial Publishing, Inc.®, 1998), 33.

---

### DISCUSSION EXERCISE 7.5

Sally and Will Cleare make $41,400 in gross annual income. They wish to purchase a $150,000 home, with $30,000 as a down payment. Fixed-rate, 30-year mortgages are at 7 percent. The monthly principal and interest payment is $798.36. Taxes for a home in this price range are approximately $1,440 per year. Insurance is approximately $540 per year. No private mortgage insurance is necessary if the loan-to-value ratio does not exceed 80 percent.

The Cleares have installment loan payments totaling $70 a month and a car payment of $320.

Using the Do-it-Yourself Prequalification Form in Figure 7.6, determine whether the Cleares qualify for this loan.

---

### DISCUSSION EXERCISE 7.6

The following role-playing skit, designed to highlight mistakes some sales associates make in their first meetings with prospective buyers, allows both spectators and participants to learn from the process. Three actors are needed—a sales associate and two buyers. The persons in the skit should be enthusiastic and as realistic as possible. During the presentation, if the sales associate says something that may violate the law or ethics, group members should shout "Zap!" to signify their disapproval. At the end of the skit, group members should be able to itemize the sales associate's errors and recommend responses to the buyers' questions.

# SKIT

## Buyers' First Meeting with a Licensee

Buyers walk in, are greeted by sales associate.

**Licensee:**  Hello, may I help you?

**Husband:**  Yes, we are here to see Lee Wilson.

**Licensee:**  I'm Lee. You must be Mr. and Mrs. Camp?

**Wife:**  Yes, we are. Very nice to meet you.

**Licensee:**  Great. Please sit down. (*Pause while they sit.*)

**Husband:**  Our mutual friends, the Joneses, recommended we get in touch with you.

**Licensee:**  Yeah, the Joneses send me lots of people. By the way, if you send me anyone who buys a house, I'll give you $50.

**Wife:**  That's what they told us. I hope you can find us a good deal, too.

**Licensee:**  I love working with buyers, Mrs. Camp, and because I'm a transaction broker, I can work harder on your behalf.

**Wife:**  Well, do you have any distress sales of houses in the $100,000 range that we could take advantage of?

**Licensee:**  As a matter of fact, my company just listed one. The listing sales associate suggested that I look at it. Confidentially, the owners' business is in trouble, and they need to sell quickly. The listing sales associate says they are desperate and probably would come off the price as much as $6,000, but we should start even lower to get the best counteroffer.

**Husband:**  Tell us about it.

**Licensee:**  Well, it's in Bent Tree Estates, close to Lake Jackson. It's got three bedrooms, two baths, a large lot, and a two-car garage. It's in absolutely perfect condition.

**Wife:**  The newspaper ran an article last week suggesting that buyers get a home inspection. Is that a good idea?

**Licensee:**  It is if you want to spend $300 for nothing. I've looked over the house, and it's just perfect. No problems whatsoever.

**Husband:**  I need to tell you that we may have a problem qualifying for a new loan. I had some credit problems last year, and we got turned down on another house we tried to buy. We really need to get an assumable loan with no qualifying.

**Licensee:**  Well, we're in luck again. If you like this house, you can buy it with less than $8,000 down. We'll have to structure a wraparound loan to beat the due-on-sale clause, but I do that all the time. Can you work with $8,000 down?

**Husband:**  I think we can come up with that much, if we can get the price right. Can we put some kind of contingency in the contract in case I can't get the money?

**Licensee:**  Hey! I can write up a contract with contingencies that will let you out at any time with no risk. Don't worry about that. But let's go see it.

**Husband:**  Should we have an attorney?

**Licensee:**  You know what's wrong with five attorneys up to their necks in sand?

**Husband:**  (*Smiles*) No, what?

**Licensee:**  Not enough sand. (*He laughs.*) Seriously, folks, you don't need an attorney. I can help you with anything an attorney can.

**Wife:**  Can we ask you some more questions first?

**Licensee:**  Sure. Go ahead.

**Wife:**  Is it a good neighborhood?

**Licensee:**  Oh, yeah, there are hardly any minorities living there!

**Wife:**  Well, I didn't mean that. I meant is it pleasant and well maintained?

**Licensee:** Uh-oh, sorry. Yes, it's really nice.

**Husband:** Do you need us to sign any disclosure forms now?

**Licensee:** No, not really. Not until we write a contract for a house.

**Husband:** Well, let's go looking. I hope it works out.

**Licensee:** I'll do everything I can for you. (*The Camps leave; to an associate in the office*) Hey, Jim! I'll be back in a while. I've got some flakes with no money again, but I'm going to show a house!

Is it possible to learn from mistakes? The mistakes made in this skit may seem ridiculous, but these statements are actually made—although probably not all in a single transaction. Sales associates must be alert in their presentations and when answering questions to avoid these mistakes.

After qualifying the buyer, the sales associate has one more step to complete before showing properties.

## PREPARING THE BUYER TO BUY

The successful sales associate will prepare the buyer for signing the contract long before the right property is found. After qualifying the buyer's needs, the sales associate should give the buyer a copy of the contract for purchase and sale and explain the more important paragraphs to the buyer.

This serves two important functions

1. If the buyer receives important information from the sales associate at their first meeting, this works to cement the buyer's loyalty to the associate.
2. Because the buyer is given a copy of the contract along with an explanation, the contract becomes the buyer's property. When the buyer becomes interested in a particular property, he or she is not startled when the sales associate pulls out a contract form.

Many successful sales associates keep a contract on a clipboard along with the MLS information on the property. It's always in sight so the buyer can see it. If the buyer asks questions like, "Can the seller leave the draperies?" the sales associate would ask, "Shall I put that in the agreement?" while writing on the contract.

## SHOWING THE PROPERTY

Once the buyer has been qualified, it is time to show properties that meet the buyer's needs. The sales associate should use the following sequence in the showing and contracting process

1. Setting the appointment
2. Previewing the properties
3. Planning the route
4. Entering and showing the properties
5. Evaluating the buyer's level of interest
6. Estimating the buyer's costs and making required disclosures
7. Writing the contract

Steps 1 through 5 are discussed in the following sections. Step 7, writing the contract, is the subject of Chapter 8. Step 6, estimating the buyer's costs and making required disclosures, is covered in Chapter 9.

## Setting the Appointment

This step is important not only for the obvious reason (nothing can happen until a meeting occurs) but also from a timing standpoint. Does the sales associate set the appointment before he has previewed prospective homes or after? Many times a sales associate will not set an appointment until he has previewed homes and is confident that good choices are available to show. The advantage of this method is that the sales associate can describe properties that meet the buyer's needs. Two disadvantages in this approach follow

1. The sales associate might spend a lot of time looking at properties, only to find that the buyer is working with another licensee.
2. If the sales associate can't find anything just right and puts the buyer off, the buyer might decide to work with another licensee.

Many sales associates say, "If you set the appointment, you'll find the properties." The premises here are that (1) showing homes helps the buyer focus on likes and dislikes and (2) showing homes that are not quite right is better than not showing homes at all. The sales associate must decide which works best in each situation.

It is important to keep in contact with the buyer regularly, based on priority status. At least weekly, the sales associate should match the buyer's profile with new listings, then call the buyer for an appointment. If the sales associate wants a Saturday showing appointment, the appointment must be made far enough in advance that the buyer can make the necessary arrangements. Saturday morning is too late to make the call. Early in the week is the best time to call for weekend showing appointments.

The best way to match a buyer with property is to use one of the client follow-up programs mentioned in Chapter 3. A separate card may be printed for each property. Match-ups between buyers and properties also are possible using some of the MLS system software. If the sales associate does not have access to a computer, it is simple to enter the buyer information on prospect cards. Spread out the cards on a tabletop and group them by price range when reviewing new listings. Listings should be matched to the buyer, and the sales associate should call the buyer about the properties. The more frequently the sales associate makes the buyer aware that the sales associate is continually searching for the right property for the buyer, the more likely it is that the buyer will call about properties he has seen.

## Previewing the Properties

The sales associate should preview properties before actually showing them to the buyers. The sales associate would be surprised and embarrassed if, after telling the buyers, "I think you'll like this next one!" takes them to a property in terrible condition.

Each time the sales associate sees a new property, whether on a showing appointment, a preview day, or an office caravan of new listings, the sales associate should match that property with a buyer, taking careful notes before contacting the appropriate buyer.

## Being Prepared to Show Properties

One of the most important factors in "closing the sale" is being prepared. That means having the objective firmly in mind that *today* you will write the contract. So before showing property, you should have in your file folder

1. a copy of the lender's good-faith estimate for the top price the buyer can qualify for so you're ready to write the buyer's estimated cost disclosure
2. all the necessary forms, including the cost disclosure estimate sheet and the contract for sale and purchase

## Planning the Route

Normally, the sales associate should show no more than five properties in one tour. However, if a Priority 1 buyer is in town for the weekend for the purpose of buying a home, the sales associate must continue to show homes or risk losing the buyer.

When setting the appointment to show properties, the sales associate must consider in which order the homes will be shown. Buyers go through a continual evaluation process during the inspection tour, and the sales associate should help that process. Many sales associates like to schedule the home they consider just the right property as the last on the tour. While there are good arguments for this procedure, there are also disadvantages. The biggest problem is that if the houses get better between numbers one and five, and five is the best, the buyer wants to see house number six. Most brokers recommend showing the best house early in the tour. This sets a standard against which all other homes are measured. It usually makes the tour faster because the buyer can decide quickly that the home shown earlier was more to his liking.

Once the route has been decided, the sales associate should make appointments for the showings with the property owners. The time scheduled for each showing should not be fixed but should fall in a range, because it is often difficult for the sales associate to judge how long the buyer will stay in each home on the tour. The seller should be asked to prepare the home for showing by opening the drapes and turning on all the lights so that the house will be bright and pleasant. The sales associate should ask the seller to vacate the property during the showing so that the buyer can have emotional possession of the property. If the sales associate has a cell phone, she should call the seller when leaving the previous house on the tour. If the seller owns a dog, the sales associate should ask that the seller make arrangements to contain the pet. If the sales associate will be later than scheduled or must cancel, common courtesy as a professional dictates that the sales associate should call the seller to explain the circumstances. Nothing is more disappointing to a seller than to needlessly prepare the home for a showing.

The route taken on the way to each property also is important. A trip past a beautiful park nearby makes the home site more interesting to the buyer, as does a trip past the shopping areas and schools closest to the home. While the initial route might avoid unsightly areas, they should be shown on the way out. Failure to show such surroundings is misrepresentation.

If the property has negative features, the licensee should discuss those features on the way to the property—for example, "When I previewed the home yesterday, the housekeeping was not up to its usual standard because the kids are out of school this week. I hope that's OK." This reduces the shock the buyer might feel when entering. Often, the buyer defends the property: "Considering everything, the house is surprisingly clean!"

The sales associate should avoid exaggerating a home's positive aspects to the buyer. This exaggeration may create an expectation that the house will not meet. It is better that the buyer be pleasantly surprised when discovering the features.

## Entering and Showing the Properties

This process depends on a property's general appearance. If the home's exterior is outstanding, the presentation should give the buyer time to appreciate this feature. Many sales associates park across the street so that a buyer's walk to a house is as pleasant as possible.

When highlighting a property's features, the sales associate must remember the most important words in any sales presentation:

- Fact
- Bridge
- Benefit
- Picture

1   The sales associate often points out facts that she believes to be important to the buyer and
2   expects the buyer to be able to translate each fact into a benefit. "This house is on a cul-de-sac"
3   might be a typical comment when driving up to the property. The sales associate believes this
4   is important information to the buyer. The buyer might be thinking, "Yes, that's quite obvious.
5   So what?" The full presentation should include fact, bridge, benefit, and picture.

6   The *fact* is that the property is on the cul-de-sac. The *bridge* might be "What that means
7   to you, Mr. and Mrs. Jones,…" The *benefit* is the rest of the sentence: "is that because there is
8   no through-traffic, automobiles travel very slowly, resulting in greater safety to your children."
9   The *picture* is a word picture: "Imagine being out here on the street while your children roller-
10  skate safely."

---

### DISCUSSION EXERCISE 7.7

Picture a house that you have been in recently. Try to think of as many features of the house as
you can, then express those features to represent fact, bridge, benefit, and picture statements.

Set up a group contest to see who can come up with the most fact-bridge-benefit-picture
statements about a house that is familiar to all of you.

---

11  The sales associate should practice this technique whenever she can: when driving in the
12  car alone, when **previewing properties,** or when on the office caravan of listings. Once it
13  becomes a habit, buyers will find the sales associate's statements clearer and more interesting,
14  and the sales associate will make more sales.

15  Many times, the listing office gives out the key to the back door, or the back door key may
16  be the only key provided in the lockbox, or **keysafe,** at the house. Although the sales associ-
17  ate must go in through the door for which she has a key, the buyer always should enter
18  through the front door.

19  Finally, the sales associate should not "overshow" a property. The buyer should be allowed
20  to discover some of the best features on his own. The classic example of overshowing is walk-
21  ing through a property making statements like, "This is the dining room."

22  ## Making the Buyers' Decision Easier

23  Normally, a sales associate will only show five to seven homes during a showing appointment.
24  This is usually recommended so the seller can have an opportunity to give feedback and not
25  become confused by a huge quantity of homes. In some cases, however, many homes are
26  shown to a buyer during one appointment. This might happen if the buyer is making a trip
27  from out-of-town and needs to find the right house during this trip.

28  If a buyer sees 20 to 30 homes in a tour, the buyer will certainly be confused about which
29  home had what feature. To make it easier, an experienced associate will have the buyer make
30  a decision after seeing each home. You would say, "Which home do you like best—this house
31  or the house on Hibiscus Lane?" If the answer were "Hibiscus Lane," you would say, "OK, for-
32  get all the other homes." At the last home on the tour, it is then easy to close with the ques-
33  tion, "Well, which home do you want to buy, this one or the one on Hibiscus Lane?"

34  If you show more homes tomorrow, and the buyer liked Hibiscus Lane best, start the tour
35  by taking the buyer back to Hibiscus Lane, with a comment like, "OK, so this is the house
36  we're ready to buy if we don't find one better today, right?"

### Evaluating the Buyer's Level of Interest

A buyer usually knows he or she is not interested shortly after entering the house. The sales associate should stop showing the property and proceed to the next. Because this is not the right house, it would be pointless to answer any of the buyer's objections. If the seller is at home, the sales associate should explain tactfully that the house does not satisfy the buyer's needs.

### Handling Objections

Some important points to remember about objections:

- An objection can be an opportunity to make the sale. Many objections can be turned into immediate selling points. "The house needs paint" could provoke an argument from an unprofessional sales associate. The empathetic sales associate simply asks, "Would you paint it yourself, or would you hire someone to paint it for you?" With a positive response from the buyer, both parties are happy.
- Be certain you understand the objection; restate it. For example, a buyer may say, "This house costs too much money!" You may follow with a question like, "If I understand you, you feel that the house is overpriced?" The buyer may answer, "No, I'm just not certain I want to buy a house at this price level." By clarifying with a question, you avoid being argumentative.

Don't answer an objection until you have isolated it; if there are many more objections, this is not a suitable property. "If it were not for the problem about the house price, would you buy this house?" A yes answer tells you, "Satisfy me regarding this problem, and I'll buy."

If you don't feel you can answer an objection to the buyer's satisfaction, especially if the objection is valid and you believe it is a "deal-breaker," you shouldn't. You should agree with the buyer and go to the next property.

Make a list of as many objections you can think of, then write out at least two plausible answers to the objection. Try them in your office sales meetings and practice them regularly.

Chapter 8 covers the legal document called a Contract for Sale and Purchase. It is very important for licensees to understand the wording of the agreement they will ask buyers and sellers to sign. Chapter 9 discusses writing and presenting an offer.

## SUMMARY

When working with buyers, a sales associate must be certain to make required agency disclosures on a timely basis. A buyer benefits most when a licensee represents the buyer and no one else. Extensive product knowledge is necessary if a sales associate is to provide the best service to a consumer. The sales associate has many ways to acquire product knowledge, but all consist of looking at properties. Index cards or client contact software helps the licensee remember properties, and a best-buys-on-the-market list helps the sales associate better exhibit her product knowledge.

Sales associates draw buyers from a number of sources: calls on ads or signs, past customers or clients, friends and family, open house visitors, canvassing, and buyer seminars. When handling an ad or a sign call, a licensee's primary objective is to get an appointment. Sales associates should prepare carefully for ad calls, know the properties advertised, and have fallback lists.

A sales associate should qualify a buyer's housing objectives and have the buyers preapproved for a loan, as well as prioritize buyers based on the immediacy of their needs. When showing properties, the sales associate should describe benefits and be careful not to overshow the properties. The sales associate can help reduce buyer confusion by helping the buyer decide which is the favored house after each house is shown.

# KEY TERMS

buyer brokerage agreement

canvassing

fallback list

keysafe

prequalification

previewing properties

qualifying

# PRACTICE EXAM

1. Most brokers recommend showing the best house:
   a. last.
   b. early in the tour.
   c. second to last.
   d. whenever—it doesn't matter.

2. Before showing properties to a buyer, a sales associate should *NOT*:
   a. qualify the buyer's financial abilities and housing needs.
   b. preview the homes to be shown.
   c. make the required brokerage relationship disclosures.
   d. find out what church they would like to live near.

3. A Priority 1 buyer is one who:
   a. has an immediate need to buy.
   b. is important but not as important as Priority 3.
   c. will not buy right away but should be contacted regularly.
   d. is not highly motivated.

4. Normally, the prospective buyer calling about a property with a "For Sale" sign wants information from the sales associate about the property's:
   a. location.
   b. lot size.
   c. price.
   d. address.

**Use the following information and Fannie Mae/Freddie Mac guidelines to answer questions 5 through 8.**

William is a new sales associate. On Saturday afternoon, the Sharpes visit his office and want to look at homes. They give William the following information:

| | |
|---|---|
| Gross income | $60,000 |
| House price | 140,000 |
| Monthly payment (PITI) | 1,350 |
| Other monthly obligations | 600 |

5. What is the Sharpes' housing expense ratio?
   a. 12 percent
   b. 27 percent
   c. 39 percent
   d. 44.4 percent

6. What is the Sharpes' total obligations ratio?
   a. 12 percent
   b. 27 percent
   c. 39 percent
   d. 44.4 percent

7. Will the Sharpes qualify for the loan?
   a. Yes, provided they escrow for taxes and insurance.
   b. No, the housing expense ratio is too high.
   c. No, the total obligations ratio is too high.
   d. No, both ratios are out of line.

8. What is the highest monthly payment the Sharpes can qualify for?
   a. $1,200
   b. $1,350
   c. $1,800
   d. $2,000

9. How does a buyer benefit by agreeing to pay a brokerage commission to her broker?
   a. The commission will be lower than if the seller has to pay a commission.
   b. The broker will automatically be the buyer's single agent.
   c. The broker will be able to work harder on the buyer's financing alternatives.
   d. The broker can show the buyer unlisted properties like FSBOs and foreclosures.

10. For a buyer to decide to work with a licensee, the most important factor probably is the licensee's:
    a. low fee.
    b. product knowledge.
    c. dress code.
    d. automobile make and model.

11. When making an appointment with a seller to show her property, a sales associate should NOT do which of the following?
    a. Set the time as a range rather than a specific time.
    b. Tell the seller to turn on the lights.
    c. Tell the seller to leave the home during the showing.
    d. Fail to call if it looks like the visit will be much later than the time specified.

12. A sales associate's primary objective when answering a sign call or an ad call is to:
    a. give out the information requested.
    b. make a friend.
    c. make an appointment.
    d. get a name.

13. A fallback list consists of:
    a. past customers.
    b. answers to objections.
    c. places to find part-time employment.
    d. properties similar to those advertised.

14. If a property is particularly attractive from the front, the best way to show the property is by:
    a. parking in the garage.
    b. parking at the street.
    c. sending a photo to the buyer.
    d. driving up and down the street first.

15. Before a buyer begins seeing properties, the sales associate should *NOT*:
    a. give the buyer a brokerage relationship notice.
    b. qualify the buyer.
    c. ask the buyer about his feelings about having minorities living in the neighborhood.
    d. find out what area of town the buyer would prefer.

16. A sales associate asks a seller to vacate the property while it is being shown because:
    a. the seller can't hear what the sales associate is saying about the property.
    b. the buyer can take emotional possession of the property during the showing.
    c. it allows the buyer's children to use the bathroom if necessary.
    d. the buyer can inspect the structure for defects without interruption.

17. Generally, the only features a sales associate should discuss with a buyer on the way to viewing a property are the:
    a. home's most outstanding attributes.
    b. negative features if any.
    c. beautiful Jacuzzi and huge master suite.
    d. features previously discussed.

18. One way to find lots of buyers at one time is:
    a. calling friends.
    b. calling past customers.
    c. canvassing.
    d. conducting buyer seminars.

19. A sales associate's statement that "the house is built of brick" should be followed immediately by the:
    a. fact.
    b. bridge.
    c. benefit.
    d. picture.

20. The safest way for a sales associate to determine whether a buyer is qualified is to:
    a. let a lender do it.
    b. use national mortgage market guidelines.
    c. use Fannie Mae/Freddie Mac underwriting guidelines.
    d. use any of the above methods.

# CHAPTER

# 8

# SALES AND OPTION CONTRACTS

<sup>1</sup> **LEARNING OBJECTIVES**

<sup>2</sup> Upon completion of this section, *you should be able to*

<sup>3</sup> **1.** discuss the unique features of a real estate contract versus a normal business contract;

<sup>4</sup> **2.** define what is meant by a valid contract;

<sup>5</sup> **3.** distinguish between an implied contract and a quasi-contract;

<sup>6</sup> **4.** distinguish between a voidable contract and a void contract;

<sup>7</sup> **5.** define what is meant by an unconscionable contract;

<sup>8</sup> **6.** distinguish the difference between the statute of frauds and the statute of limitations;

<sup>9</sup> **7.** explain the exceptions to the statute of frauds that are recognized as valid real estate transactions;

<sup>10</sup> **8.** list at least three transactions that are *not* suitable for using the Florida Association of REALTORS®
<sup>11</sup>   Residential Sale and Purchase Contract;

<sup>12</sup> **9.** describe the legal test for the sufficiency of a legal description;

<sup>13</sup> **10.** name and explain at least ten important sections or provisions in a real estate sales contract;

<sup>14</sup> **11.** complete a sales contract; and

<sup>15</sup> **12.** list the requirements for completing an option contract.

<sup>16</sup> **OVERVIEW**

<sup>17</sup> Contracts are part of our everyday lives. When a person orders telephone service, buys a refrigerator, or
<sup>18</sup> pays for an airline ticket, a contract has been formed.

<sup>19</sup> Licensees regularly work with many different kinds of contracts. The broker's employment agreement, listing
<sup>20</sup> contracts, buyer brokerage agreements, leases, options, and sales contracts are just a few. Understanding
<sup>21</sup> the information in a contract and being able to correctly explain it to sellers and buyers is an important
<sup>22</sup> function of a sales associate. Licensees may legally prepare listing contracts, sales contracts, and option
<sup>23</sup> contracts. Preparing notes, mortgages, or deeds is unauthorized practice of law. ■

# ANALYSIS OF REAL ESTATE CONTRACTS

A **contract** is a promise or set of promises that must be performed. Once the promise is given, the law recognizes performance of that promise as a duty. If the promise is broken or breached, the law provides a legal remedy for the injured party. However, one promise, standing alone, does not constitute a contract. Some specific act by the party to whom the promise is made, or a mutual promise from that party, is required to conclude a contract. For example, if you promise to fix your neighbor's roof and the neighbor thanks you, no contract exists because you asked for nothing in return for your promise. If your neighbor promises to give you $1,000 to fix her roof and you promise to do it, mutual promises have been exchanged, and a contract has been made.

## Types and Legal Standings of Contracts

A number of contract types and classifications exist, each having certain legal effects. Newly licensed sales associates will remember having been exposed to certain classifications of contracts and to the fact that a contract can change from one classification to another as **performance** progresses.

A **bilateral contract,** the most common type, is a mutual agreement by both sides to perform. A real estate sales contract is an example of a bilateral contract because the seller promises to sell a parcel of real property and to deliver title, and the buyer promises to pay a certain sum of money for the property. A **unilateral contract,** on the other hand, is a one-sided promise. One party makes an obligation to perform without receiving a promise to perform from the other party. In effect, it is an offer that can be accepted only by performance on the terms offered. An example of a unilateral contract is the ordinary option, in which the person granting the option (optionor) is obligated not to sell to anyone but the person asking for the option (optionee) during the life of the option. The optionee is not required to buy.

Two additional examples of a unilateral contract are

1. an open listing agreement, where the seller agrees to pay a commission if the broker performs, but the broker makes no promises to market the property and
2. a broker's promise to pay a $5,000 bonus to the sales associate who sells the most homes in a subdivision

An **express contract** is a mutual agreement between parties stated in words, either oral or written. An **implied contract** is an unwritten agreement inferred from the actions or conduct of the parties that shows intent to be bound by the agreement. For example, if a broker personally buys property on behalf of his principal, a promise is implied on the broker's part to deliver the property to the principal. A second example of an implied contract is a situation in which a broker tells a seller that she has a buyer willing and able to pay for the seller's property, and the seller accepts the buyer's offer. The law usually requires that the seller pay the broker a typical rate of commission because of the parties' acts.

An **executory contract** is an agreement in which some future act remains to be done by one or both parties. For example, a real estate sales contract, between signing and title closing, is an executory contract. An **executed contract,** on the other hand, is an agreement in which the parties have fulfilled their promises and thus performed the contract. For example, a sales contract becomes an executed agreement after title closing and after all parties have fully performed. (*Note:* Do not confuse the term *executed contract* with the use of the word *execute,* which refers to the signing of a legal document such as a contract.)

A **valid contract** is an agreement that contains all of the essential elements—contractual capacity, offer and acceptance, lawful purpose, in writing and signed, and consideration (COLIC)—and is binding and enforceable on both parties in a court of law.

A **quasi-contract** is an obligation imposed by law in the absence of a contract to prevent unjust enrichment. Thus, it is not a contract at all because it does not depend on the parties' intentions; it was "invented" to allow the courts to preserve justice and fair dealing. For example, if a person comes into the possession of money that belongs to another, the law infers the existence of a promise to pay the money to the person entitled to it.

A **voidable contract** is an agreement that appears to be valid and enforceable but may be rescinded by one of the parties. For example, an agreement entered into with a minor usually is voidable by the minor. The competent parties element of a valid contract is absent. For another example, a contract may contain a clause (provision) related to time of performance by both parties. If either party fails to perform on or before a specified date, the other party has the right to void or nullify the contract. Thus, a voidable contract may be seen as midway between a valid contract and a void contract: It remains valid until the party with the power to void the agreement chooses to do so. A **void contract** is an agreement that is unenforceable under the law. It has no legal force because it does not contain the essential elements of a contract. For example, a listing contract in which a broker agrees to illegal discrimination based on race, sex, color, religion, national origin, family status, or handicap probably voids the document.

An **unconscionable contract** is an agreement that, if the contract were enforced, would be too harsh on or oppressive to one of the parties. The word *unconscionable* means unreasonable or excessive. The Uniform Commercial Code (UCC) provides that a court may refuse to enforce an unconscionable contract, may strike out an unconscionable clause, or simply may tailor enforcement of a contract to prevent an unconscionable result. This interpretation of the UCC by the courts is an example of the rapidly growing judicial trend toward preventing informed and knowledgeable parties from taking advantage of uninformed parties. It is not necessary that fraud be an element in a dispute for the provisions of the law to be applied. Any agreement or clause in a contract related to consumer credit, a consumer lease, or a consumer loan is void if the agreement or clause is unconscionable. For example, a seller may insist on an "as is" provision in the sales contract. A buyer compelled to sign the contract with the clause "Buyer represents that he or she has examined the entire property and declares that he or she has not relied on any representation made by the Seller" seemingly is being prevented from raising a defense of fraud or misrepresentation should its existence be revealed later. Any contract that appears to create a one-sided bargain is in danger of being declared unconscionable.

---

### DISCUSSION EXERCISE 8.1

You are a sales associate who has listed John Wilson's home in Foxcroft. Mr. Wilson would rather not repair several property defects (such as a cracked foundation). He suggests the use of an "as is" clause in the contract so that a buyer can do any inspection desired. "Based on this clause," Wilson tells you, "we have no need to disclose."

Does the use of an "as is" clause in a sales contract excuse a broker from disclosing material facts regarding a property? Explain.

---

## Statute of Frauds

Before the enactment of the **statute of frauds,** it was not uncommon for a person to pay "witnesses" to falsify testimony to support a nonexistent oral contract for the sale of real property. The law commonly called the *statute of frauds* requires that certain types of contracts, in order to be enforceable, be in writing and be signed by the party against whom enforcement is sought. Contracts that must be in writing and signed are of two general types: those that will not be performed fully within a short period of time and those that deal with specific subjects.

In Florida, an agreement or a promise that cannot be performed by both parties within one year after the contract date must be evidenced by a written document. Also, an agreement to sell or the actual sale of any interest in real property is subject to the statute of frauds and must be in writing and signed by all parties bound by the contract to be enforceable. Witnesses are not required.

Two common exceptions to the statute of frauds are recognized:

1. *Executed contracts.* Performance of the promise made proves the contract existed; therefore, the function of the statute of frauds has been accomplished, and a written form is not required.
2. *Partial performance.* Usually, the statute of frauds does not apply to partially performed contracts as long as two conditions have been met: (1) partial or full payment has been made and (2) the buyer has either taken physical possession of or made improvements to the subject property. For example, if a buyer has evidence of a $500 payment toward the purchase of a parcel of land, then moves onto the property and plants a crop of tomatoes, the statute's function has been accomplished. The payment and possession are regarded as evidence that a valid contract exists.

## SALES CONTRACTS

A **sales contract,** also referred to as a *purchase and sale contract* or a *contract for sale and purchase*, is a written agreement setting forth the terms for the transfer of real property from seller to buyer, with both signing the document. The standard contract for sale and purchase developed by the Florida Association of REALTORS® (Residential Sale and Purchase Contract) is the most widely used preprinted sales contract form in the state. (See the Forms-To-Go Appendix.) This section of the chapter presents specific instructions for the correct preparation of that contract, providing licensees with hands-on practice in preparing contracts to increase their professional skills. If licensees in your area use a different sales contract form, substitute that form for the FAR contract. The discussion that follows applies to your contract form as well.

### Online Contracts for REALTORS®

Members of the Florida Association of REALTORS® have a very helpful tool called "On-Line Gold Web-Based Account," containing a library of forms. Using this Web site, users can

- Fill in forms such as listing and sales contracts
- Save forms as internal data or flat .PDF files
- Print forms
- E-mail forms to customers
- Link common information between forms, providing the quick processing of contract-related forms
- Create a Form Transaction, managing forms as a group and auto-filling in information common to the deal
- Save their own special clauses to insert into contracts
- Use their contact list information on customers, cooperating licensees, title companies, and loan institutions to automatically populate their contracts, and
- Set up a brokerage office database account so the broker can review all contracts

### Whether to Use a Printed Form

No two real estate transactions are exactly alike. Even two nearly identical houses located adjacent to one another may require different contractual handling. The earnest money deposits, mortgage sources, and prices, as well as many other items, must be considered. Even the tried-and-proven clauses in a standard form may need to be adapted to the requirements of a particular transaction. Therefore, licensees should use printed form contracts cautiously. Two contracts are widely used by licensees: the FAR Residential Sale and Purchase Contract and the FAR/BAR Contract for Sale and Purchase. This text will describe the features of the FAR contract. Both contracts are similar and intended for use in routine transactions involving the sale of single-family dwellings or unimproved real property. If a licensee is involved in any one of the following types of transactions, the contracts are *not* suitable:

- Business purchase or sale
- Construction or improvements contract
- Contract for deed (installment contract, agreement for deed)
- Exchange agreement (contract for exchange of real property)
- Lease with option to buy
- Option contract (to be described later in this chapter)
- Unique or complex transactions

If vacant land (other than a single-family vacant lot) is involved in a transaction, special provisions should be included in the contract concerning the concurrency status of the property for development purposes, as well as suitability for its intended use relative to the area's comprehensive plan.

## Responsibility for Preparation

The sales contract is the most important instrument for closing a real estate transaction. Because it is the final agreement after all the offers and negotiations that have taken place, a licensee must be very careful when preparing it. Any time a licensee is not certain whether an attorney is required in preparing any special clause or type of contract, the best course of action is to advise the buyer and seller to consult an experienced real estate attorney.

The sales associate and his or her employer may be held financially responsible for any mistakes in the agreement. If any errors, omissions, or ambiguities exist regarding material terms, the courts will not go outside the contents of the contract to determine intent. The licensee who prepared the contract will not be allowed to explain later intent not indicated in the contract contents. If the contract is vague and unenforceable, the result could be no transaction at all, loss of commission, and a possible civil lawsuit against the licensee.

## "Time Is of the Essence" Provision

A single sentence in Paragraph 11, "**Time is of the essence** for all provisions of this Contract," has important legal effects. If a party fails to perform the duties or promises made within the exact time limits in the contract, it causes an automatic default. This default then creates a right of cancellation on the part of the other party (voidable contract). Because of the importance of meeting requirements with dates and times, licensees should

- use realistic time periods
- check that the time periods complement and are consistent with times in other blank spaces, and
- set up calendar deadlines in the file to monitor performance by the parties to the sales contract once it has been signed. (See Figure 8.1)

## Gathering Contract Data

Collecting the information required to complete all of the entry blanks in the FAR contract is a sizable task. Information may become available or should be obtained as the real estate lic-

**F I G U R E  8.1  ■  Stated Performance Dates**

Some important contract performance dates and deadlines are in Paragraph:

- 2(b)  Additional deposit;
- 3(b)  Financing period: time for buyer to qualify for and obtain financing;
- 3  Buyer to apply for financing;
- 4  Closing date;
- 6 and 8  Inspection period and wood-destroying organisms report;
- 7(c)  Buyer cancellation period for flood zone floor level problems;
- 10  Delivery of title evidence;
- 11  Effective date definitions;
- 16  Dispute resolution;
- Signature  Offer, counteroffer, and effective date of contract.

ensee helps negotiate the contract. Once the licensee gathers all of the information, she must verify it for accuracy and currency. Including obsolete information in a contract may be more harmful to a successful closing than having insufficient information to complete the contract. The licensee should pay particular attention to and be sure to verify the following two categories of data:

1. *The owner/seller's name and address and the property's legal description.* MLS data, property appraiser information, and even listing agreements have been in error on occasion. Place more reliance on an existing or a prior title insurance policy, a deed, or a survey for the information.
2. *Financial information.* Financial data tend to change frequently and require last minute updating. Check with local lenders to make certain that times allowed for obtaining financial commitments are realistic and that the rates and terms contemplated actually are available.

## PREPARING SALES CONTRACTS

While the following guidelines are provided as an aid in understanding and preparing each element in the FAR Residential Sale and Purchase Contract, these instructions are generic in description and should apply to most other sales contracts. Each specific provision of the form is described separately to help licensees examine the contract thoroughly. Paragraph numbers in this section refer to contract paragraph numbers. The current FAR Residential Sale and Purchase Contract is reproduced in its entirety in the Forms-To-Go Appendix.

### Residential Sale and Purchase Contract

**1. Sale and Purchase**

**Seller:** Seller's name(s) should be shown in the manner in which title is held, showing the marital status of each seller. You can get this information from the seller's title insurance policy or a copy of the recorded deed.

*Residence:* If a married person owns the property individually, you should obtain the signature of the spouse to avoid possible future litigation.

*Joint Ownership:* If the property is jointly owned, obtain the signatures of all joint owners. If a residence is located on the property, obtain the signatures of joint owners and their spouses.

*Corporations, Partnerships, Estates, Trusts, and Use of Powers of Attorney:* Each requires special attention and instructions. Seek broker or legal counsel, as appropriate.

**Buyer:** Buyer's name(s) should be shown in the same manner as the buyer wishes title to be taken at closing. Other points to consider include:

- Each buyer shown on the contract must execute the contract.
- If the buyer later desires to take title in some other manner and this is permitted by the contract, an appropriate assignment or amendment to the contract should be obtained at closing.
- Buyers often seek advice as to the manner in which they should take title to property—for example, tenancy by the entireties, tenants in common, and so on. If the buyer asks how title should be taken, advise him to see his attorney. Under no circumstances express an opinion.
- *Non–U.S. Corporations, U.S. Corporations, Partnerships, etc.:* Seek broker or legal counsel, as appropriate.
- *Addresses and Telephone Numbers:* Include complete information concerning these items to make handling the transaction easier for all involved.
- *Address:* If the street address, city, and ZIP code are available, insert them. This may render an otherwise insufficient legal description legally sufficient.

**Legal Description:** *Material Term:* The legal description of the property to be sold is an essential provision of the contract. A defective legal description can render the contract unenforceable.

*Sufficiency Test:* The classic test of the sufficiency of a legal description is whether a surveyor can locate the property by reference to the description used.

*Reliable Information:* Do not rely on tax roll descriptions. The tax rolls are filled with errors and abbreviated descriptions that could be regarded as legally insufficient. Also, do not rely on descriptions contained in MLS listing sheets because they may only repeat errors others have made. Instead, rely on copies of prior deeds, prior title insurance policies, or prior surveys.

*Description Not Known at Time of Contract:* If any question remains as to the property's exact location, size, or description, and if the question cannot be resolved before the execution of the contract, agreement must be reached as to the survey of the property and as to who will bear the expense of the survey. Furthermore, agreement must reflect that the contract will be amended to conform to the legal description. The buyer also should have the right to terminate the contract if the property location and size are not substantially as represented.

*Easements, Other Interests:* The legal description should include any interest in the property being conveyed—for example, private right-of-way or common elements. This information usually is found on the deed or title insurance policy.

*Quantity:* From the seller's point of view, references to exact acreage in the legal description should be avoided. This could give rise to a right on the part of the buyer either to cancel the contract or to reduce the purchase price should the actual acreage prove to be materially different.

Minimum Description Requirements—Platted Subdivision

- County in which property is located
- Lot and block numbers
- Name of subdivision (include phase or unit if applicable)
- Plat book and page number of recorded plat

Minimum Description Requirements—Condominium

- County in which property is located
- Condominium unit or parcel number

- Name of condominium complex
- Identification of common elements—for example, parking spaces and storage spaces if applicable
- Recording information (official record book and page number) of original declaration of condominium and any amendments
- Reference to ground lease or recreational lease and recording information if applicable

Minimum Description Requirements—Unplatted Property

- County in which property is located
- Legal description provided by survey or prior deed(s)
- Reference to section, township, and range

**Improvements and Attachments:** The contract includes all improvements and attached items, and further describes fixtures, built-in furnishings, built-in appliances, ceiling fans, light fixtures, attached wall-to-wall carpeting, rods, draperies, and other window coverings (unless any of these items are specifically excluded). It has a section to add other items of personal property. If personal property is to be included, you should prepare an accurate description. Personal property may be regarded as a material term of the contract, so inaccurate, incomplete, or insufficient descriptions can render the contract voidable or unenforceable. To reduce appraisal problems and potential sales tax liability, the contract has words "Personal property listed in this contract is included in the purchase price, has no contributory value, and is being left for Seller's convenience."

*What to Include:* In the normal residential transaction, a detailed inventory of all personal property (with defects disclosed if applicable) should be prepared and attached to the contract. The list should include all kitchen equipment and appliances, plus other equipment and appliances, such as outside television antennas and satellite dishes, pool equipment, lawn furniture, and other easily removable "fixtures." Quantify items where applicable. Failure to provide an accurate and complete inventory of all property included in the sale can lead to closing day problems, and the broker may have to make up any difference to close the transaction.

*Florida Sales Tax on Personal Property:* The Florida Department of Revenue has made several rulings on the tax liability of personal property included in the sale of real property. If itemized in the sales contract, with a separately stated value for each item, sales tax must be paid. No sales tax is due if the contract simply lists the property, such as a "refrigerator, range, microwave, and washer/dryer combination."

## Price and Financing

### 2. Purchase Price

**Fixed Purchase Price:** The format of the preprinted contract calls for a fixed purchase price to be expressed in monetary terms.

**Variable Price:** If the full purchase price cannot be expressed in monetary terms, the manner in which it might be determined accurately should be stated in the contract in an addendum. For example, if acreage is involved and the parties agree on a price per acre, that price per acre should be set forth in an addendum (under "Special Clauses," check "Addendum is attached") together with a provision for an accurate survey determination. Whenever an addendum is used, it should have the date of the original contract, the complete names of the parties, and a complete legal description. It also must be dated and signed by the parties.

**Method of Payment:** The subparagraphs set forth the manner in which the purchase price is to be paid. The sum total of the monetary amounts set forth in these subparagraphs should equal the purchase price.

---

### DISCUSSION EXERCISE 8.2

You are writing a contract for the purchase of a tract of land that is to be subdivided. The parties mark on the actual property lines where the division is to be made but can only estimate the size of the property at about 24 acres. Both parties agree on a price of $12,500 per acre.
Write a special clause that will set forth the parties' agreement and be legally binding.

---

**Deposit Received**

*2(a):* with the amount of the deposit, the date, and the escrow agent.

*2(b):* This line is used when the payment of the deposit is split between the initial deposit and an additional deposit. Typically, the second deposit is much larger than the initial deposit. The amount of the additional deposit and the date or the number of days within which it must be made should be inserted. The contract allows the seller to recover not only the initial deposit but also any unpaid deposit. If the buyer defaults by failing to make the additional deposit, the seller is faced with having to initiate litigation to recover the balance. While the seller has an alternate remedy of specific performance, the seller's best remedy in the event of buyer default is a forfeiture of the deposit.

*2(c):* Enter the amount of total financing in this line. It can be shown as a dollar amount or as a percent, but a dollar amount is usually better to determine whether the balance to close is correctly added.

*2(d):* This line can be used for items that are not cash or financing. For example, it could be a boat taken as part of the purchase price.

*2(e):* State the balance of the cash to be paid after deducting from the purchase price the cash deposit, financing, and other payments. Note that this figure does not include closing costs, prepaid items, or prorations. The contract requires either cash or a locally drawn certified or cashier's check, not a personal check, in order to speed up disbursement of funds at closing.

### 3. Financing

There are two options that can be selected in this section

(a) A cash transaction with no financing contingency

(b) A financing commitment no later than the date specified or the closing date, whichever is sooner, by
 1. a new loan (fill in the amount or percentage of value) or
 2. seller financing (use an addendum to describe).

**Prompt Application:** The number of days the buyer will have to make an application is inserted. Except under unusual circumstances, it should be possible for the buyer to make an application for the mortgage almost immediately. The broker or sales associate should ensure that the buyer proceeds diligently to make a loan application. Keep in mind that paragraph 11 of the contract makes time of the essence, and failure to make a timely application may be a default.

**Monitor the Buyer:** It is in the licensee's interest to monitor the steps the buyer is taking to obtain a loan commitment pursuant to the contract terms. If the buyer fails to use reasonable diligence under this provision, the seller may declare a default and require the buyer to forfeit the deposit. If additional time is needed to obtain a loan commitment and the parties agree, amend the contract to extend the time.

**New Mortgages**

*Financing Contingency:* If the buyer cannot qualify for the loan in time after making all necessary good-faith efforts or if the buyer is turned down, the buyer may elect not to proceed, return all seller's documents, and, after all interested parties agree, get the deposit back.

*Know the Mortgage Market:* All active licensees should have current information on the local mortgage market, including data on available interest rates (fixed and adjustable), points, time for processing applications, and so on.

*Contingency Should Be Broad:* Whether the buyer or the seller is the principal, make certain that the financing contingency clause describes a mortgage that is obtainable by the buyer.

*Time to Get Commitment:* The number of days the buyer has to obtain a loan commitment is sometimes based on how much time the seller will give the buyer to find financing. In any event, the broker or sales associate should know approximately how long local institutions take to process loan applications. Then a reasonable period of time should be inserted.

*Type of Mortgage:* A mortgage loan can be obtained on the basis of either a fixed rate or an adjustable rate, and the appropriate box should be checked. If the buyer has not decided, the third block should be checked, indicating that the buyer will seek a commitment for either a fixed-rate or an adjustable-rate loan. If the buyer seeks a different type of mortgage, address this in an addendum.

*Principal Amount:* The principal amount of the third-party mortgage that the buyer seeks is inserted. Licensees should have a working knowledge of what is available in the local financial market.

*Relation of Financing Commitment to the Closing Date:* Standard P provides that if the lender imposes requirements relating to place, time of day, and procedures for closing and disbursing mortgage proceeds, those requirements control and supersede other contrary contract provisions. This does not mean that the title closing date may be extended by the lender's requirements. If delays occur as a result of loan application processing or loan closing, it may be necessary to amend the contract to extend the title closing date.

## Closing

### 4. Closing Date; Occupancy

**Time Is of the Essence:** The failure of either party to close on the closing date, assuming the closing date is not extended, causes a default.

**Conditions:** The closing date should be set for a reasonable period of time after any conditions have been satisfied and the title evidence delivered.

---

### DISCUSSION EXERCISE 8.3

You are writing a FAR/BAR contract for the sale of a 160-acre farm and home. All parties have agreed that the buyer should have 40 days from the contract date to produce a written commitment for financing the purchase.

What would be an optimum time for the contract closing date?

---

**Extensions:** Note the phrase "unless extended by other provisions of this Contract." As previously stated, the contract sets forth many deadlines for performance. Where any of these provisions would require or allow performance to take place after the closing date, the closing date will be deemed extended.

**Swept Clean:** Notice that the seller's personal items are to be removed by the closing date and the property swept clean. Junk items that are not included in the sale should be removed from the property.

**Insurance suspension:** When a hurricane is in a specific geographic area called the "box" (see Chapter 12), insurance underwriters no longer issue policies. This provision allows the date of closing to be extended for up to five days after the suspension is lifted. The buyers should be advised to get insurance coverage well before closing.

**5. Closing Procedure: Costs**

This section allows an electronic closing. If there is gap title insurance during the period from closing to recording, the closing agent will disburse at closing to the seller and the broker.

**(a) Seller Costs:** This section shows the expenses to be paid by the seller, including documentary stamps on the deed, repairs up to 1.5 percent for both repairs and wood-destroying organism treatment, and repairs.

**(b) Buyer Costs:** Buyer agrees to pay taxes on notes and mortgages and recording fees on deed and financing statements. Buyer also agrees to pay for lender's title insurance, inspections, survey, and flood insurance.

**(c) Title Evidence and Insurance:** This section lets the parties determine what type of title evidence is appropriate and who will pay for title insurance.

**(d) Prorations:** Expenses of the property will be prorated between the parties. The buyer agrees to be responsible for property tax increases due to a change in ownership. The intent of this is to protect the seller in case the property taxes have been capped under the "Save Our Homes" amendment.

**(e) Tax Withholding:** Parties agree to abide by the Foreign Investment in Real Property Tax Act if the seller is a "foreign person," as described in the law.

**(f) Home Warranty:** The parties may agree on a homeowners' warranty and who will pay for it.

## Property Condition

**6. Inspection Periods**

This paragraph sets the date by which all inspections must be completed.

**7. Real Property Disclosure**

This paragraph requires that the seller disclose all known defects that materially affect the value of the property other than those that are readily observable.

Other disclosures are required, including energy efficiency, radon gas, flood zone, and the homeowners' association disclosure.

**8. Maintenance, Inspections, and Repair**

**(a) Warranty, Inspections, and Repair:** This section requires the seller to keep the property in the same condition until closing except required repairs. If seller can't complete the repairs by closing, the seller must pay for the repairs at closing.

(1) *Warranty:* Seller warrants that appliances; heating, cooling, mechanical, electrical, security, sprinkler, septic, and plumbing systems; seawall; and dock and pool equipment are in working order at closing.

Seller need not repair any cosmetic conditions, as defined in the contract, nor bring any item into compliance with existing building code regulations.

(2) *Professional Inspection:* Buyer may have an inspection made of warranted items and has five days after the inspection period to notify seller of items that are not in the condition warranted. After five days, the buyer must accept the items "as is."

(3) *Repair:* This section describes remedies if the seller disagrees with the buyer's inspection results. It also describes the process if the repair costs exceed the amount the seller had agreed to pay.

(b) **Wood-Destroying Organisms:** This section describes the WDO inspection and the steps a seller must take if damage or active infestation is discovered.

(c) **Walk-Through Inspection:** The walk-through inspection is solely to determine that the seller has made the required repairs and has met the contractual obligations. If the buyer does not make the walk-through inspection, the seller's repair and maintenance obligations are deemed fulfilled.

## 9. Risk of Loss

This section describes the remedies available in case the improvements are destroyed before closing.

## Title

### 10. Title

Either the seller or the buyer may pay the cost of either a **title insurance** policy or an up-to-date **abstract** of title. The title insurance premium must be charged for the title insurance commitment or binder whether or not a policy is issued. There is no charge for a policy issued pursuant to an issued commitment.

(a) **Title Evidence:** The time limit for delivery of title evidence may depend on several factors, such as the satisfaction of contingencies. Generally speaking, however, it is desirable to provide for delivery of title evidence as quickly as possible so that if any title problems are discovered, there will be as much time as possible to deal with them. Where the time period between the date of the contract and the closing date is prolonged, it is desirable to provide in the contract a provision that the title insurance binder will be updated by endorsement to reflect any intervening title matters that might have arisen.

(b) **Title Examination:** This paragraph describes the steps available to the buyer in case title is found to be defective.

(c) **Survey:** The contract provides that if the survey shows an encroachment or a violation, the fact of such encroachment or violation will be regarded as a title defect, and the curing provisions of Paragraph (b) will apply. If, for example, zoning setback violations are found, these curing provisions would give the seller an opportunity to seek an appropriate variance from zoning authorities. There is also a sentence requiring compliance with the coastal construction control line.

## Miscellaneous

### 11. Effective Date; Time

This paragraph makes the effective date the date that the last of the parties initialed or signed the latest offer. It also has the wording that "time is of the essence." Time periods do not include Saturdays, Sundays, or holidays, and the periods end at 5 P.M.

### 12. Notices

Notices may be made by mail, personal delivery, or electronic media. The paragraph emphasizes that if the buyer does not make the required notices about contingencies to the seller on time, the contingency will no longer exist.

### 13. Complete Agreement

Except for brokerage agreements, this is the only agreement between the parties. Handwritten portions of the agreement supersede preprinted portions if the two conflict. This sentence is meant to protect the contract if a licensee fails to delete an inconsistent provision covered in handwritten clauses or to protect any riders or addenda that are designed to show the parties' true intent. To know whether it is necessary to revoke, amend, or replace a printed provision, a licensee must know the content of the printed provisions.

### 14. Assignability; Persons Bound
The contract may not be assigned without the seller's consent.

## Default and Dispute Resolution

### 15. Default

(a) **Seller Default:** If the seller defaults, buyer can either get the binder back and cancel the contract or seek damages, or can sue for specific performance. Seller will also owe the broker a commission.

(b) **Buyer Default:** If the buyer defaults, the seller can collect the deposits as liquidated damages, agreeing to pay the broker 50 percent of the deposits up to the full brokerage fee.

### 16. Dispute Resolution

(a) **Disputes Concerning Entitlement to Deposits:** In case of disputes over the escrow deposits, buyer and seller can go through mediation for up to 30 days. If that fails, the escrow agent will submit the dispute to arbitration, a Florida court, or the Florida Real Estate Commission for a resolution.

(b) **All Other Disputes:** In disputes other than over escrow deposits, the parties have 30 days to go through mediation, after which they must seek binding arbitration of the issues.

(c) **Mediation and Arbitration; Expenses:** The parties agree to equally split the fees paid to mediators or arbitrators.

## Escrow Agent and Broker

### 17. Escrow Agent
This paragraph authorizes the escrow agent to accept and disburse funds and releases the escrow agent from liability unless there has been willful breach of the contract or gross negligence. If the escrow agent has to interplead the subject matter with a court, the court costs and attorney's fees may be paid from the deposit.

### 18. Professional Advice; Broker Liability
This section advises the buyer to get legal and other professional advice. The buyer agrees to look solely to the seller for property condition, square footage, and other facts that affect property value. If the buyer or seller makes misstatements, the broker is entitled to collect court costs and attorney's fees to defend against damage claims.

### 19. Brokers
Parties agree in this paragraph that the broker is the procuring cause of the sale, and direct the closing agent to disburse brokerage fees according to the brokerage agreements and the cooperating broker arrangements for commission splits. In the absence of such brokerage agreements, the paragraph is set up to fill in the brokers' names and the amount of their commissions.

## Addenda and Additional Terms

### 20. Addenda
Licensee should check the appropriate boxes for addenda that apply to this agreement. The

Comprehensive Addendum to the Residential Sale and Purchase Contract has many of the most common clauses. Various laws and regulations require that some riders be attached to the contract and that other riders expand and clarify contract terms. All of the riders listed are available as preprinted forms.

**21. Additional Terms**
This is the area for special clauses specific to the needs of this particular transaction.

### Practicing with the Contract for Sale and Purchase

This discussion was meant to familiarize the student with some of the contract language. In the next chapter, the student will have an opportunity to complete a FAR Residential Sale and Purchase Contract along with a cost disclosure statement.

## OPTION CONTRACTS

An **option contract** is a contract between a property owner (optionor) and another (optionee) in which the optionee, for a consideration, has the right (not the obligation) to purchase or lease the property at a specified price during a designated period. To be enforceable in Florida, an option must contain all of the essential elements of a contract.

Strictly speaking, it is important to distinguish between an *option contract* and an *option* (in actual practice, the terms are often used interchangeably). If you offer to sell your house to a friend for $100,000 and your friend says she wants to think about the offer for a day or so, your friend might have an option, but she does not have an option contract. Therefore, you could revoke your offer to sell and no breach of contract would occur because no contract exists when there is a lack of consideration (exchange of promises). Had your friend paid you $1,000 in consideration of a 30-day or 60-day period to decide about your offer and you agreed to those terms, an option contract would have been concluded. The consideration given legally may be applied as part of the purchase price in the event the option is **exercised.**

An option creates a contractual right; it does not create an estate in the optioned property. When first written and executed, an option contract is unilateral. The owner/optionor is obligated to sell if given proper notice by the buyer/optionee, but the buyer/optionee is not obligated to purchase and may allow the option to expire. Options frequently are used to give a developer or buyer time to resolve problems related to financing, zoning, title, or feasibility before committing to purchase or lease. Options also are useful instruments in the land assemblage process.

In addition to the required information in an option contract, other provisions should or may be included. For example, a statement of the method of notice required to exercise the option normally is provided. Also, some provision should be included concerning the option money (the consideration) if the option is not exercised. Unless expressly prohibited by the wording of the terms, an option normally is assignable.

Option contracts often are written with less care and attention than they deserve. Keep in mind that an option contract is converted into a sales contract when the option is exercised. However, if the option fails to include all the terms material to the transaction and leaves some terms or decisions for future agreement, the option contract normally is not enforceable. For example, if the option calls for a purchase-money mortgage as part of the method of payment and does not include the mortgage interest rate or the duration, courts normally would refuse to enforce the contract. Generally, it pays to have a competent real estate attorney construct an option agreement.

---

> ### DISCUSSION EXERCISE 8.4
>
> Oscar paid Silvio $2,000 for a 30-day option to buy Silvio's house for $160,000. Two weeks later, Silvio sold his house to Benny for $175,000.
>
> Can Oscar enforce his option and require the property to be sold to him? Why or why not?

---

1   The optionee may wish to record the option. This establishes the optionee's rights back to
2   the option date and gives priority over subsequent rights of third parties. Good title practice
3   requires that a release of option be recorded later in the event a recorded option is not exer-
4   cised. Otherwise, the expired option may create a cloud on the title. Many times, an option is
5   constructed to include a defeasance clause stating that the recorded option will automatically
6   cease to be a lien on the property upon expiration of the exercise date.

## SUMMARY

A contract is a legally enforceable agreement that can be classified in a number of ways, such as bilateral, unilateral, express, implied, executory, executed, quasi, voidable, and void. Each classification has specific legal effects in a court of law. The licensee is permitted to "prepare" three types of real estate contracts: listing, sales, and option contracts. A sales contract is an agreement for the sale and purchase of real property. The various provisions and standards contained in a sales contract include information on the parties to the agreement, a legal description of the property, the purchase price and method of payment, deadline times and dates, information about financing, and riders to the contract.

## KEY TERMS

abstract

bilateral contract

contract

cross-defaulting clause

executed contract

executory contract

exercised

express contract

FAR Residential Sale
  and Purchase Contact

implied contract

option contract

performance

quasi-contract

sales contract (contract for
  sale and purchase)

statute of frauds

time is of the essence

title insurance

unconscionable contract

unilateral contract

valid contract

voidable contract

void contract

# PRACTICE EXAM

1. Your neighbor promises to paint your house while you are on vacation. Responding to a question about the color desired, you answer "white." At that point, your neighbor and you have:
   a. an implied contract.
   b. no contractual agreement.
   c. an employment contract.
   d. an option contract.

2. A valid contract that creates a one-sided bargain, heavily weighted in favor of one party and against the interests of the other party, is termed a(n):
   a. voidable contract.
   b. quasi-contract.
   c. unilateral contract.
   d. unconscionable contract.

3. The FAR Residential Sale and Purchase Contract is LEAST suitable for transactions involving the sale of a:
   a. single-family home.
   b. condominium dwelling unit.
   c. vacant residential site.
   d. business.

4. Tim Palmer was a buyer who was trying to close on his new home. The required closing date was August 26. The previous day, a hurricane in the Caribbean caused insurance underwriters to suspend writing new policies. If Tim fails to close on the 26th, what effect will this have on Tim's FAR contract?
   a. His contract will be void.
   b. His contract will be voidable by the seller.
   c. He has three days to close after the suspension is lifted.
   d. He has five days to close after the suspension is lifted.

5. When "time is of the essence," failure of any party to perform within established time limits can result in automatic:
   a. cancellation of the contract.
   b. liability for damages.
   c. default by the tardy party.
   d. forfeiture of all contractual rights and deposits.

6. When a licensee verifies contract information, one of the preferred sources regarding the owner/seller and the legal description is:
   a. the MLS databank.
   b. a previous title insurance policy.
   c. the listing agreement.
   d. the latest appraisal report.

7. Which statement is NOT correct regarding a violation of the statute of frauds?
   a. It may not constitute an illegal act, but it invalidates a sales contract.
   b. It carries with it prescribed time frames for enforcement.
   c. It questions the contract's validity.
   d. It normally has to do with whether a contract is in writing.

8.  What is *FALSE* about a valid real estate sales contract?
    a.  It is legally enforceable in a court of law.
    b.  It has five essential elements.
    c.  It requires witnessing.   ✗
    d.  It deals with the transfer of an interest in real property.   ✓

9.  An adult contracting with a minor is an example of noncompliance with which of the following essentials of a real estate contract?
    a.  Legal purpose
    b.  Offer and acceptance
    c.  Contractual capacity
    d.  In writing and signed

10. Rob purchased a home using the FAR Residential Sale and Purchase Contract. Before closing, he was approached by an investor who offered him a substantial profit if he would sell him his contract. Which is correct about the contract's assignability?
    a.  He can freely assign the contract.
    b.  He cannot assign the contract without the seller's written consent.
    c.  He cannot assign the contract because it would violate Florida law.
    d.  He can assign the contract as long as the property is not the seller's homestead.

11. A prospective buyer signs a sale and purchase contract form offering to pay the seller $175,000. When the listing sales associate presents the offer to the seller, the seller counteroffers for the full list price of $190,000. The buyer refuses the counteroffer and begins looking for another property. Later the seller agreed to the original contract. Which is correct?
    a.  No enforceable contract exists. The counteroffer terminated the original offer.
    b.  The contract is enforceable.
    c.  The seller owes the broker a commission.
    d.  The buyer owes the broker a commission.

12. Sharon wrote a special clause into paragraph 21 of the FAR Residential Sale and Purchase Contract. To her horror, she later found that it was in direct contradiction with one of the preprinted clauses in Paragraph 4. The special clause as written:
    a.  has no effect.
    b.  has no effect because she failed to cross out the preprinted clause.
    c.  is valid and binding.
    d.  was improper and is considered unauthorized practice of law.

13. What is the classic test of the sufficiency of a legal description?
    a.  It is the one used on the property tax bill.
    b.  It is the one recorded in the clerk's office.
    c.  It includes the address as shown by the U.S. Postal Service.
    d.  A surveyor can locate the property by reference to the description.

14. Under the Florida Association of REALTORS® Residential Sale and Purchase Contract, the party responsible for a property tax increase because of a change in ownership is the:
    a.  buyer.
    b.  seller.
    c.  both parties equally.
    d.  broker, if the broker did not specifically write the provision into the contract.

15. The minimum description requirement in a contract for a platted subdivision does *NOT* include the:
    a.  lot and block number.
    b.  number of acres in the parcel.
    c.  plat book and page number of recorded plats.
    d.  county in which the property is located.

16. The date of the FAR contract is the date the:
    a.  buyer signs the contract and gives the earnest money deposit.
    b.  seller signs the contract.
    c.  transaction will close.
    d.  last one of the buyer or seller signs the contract and communicates it to the other.

17. If the buyer asks to have occupancy of a house before closing, what is the best suggestion from the sales associate to the seller?
    a.  "Let's put the early occupancy in the contract so that if the sale falls through, the buyer easily can be required to vacate."
    b.  "We should require that the buyer give an additional deposit of up to $1,000."
    c.  "Don't let them move in if you can avoid it."
    d.  "Because I know the buyers, I'm sure it will be OK."

18. An option contract is:
    a.  bilateral and binds the optionor.
    b.  bilateral and binds the optionee.
    c.  unilateral and binds the optionor.
    d.  unilateral and binds the optionee.

19. Calvin Goin, a sales associate, writes up a six-month option agreement for Ricky Field on property located on Capital Circle. Ricky pays $2,000 option money. Calvin writes, "Terms of owner financing will be negotiated when this option is exercised." When Ricky later exercises the option, the seller wants a higher interest rate and a shorter loan term than Ricky will accept. In this case, which is correct?
    a.  Ricky can sue and the court will force the seller to a lower interest rate.
    b.  If Ricky sues, the court probably will decide that the option contract is not enforceable because it is too vague.
    c.  The seller can sue Ricky and force him to close at the higher interest rate.
    d.  The parties must go to binding arbitration.

20. Jimmy Padron purchases an option on property located on Dale Mabry Highway. He requires that the option contract be acknowledged and recorded. The seller asks June Cullars, his agent, about the best way to proceed. How should June answer?
    a.  Option contracts cannot be recorded under Florida law.
    b.  Don't ever sell an option because they never close.
    c.  The option should include a defeasance clause stating that the recorded option will automatically cease to be a lien on the property upon expiration of the exercise date.
    d.  Option contracts are illegal in Florida.

21. An insulation rider is required when the property:
    a.  has residential improvements.
    b.  has new residential improvements.
    c.  was constructed before 1978.
    d.  may be in an area with high levels of radon gas.

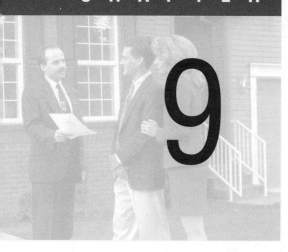

# WRITING AND PRESENTING THE OFFER

<sup>1</sup> **LEARNING OBJECTIVES**

<sup>2</sup> Upon completion of this section, *you should be able to*

<sup>3</sup> **1.** prepare and explain a buyer's cost disclosure;

<sup>4</sup> **2.** write a contract for sale and purchase and be able to explain it in easy-to-understand language;

<sup>5</sup> **3.** list the steps involved in presenting an offer;

<sup>6</sup> **4.** list the three possible seller responses to an offer;

<sup>7</sup> **5.** prepare a counteroffer using information given in the problem; and

<sup>8</sup> **6.** describe the process involved when a seller makes a counteroffer.

<sup>9</sup> **OVERVIEW**

<sup>10</sup> Licensees hope that at the end of the showing process, the buyers will have found a house to buy.
<sup>11</sup> Sometimes the buyers will tell the licensee, "This is the house; we'd like to make an offer." More often, a
<sup>12</sup> buyer will say "This is our favorite so far, but we'd like to think it over." The professional licensee can help the
<sup>13</sup> buyer make the decision, by providing the buyer with information about financing, closing costs, and the
<sup>14</sup> process involved in making an offer. This chapter will help sales associates become familiar with that
<sup>15</sup> process. ■

## ESTIMATING THE BUYER'S COSTS AND MAKING REQUIRED DISCLOSURES

Most buyers are reluctant to make a buying decision until they see cash required to close and the monthly payment amount. To move the buyer closer to buying, the licensee should give the buyer a cost-disclosure statement. The licensee should get the good-faith estimate from the lender. Many sales associates go over this disclosure during the initial meeting so the buyers know what to expect. The following exercise shows how to prepare a buyers' cost disclosure.

---

### PRACTICE EXERCISE 9.1

Using the blank form in Figure 9.1, estimate the buyer's closing costs and monthly payments based on the following information:

| | |
|---|---|
| Purchaser | Kyle and Kari Buyers |
| Property address | 1460 Lime Drive |
| | Orlando, FL |
| Date of contract | March 20, 2005 |
| Mortgage lender | Security First |
| Prepared by | (Your name) |
| Sales price | $200,000 |
| First mortgage: | $160,000 |

**Closing Costs:**

| | |
|---|---|
| Title insurance | $ 1,250 |
| Origination fee | 1% |
| Discount points | ½ |
| Recording fees | $ 60 |
| Credit report | $ 50 |
| Appraisal fee | $ 300 |
| Survey | $ 180 |
| Underwriting fee | $ 125 |
| Express mail fee | $ 20 |
| Attorney's fee | $ 300 |

**Escrow/Prepaid Items:**

| | |
|---|---|
| Taxes—3 months | $ 600 |
| Hazard insurance (1 year) | $ 900 |
| Hazard insurance (2 months) | $ 150 |
| Monthly mortgage insurance premium (2 months) | $ 44 |
| Prepaid interest (1 month) | $ 935 |

Mr. and Mrs. Buyers will give a deposit of $4,000. The principal and interest on the 7 percent, 30-year, fixed-rate loan amount is $1,064.48.

---

## WRITING THE REAL ESTATE CONTRACT

In the case study below, you will complete the cost disclosure forms and the contract. You are a sales associate for Sunny Hills Realty, Inc. In March of this year, a past customer referred Bob and Sandy Smith to you. At your request, they visited Security Atlantic Mortgage Company, which preapproved them for a mortgage loan of up to $200,000.

You learned that they wanted a three- or four-bedroom home with two baths and a two-car garage. They wanted a home in the northeast less than five miles from the regional hospital, where Bob is a pharmacist.

**F I G U R E   9.1  ▪  Real Property Sales Disclosure**

PURCHASER: _____     PROPERTY ADDRESS: _____

Date of Contract: _____     Sales Price $ _____         $ _____

Mortgage Lender: _____     1st Mortgage $ _____ + _____   $ _____

Prepared by: _____     2nd Mortgage $ _____  FHA MIP OR FUNDNG   TOTAL LOAN AMOUNT

                                                                              $ _____

**Estimated Down Payment**          **(1)**   $ _____

**Estimated closing costs:**

1. Title Insurance: ❑ owner's ❑ mortgagee's        _____
2. Title Insurance Endorsements                    _____
3. Origination fee _____%                          _____
4. Discount points estimated _____%               _____
5. Intangible Tax ($.002/$1) on new mortgage       _____
6. Documentary Stamps ($.35/$100) on all notes     _____
7. Recording Fees . . . . . . . . . . . . . . . . . . . .   _____
8. Credit Report . . . . . . . . . . . . . . . . . . . . .   _____
9. Appraisal Fee                                   _____
10. Survey                                         _____
11. Document Preparation Fee                       _____
12. Tax Service Fee                                _____
13. Underwriting Fee                               _____
14. Express Mail Fee(s)                            _____
15. VA Funding Fee at _____%                      _____
16. Assumption Fee on Existing Mortgage            _____
17. Purchase of Escrow Account                     _____
18. Home Inspection Fee                            _____
19. Homeowner's Warranty _____                 _____
20. Attorney's Fee (if any)                        _____
21. _____                 _____
22. _____                 _____

**Total Estimated Closing Costs**          **(2)**   $ _____

**Estimated escrow/prepaid items:**

1. Taxes _____ months                  _____
2. Hazard Insurance, 1 year            _____
3. Hazard Insurance, 2 months          _____
4. First year Mortgage Insurance       _____
5. Mortgage Insurance, 2 months        _____
6. Flood Insurance, 14 months          _____
7. Prepaid Interest                    _____
8. Homeowner's Assn. Dues              _____

**Total Estimated escrow/prepaid items**          **(3)**   $_____

| ESTIMATED MONTHLY PAYMENTS |
| --- |
| ❑ Fixed   ❑ ARM   ____% Interest Rate   ____Years |
| Principal & Interest $_____ |
| Property Taxes_____ |
| Hazard Insurance_____ |
| Mortgage Insurance_____ |
| Other _____ |
| TOTAL$_____ |
| Other Association fees may be due monthly |

**Total Lines 1, 2 and 3**      $_____

**Less: Deposit money**         $_____

Estimated Total due at Closing   $_____

(Must be tendered in cash or certified funds)

---

**DISCUSSION EXERCISE 9.1**

After the disclosure has been completed, do a role-playing session in class, with two students playing Mr. and Mrs. Buyers and one student playing the sales associate. The sales associate should present the completed form to the buyers, who should ask some simple questions in a positive way.

---

1  You described the entire process of buying a home, from showing homes through moving
2  into their new home. You told them it is a sellers' market, and that listings sell almost as soon
3  as they go on the market.

4  You went over the lender's good-faith estimate with them, and discussed the important
5  clauses in the purchase agreement. You gave them copies of the paperwork along with a trans-
6  action broker notice. Because they have enough cash for a 20 percent down payment (80 per-
7  cent loan), you can show homes in the $250,000 range ($200,000 ÷ 0.80).

## 8  Finding the Right Home

9  You set a showing appointment for Saturday and begin previewing homes that might satisfy
10  their requirements. You find five houses that seem like real possibilities; one of them is just
11  about perfect. It is located at 816 Harrison Court, a quiet street in a well-kept neighborhood,
12  just two miles from the hospital. The owners have kept it in wonderful condition. And it has
13  great "curb appeal." It was listed by Blue Sky Realty, Inc., and is priced at $255,000. Perfect!
14  You make appointments with the sellers to show the homes.

15  On Saturday morning you show your favorite home first. They both love everything about
16  it. You give them a copy of the sellers' disclosure statement that was available on the kitchen
17  counter. It has no apparent problems. After entering each house after that, it doesn't take long
18  to walk through, because they love the first home. You suggest a return visit and clear it with
19  the sellers. The sellers tell you they are going out for several hours and the house will be avail-
20  able most of the day. After returning to the home, you stay unobtrusive and let the Smiths dis-
21  cover more features of the home. They want to think it over. You cover the market conditions
22  with them again and explain that if they love it, it is likely that other buyers will, too.

## 23  Writing the Offer

24  You suggest that, even if they end up "sleeping" on the decision, it might be helpful if they
25  had the contract filled out. Bob says to make the paperwork out as if they were paying
26  $245,000. Bob wants to see the backyard again, so you suggest they look around some more
27  while you complete the paperwork.

28  You will ask the buyers to give you a good-faith deposit of $5,000. Based on previous con-
29  versations, the Smiths will want to be in the home in 20 days. Because the sellers are in town,
30  and because the market is so active, you will give them until 10 P.M. tonight to accept or
31  reject the offer.

32  You pull out the MLS data from the house that shows the following information:

33  Sellers' names: Larry and Wilma Palmer
34  Street address: 816 Harrison Court, Sunny Hills, FL
35  Legal description: Lot 18, Block C, Old Hills as recorded in book 126, page 368, Houser
36  County.

37  Personal property included: range, draperies, rods, and window treatments (as shown by
38  the MLS information). The buyers also want to include the refrigerator, washer, and dryer,

1 and the riding lawn mower. You explain that these items are not included in the sale, but they
2 want to try for them anyway.

---

**PRACTICE EXERCISE 9.2**

**Preparing the Cost Disclosure Statement.** Using the Real Property Sales Disclosure in the Forms-To-Go Appendix, estimate the buyer's closing costs and monthly payments based on the following information given on a good-faith estimate given to the buyers by Security Atlantic Mortgage Co.

**Closing Costs:**

| | |
|---|---|
| Title insurance | $1,550 |
| Origination fee | 1% |
| Discount points | ½ |
| Recording fees | 60 |
| Credit report | 50 |
| Appraisal fee | 350 |
| Survey | 250 |
| Underwriting fee | 125 |
| Express mail fee | 20 |
| Attorney's fee | 300 |

**Escrow/Prepaid Items:**

| | |
|---|---|
| Taxes—3 months | 800 |
| Hazard insurance (1 year) | 1,200 |
| Hazard insurance (2 months) | 200 |
| Monthly mortgage insurance premium (2 months) | 52 |
| Prepaid interest (1 month) | ? |

The principal and interest on the 6 percent, 30-year, fixed-rate $200,000 loan amount is $1,199.10.

---

**PRACTICE EXERCISE 9.3**

**Preparing the FAR Residential Sale and Purchase Contract.** (Remove the Residential Sale and Purchase Contract from the Forms-To-Go Appendix and complete the form with the information you have been given so far.)

Just as you are finishing the contract, Sandy and Bob return to the kitchen. You tell them it's a great home, and well priced at $255,000. You ask if there is anything they want to do to the home after they buy it and Bob says he wants to pour a concrete patio. At your request, they write a short note to the sellers about why they want to buy this house, then both sign it.

You go over the cost-disclosure statement, and attach it to the lender's good-faith estimate. Then you go over the contract form carefully. Sandy says it all looks good. You say "You could go home and worry about this tonight, or I could take this to the seller and you might have great news to celebrate tonight. Wouldn't it be better if we went ahead?" Wait for the answer, because in many cases, the buyer will agree.

If the Smiths agree, ask them to

1. approve the cost disclosure first
2. sign a receipt for the sellers' property disclosure statement, and
3. approve the agreement with their signatures

Ask for the good-faith deposit and clip all the paperwork together. To prepare them for a counteroffer, ask that they not be too disappointed if the seller does not accept the offer at $245,000. After dropping them off, you should immediately contact the listing agent, Hillary Jenkins.

## Presenting the Offer

Hillary answers her mobile phone right away. After you tell her that you have an offer that expires at 10 P.M., she asks if you'd like to fax it to her office. Because you want to present the offer with her, you arrange to meet at her office 45 minutes before the appointment. You ask if there are any other offers to be presented, and she says there are not. You request that you be called if that situation changes, and she agrees. In some cases, especially if you are a buyers' agent, the listing sales associate will be reluctant to let you present your offer. Explain that you will not stay during the discussions, but that it may be helpful if you tell them about the buyer, present the offer, and see if they have any questions about the flexibility of the buyers, for example, on the closing date.

Hillary calls back and says she has an appointment with the Palmers at 7 P.M., and will see you at her office at 6:15 P.M.

## Going to the Sellers' House

You make extra copies of the offer, gather all the documents, and arrive at the Blue Sky Realty office at 6:15 P.M. You show Hillary the bank's preapproval letter and give her a copy of the offer. If she has no questions about the offer, you ask if she'd like you to present it to the sellers and she agrees. She also suggests that after presenting the contract, if the sellers have no questions, that you might excuse yourself so they have time to discuss the offer. This is very gracious on her part as she will not ask to you leave; it will be your idea.

You go in separate cars to the house. Hillary waits outside so you can go in together. You smile when you see her carrying a "sold" sign on top of her file folder.

At the door Hillary introduces you to the seller and takes charge, asking if we can all sit at the kitchen table. The sellers agree.

Hillary starts the presentation by complimenting you. You look at her with gratitude and admiration, beginning to understand why she is successful.

She continues: "I'm going to let _____ tell you a little about the prospective buyers and go over the offer with you, if that's OK." The sellers nod in agreement and look in your direction.

"Hi, Mr. and Mrs. Palmer," you say. "I'd like to say how pleased I am to be working with Hillary again. You made a great choice when you listed your home with her. Before I go over the offer, I'd like to tell you a little about the buyers. Their names are Robert and Sandy Smith. Robert is a pharmacist at Sunny Hills Regional Hospital. They have two children, Mary, who's 3, and Brett, who's 1.

"They have owned a condominium since they've been married, so this is their first home. They have been approved for financing by the bank to buy your home. And they love it! They have written you a note about your house and why they want to buy it." Hand them the note. (See Figure 9.2.)

Mrs. Palmer says, "That is the sweetest thing! Larry, I hope this couple buys this house."

Mr. Palmer says, "Yes, they sound like pretty nice people. But let's see what they're willing to pay."

And you present the contract. Save the offered price until last. Ask if they will let you cover the highlights before starting a discussion on any one item, and that you'll give them copies of the agreement in a moment. Then cover the contingencies first before talking about price.

**FIGURE  9.2  ■  Handwritten Note**

---

*Dear Mr. and Mrs. Palmer,*

    *We just want to tell you how much we love your home. We can tell that you love it too, by the way you keep it so beautiful.*

    *We can't think of a home that would be better to raise our two young children in. Their names are Mary and Brett.*

    *We hope you will let us have it.*

    *And we hope you'll be happy in your new home, too.*

*Sandy Smith*
*Bob Smith*

---

"The buyers need to close and move in 20 days. I've spoken with the lender who says they can close it on time.

"They're including your refrigerator, range, washer-dryer, riding mower, and the window treatments.

"They're getting new financing and have been preapproved for their loan."

Now tell them the offer is $245,000. Reassure the sellers that the buyers' offer is not meant to insult them, but they can qualify to buy a $250,000 home and are hoping to keep $5,000 to build a concrete patio. Give statistics about sales: price ratios in the MLS ("Listings sell at 96 percent of list price," etc.), so this offer is right on target.

Tell the sellers that if they have no questions for you about the buyers or the offer, you'd like to excuse yourself to give them an opportunity to discuss the offer with Hillary. You can tell them you have some calls to make anyway, and will do it from your car, so you'll be close by if any other questions arise.

## Sellers' Responses to an Offer

Sellers who receive an offer on their home have several possible responses:

■ Acceptance
■ Rejection
■ Counteroffer

**Acceptance.**  Obviously, the selling sales associate hopes the response will be an acceptance. The offer is signed and becomes a contract between the buyer and the seller.

**Rejection.**  If the price offered is very low, and is obviously a "fishing expedition," the seller may be advised to reject the offer outright. A better approach might be to reject the offer with an invitation to come back with a more serious offer. Recently many coastal areas in Florida have experienced strong sellers' markets with many buyers bidding for the same properties. Brokers report that more sellers have been rejecting offers unless they are very close to the asking price.

**Counteroffer.**  If the offer is not acceptable but is close enough to be considered serious, a **counteroffer** should be used. A counteroffer keeps the parties "at the table," making continued negotiations easier.

During the discussions about the offer, it is probably best to keep notes rather than marking on the contract form. When the terms of the counteroffer are fully understood, that's when the listing agent should begin writing and making the formal changes. While some bro-

**FIGURE  9.3  ■   Counteroffer Stamp for Initials**

Initial Here

1   kerage firms have a policy of using a counteroffer form rather than changing anything on the
2   form, most counteroffers are made directly on the contract form. Each change should be care-
3   fully made, and a symbol for initials should be drawn or stamped adjacent to the change.

4       Some sales associates use a quarter to draw a circle, then put a horizontal and a vertical
5   line in the circle to make room for sellers' and buyers' initials. Some title insurance companies
6   have small stamps that look more professional, or you can have your own stamp made. See
7   Figure 9.3 for a sample that can be made into a rubber stamp.

8       In 15 minutes, Hillary comes to the door and motions you inside. Back at the table, Hill-
9   ary says, "Mr. and Mrs. Palmer want the Smiths to have this home, but want to make several
10  changes. First, they feel the house is worth the asking price of $255,000, but they will split the
11  difference with the buyers at a price of $250,000. They will include the range and window
12  treatments, but want to take the other items of personal property. Also, because they cannot
13  get into their new home, the closing date will have to be 30 days from now. Do you think you
14  can help me change the forms so we can get several copies of the counteroffer?" You agree to
15  help her make the changes.

> **PRACTICE EXERCISE   9.4**
>
> **Preparing the Counteroffer.**  Make the appropriate changes to the offer on the FAR Residen-
> tial Sale and Purchase Contract and draw the circles for the sellers' initials.

16      After all changes have been made to the counteroffer, the sellers should initial each change
17  and sign at the signature lines in the offer. Since the buyers have already signed the offer, all it
18  will take to make the offer into a contract will be the buyers' initials on the changes.

19      When the sellers have initialed and signed the counteroffer, you say, "Thank you all so
20  much for your courtesy. I'll do everything I can to sell your home. Hillary, I'll call you as soon
21  as I've spoken with the buyers."

22      When you arrive at the Smiths' house, tell them you have great news. "The sellers came
23  off the price by $5,000! Let's go over their counteroffer."

24      They agree to all terms of the counteroffer. You change the cost disclosure statement to
25  reflect the new price, and have them initial all changes on your copies. Call Hillary and tell her
26  you'll take the contract to her office or her house, and she should get it to the seller. She agrees.

27      You have sold the house and made several people very happy.

28  **Additional Points on Writing and Presenting Offers**

29      ■   If the buyers' offer will be much lower than the asking price, strongly recommend that
30          the buyers not add many contingencies to the offer. Boil all the requirements into the
31          offering price.

- If the market is very strong and there might be multiple offers for the property, don't add too many contingencies. Sometimes even if the offering price is good, a buyer may accept another offer that is simpler and more certain to close.
- If the market is very strong and you are aware that there will be competing offers for the property, recommend that the buyers not only remove most contingencies, but also consider making an offer that is higher than the asking price.
- Make the acceptance date fairly short so the seller makes a decision quickly, rather than waiting to "shop" the offer.
- Go with your contract. Present it with the listing agent. You may be busy, but you'll have many more accepted contracts if you help in the presentation. You are the only one who can answer questions about the buyers, and give the buyers a "face" in the minds of the sellers. Sure, it takes more of your time. But this is top priority time, and your customer's lives and lots of your money is riding on your performance.
- If you are the listing associate and another associate has the offer, you want the cooperating associate to be with you when you present. You're a team. It also stops second-guessing about the quality of your presentation if the other associate's offer is not accepted. If the other associate is a buyers' agent, you should tell your sellers not to give any reaction during the presentation of the offer, as it may affect their negotiating position.
- If you are the listing sales associate, prepare your sellers for a low offer before the cooperating sales associate arrives to present the offer. If a seller has raised expectations, a low offer may insult the sellers and make it very difficult to put a transaction together.
- If the parties are far apart on the offered price, try to keep the buyers and sellers from taking it personally. It is your job to be sure personalities are not a factor in the negotiations.
- Be courteous to the cooperating sales associate. Nothing can derail the presentation of an offer more than distrust and dissension between the licensees.
- Don't give the offer out to all parties until you have summarized the important parts. It is hard to maintain control if the parties are all looking at different parts of the contract, interrupting by asking questions.
- Make enough documents for everyone who will be at the presentation so they don't have to read over your shoulder.
- Give the seller a copy, never the original offer, until it is determined exactly what the counteroffer will be. Sellers sometimes mark up a contract before thinking it through.
- Cover all points of the agreement, making price last. Have all the buyers' requirements depend on "getting the price right."
- Work the contract until it's either accepted or dead. Don't stop working it because it's nearly midnight. Sellers want to sell and buyers want to buy, and respect professionals who work hard. Working late brings an urgency that gets lots of offers accepted.
- If you are the listing associate and the cooperating associate brings in a very low offer, have the cooperating associate present the offer to your sellers.
- If the offer is low and the sellers are angry, let them vent their frustration before starting to work on a counteroffer.
- If you are the listing associate and there are multiple offers from both your company and other companies, you should get your broker involved. Especially if your company has an offer, ask the other associates not to fax their offers. You don't want to know, and thus cannot be suspected of "shopping" the offer. The broker should meet with all the associates before the presentation to establish the ground rules. The broker should arrange for each selling associate to present his or her offer in the order received. Everything should be scrupulously fair and transparent.

## SUMMARY

Because buyers are reluctant to commit to buy without understanding the financial commitment they must make, a sales associate should understand how to prepare a cost disclosure statement. To reduce liability, the statement should be based on a lender's good-faith estimate of settlement costs.

A licensee should practice preparing offers on different types of properties with a variety of financing programs. Once the practice offer is written, you should role-play the explanation of the offer. Practice will give you the skills to help you get more transactions to the closing table.

A seller has three possible responses to a counteroffer: acceptance, rejection, or counteroffer. To counteroffer, the seller makes the appropriate changes, initials each change, and then signs the offer. To accept the counteroffer, a buyer need only initial the changes.

## KEY TERM

counteroffer

# PRACTICE EXAM

1. John is preparing a buyer's cost disclosure statement. Because he wants to protect himself from later problems, he should:
   a. use a disclosure form for a similar house from the office closed-sales files.
   b. talk to several licensees in the firm to get their ideas on current costs.
   c. ask his broker for the information on closing costs for a new loan.
   d. get the information from the lender's good-faith deposit.

2. A buyer has been prequalified for a $160,000 mortgage. If the buyer has enough cash for a 20 percent down payment, he or she can get a house priced at:
   a. $320,000.
   b. $240,000.
   c. $220,000.
   d. $200,000.

3. According to the text, the sales associate who is presenting the offer should normally give copies of the offer:
   a. before starting to present the information.
   b. only after summarizing the important parts of the offer.
   c. just before asking for a signature.
   d. to the listing sales associate by fax as soon as the associate is notified of the offer.

4. When presenting an offer, the sales associate should *NOT*:
   a. give the seller the offer with the original signatures.
   b. make copies for all the parties who are present.
   c. work the offer until it's accepted or dead.
   d. present all terms of the offer before discussing the price.

5. When the seller wants to make a counteroffer:
   a. it should be made verbally.
   b. the seller should initial the changes but should not sign the offer.
   c. the seller should initial the changes and sign the offer.
   d. the sales associate should strongly object and try to get the original offer accepted.

6. If you are the listing sales associate and there are multiple offers to be presented, both from your company and other companies, you should:
   a. present your company's offers first.
   b. tell the sales associates in your company the details of the other offers.
   c. get your broker involved.
   d. get the associates from the other companies to fax their offers.

7. When presenting an offer to the sellers, it is helpful to:
   a. tell them first what price is being offered.
   b. make only one copy of the offer in order to keep better control of the presentation.
   c. get them to like the buyers.
   d. tell them nothing about the buyers.

8. If you have an offer to present to a seller, and you are not the listing sales associate, you should:
   a. excuse yourself after making the presentation, making sure the sellers have no further questions for you.
   b. require that the listing broker be present in case there is a problem during the presentation.
   c. not attend or present your offer, but instead let the listing agent do so.
   d. first give the good-faith deposit to the listing agent for deposit, if the offer is accepted.

9. When buyers just want to "sleep on the decision," and you want them to make an offer on a home they love, the best way to help them make the decision is to:
   a. tell them there are three other buyers interested, whether or not that's true.
   b. prepare the paperwork, then explain the sales agreement and the offer process.
   c. tell them you'll be out of town for the rest of the week.
   d. offer to pay their closing costs.

10. Principal and interest on a new loan is $1,564.90. Annual taxes are estimated to be $3,575, and insurance is estimated to be $1,289 annually. What is their monthly payment?
    a. $6,428.90
    b. $5,139.90
    c. $1,970.23
    d. $1,862.82

## APPLY WHAT YOU'VE LEARNED!

The authors suggest the following actions to reinforce the material in *Section III—Selling Real Property:*

- ❏ Preview at least five homes in your favorite price range. Try to see five each day for the next five days. Use a tape recorder to describe each home thoroughly, and try to match it with a prospective buyer or type of buyer.

- ❏ From your preview visits, list the best homes on the market. Pick your favorite home from that list.

- ❏ Describe every characteristic of *your* favorite home from your preview trips as if you were writing a book on the house. Try to remember colors, room sizes and arrangements, and garage size. Describe each room in as much detail as possible. If you can't do it, go back to the house again and make careful notes. Try to increase your observation powers every time you preview homes.

- ❏ When you visit a vacant home, thoroughly describe each room aloud as if your buyer were sight-impaired.

- ❏ Keep a tape recorder near your phone. The next time you answer a call from a prospective buyer, turn on the recorder. (You must observe the law, however; record only *your* side of the conversation.) When you have completed the call, listen to the tape. Make written notes about what you would change about your side of the conversation.

- ❏ Ride through a neighborhood you have not yet explored, describing into your tape recorder the details you see. Then do the same thing in the surrounding area to find shopping areas, libraries, car washes, schools, and churches.

- ❏ Write the features you think some close friends would like in a home. From memory, list the properties you would show them and give reasons for your decisions. Make a buyer's cost statement based on a 90 percent conventional loan.

- ❏ Call your friends and tell them about the previous exercise. Ask whether they will let you show them the homes you chose for them. How well did you judge their tastes?

# FINANCING AND CLOSING REAL ESTATE TRANSACTIONS

CHAPTER 10.    EXPLORING MORTGAGE ALTERNATIVES

CHAPTER 11.    ACQUIRING FINANCING FOR THE PROPERTY

CHAPTER 12.    CLOSING REAL ESTATE TRANSACTIONS

---

Licensees often are asked for advice about the most appropriate type of loan for a buyer. This requires an understanding of the advantages and disadvantages of each mortgage type and the situations that make certain mortgages more suitable.

Sales associates must understand the loan application and underwriting process completely to effectively assist a buyer when dealing with lenders. This section will give licensees a better idea of the steps required to take a loan from application to closing.

The closing is often the most troublesome part of a real estate sale. This section is intended to give licensees information on how to reduce stress levels at closings and to make the licensees more efficient and professional. Many problems result from communication failures between cooperating brokers and sales associates. This section explores methods of tracking the necessary components of the closing to ensure that everything is completed on time.

Sales associates are expected to oversee closings and to review the closing documents, particularly the closing statement. A sales associate must understand each part of the statement. This section provides hands-on practice for the sales associate in preparing closing statements. ■

# 10

# EXPLORING MORTGAGE ALTERNATIVES

## LEARNING OBJECTIVES

Upon completion of this chapter, *you should be able to*

1. describe the components of the lender's required annual percentage rate (APR) disclosures;

2. calculate the effective interest rate on 30-year, fixed-rate loans and on loans for shorter periods;

3. calculate the PITI payment for a borrower;

4. compare the interest savings on a 15-year, fixed-rate mortgage versus a 30-year, fixed-rate mortgage;

5. compare the interest savings on a biweekly mortgage versus a 30-year, fixed-rate mortgage;

6. discuss the pros and cons of an adjustable-rate mortgage (ARM);

7. explain the five components of an ARM;

8. explain the advantages of FHA interest rate caps over conventional ARM caps; and

9. calculate the interest rate adjustments.

## OVERVIEW

The mortgage market has seen many significant changes in recent years. Twenty years ago, commercial banks and savings associations originated more than 80 percent of home mortgages. That share has dropped sharply, and today mortgage companies are the dominant factor in the market, originating more than 50 percent of all home loans. Driven by market forces, lenders offer a wide variety of mortgage products tailored to the needs of consumers. Experts expect the changes to accelerate in the future.

A general knowledge of these changes can enhance the opportunities available to the real estate professional. Developing strong relationships with lenders who preapprove loans for prospective buyers saves licensees time and can significantly increase their income. ■

# STEPS BEFORE LOAN APPLICATION

Before buyers begin calling or visiting lenders, they should have a good understanding of their own financial capabilities and housing objectives. Licensees should explain both issues to their customers to help them understand the importance of prequalifying. This is important because if a loan application is denied, the applicant may lose the opportunity to buy the desired home. In addition, some expense is involved in applying for a loan. Fees may range from $150 to $500, depending on the property and circumstances.

## Mortgage Shopping

In shopping for a mortgage, licensees should advise buyers to look for competitive rates and a lender with a reputation for integrity and good service.

Surveys show that mortgage interest rates and closing costs vary in metropolitan markets for the same mortgage product. Comparing prices obviously is important, but it is not an easy task. Lenders charge a variety of fees a borrower may be asked to pay when she submits a loan application. Discount points, usually one of the largest fees lenders charge, also vary from lender to lender in the same market area. The points change the effective interest rate, and just two points more on a loan can mean significant additional expense to the borrower.

Licensees must learn which lenders can be trusted to act with speed and service to borrowers. Licensees should use and recommend only those that provide good service.

## Seller-Paid Closing Costs

A buyer must have the necessary income and debt ratios to afford a mortgage payment. Coming up with enough cash to close is another big hurdle. The closing costs and prepayments on a typical mortgage loan for $120,000 can reach $5,000 in addition to the down payment. Many qualified buyers are forced to rent in order to accumulate the savings necessary to close. Licensees who know lender standards on seller-paid closing costs are able to sell to these buyers much sooner. The seller can pay part of the closing costs for conventional, FHA, and VA mortgage loans. Figure 10.1 shows the current allowed percentages.

A seller who could pay only 3 percent of the buyer's closing costs on a low down payment conventional loan for $120,000 would contribute $3,600. If a two-income family is saving $300 per month, the home purchase could be made 12 months sooner.

**FIGURE  10.1  ■  Maximum Seller-Paid Closing Costs That Can Be Applied to Buyer's Closing Costs, Prepaid Items, and Reserves, Expressed as a Percentage of the Purchase Price**

| Type of Loan | Percent |
|---|---|
| Conventional | |
| Less than 10% down payment | 3 |
| 19% or greater down payment | 6 |
| FHA | 6 |
| VA | 6 |

Do you think most licensees guide potential borrowers to lenders with which they have built relationships or to lenders that have the best mortgage rates on a given day?

## Annual Percentage Rate (APR)

The Truth-in-Lending Act requires that mortgage lenders disclose their annual percentage rates to potential borrowers. The **annual percentage rate (APR)** is a standard expression of credit costs designed to give potential borrowers an easy method of comparing lenders' total finance charges. These financing costs include points and any other prepaid interest or fees charged to obtain the loan in addition to the contract interest cost. The APR must be, by law, the relationship of the total financing charge to the total amount financed, and it must be computed to the nearest one-eighth of 1 percent. Perhaps the best and most accurate definition of the APR is that it is the effective interest rate for a mortgage loan repaid over its full term.

The law allows a lender three days after loan application to inform the applicant of the APR. When a lender gives the borrower a good-faith estimate of the annual percentage rate, the consumer should be aware that this is not a legally binding document; it is simply an estimate. Licensees should avoid lenders who frequently estimate a lower APR than the rate available at closing.

Another feature of this act is that it assumes that borrowers will keep their loans for the full number of years for which the loans are written. Records of mortgage lending, however, show that most borrowers either sell or refinance their homes in less than 12 years. The actual (effective) interest rate paid depends on the number of years a loan is kept.

**EXAMPLE:** If the borrower expects to keep the loan for longer than 12 years, divide the points by 8 and add the result to the note interest rate. For example, if a lender has offered a first mortgage for 30 years at 7.5 percent and 3 points, the effective interest rate would be 7.875 percent, computed as follows:

$$\text{Note rate} + (\text{points} \div 8) = \text{Effective interest rate}$$
$$7.5\% + (.03 \div 8) = 7.5\% + 0.375\% = 7.875\%$$

When the lender gives a prospective borrower a rate quote, the borrower is often undecided about whether to pay discount points. Discount points can be considered prepaid interest that will reduce the interest rate on the note. In effect, a borrower has a "menu" of interest rates based on the amount paid as discount points. Figure 10.2 shows a sample market quote for a 30-year fixed-rate loan. Fluctuations in the market cause differences from day to day in the differential of discount points and yield.

**FIGURE  10.2  ■  $100,000 30-Year Fixed-Rate Mortgage Comparison of Rates and Discount Points**

|  | A. Interest Rate | B. Discount Points | C. Principal and Interest Payment | D. Payment Difference from 7% Rate | E. Amount Paid in Discount Points | F. Months at Lower Rate for Points Payback (E ÷ D) |
|---|---|---|---|---|---|---|
| 1. | 7.000 | 0 | $665.30 | — | $ 0 | 0 |
| 2. | 6.875 | 0.5 | 656.93 | $ 8.37 | 500 | 59.7 |
| 3. | 6.750 | 1.2 | 648.60 | 16.70 | 1,200 | 71.9 |
| 4. | 6.625 | 1.7 | 640.31 | 24.99 | 1,700 | 68.0 |
| 5. | 6.500 | 2.3 | 632.07 | 33.23 | 2,300 | 69.2 |

1  From the example, it's obvious that a person who intends to occupy the property for three
2  years should avoid paying points because it will take almost six years to break even. In some
3  cases, a borrower should ask the lender to raise the interest rate not only to avoid discount
4  points but also to avoid paying an origination fee.

5  If a person expects to remain in the property for the full 30-year period and will not be
6  refinancing or making an early loan payoff, the savings could be worth paying points. At line
7  5, for instance, the borrower breaks even at 69 months. The difference in payments of $33.23
8  for the remaining 291 months would total $9,670, well worth paying the points.

9  Of course, the better way to analyze points is by considering the time value of money.
10  Using the 6.5 percent rate on line 5, the borrower pays $2,300 in *today's* dollars (that could be
11  invested to return some interest) to get a savings sometime in the *future*. A financial calcula-
12  tor approach shows the payback period is longer (87 months versus 69.2 months).

---

**Financial Calculator Keystrokes To Find Payback Period for $2,300 in Points with a 6.5 percent Yield**

| %I | PMT | PV | FV | Solve for N |
|---|---|---|---|---|
| .54167 | 33.23 | 2,300 | 0 | 87 months |

Where:     % = *monthly* market interest rate: 6.5% ÷ 12 months = .54167
                PMT = savings per monthly payment = −$33.23
                PV = Dollars paid in points = $2,300
                FV = input zero for this problem = 0

Solve for:     N = Number of months to pay back points

**Solution is 87 months**

---

**DISCUSSION EXERCISE 10.2**

John has been transferred to Miami and expects to be in the location for about three years
before being transferred again. He needs to borrow $200,000 for his new home. With no points,
he can get a 7.5 percent fixed-rate mortgage with principal and interest payments of $1,398.43.
The lender offers him a 7.125 percent mortgage (payments of $1,347.44) with two points.
     Should John take the lower interest rate mortgage?
     Using simple math, how many months will it take John to break even by paying the
points if he takes the lower interest rate?

---

13  ## PITI Payment

14  Customers often ask licensees to calculate the monthly mortgage payment for a possible pur-
15  chase or sale. Most lenders require an amount each month that includes principal and interest
16  plus escrow items—property taxes, homeowner's insurance, and possibly mortgage insurance
17  or homeowners'/condominium association dues. This entire package of payments commonly
18  is referred to as the **PITI payment.**

19  Principal and interest payments on the mortgage are the largest part of the monthly PITI
20  payment. Using the mortgage payment factor table shown in Table 10.1, multiply the loan
21  amount by the appropriate factor to get the principal and interest portion of the payment.

22  For example, the payment factor for a 30-year mortgage at 8.5 percent is .0076891. To cal-
23  culate the monthly principal and interest for a 30-year loan of $98,000 at 8.5 percent, use the
24  following equation:

25  $$\$98,000 \times .0076891 = \$753.53$$

**T A B L E   10.1  ■   Mortgage Payment Factor Table**

Multiply the mortgage principal times the factor to solve for the mortgage payment.

| Interest Rate | Term of Loan | | | | |
|---|---|---|---|---|---|
| | 10 years | 15 years | 20 years | 25 years | 30 years |
| 5.00% | 0.0106066 | 0.0079079 | 0.0065996 | 0.0058459 | 0.0053682 |
| 5.25% | 0.0107292 | 0.0080388 | 0.0067384 | 0.0059925 | 0.0055220 |
| 5.50% | 0.0108526 | 0.0081708 | 0.0068789 | 0.0061409 | 0.0056779 |
| 5.75% | 0.0109769 | 0.0083041 | 0.0070208 | 0.0062911 | 0.0058357 |
| 6.00% | 0.0111021 | 0.0084386 | 0.0071643 | 0.0064430 | 0.0059955 |
| 6.25% | 0.0112280 | 0.0085742 | 0.0073093 | 0.0065967 | 0.0061572 |
| 6.50% | 0.0113548 | 0.0087111 | 0.0074557 | 0.0067521 | 0.0063207 |
| 6.75% | 0.0114824 | 0.0088491 | 0.0076036 | 0.0069091 | 0.0064860 |
| 7.00% | 0.0116108 | 0.0089883 | 0.0077530 | 0.0070678 | 0.0066530 |
| 7.25% | 0.0117401 | 0.0091286 | 0.0079038 | 0.0072281 | 0.0068218 |
| 7.50% | 0.0118702 | 0.0092701 | 0.0080559 | 0.0073899 | 0.0069921 |
| 7.75% | 0.0120011 | 0.0094128 | 0.0082095 | 0.0075533 | 0.0071641 |
| 8.00% | 0.0121328 | 0.0095565 | 0.0083644 | 0.0077182 | 0.0073376 |
| 8.25% | 0.0122653 | 0.0097014 | 0.0085207 | 0.0078845 | 0.0075127 |
| 8.50% | 0.0123986 | 0.0098474 | 0.0086782 | 0.0080523 | 0.0076891 |
| 8.75% | 0.0125327 | 0.0099945 | 0.0088371 | 0.0082214 | 0.0078670 |
| 9.00% | 0.0126676 | 0.0101427 | 0.0089973 | 0.0083920 | 0.0080462 |
| 9.25% | 0.0128033 | 0.0102919 | 0.0091587 | 0.0085638 | 0.0082268 |
| 9.50% | 0.0129398 | 0.0104422 | 0.0093213 | 0.0087370 | 0.0084085 |
| 9.75% | 0.0130770 | 0.0105936 | 0.0094852 | 0.0089114 | 0.0085915 |
| 10.00% | 0.0132151 | 0.0107461 | 0.0096502 | 0.0090870 | 0.0087757 |
| 10.25% | 0.0133539 | 0.0108995 | 0.0098164 | 0.0092638 | 0.0089610 |
| 10.50% | 0.0134935 | 0.0110540 | 0.0099838 | 0.0094418 | 0.0091474 |
| 10.75% | 0.0136339 | 0.0112095 | 0.0101523 | 0.0096209 | 0.0093348 |
| 11.00% | 0.0137750 | 0.0113660 | 0.0103219 | 0.0098011 | 0.0095232 |
| 11.25% | 0.0139169 | 0.0115234 | 0.0104926 | 0.0099824 | 0.0097126 |
| 11.50% | 0.0140595 | 0.0116819 | 0.0106643 | 0.0101647 | 0.0099029 |
| 11.75% | 0.0142029 | 0.0118413 | 0.0108371 | 0.0103480 | 0.0100941 |

1   While the factor table has been included in this text so that all students can calculate the
2   monthly payment, most real estate licensees use a financial calculator to obtain the monthly
3   mortgage payment of principal and interest.

4   In the example shown above, the licensee with a financial calculator would solve the
5   problem as shown below:

| N | %I | PV | FV | Solve for: PMT |
|---|---|---|---|---|
| 360 | .70833 | 98,000 | 0 | $753.53 |

Where:
N = number of monthly periods in loan term
%I = interest rate (8.5% ÷ 12 months = .70833)
PV = loan amount
FV = input zero when solving for present value

Solve for: **PMT = monthly mortgage payment**

Note: %I is calculated by dividing 8.5% by 12 months.

A PITI worksheet that licensees can use in helping their clients and customers calculate at the PITI amount for a potential loan is shown in Figure 10.3.

# FIXED-RATE MORTGAGES

Any mortgage written to preclude change in the interest rate throughout the entire duration of the loan is a **fixed-rate mortgage.** The term includes the traditional 30-year mortgage, the 15-year mortgage, and the biweekly mortgage. The use of a due-on-sale clause in a fixed-rate mortgage reserves the lender's right to make an interest rate change if a transfer of ownership takes place. Practically all conventional mortgages issued since the early 1980s contain such a clause.

## Traditional 30-Year Mortgage

The fixed-rate, fully amortizing mortgage loan has been the standard of the real estate finance industry for the past 50 years. A 30-year term provides a reasonably low payment for the amount borrowed, while the interest rate, payment amount, and repayment schedule are set permanently at the beginning of the loan period. Fixed-rate loans often are sold in the secondary market because they appeal to pension funds and other investors searching for a relatively safe investment with a known interest rate and a long duration.

**Advantages of a 30-Year Mortgage.** Monthly payments on the loan are spread over 30 years, offering the borrower protection against future increases in interest rates and inflation rates

**F I G U R E  10.3  ■  PITI Worksheet**

Mortgage amount      $ _____
Interest rate        _____ %
Term of loan         _____ years
Mortgage payment factor _____

Principal and interest payment:                    $ _____
($ _____ × _____)
    (mtg. amt.)        (factor)                     _____
Property taxes: $ _____ ÷ 12
Hazard insurance: $ _____ ÷ 12              _____
Mortgage insurance:
$ _____ × _____ ÷ 12                 _____
(mtg. amt.)    (premium rate)

TOTAL MONTHLY MORTGAGE PAYMENT (PITI)               $ _____

Source: Adapted by permission from Thomas C. Steinmetz, *The Mortgage Kit,* 4th ed. (Chicago: Dearborn Financial Publishing, Inc.®, 1998), 163.

while providing for the orderly repayment of the amount borrowed. Household budgets are easier to manage when the borrower does not have to plan for changing payment amounts or interest rates.

**Disadvantages of a 30-Year Mortgage.**  If overall interest rates drop, as they did in 2000–2001, the rate on a fixed-rate mortgage will not go down with them. To take advantage of lower interest rates, the original loan must be repaid with the proceeds of a new loan taken out at the lower rate. This procedure, called **refinancing,** usually requires that the borrower pay substantial closing costs on the new loan.

## 15-Year Mortgage

The 15-year fixed-rate mortgage has become popular with both lenders and borrowers in recent years. It is just like a traditional 30-year loan, except that its monthly payment is higher, its interest rate typically is slightly lower, and it is paid off in 15 years. The 15-year mortgage saves the borrower thousands of dollars in interest payments.

The popular press sometimes compares the two mortgage plans, showing dramatic savings from the 15-year plan. The gross savings, however, usually are overstated. The higher payments on the 15-year plan have an opportunity cost. If the difference were invested, the return on the investment would reduce the net cost of the 30-year mortgage. The tax savings from mortgage interest deductions also would reduce the savings.

For many borrowers, the 15-year mortgage may be the best way to finance a home because in addition to the overall savings in total cost, it forces a monthly saving in the form of extra equity and allows a person who needs it a sense of confidence that her home will be paid off in 15 years. This is true for those planning in advance for retirement. Also, many in the baby boomer generation are in their 40s, with a growing number eager to end their mortgage payments and own their homes free and clear.

Licensees should point out, however, that the 15-year mortgage robs the borrower of some flexibility. A 15-year mortgage cannot be extended to 30 years, but a 30-year mortgage can be paid off in 15 years if the borrower accelerates monthly payments to create a 15-year loan or remits a lump-sum payment on principal each year. The borrower retains the right to decide when, or if, he will make extra payments. Borrowers must evaluate the benefits of the 15-year mortgage based on their personal situations.

**Advantages of a 15-Year Mortgage.**  Because lenders get their money back sooner than they do with traditional 30-year mortgages, they charge slightly lower rates for 15-year loans. Also, the loans are paid off faster, less money is borrowed for less time, and less total interest is paid over the lives of the loans—more than 50 percent less. As with a 30-year, fixed-rate loan, the interest rate on a 15-year mortgage does not change, and the monthly principal and interest payment does not go up. Finally, the higher monthly payment results in forced savings in the form of faster equity buildup.

**Disadvantages of a 15-Year Mortgage.**  The monthly payment on a 15-year loan is higher, and the borrower forgoes investment opportunities voluntarily for the extra dollars paid on the loan each month. Some income tax advantages related to home mortgages and investment opportunities are lost. Flexibility of mortgage payment is sacrificed, and any future increase in income tax rates could increase the 15-year mortgage's net costs.

## Biweekly Mortgage

The development of computer programs to service biweekly mortgages properly, the creation of a secondary market (Fannie Mae), increased familiarity with the product, and growing consumer demand all are combining to bring about a comeback for the biweekly mortgage. The **biweekly mortgage** alternative is a fixed-rate loan, amortized over a 30-year period, with payments made every two weeks instead of every month. Borrowers pay half the normal monthly payment every two weeks, which means a total of 26 payments each year, or the equivalent of 13 monthly payments. The extra month's payment each year reduces the principal faster and results in considerable savings in interest, as well as a reduction in the duration of the loan to between 19 and 21 years.

Normally, interest rates for biweekly mortgages are comparable to the rates charged for traditional 30-year mortgages. Most biweekly loans are scheduled to mature in 30 years even though the actual number of years to maturity depends on the interest rate. The higher the interest rate, the larger the monthly payment, and the more that is applied to reducing mortgage principal. A biweekly mortgage with a 7 percent interest rate, for example, would be paid off in approximately 23 years, 9 months.

*Consumer Reports Magazine* analyzed several mortgage options and concluded that a $100,000 biweekly mortgage at 8 percent interest would save a borrower approximately $34,000 in interest, when compared with a traditional 30-year, fixed-rate mortgage at the same interest rate.

Table 10.2 compares the results of making scheduled payments on a traditional 30-year mortgage, of adding different amounts of additional principal payments each month, and of making scheduled payments on a biweekly mortgage amortized over 30 years.

**Advantages of a Biweekly Mortgage.** A biweekly mortgage combines the benefits of the 30-year loan and the 15-year loan without the increased payments of the 15-year loan. It offers borrowers the affordability of the 30-year loan because the two biweekly payments come within a few pennies of the one monthly payment on a 30-year loan.

Also, Fannie Mae requires that payments be deducted automatically from a borrower's checking or savings account every two weeks. Because more than half of the nation's workforce is paid on a biweekly basis, it is compatible with a large number of paychecks. Some lenders include a conversion clause that permits a borrower to change a biweekly mortgage to a traditional 30-year, fixed-rate, amortized mortgage at little or no cost with only 30 days' advance notice.

**Disadvantages of a Biweekly Mortgage.** The biweekly mortgage has the same disadvantages as other fixed-rate mortgages. In addition, the biweekly loan threatens those borrowers who do not maintain stable checking or savings account balances. The biweekly mortgage also locks borrowers into payment plans that they could set up themselves, at their own discretion, with a traditional 30-year loan. Some lenders also charge a set-up fee.

**T A B L E   10.2  ■   Comparison of Interest Costs for Various Mortgage Plans for a $100,000 Loan at 8% Interest**

| Payment Pattern | Regular Payment Amount | Total Paid Each Year | Time Until Paid Off | Total Interest Paid |
|---|---|---|---|---|
| 30-Year Mortgage | $733.76 | $ 8,805 | 30 years | $164,155 |
| Added $25/Month | 758.76 | 9,105 | 26 yrs. + 6 mos. | 141,286 |
| Added $100/Month | 833.76 | 10,005 | 20 yrs. + 2 mos. | 101,770 |
| Biweekly Mortgage | 366.88 | 9,539 | 22 yrs. + 10 mos. | 117,804 |
| 15-Year Mortgage | $955.65 | $11,468 | 15 yrs. | $ 72,017 |

> ### DISCUSSION EXERCISE 10.3
>
> If the biweekly mortgage combines the good features of both the traditional 30-year, fixed-rate mortgage and the 15-year, fixed-rate mortgage, why is it so seldom used, comparatively speaking, to finance residential purchases?

# ADJUSTABLE-RATE MORTGAGES

The **adjustable-rate mortgage (ARM)** has become a widely accepted alternative to the traditional 30-year, fixed-rate, level-payment mortgage. The popularity of ARMs noticeably increases when interest rates rise, and they lose favor when interest rates fall. An adjustable-rate mortgage is, as the term implies, a financing instrument that allows the lender to increase or decrease the interest rate based on the rise or fall of a specified index.

## Components of Adjustable-Rate Mortgages

The primary elements in determining the acceptability of an ARM from the borrower's viewpoint are the index, the lender's margin, the calculated interest rate, the initial interest rate, and the interest rate caps.

Lending institutions are permitted legally to link the interest rate of a conventional ARM to any recognized **index** (indicator of cost or value) that is not controlled by the lender and is verifiable by the borrower. The **margin,** also called the *spread,* is a percentage added to the index. The margin usually remains constant over the life of the loan, while the selected index may move up or down with fluctuations in the nation's economy. The calculated (or actual) interest rate is calculated by adding the selected index to the lender's margin (index plus margin equals calculated interest rate). This calculated interest rate may be discounted during the initial payment period, but it is the rate to which all future adjustments and caps apply.

To be competitive, lenders sometimes reduce the first year's earnings by discounting the calculated interest rate, thus creating a lower initial interest rate. This helps to qualify potential buyers at artificially low interest rates, which may or may not be a service to the borrowers, and establishes the amount of the monthly loan payment during the first time period of the loan. Be aware that many lenders now use the second year's interest rate rather than the discounted rate as the qualifier. Both Fannie Mae and Freddie Mac require borrowers with less than a 20 percent down payment on one-year, adjustable-rate loans to be qualified at the initial interest rate plus 2 percent.

The main appeal of ARM loans is the lower-than-market initial interest rates offered as inducements (teasers). But without some type of protection from unacceptable increases in interest rates, borrowers would be in danger of being unable to make future mortgage payments. To prevent this, most lenders and all federal housing agencies have established standards calling for ceilings on increases. Three types of **caps** (ceilings) limit increases in the calculated interest rates of ARM loans:

1. Amount of increase that can be applied at the time of the first adjustment (for example, cap of 1 percent or 2 percent per adjustment period)
2. Amount of increase that can be applied during any one adjustment interval (for example, no more than 2 percent during any one-year period)
3. Total amount the interest rate may be increased over the life of the loan (for example, no more than 6 percent)

Borrowers should be cautious when payments are capped and interest rates are not because of the probability that **negative amortization** will be involved in the loan. Negative amortization occurs when the monthly payment is not enough to pay the interest on the loan. The shortfall is added to the mortgage balance.

Lenders must provide potential borrowers with a worst-case example at loan application. This disclosure must show the maximum possible payment increases if conditions should warrant maximum interest rate increases at the earliest opportunities.

## Conventional ARM

To help you better understand adjustable-rate versus fixed-rate mortgages, Table 10.3 compares two approaches to a $100,000 conventional mortgage using a worst-case scenario for interest rate increases.

In this example, all monthly payment amounts are for principal and interest, and the amounts are rounded to the nearest dollar. The upfront costs of points and fees will be discussed later.

ARM loans have lower initial rates than fixed-rate mortgages, primarily because lenders can avoid the risk of market interest changes for the full 30 years of the loan period. ARM loans reduce the risk, so lenders don't need as much cushion for contingencies. New ARM products are available that combine the ARM features of lower initial interest rate with a longer fixed-rate period between adjustments. For example, three-year, five-year, or ten-year ARMs are available at slightly higher initial rates than one-year ARMs, but at lower rates than 30-year fixed mortgages.

---

**DISCUSSION EXERCISE 10.4**

In your opinion, do the lower initial rates offered on ARM loans cause borrowers to take on more mortgage debt than they can afford? Why or why not?

---

**Interest Rates and Recognized Indexes.** The index to which a conventional ARM is tied can increase or decrease the volatility of interest rate changes. There are four principal indexes used for residential mortgages:

- The LIBOR (London Interbank Offered Rate) index is the base interest rate paid on deposits between banks in the Eurodollar market.
- MTA—Monthly Treasury Bill Average—This stable, slow-moving index is a 12-month moving average of the U.S. One-Year Treasury Bill.

**T A B L E   10.3  ■    $100,000 Mortgage Loan, 30-Year Term, 8% Fixed-Rate Versus 5.5% Adjustable-Rate Mortgage (Annual Cap 2%, Lifetime Cap 6%)**

| | Fixed Rate | | Adjustable Rate | | ARM Savings (Loss) | |
|---|---|---|---|---|---|---|
| Year | Payment | Rate | Payment | Rate | Monthly | Accumulated |
| 1 | $734 | 8% | $568 | 5.5% | $166 | $1,992 |
| 2 | 734 | 8 | 699 | 7.5 | 35 | 2,412 |
| 3 | 734 | 8 | 841 | 9.5 | (107) | 1,128 |
| 4* | 734 | 8 | 990 | 11.5 | (256) | (1,944) |

*ARM savings exhausted in fifth month of year 4.

- COFI—11th District Cost of Funds Index—Another stable, slow-moving index, consisting of the weighted average of deposits and borrowings between banks in the Federal Home Loan Bank District of San Francisco.
- PRIME rate is the rate charged to most favored customers by major banks. This rate is commonly used for adjustments to home equity or second mortgages and can be quite volatile.

Lenders must provide consumers with details on conventional ARMs to assist them in comparison shopping. Potential borrowers must be informed of the index used, how often the loan will be adjusted, and the maximum amount of loan payment increase allowed.

When helping prospective borrowers sort through the many factors to be considered in selecting a conventional adjustable-rate loan, licensees should make sure the borrowers know

- what rate will be used when interest rate caps are applied to an ARM loan;
- that the margin is one of the most important benchmarks in comparing lenders (most other ARM features are relatively similar, but the margins can vary considerably):
- to seek another lender if the one they are considering has policies that call for ARM increases exceeding the 2 percent annual cap or the 6 percent lifetime cap;
- not to consider loans that call for negative amortization;
- to compare upfront costs, such as underwriting fees, points, and origination fees, because some lenders offer lower interest rates but make up for it with inflated upfront costs; and
- not to stretch their borrowing to the limit, as they could with a fixed-rate loan, because the payments remain fixed and income should increase. Borrowing to the limit can become a disaster when an ARM is involved. Prospective borrowers should calculate their first-year payments at the initial interest rate plus 2 percent; otherwise, the first adjustment could hurt them financially.

**Advantages of the ARM Loan.** The ARM's low initial interest rate and the borrower's ability to qualify for a larger mortgage top the list of advantages of adjustable-rate mortgages. ARMs appear to be most appropriate for those who plan to hold the mortgage loans for no more than four years. Also, anytime the interest rate gap between a fixed-rate loan and an adjustable-rate loan reaches 3 percent in favor of the ARM, an ARM loan with interest rate caps and a one-year Treasury bill constant maturity index should make sense to homebuyers. Many ARMs are now written with conversion privileges, allowing the mortgagors to convert to fixed-rate loans for a modest fee during a specified period. This enables borrowers to take advantage of falling interest rates if they desire to do so. One of the standard features of ARMs is no prepayment penalty.

***Longer Adjustment Periods Are Available.*** Many borrowers prefer an ARM loan that won't adjust for periods longer than a year. For example, the low initial rate may last for three, five, or seven years, then adjust once each year. Such loans would be called 3/1, 5/1, or 7/1 ARMs. Other options would be for loans that had an initial rate that lasted five years, then went to a fixed-rate loan at the prevailing rates available for the fifth year. This would be called a 5/25. There are 3/27s, 5/25s, 7/23s, or 10/30s. No one program is better for everyone, so each borrower must evaluate the possibilities based on his or her personal situation.

---

**DISCUSSION EXERCISE 10.5**

Cindy has been transferred to Tampa, and is expecting to be in that location for about three years before being transferred again. She can get a 7½ percent fixed-rate mortgage with no discount points or a 5 percent one-year adjustable-rate mortgage with no points. The ARM has a 2 percent annual and a 6 percent lifetime cap. She asks for your recommendation.

What should Cindy do based on her situation?

What calculations did you use to make your recommendation?

**Disadvantages of the ARM Loan.** ARM borrowers bet against the lenders that interest rates will not rise to the extent that the maximum interest rate caps will be needed. The main disadvantages of the ARM loan are the uncertain amounts of future mortgage payments and the difficulty in calculating adjustments in interest rates as they occur. Lenders, of course, do the actual calculation of adjustments, but they have been known to make mistakes, and such mistakes can be expensive to the borrowers. Calculation details are spelled out in each loan document, but they are somewhat complicated and require the use of either a financial calculator or a handbook of ARM payment tables. For a borrower who wants to audit a lender's ARM adjustments without going to the trouble of research and math calculations, Loantech, Inc., a Gaithersburg, Maryland, mortgage consulting firm (1-800-888-6781), will do a complete individual ARM adjustment review for a fee, based on the terms of the loan document submitted.

## FHA Adjustable-Rate Mortgage

Section 251 of the National Housing Act authorizes the Federal Housing Administration (FHA) to insure adjustable-rate mortgages on single-family properties. The interest rate is the sum of the index and the margin. The index changes, but the margin will remain the same over the life of the loan. The initial interest rate may be a result of combining the current one-year Treasury bill index with the margin at the time the loan is closed. This combination of components produces what is often called the **calculated interest rate.** Each FHA-approved lender is allowed to discount the calculated interest rate to a lower figure if local competition requires it, or the calculated interest rate may become the initial interest rate. The initial interest rate cannot be a rate higher than the current index plus margin.

Once the initial interest rate is set, annual adjustments to FHA ARMs must be calculated. The first interest rate adjustment may not occur sooner than 12 months from the due date of the first monthly payment or later than 18 months from that first designated payment date. In other words, the first adjustment must be made during a six-month period or it is forfeited. This time frame permits lenders to complete the collection or pooling of many mortgages for sale to secondary market institutions. Whatever date is designated as the initial interest rate adjustment date, all subsequent rate adjustments must be made on the anniversary of that first adjustment date.

Unlike the conventional ARM choice of index, all FHA ARMs must use the published "Constant Maturity of the One-Year Treasury Security" index, using the most recently available figure that applied exactly 30 calendar days before the designated change date. The new current index plus the constant margin rounded to the nearest one-eighth of one percentage point is the new calculated interest rate. It is then compared with the existing interest rate. If it is the same as the existing interest rate, no change is made to the existing rate. If it is up to 1 percent higher or lower than the existing interest rate, the new calculated interest rate becomes the new adjusted interest rate. If it is more than 1 percent higher or lower than the existing interest rate, the new adjusted interest rate is limited to a 1 percent increase or decrease of the existing interest rate.

The new adjusted interest rate becomes effective on the designated change date and is regarded as the existing interest rate until the next allowable change date. In no event may any future combination of interest rate adjustments exceed five percentage points higher or lower than the initial interest rate.

The FHA considers interest payable on the first day of the month following the month in which the interest accrued. Therefore, adjusted monthly mortgage payments resulting from the adjusted interest rate are not due until 30 days after the designated change date. No negative amortization is allowed with FHA ARMs. The FHA requires that payments be recalculated each year to provide for complete amortization of the outstanding principal balance over the remaining term of the loan at the new adjusted interest rate. Lenders must give borrowers at least 30 days' notice of any increase or decrease in the monthly mortgage payment amount. The adjustment notice must contain the date the adjustment notice is given, the ARM change date, the new existing interest rate, the amount of the new monthly mortgage payment, the current index used, the method of calculating the adjustment, and any other information that may be required to clarify the adjustment.

**FHA Required Disclosure Statement.** All approved lenders making FHA adjustable-rate loans must provide each borrower with a mortgage loan information statement that includes a worst-case example form. The borrower must receive this statement and be given an opportunity to read the informative explanation before signing the borrower's certification on the loan application. Licensees are urged to obtain personal copies of the FHA adjustable-rate mortgage disclosure statement to use when counseling clients or advising customers.

**Advantages of the FHA ARM.** An FHA ARM has several advantages over a conventional ARM. Often, an FHA ARM bears a slightly lower interest rate because of the government insurance provided the lender. In addition, the FHA commonly uses more lenient qualification formulas. The down payment (required investment) also is lower in many cases, and the interest rate increase each year is limited to 1 percent, with an overall cap of 5 percent (conventional caps usually are 2 percent per year, with a 6 percent overall cap). FHA loans continue to be easier to assume than conventional loans, although the FHA has increased the requirements for assumption of FHA loans. The FHA now requires a review of the creditworthiness of each person seeking to assume an FHA-insured loan.

**Disadvantages of the FHA ARM.** The FHA imposes a maximum loan amount that differs from region to region, depending on the cost of living in each region. Also, the FHA requires an upfront mortgage insurance premium (UFMIP) of 1.5 percent, although this cost may be financed along with the mortgage. If FHA loans are repaid early, mortgagors may apply for partial refunds of the mortgage insurance premiums.

### Bond Money for First-Time Homebuyers

States, counties, and cities can offer below-market mortgage financing by selling tax-free bonds. These loans are available to first-time homebuyers (who haven't owned a home for the previous three years). Sometimes divorced persons who want to buy their own home also qualify. These programs come and go, so check with local lenders for availability.

## MORTGAGE INSURANCE

Conventional lenders usually require that the borrower pay for private mortgage insurance (PMI). PMI protects the lender if the borrower defaults on the loan. The *Homeowners Protection Act of 1998*, which became effective in 1999, established rules for automatic termination and borrower cancellation of PMI on home mortgages. These protections apply to certain home mortgages signed on or after July 29, 1999. These protections do not apply to government-insured FHA or VA guaranteed loans or to loans with lender-paid PMI.

For conventional home mortgages signed on or after July 29, 1999, PMI must, with certain exceptions, be terminated *automatically* when the borrower has achieved 22 percent equity in the home *based on the purchase price,* if the mortgage payments are current. PMI also can be canceled when the borrower *requests it*—with certain exceptions—when the borrower achieves 20 percent equity in the home based on the original property value, if the mortgage payments are current.

There are three exceptions for which the PMI may continue:

1. If the loan is "high-risk"
2. If the borrower has not been current on the payments within the year prior to the time for termination or cancellation
3. If the borrower has other liens on the property

The FHA Homebuyer Savings Plan has also reduced mortgage insurance premiums on loans originated after January 1, 2001, to 1.5 percent of the original loan amount from 2.25 percent. FHA has also eliminated the .5 percent premium for borrowers who have achieved 22 percent equity in their house, based on the lower of the purchase price or the appraisal.

---

**WEB LINKS**

Fannie Mae Home Page: www.fanniemae.com

Freddie Mac Home Page: www.freddiemac.com

U.S. Department of Housing and Urban Development: FHA: www.hud.gov/fha/fhahome.html

Federal Reserve Board: www.federalreserve.gov

U.S. Department of Veterans Affairs: www.va.gov

---

## SUMMARY

Real estate licensees should assist their clients and customers in the initial two steps of prequalifying and shopping for a mortgage loan. Too often, the process begins instead with the loan application. Various proven tools and techniques exist for doing both before applying to a lender for a loan.

Fixed-rate mortgages remain popular. While the 30-year, fixed-rate mortgage is the most common, 15-year and biweekly mortgages are gaining in popularity. Adjustable-rate mortgages also are popular among lenders and borrowers. Conventional and FHA adjustable-rate mortgages are available. Each financing instrument has its own advantages and disadvantages, and licensees who understand the current and ever-changing mortgage market increase their chances for success in the business.

## KEY TERMS

| | | |
|---|---|---|
| adjustable-rate mortgage (ARM) | cap | negative amortization |
| annual percentage rate (APR) | fixed-rate mortgage | PITI payment |
| biweekly mortgage | index | refinancing |
| calculated interest rate | margin | |

# PRACTICE EXAM

1. The FHA-required disclosure statement indicates the initial interest rate for an FHA ARM loan may remain in effect for up to how many months?
   a.  12
   b.  18
   c.  24
   d.  30

2. The primary elements a borrower uses to determine whether to accept an adjustable-rate mortgage are the index, the lender's margin, and the:
   a.  seller's income and credit history.
   b.  housing expense ratio and total obligations ratio.
   c.  calculated interest rate, initial interest rate, and interest rate caps.
   d.  amount of the buydown and amount of negative amortization.

3. Of the recognized indexes used on ARM loans, which of the following is most volatile?
   a.  Prime rate charged by money center banks
   b.  One-year Treasury bill index
   c.  LIBOR index
   d.  Cost-of-funds index of the Federal Home Loan Bank, 11th District

4. Total interest rate increases on an FHA adjustable-rate loan may not exceed what percentage over the life of the loan?
   a.  5 percent
   b.  3 percent
   c.  2 percent
   d.  1 percent

5. On January 10, the one-year Treasury bill index was 7 percent. Southern Federal Savings Association used that index to write a new one-year adjustable-rate mortgage that included a 2 percent cap on annual interest rate increases. The margin was $2\frac{1}{2}$ percent. What is the calculated interest rate contained in the new ARM loan above?
   a.  7 percent
   b.  9 percent
   c.  $9\frac{1}{2}$ percent
   d.  11 percent

6. Using the information in question 5, assume the index rose to $9\frac{1}{2}$ percent in year two. What interest rate will be charged in year two?
   a.  11 percent
   b.  $11\frac{1}{2}$ percent
   c.  12 percent
   d.  $9\frac{1}{2}$ percent

7. Phyllis takes out a $127,000, 30-year, fixed-rate mortgage at $9\frac{1}{2}$ percent. The mortgage payment factor is .0084085. Taxes for the year are $2,400, and insurance is $600. What will Phyllis pay in monthly PITI payments?
   a.  $1,267.88
   b.  $1,067.88
   c.  $1,245.89
   d.  $1,317.88

8.  The component of an adjustable-rate mortgage that does NOT usually change is the:
    a.  margin.
    b.  index.
    c.  points.
    d.  calculated rate.

9.  Jack purchased a new home at the FHA appraisal amount of $100,000 and financed it with an FHA mortgage loan. To what amount must he reduce the outstanding loan balance before he no longer has to pay the ½ percent annual mortgage insurance premium?
    a.  $90,000
    b.  $85,000
    c.  $78,000
    d.  $80,000

10. What is the index measuring the base interest rate paid on deposits between banks in the Eurodollar market that is used in many adjustable-rate mortgages?
    a.  COFI
    b.  MTA
    c.  PRIME
    d.  LIBOR

11. A borrower who is shopping for an acceptable ARM probably should reject a loan that has:
    a.  annual caps of more than 2 percent.
    b.  a lifetime cap greater than 4 percent.
    c.  a margin greater than 2 percent.
    d.  annual caps of 2 percent.

12. What is the maximum amount of a buyer's closing costs that can be paid by the seller under conventional lending standards when the borrower is making a 5 percent down payment?
    a.  6 percent of the purchase price
    b.  4 percent of the loan amount
    c.  3 percent of the purchase price
    d.  3 percent of the loan amount

13. Millie Proffit is buying a new home and will make a 10 percent down payment. The beginning interest rate on her ARM loan is 7 percent. Sara, her sales associate, prequalified Millie based on a payment from the factor table at 7 percent, plus escrow items (PITI). Which is correct?
    a.  Sara should have qualified Millie without the escrow items in the payment.
    b.  Sara should have qualified Millie at a 9 percent payment factor plus escrow items.
    c.  Millie can't get a 90 percent ARM loan; 80 percent is the maximum loan-to-value ratio.
    d.  Sara should have qualified Millie at a 9 percent payment factor without escrow items.

14. Marian is shopping for a new $150,000 mortgage. She expects to live in her new home for about four years. She can get a 30-year, 7.75 percent fixed-rate mortgage with principal and interest payments of $1,074.62 with no points. She can also get a 7.25 percent mortgage loan (payments of $1,023.26) with three points. How many months will it take Marian to break even on the points if she takes the lower interest rate loan, using simple arithmetic?
    a. 48.5
    b. 58.6
    c. 87.6
    d. 89.2

15. ARM loans are more popular:
    a. than fixed-rate mortgages in most markets.
    b. when interest rates are low.
    c. for people who are risk-averse.
    d. when interest rates are high.

16. Wade Pitts is shopping for a new loan and has narrowed the field to two choices. One is a 30-year, fixed-rate loan that has principal and interest payments of $940 per month. The other is a biweekly mortgage. What is the difference in Wade's annual payments based on this information?
    a. $940
    b. No difference in payments but a big difference in interest saved
    c. No difference in payments and no difference in interest saved
    d. $470

17. When compared with a 30-year mortgage, a 15-year mortgage:
    a. is more flexible in repayment possibilities.
    b. has slightly higher interest rates.
    c. has slightly lower interest rates.
    d. has lower monthly payments.

18. Popular literature shows dramatic interest savings from a 15-year loan versus a 30-year loan. What is true about most of these analyses?
    a. Amounts saved usually are less because income tax effects are not factored in.
    b. Amounts saved usually are less because opportunity costs of the additional payments required are not considered.
    c. They usually show that the amounts of interest saved are not substantial.
    d. Both a and b

19. Disclosure of the annual percentage rate of interest need *NOT*:
    a. be given to the borrower within three days of loan application.
    b. be computed to the nearest one-eighth of 1 percent.
    c. show the total financing cost in relation to the amount financed.
    d. be given to a prospective buyer of a single-family home who is paying all cash.

20. Which is true about a loan's effective interest rate?
    a. Each point equals a ½ percent increase in the lender's yield.
    b. Origination fees should be added to the points charged in making the calculation.
    c. Each point equals one-eighth of a 1 percent increase in the lender's yield, even if the loan is in force for less than five years.
    d. Origination fees should not be considered on an ARM based on index changes.

# 11

# ACQUIRING FINANCING FOR THE PROPERTY

## LEARNING OBJECTIVES

Upon completion of this chapter, *you should be able to*

**1.** list three federal statutes that control the information a lender may obtain and consider when qualifying an applicant;

**2.** list the four basic loan processing procedures;

**3.** list two of the latest trends in mortgage lending due to computer technology;

**4.** describe the difference between qualifying the borrower and qualifying the property;

**5.** describe how lenders are using credit scoring to assist in the underwriting process;

**6.** itemize at least three sources of income that will be counted when qualifying a buyer;

**7.** explain what *analyzing the title* means and how it is accomplished;

**8.** list the components of a full title report;

**9.** list the two methods of obtaining assurance of good title; and

**10.** describe the differences between an owner's title insurance policy and a lender's title insurance policy.

## OVERVIEW

The origination of a home mortgage is subject to a number of federal statutes, particularly the **Equal Credit Opportunity Act (ECOA),** the **Consumer Credit Protection Act** (Title I: Truth-in-Lending Act), and the **Real Estate Settlement Procedures Act (RESPA).** Together, these laws control the information a lender may obtain and consider in qualifying consumer mortgage loan applicants. They also dictate both the content and the form of information lenders must present to borrowers, the procedure for closing mortgage loan agreements, the documents to be used in closings, and the fees that may be charged.

In today's environment, lenders are required by the Civil Rights Acts, and the amendments to them, not to discriminate against consumer mortgage loan applicants on the basis of race, color, national origin, religion, sex, age, family status, or handicap. In addition, borrower rights have been better protected since passage of the Equal Credit Opportunity Act and the *Federal Reserve Board of Governor's Regulation B*, which implemented the act. The act requires fair consideration of consumer loan applications from women, minority races, part-time employees, and others who may have suffered prejudicial treatment in the past.

As a result of increasing concern about protection of consumer rights, most mortgage lenders have developed specific guidelines for loan underwriters to follow to ensure compliance with federal laws affecting consumer mortgage lending. Although the guidelines are protective of consumers' rights, they do not interfere with the analysis of an applicant's credit standing. The purpose of such guidelines is to prevent homebuyers from being victimized, not to guarantee that a loan will be approved. In the final analysis, good underwriting policies and practices by a lender combine compliance with the continual search for financial safety and streamlined processing. Licensees can serve themselves and their customers well by becoming knowledgeable about residential mortgage loan processing and closing.

To accomplish the above-stated goals of government agencies and originating lenders, four basic **loan processing procedures** have been developed:

1.  Determining a borrower's ability to repay the loan
2.  Estimating the value of the property being pledged as collateral to guarantee this repayment
3.  Researching and analyzing the marketability of the collateral's title
4.  Preparing the documents necessary to close the loan transaction

Most lenders follow loan processing procedures that reflect a combined concern for the borrower's credit ability and the collateral's value. Some loan transactions require an emphasis of one factor over the other, but generally both borrower credit and collateral value are essential determinants in the real estate finance loan processing equation.

**Loan underwriting** is the evaluation of the risks involved when issuing a new mortgage. This process involves qualifying the borrower and the property to determine whether they meet the minimum requirements established by the lender, investor, or secondary market in which the loan probably will be sold. ∎

## TRENDS IN THE MORTGAGE MARKET

The mortgage market is changing as rapidly as many other sectors of the real estate industry, and technology is the engine of the change. The last two years have seen many lenders migrating their loan programs to the Internet. Almost immediate loan approval is possible on the Web. *Credit scoring*, discussed later in this chapter, is changing the way mortgage interest rates are quoted. Appraisers can make restricted "drive-by" appraisals when a loan application is strong.

### Automated Underwriting

With **automated underwriting** a lender can enter loan application information into Fannie Mae's Desktop Underwriter software and receive a decision almost immediately. If the software determines that the buyer and the property are qualified, Fannie Mae is required to purchase the loan from the originator.

Because of the huge growth of people using the Internet and the public's acceptance of the technology, lenders are moving toward so-called **paperless mortgages.** For example, a person who applies for a mortgage online can expect to take 15 minutes to complete the application, and the applicant will get an automatic decision almost immediately. This bypasses the need for a lender to take the application. How does all this work? With **computer valuation** (appraisals) and credit scoring.

## Automated Valuation

Some years ago, a consortium of lending organizations including Fannie Mae, Freddie Mac, Citibank, Countrywide Funding, and others formed an organization called the *National Property Data Service*. The purpose was to reduce time and costs for both consumers and lenders through **automated valuation.**

Each lender contributed all its residential appraisals to create a huge database of property descriptions and sale prices. A review of the database might show, for example, that 74 percent of all the homes in a given subdivision had been the subject of an appraisal over a ten-year period.

An appraiser employs matched pair analysis using two or three pairs of properties to estimate the value of a fourth bedroom, a swimming pool, or another feature. The Desktop Underwriter uses multiple linear regressions to do the same thing for that neighborhood. It uses precise dollar adjustments and, depending on the buyer's credit score, may allow an appraiser to do a "streamlined property inspection" (exterior only) to make an estimate of value. When Fannie Mae uses this method, it has judged the reasonableness of the sales price and has relied on the property value generated by the software.

## QUALIFYING THE BORROWER

The framework for current real estate financing is the 30-year amortization schedule and regular monthly payments of principal and interest. In addition, mortgagees currently can lend up to 100 percent of a property's value. High loan-to-value ratios combined with long-term loan amortization payment schedules require that a lender look to the credit of the borrower as the primary protection.

Even though lenders using insured or guaranteed programs of real estate finance do not bear the risks of default directly, they still must follow the directions of their guaranteeing agencies and carefully screen loan applicants to derive some reasonable estimate of borrowers' ability to pay and their inclinations to meet their contractual obligations responsibly. Thus, a great effort is made to check and evaluate thoroughly a potential mortgagor's credit history and current financial status to predict her future economic stability. The mortgage loan process is shown in Figure 11.1.

### Loan Application

When a licensee works with a buyer, one of the services the licensee can offer is that of helping the buyer obtain financing. Before the buyer goes to the lender to make an application, the licensee should provide a list of items the buyer will need. A Mortgage Loan Application Checklist is shown in the Forms-To-Go Appendix in the back of the book.

**Data Verification.** The loan processor will verify the information included in the application by actually checking with the various references given, the banks where deposits are held, and the applicant's employer.

**Deposits.** The borrower must sign a separate deposit verification form for each bank account, authorizing the bank to reveal to the lender the current balance in the borrower's account. Under the *Federal Right to Privacy Act,* the bank cannot release such confidential information without a verification form. The knowledge that the loan processor can verify account amounts usually is enough incentive for the borrower to be truthful in reporting financial information. When the deposit balances are verified, the appropriate entries are made in the applicant's file.

**FIGURE  11.1  ■  Mortgage Loan Process**

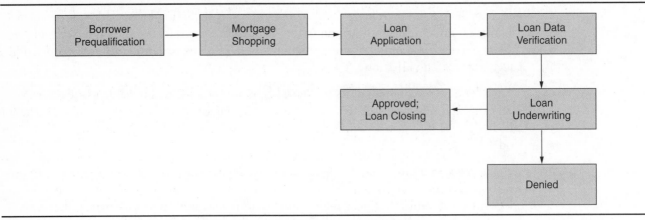

SOURCE: Adapted by permission from Thomas C. Steinmetz, *The Mortgage Kit,* 4th ed. (Chicago: Dearborn Financial Publishing, Inc.®, 1998), 7.

**Employment.** The applicant also is required to sign an employment verification form authorizing the employer to reveal confidential information concerning the applicant's job status. Not only will the applicant's wages or salary and length of employment be verified but the employer also will be requested to offer an opinion of the applicant's job attitude and give a prognosis for continued employment and prospects for advancement. Employment may be checked again before closing.

**Credit Report.** Simultaneously with the gathering of financial and employment information, the loan processor sends a formal request for the borrower's credit report to a local company offering this service. The credit report is a central part of the loan approval process, and the lender relies on it heavily. Of the two types of credit reports, consumer credit and mortgage credit, the discussion here centers on the latter.

A credit report is the result of the compilation of information accumulated from a thorough check of the creditors indicated on the loan application, as well as a check of the public records to discover whether any lawsuits are pending against the applicant. When completed, the credit search company sends the loan processor a confidential report of its findings.

This report usually states the applicant's (and co-applicant's) age, address, status as a tenant or owner, and length of residency at his current address and includes a brief employment history and credit profile, both past and present. The credit profile itemizes the status of current and past accounts, usually identified by industry, such as banks, department and specialty stores, and finance companies. In addition, it indicates the quality and dates of the payments made, and their regularity; delinquency, and any outstanding balances also are reported. This payment history is the most important part of the report because it indicates how well the applicant has managed debt over time. Underwriters view a person's past behavior as the best indicator of future attitude toward debt repayment. Research tends to reinforce these opinions, indicating that slow and erratic payers generally retain those attitudes when securing new loans and that prompt and steady payers also are consistent in meeting their future obligations. As a result, lenders pay careful attention to the last section of a credit report, which indicates an applicant's attitude toward debt and his or her payment pattern.

When a credit report is returned revealing a series of erratic and delinquent payments, the loan is usually denied at this point and the file closed. If an applicant is denied a loan because of adverse information in a credit report, the applicant has the right to inspect a summary of that report, to challenge inaccuracies, and to require corrections to be made (see the most current RESPA-required brochure, *Settlement Costs: A HUD Guide*). If one or two unusual entries stand out in a group of otherwise satisfactory transactions, the applicant will be asked to explain these deviations.

As with many standardized procedures, credit reporting has become computerized, dramatically shortening the time needed for completing a check. In exchange for time efficiency, however, credit-reporting bureaus risk sacrificing the borrower's confidentiality. The fraudulent use of credit reports is increasing now that information is so easily accessed. Credit reports should be used only by the persons or institutions requesting the information and only for the purposes stated. As a result of increased seller financing, credit bureaus are receiving more requests from agents and sellers to check the credit of potential purchasers. To protect a buyer's confidentiality, most credit agencies insist on seeing the buyer's written permission before issuing any information.

After the deposit and employment verifications are returned with acceptable information and a favorable credit report is obtained, the lending officer makes a thorough credit evaluation of the data collected before continuing with the loan process.

## Evaluation of Credit Ability

Despite the standardization of the detailed guidelines used in the lending process, the one area allowing for the greatest amount of latitude in interpretation is the analysis and evaluation of a borrower's credit ability. A degree of subjective personal involvement may be introduced into an otherwise strongly objective and structured format by an evaluator's unintentional bias or by a loan company's changing policies.

In addition, credit standards are altered periodically to reflect a lender's changing monetary position. When money is scarce, standards are more stringent; when money is plentiful, standards are lowered. An applicant who qualifies for a loan at one time may not at another. Thus, although a credit analyst is governed by guidelines, rules and regulations, the criteria fluctuate with the analyst's discretionary powers. In the long run, a lender's success is demonstrated by a low rate of default on approved loans and by the fact that no discrimination complaints have been filed.

## Credit Scoring

One of the most significant changes in mortgage lending has been the use of credit scores to better evaluate a borrower's ability to repay. Many borrowers who would have been turned down for a loan five years ago can buy today, but at higher rates.

A major reason Fannie Mae and Freddie Mac lenders are willing to make immediate loan decisions is credit scoring. **Credit scoring** uses statistical samples to predict how likely it is that a borrower will pay back a loan. To develop a model, the lender selects a large random sample of its borrowers, analyzing characteristics that relate to creditworthiness. Each of the characteristics is assigned a weight based on how strong a predictor it is. Credit scores treat each person objectively because the same standards apply to everyone. Credit scores are blind to demographic or cultural differences among people.

The most commonly used credit score today is known as a **FICO score,** named after the company that developed it, Fair, Isaac & Co. FICO scores range from 300 to 850. The lower the score, the greater the risk of default. A recent study by the Federal Reserve Board found that borrowers with low credit scores accounted for 1.5 percent of new mortgages, but 17 percent of the delinquencies.

Freddie Mac has found that borrowers with credit scores above 660 are likely to repay the mortgage, and underwriters can do a basic review of the file for completeness. For applicants with scores between 620 and 660, the underwriter is required to do a comprehensive review. A very cautious review would be made for persons with credit scores below 620.

**Is Credit Scoring Valid?** With credit scoring, lenders can evaluate millions of applicants consistently and impartially on many different characteristics. To be statistically valid, the system must be based on a big enough sample. When properly designed, the system promotes fast, impartial decisions.

Fair, Isaac has recently completed *NextGen*®, designed to more precisely define the risk of borrowers because it analyzes more criteria than the old model. Using the new model, lenders can evaluate credit profiles of high-risk borrowers in terms of degrees, rather than lumping them into the same category.

**What Information Does Credit Scoring Use?** The scoring models use the following information when evaluating a score:

- 35 percent of the score is determined by payment history with higher weight for recent history. If late payments, collections, and/or bankruptcy appear in the credit report, they are subtracted from the score.
- Outstanding debt is very close in importance to payment history (30 percent of the total score). Many scoring models evaluate the amount of debt compared with the credit limits. If the amount owed is close to the credit limit, it affects the score negatively.
- 15 percent is the result of credit history. A long history is better if payments are always on time.
- 10 percent is very recent history and "inquiries" for new credit. If the applicant has applied for credit in many places recently, it will negatively affect the score. This problem occurs when a person goes car shopping. Sales associates at each car lot will ask for the consumer's Social Security number in order to pull a credit report ("no charge"). The shopper has no idea that as more reports are ordered, the shopper's credit rating declines.
- 10 percent is based on the mix of credit, including car loans, credit cards, and mortgages. Too many credit cards will hurt a person's credit score. In some models, loans from finance companies or title loan companies will also hurt the score.

To improve the credit score, persons should pay bills on time, pay down outstanding balances, and not take on new debt. It may take a long time to improve the score significantly. See Figure 11.2 for examples of the effects on the FICO credit score caused by actions a potential borrower might take.

**How Is Credit Scoring Being Used?** Residential lenders now use credit scoring the same way it is used in automobile financing and consumer loans. Interest rates on home mortgages will be based on the credit score. In theory, a person with a very high score should expect to get the best rate, but typically the rate is the same for anyone with a FICO score higher than 620. Below the 620 line, several grades and interest rates have resulted.

As an example, when an A+ borrower could obtain a 30-year fixed rate mortgage at 7 percent, an A– borrower paid 8.4 percent, a B borrower paid 8.7 percent, a C borrower paid 9.15 percent, and a D borrower paid 9.95 percent. Before credit scoring, however, these borrowers might not have been able to get a loan at all.

Many people who go to subprime lenders have only slight credit problems and end up paying 2 percent higher than they need to. Those borrowers may qualify for standard rates, and should find out their credit scores before making a decision on a lender. If individuals cannot get their FICO score, E-Loan Corp. provides a credit score using basically the same techniques. Individuals can get one free credit score by logging into E-Loan and requesting the information.

**F I G U R E  11.2  ■  Results on FICO Score from Certain Financial Decisions**

Assume that your current FICO score is 707 (very good).
This table shows the likely effect on your score based on the following actions:

| Action | New FICO Range |
|---|---|
| **You currently have a combined revolving balance of $2,230 and you pay down $750 on the balance**<br>Paying your bills on time is a substantial factor affecting your FICO score. Generally speaking, if you have no negative items on your file, your score will remain fairly stable as you continue to pay your bills on time.<br><br>If you have some history of late payments, how recently they occurred is important. The more recently they happened, the more impact they will likely have on your score. As they age, their impact on your score will gradually lessen. | 707 to 727 |
| **Max out your credit cards**<br>Carrying extremely high balances on all of your revolving accounts makes you look "maxed out" on your available credit. It is often considered a high-risk trait by lenders and the FICO score.<br><br>In this simulation, the impact to your FICO score will depend on how high your current balances are on your revolving accounts. If you already carry high balances, the impact will probably be minimal. The impact will be more noticeable if you currently have a low or medium balance. | 637 to 687 |
| **Apply for and receive a new credit card with a credit limit of $3,000**<br>Consumers seeking and obtaining new credit are generally riskier than consumers who are not. The impact on your FICO score will vary, depending on your current credit profile. The score takes into consideration the level of your existing credit history (recently opened files versus more mature files, for example), the amount of recently opened credit you currently have on file, and other factors.<br><br>This simulation is based on your applying for and receiving a new credit card with a limit of at least $3,000. | 697 to 717 |
| **Miss payments on all accounts with a payment due**<br>FICO scores evaluate late payment information in a variety of ways—in terms of the *frequency* of missed payments, the *recency* of the missed payments and the *level of delinquency* (how late the payment is).<br><br>In this simulation, the impact on your score of missing a payment will depend on your current status and the level of the delinquency. For example, the impact will probably be more substantial if you miss a payment this month, and you currently have a spotless or relatively clean credit report. There will be less impact on the score if you currently have multiple negative items on your credit report. | 582 to 632 |

SOURCE: Fair, Isaac & Co.

**WEB LINK**

1   E-Loan (for prequalifying and credit scores): www.eloan.com

2   HSH Associates, Financial Publishers: www.hsh.com

3   Fannie Mae Home Page: www.fanniemae.com

4   Freddie Mac Home Page: www.freddiemac.com

5   FHA Home Page: www.hud.gov/fha/fhahome.html

6   Federal Reserve Board: www.federalreserve.gov

7   U.S. Department of Veterans Affairs: www.va.gov/

8   Fair, Isaac & Co.: www.fairisaac.com

The quantity and quality of an applicant's income are the two major considerations in determining ability to support a family and make the required monthly loan payments. Analysts consider the **quantity of income**—the total income—when they review a loan application. Not only is the regular salary of a family's primary supporter basic to the analysis but also a spouse's full income usually is accepted. Extra sources of income also may be included in the analysis if circumstances warrant it.

Any bonuses will be accepted as income only if they are received on a regular basis. If commissions are a large part of an applicant's income base, the history of past earnings will be scrutinized to estimate the stability of this income as a regular source for an extended time period. Overtime wages are not included in the analysis unless they have been—and will be—earned consistently. Pensions, interest, and dividends are treated as full income, although it is recognized that interest and dividends fluctuate over time and could stop if an investment were cashed out.

A second job is accepted as part of the regular monthly income if it can be established that the job has existed for approximately two years and there is good reason to believe it will continue. Child support also can be included in the determination of monthly income, but only if it is the result of a court order and has a proven track record. Government entitlement funds must also be considered.

In addition to its total quantity, a loan analyst pays careful attention to the **quality of income.** An applicant's employer will be asked for an opinion of job stability and possible advancement. Length of time on the job no longer carries the importance it once did. Applicants whose employment records show frequent shifts in job situations that result in upward mobility each time will be given full consideration. Lenders will, however, be wary of an applicant who drifts from one job classification to another and cannot seem to become established in any specific type of work.

When the accumulated data strongly support a positive or negative decision, the loan underwriter's decision is easy, and minimal use of discretion is needed. However, numerous borderline cases make it difficult for a loan officer to form objective judgments. In such a case, the loan officer schedules an in-depth personal interview with the applicant during which questions regarding data appearing on the credit report are clarified or mistakes in bank balances can be explained. More often, however, the loan officer merely wishes to visit with the applicant to observe and probe her attitudes regarding the purchase of the property and the repayment of the prospective loan. Thus, although a person's credit character can be measured objectively, personal character is subject to interpretation.

After reviewing all of the information provided in the application as well as the other data collected, the loan officer decides either to approve or to disapprove the loan application. If the officer judges a loan application to be unacceptable, he states the reasons for the rejection, the parties to the loan are informed, and the file is closed.

## QUALIFYING THE COLLATERAL

Despite the current trend toward emphasizing a borrower's financial ability as the loan-granting criterion, real estate lenders and guarantors are practical and fully understand that life is filled with events beyond one's control. Death is a possibility that can abruptly eliminate a family's wage earner. Economic conditions can exert devastating financial impact. Corporate downsizing and layoffs have resulted in hardship for many families. Honest mistakes in personal decisions can result in bankruptcies, often damaging or destroying credit.

---

### DISCUSSION EXERCISE 11.1

You are at an open house on Sunday afternoon. A young couple asks whether they could qualify to buy the house. Based on the home's price of $156,000, you estimate a 90 percent loan would be about $140,000. You tell them you can give them your best estimate, but that they will know for sure only after they see a lender to become preapproved. They give you the following monthly financial information:

| | |
|---|---|
| Gross monthly income | $4,300 |
| Mortgage principal and interest payment @ 6% for 30 years | $ 839 |
| Real estate tax escrow | $ 150 |
| Homeowner's insurance escrow | $ 50 |
| Private mortgage insurance | $ 45 |
| Car payment | $ 250 |
| Credit card payments (average) | $ 50 |
| The borrower's housing expense ratio is: | _____ |
| The borrower's total obligations ratio is: | _____ |
| What is your informal opinion on their chances to buy? | _____ |

---

1  To reduce the risk of loss, real estate lenders look to the value of the collateral (the real prop-
2  erty) as the basic underlying assurance for recovery of their investments in a default situation.

3  Unique financing terms or an active local housing market in which the number of poten-
4  tial buyers briefly exceeds the number of available properties may cause prices to rise above
5  actual market values. Therefore, each parcel of property pledged for collateral must be
6  inspected and appraised carefully to estimate its current market value because this amount
7  will be used as the basis for determining the mortgage loan amount. Depending on the type of
8  loan to be issued and its loan-to-value ratio, either the amount determined through the for-
9  mal or certified appraisal made as part of the loan process or the purchase price, whichever is
10  less, determines the loan's amount.

11  Some financial institutions maintain appraisers on their staffs, but most lenders engage
12  certified appraisers for estimates of value. All three approaches to estimating a property's
13  value are addressed. When an appraisal is completed, it is delivered to the loan officer to aid
14  in the final loan decision. As noted previously, a loan amount is based on the lesser of either
15  this appraised value or the purchase price of the property.

---

### DISCUSSION EXERCISE 11.2

Which do you consider the more important factor in granting or denying a mortgage applica-tion: the borrower's ability to make the required payments or the value of the collateral? Why?

---

## 16  ANALYZING THE TITLE

17  The assurance of good title is as essential to a loan's completion as are the borrower's credit
18  and the collateral's value. In anticipation of issuing a loan, the loan officer secures a title
19  report on the collateral property. The components of a full title report are a survey, a physical
20  inspection of the collateral, and a search of the records to determine all the interests in a
21  property. Normally, property interests are perfected through the appropriate filing and record-
22  ing of standard notices. A recorded deed notifies the world that a grantee has the legal fee
23  simple title to the property. A recorded construction lien, for example, is notice of another's
24  interest in the property.

In Florida, two methods have been used to obtain assurance of good title: (1) the abstract and opinion of title and (2) title insurance. Lenders prefer title insurance, but whichever method is used, the title report should provide the loan officer and the lender's attorney with all available information relevant to the legal status of the subject property, as well as any interests revealed by constructive notice. This title search requirement represents another effort by the lender to protect the loan investment. Because title insurance is most lenders' and buyers' method of choice, it is discussed here.

## Title Insurance

Title insurance companies combine the abstracting process with a program of insurance that guarantees the validity and accuracy of the title search. A purchaser of title insurance can rely on the insurance company's assets to back up its guarantee of a property's marketable title. This guarantee is evidenced by a policy of title insurance. Most financial institutions now require that a title policy be issued to them for the face amount of a loan. Insurance is defined simply as coverage against loss.

When a title insurance policy is issued to a lender, it is usually in the American Land Title Association (ALTA) form. While a standard title policy insures against losses overlooked in the search of the recorded chain of title, an ALTA policy expands this standard coverage to include many unusual risks, such as forgeries, incompetency of parties involved in issuing documents pertaining to the transfer of ownership, legal status of parties involved in the specific loan negotiations, surveying errors, and other possible off-record defects. Some additional risks can be and usually are covered by special endorsements to an insurance policy. These could include protection against any unrecorded easements or liens, rights of parties in possession of the subject property, mining claims, water rights, and additional negotiated special items pertinent to the property involved. Participants in the secondary mortgage market (Fannie Mae, Freddie Mac, and Ginnie Mae) generally require the expanded ALTA policy for the added protection it provides. Many lenders use the phrase "an ALTA policy" when describing an extended-coverage policy.

## Surveys

Whether the abstract and opinion of title method or the title insurance policy method is used, a property's title is searched by an experienced abstractor who prepares a report of those recorded documents that clearly affect the quality of ownership. In addition, lenders usually require a survey of the collateral property as a condition for a new loan. Although many properties are part of subdivisions that have been engineered and described by licensed and registered surveyors and engineers, some owners might have enlarged their homes or made additions to the improvements since the original survey. These might not meet the various setback restrictions set forth in the local zoning laws. Some properties might have been resubdivided, while others now might have encroachment problems.

## Defects

If a defect is found, sometimes called a *cloud on the title*, the loan process does not continue until this cloud is cleared to the lender's satisfaction. Such a cloud could be an unsatisfied construction lien, an income tax lien, a property tax lien, an easement infraction, an encroachment, or a zoning violation. Sometimes a borrower's name is not correct on the deed, an error exists in the legal description, or the deed has a faulty acknowledgment or lacks the appropriate signatures. Because of the many complexities in a real estate transaction, there are possibilities for defects to appear in a title search and property survey. It is the abstractor's responsibility to discover and report them.

1    In certain instances where clouds are difficult to remove by ordinary means, they must be
2    cleared by filing suits to quiet title. After appropriate evidence is submitted, a judge removes
3    or modifies an otherwise damaging defect in a title. The loan process can continue when a
4    clear chain of title is shown on the public records.

## SUMMARY

The process of obtaining a real estate loan includes four steps: qualifying a borrower, evaluating the collateral, analyzing the title, and closing the loan transaction.

Beginning with an application to obtain a loan, the borrower's credit, financial condition, and personal attitudes are analyzed to determine his or her ability and willingness to honor debts and repay the loan as agreed. Current assets and employment are verified, a credit rating is obtained, and often a private interview is held between the borrower and loan officer to estimate certain credit characteristics. Other basic criteria used to determine the applicant's creditworthiness include gross monthly earnings of approximately four times the required monthly mortgage payment (sometimes higher for large loans), stability of earnings, and a good prognosis for continued employment and advancement.

Once the loan applicant's credit is accepted, either a staff appraiser or an independent fee appraiser analyzes the value of the real estate to be pledged as collateral. A certified appraisal report offering the appraiser's opinion of the subject property's value is submitted to the loan officer.

After the borrower's credit and the collateral's value are verified, the legal status of the property's title is examined and analyzed carefully, usually by a trained abstractor. The abstract is delivered to the lender's attorney for an opinion of accuracy and validity. Because of the growing activity of this nation's secondary mortgage market and its concurrent necessity for added protection, lenders generally require title insurance to guarantee the title search.

Finally, after approval of the borrower's credit, the collateral's value, and the title's marketability, the loan processor prepares the documents necessary for closing. With the delivery of the funds to the seller and the recording of the necessary papers transferring title, the loan transaction is completed.

## K E Y   T E R M S

| | | |
|---|---|---|
| automated underwriting | loan processing procedures | paperless mortgage |
| automated valuation | FICO score | quality of income |
| computer valuation | loan underwriting | quantity of income |
| credit scoring | | |

# P R A C T I C E   E X A M

1. Qualifying the buyer has to do with income and assets. Qualifying the property has to do with the:
   a. income, credit report, and appraisal.
   b. appraisal, survey, and title report.
   c. appraisal, title report, and credit report.
   d. survey, title report, and income.

2. A lender, interested in evaluating an applicant's willingness to pay, reviews:
   a. income.
   b. assets.
   c. the credit report.
   d. All of the above

3. A federally related loan transaction is covered under RESPA guidelines if it:
   a. involves a 100-acre tract of land.
   b. involves an apartment complex of 60 units.
   c. involves a one-family to four-family home.
   d. All of the above

4. Rob has a FICO credit score of 725. He pays an additional $1,000 down on his installment debt. His FICO score will most likely:
   a. decline because he has less debt.
   b. increase because he has less debt.
   c. decline because he has less credit.
   d. be unaffected unless he does this for at least three months running.

5. What is given greatest weight in calculating the FICO credit score?
   a. Outstanding debt
   b. Credit history
   c. Payment history, with higher weight for recent history
   d. Recent "inquiries" for new credit

6. What percent of delinquent mortgage payments is the result of loans to persons with low credit scores?
   a. 1.5%
   b. 10%
   c. 17%
   d. 40%

7. When Jim applies for a loan, he has more than enough income to qualify. His credit history also has been good. However, two late notices from creditors that have since been paid remain on the credit report. Under these circumstances, Jim's loan likely will be:
   a. denied.
   b. approved without further questions.
   c. approved after Jim explains the discrepancies.
   d. reduced to a maximum 80 percent loan-to-value ratio.

8.  Joan earns $1,000 per week. Based on Fannie Mae's 28 percent housing expense ratio guidelines, what monthly payment would she qualify for?
    a.  $1,213.33
    b.  $1,120.00
    c.  $1,000.00
    d.  $867.33

9.  Bonuses are acceptable as income on a loan application, provided that they:
    a.  are actually collected.
    b.  are regular occurrences.
    c.  exceed $2,000 per year.
    d.  total less than $2,000 per year.

10.  A second job will *NOT* be counted as a source of income on a loan application if it:
    a.  pays less than $2,000 per year.
    b.  is likely to continue.
    c.  has been held for at least two years.
    d.  is temporary.

11.  The guidelines for loan underwriting are tightly structured. The one facet that allows the most subjectivity on the part of the lender's evaluation is the:
    a.  credit ability.
    b.  amount of debt.
    c.  asset valuation.
    d.  income quantity.

12.  The primary assurance to the lender if the borrower defaults on the loan, is the:
    a.  borrower's income.
    b.  borrower's assets.
    c.  borrower's net worth.
    d.  property value.

13.  A title policy offering coverage over and above the standard coverage is which of the following types of policies?
    a.  Mortgagor's
    b.  Fannie Mae
    c.  Owner's
    d.  ALTA

14.  When money is scarce, lender standards tend to be more:
    a.  lenient.
    b.  strict.
    c.  relaxed in the evaluation of credit.
    d.  relaxed in the evaluation of income.

15.  When a loan officer evaluates a credit report, the most important part of the report is the:
    a.  employment history.
    b.  payment history.
    c.  public records section.
    d.  applicant's current address.

16. The employment verification is a *NOT* a check on the applicant's:
    a. length of employment.
    b. salary.
    c. prognosis for continued employment.
    d. assets.

17. The components that together make a title report complete are a physical inspection of the collateral property, a search of the public records, and a(n):
    a. abstract of title.
    b. title insurance policy.
    c. satisfaction of previous mortgage document.
    d. survey of the property.

18. Which action will *NOT* negatively affect a FICO score?
    a. Applying for credit in several places
    b. Slow payment history
    c. High balances on credit cards
    d. Paying down debt

19. If a cloud on title exists that cannot be easily removed by ordinary means, a court case is often the result. The legal action is called a suit:
    a. for certiori.
    b. to quiet title.
    c. for partition.
    d. for declaratory judgment.

20. The most common credit scoring used by lenders today was developed by:
    a. Fanning and Investors Company.
    b. ING Investments.
    c. Fannie Mae.
    d. Fair, Isaac & Co.

# CHAPTER

# 12

# CLOSING REAL ESTATE TRANSACTIONS

LEARNING OBJECTIVES

Upon completion of this chapter, *you should be able to*

1. name the steps that a sales associate must follow after writing a contract to ensure a timely closing;

2. list the things that a sales associate should do after a closing;

3. describe the reasons why a licensee might not want to personally order repairs on a property and what steps can be taken to protect the sales associate from liability;

4. list at least four objectives of a preclosing inspection;

5. describe the reasons a real estate sales associate should provide closing documents to the buyer and seller at least one day in advance of a closing;

6. list the proration items paid in advance and those paid in arrears;

7. prorate rent, interest, and property taxes;

8. describe the methods lenders use to set up an escrow account for prepaid taxes, hazard insurance, and private mortgage insurance;

9. calculate prepaid interest for a new loan;

10. calculate the expenses on the closing statement; and

11. prepare and review a HUD-1 Settlement Statement.

# THE CLOSING PROCESS

Once the real estate contract has been signed, the licensee's work has just begun. The parties to a transaction expect their sales associate personally to monitor and coordinate all the details of their closing. While the licensee may believe he has "passed the torch" to the next group of professionals (lenders and closing agents), the buyer and seller continue to look to their sales associate to coordinate all the details of the transaction. A smooth transition from contract to closing enhances the reputations of the firm and the sales associate. This section is intended to help licensees better understand the process and to follow the "road to closing" successfully. (See Figure 12.1.)

Some important steps a licensee may take to reduce problems with title closing include:

- Disclose everything to all parties that will affect their decisions before the buyer and seller sign the contract. Surprises after a contract is signed almost certainly will result in one party wanting to get out of the contract.
- Write the contract carefully and properly explain it to the parties.
- Recommend that buyers and sellers select lenders and title closing agents who are organized professionals able to meet deadlines.
- Tell the loan officer and closing agent what the licensee expects in the way of communication and performance.

**F I G U R E   12.1   ■   The Road to Closing**

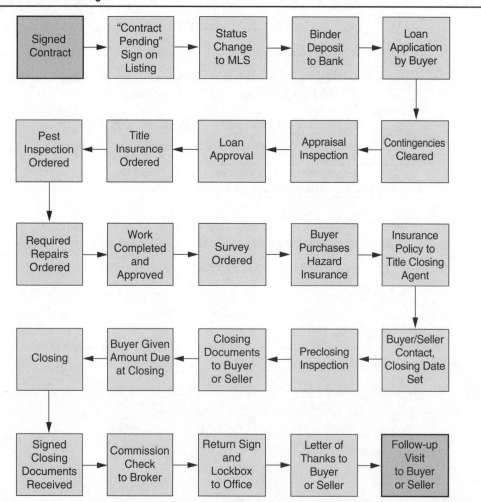

- Prepare a Property Sale Information Sheet similar to the one in the Forms-To-Go Appendix.
- Give the closing agent a copy of the prior title insurance policy, if possible.
- Provide a complete legal description of the property to the closing agent.
- Ask a lender and title agent to communicate by e-mail, speeding the process while also giving written documentation of the transaction.
- Use a checklist of duties, such as the Closing Progress Chart provided in the Forms-To-Go Appendix.
- Ask the closing agent to close the buyer's and seller's sides separately to reduce confusion during the closing.

A sales associate must be familiar with the documents that will be presented to the parties at the closing table. One of the most important documents, the HUD-1 Settlement Statement, relates to the financial side of the transaction. A closing statement is, in effect, the purchase and sales agreement reduced to numbers. The sales associate must understand each number in the statement and be able to explain it clearly to the buyer or seller. This chapter is designed to make the process easier.

## THE SALES INFORMATION SHEET

To organize the work program, the sales associate needs to complete the Property Sale Information Sheet (see the Forms-To-Go Appendix). It provides necessary data about the sale, the cooperating agent, the lender, the title company, and more. This form should be clipped inside the closing file and referred to as necessary when servicing the sale.

### Establishing a Plan of Action

One of the first steps after both buyer and seller sign the contract is to set up a plan for closing. This step is even more important if another sales associate is involved because miscommunication often delays closings and causes unnecessary problems. Organization and attention to detail are key to a successful closing.

## THE CLOSING PROGRESS CHART

The Closing Progress Chart will help the licensee organize the details of the closing. If there is a cooperating licensee, the chart should be a joint effort so that licensees agree about which licensee will handle certain duties and when the tasks should be completed. Once agreement has been reached, each sales associate should place a copy of the chart in the closing file. Additionally, each date scheduled should be transferred to the sales associate's appointment book. As each task is completed, the sales associate should place a check mark in the appropriate row. An "X" in the chart indicates that comments have been made on the back of the form. A discussion of each item follows.

### Preclosing Duties

**"Sold" or "Sale Pending" Sign on Listing.**  Placing a "sold" or "sale pending" sign on the listed property is a function of the listing sales associate. Until recently, Florida Real Estate Commission (FREC) rules prohibited placing a "sold" sign on property until the sale had been closed, but that rule was repealed, and licensees now have their choice of signs. Some sellers prefer a "sold" sign so that prospective buyers are no longer escorted through the property, while others do not want to discourage activity until at least after the buyer's loan approval.

**Notice of "Under Contract" to MLS.** Most multiple-listing services (MLSs) require that all offices be notified of a listed property's status. Failure to change the status to "under contract" can result in agents from other offices appearing at the property with customers or clients. This wastes both the sales associate's and the prospective buyers' time, and reflects poorly on the listing office.

**Binder Deposited in Bank.** A sales associate must give the earnest money deposit to the broker no later than the end of the next business day. FREC rules require that the buyer's good-faith deposit be placed in a bank no later than three business days after receipt of the funds. The broker might deposit the funds immediately or wait until the seller accepts the contract (in no case, however, may the broker wait longer than three days). If a title-closing agent will hold the deposit, the broker must deliver the deposit to the title-closing agent within the same time frames allowed by FREC for depositing the funds in a brokerage account. The broker should get a receipt for the funds.

**Additional Binder Received, if Required.** If the contract requires that the buyer put up additional funds as a good-faith deposit, it is the sales associate's responsibility to ensure that the funds are received and deposited on a timely basis. The buyer's failure to comply with contract requirements is a default. The seller must be notified and the seller's instructions followed.

**Loan Application Made by Buyer.** The FAR contract requires that the buyer make application for the loan by a certain date. The buyer's failure to comply with contract terms is a default, and the seller must be notified.

**Contingencies Cleared in Writing.** The sales associate must ensure that **contingencies** are satisfied as soon as possible. Some normal contingencies include a home inspection, a soil test, a roof inspection, and financing. If a problem arises with one of the contingencies, the sales associate should do everything within her power to correct the problem, and all parties should be made aware of the situation.

**Appraisal.** The appraisal normally is ordered and paid for at the time of loan application. The sales associate wants to be certain that the appraiser selected by the financial institution has complete cooperation, particularly with respect to access to the property. Failure to provide access wastes the appraiser's time and may delay the closing.

**Loan Approval.** The FAR contract requires a loan commitment within a certain number of days from the contract's effective date. The licensee must monitor the lender's progress and provide to the lender without delay any information or documents requested. The lender's failure to provide the commitment within the required time may allow the buyer or the seller to void the contract.

**Title Insurance Ordered.** Many lenders permit the sales associate to select the title-closing agent, provided the company is on the lender's approved list. The seller or buyer also may have a preference in making the decision, based on who will pay for the policy. Many title companies prefer that the agent deliver the contract and financing information even before loan approval is obtained so that the title search can begin. Often little time is available from loan approval to closing, and the companies like a head start. If that is the case, the licensee must verify that the title company agrees to take the risk of a failed closing and that it will not charge a fee if the sale does not close.

The licensee should give the title-closing agent the following items when a title insurance order is placed:

- A signed and dated sales contract
- A previous title insurance policy on the property, if available
- Enough information about the sellers, buyers, property, and lender to process and close the transaction, including:

      a. the sellers' and buyers' marital status

      b. a complete legal description, for example, lot, block, subdivision name, phase or unit, recording information, and county

      c. street address including ZIP code

      d. terms of any purchase-money mortgage the title company must prepare

      e. closing date and information about whether all parties will attend, and

       f. information on commission to broker and commission splits between brokers

**Wood-Destroying Organisms Inspection Ordered.** As soon as possible after loan approval, the wood-destroying organisms (WDO) inspection should be ordered. When it is completed, copies of the report should be delivered to the buyer, lender, and title-closing agent. If treatment or repairs are required, agents working with the buyer and seller should communicate and agree on the details. A sample report that indicates infestation is shown in Figure 12.2. If a structural inspection is required, a licensed contractor should be engaged to report on and estimate repair costs. Normally, the lender requires that treatment and repairs be completed satisfactorily before closing, so parties should act without delay in having the work performed.

**Required Repairs Ordered.** Many contracts require repairs other than those covered by termite damage. The appraisal could show the need for a new roof, or the buyer may have made the contract contingent on the seller's replacing a swimming pool vinyl liner, for example. As soon as loan approval is obtained, the work should be ordered.

**A Note of Caution to Licensees.** A licensee sometimes orders major repair items without the seller's authorization to do so. A failed closing can have adverse financial consequences for the sales associate aside from the loss of commission. While a sales associate might facilitate some of the legwork required in getting estimates, he should not order the work without written approval. The seller or buyer, as appropriate, should contract for the work. This also makes the contractor responsible to the appropriate party if any warranty work is necessary later. A sample form, the Authorization for Sales Associate to order work, is in the Forms-To-Go Appendix.

**Required Repairs Completed and Approved.** When the work has been completed, the appropriate party should inspect the work to be sure that it has been done properly. A licensee who takes on this responsibility may be held responsible if deficiencies are discovered later.

**Survey Ordered.** The lender or the title-closing agent often orders the survey after loan approval. A licensee who orders the survey without written approval may be liable for the fee if the sale does not close. In case of survey problems such as encroachments, the sales associate must act quickly to help clear up the problems.

**Buyer Purchases Hazard Insurance.** The buyer should purchase the insurance policy as soon as possible in the transaction, especially during Florida's hurricane season. If a hurricane or tropical storm develops anywhere within the "box," as shown in Figure 12.3, insurance companies stop writing insurance until the danger has passed. If there are several hurricanes at sea, the delay could be for a week or more, and could cause significant delay of a closing.

**Buyer/Seller Contacted for Closing Appointment.** Soon after loan approval, the title-closing agent should be able to set a closing date and time. The sales associate should coordinate with the buyer and seller in setting a time agreeable to all. All parties should be notified of the date, time, and place of the closing as far in advance as possible.

**Preclosing Inspection.** The buyer should make a **preclosing walk-through inspection.** The inspection is to ensure that

■ the property is ready for occupancy;

■ personal property the seller is required to leave remains on the property;

# FIGURE 12.2 ■ Wood-Destroying Organisms Inspection Report

Section 482.226, Florida Statutes

Licensee name _Mickey's Pest Control_                    License number _4411_

Licensee address _2102 Village Rd._

Inspector _Luke Gast_      Inspection date _1/15/95_      Identification Card No. _____

Requested by _Arthur Cody_                    (address)
                    (name)

Property inspected _180 Bliss St._
                                        (address)

Specific structures inspected _Residence_

Structures on property NOT inspected _None_

Areas of structure(s) NOT inspected _① Attic  ② Wood on or below ground._

Reason NOT inspecting _____

## SCOPE OF INSPECTION

"Wood-destroying organism" means arthropod or plant life which damages and can reinfest seasoned wood in a structure, namely termites, powder-post beetles, old-house borers, and wood decaying fungi.

THIS REPORT IS MADE ON THE BASIS OF WHAT WAS VISIBLE AND ACCESSIBLE AT THE TIME OF THE INSPECTION and is not an opinion covering areas such as, but not necessarily limited to, those that are enclosed or inaccessible, areas concealed by wall coverings, floor coverings, furniture, equipment, stored articles, or any portion of the structure in which inspection would necessitate removing or defacing any part of the structure.

THIS IS NOT A STRUCTURAL DAMAGE REPORT. A wood-destroying organisms inspector is not ordinarily a construction or building trade expert and therefore is not expected to possess any special qualifications which would enable him to attest to the structural soundness of the property. IF VISIBLE DAMAGE OR OTHER EVIDENCE IS NOTED IN THIS REPORT (ITEM NUMBER (3) OF THIS REPORT), FURTHER INVESTIGATION BY QUALIFIED EXPERTS OF THE BUILDING TRADE SHOULD BE MADE TO DETERMINE THE STRUCTURAL SOUNDNESS OF THE PROPERTY.

THIS REPORT SHALL NOT BE CONSTRUED TO CONSTITUTE A GUARANTEE OF THE ABSENCE OF WOOD-DESTROYING ORGANISMS OR DAMAGE OR OTHER EVIDENCE UNLESS THIS REPORT SPECIFICALLY STATES HEREIN THE EXTENT OF SUCH GUARANTEE.

## REPORT OF FINDINGS

(1) Visible evidence of wood-destroying organisms observed: No ☐ Yes ☒ _Sub-termites  ② Carpenter bees_
                                                                    (Common name of organisms)

Locations: _① under back deck in debris_

(2) Live wood-destroying organisms observed: No ☐ Yes ☒ _Siding left and right of sliding glass door._
                                                    (Common name of organisms) _Trim left_

Locations: _and right of sliding glass door.  2x4 under sliding glass door_

(3) Visible damage observed: No ☒ Yes ☐ _____
                                        (Common Name of organisms causing damage)

Locations: _____

(4) Visible evidence of previous treatment was observed: No ☒ Yes ☐ _____

Explain: _____

(5) This company has treated the structure(s) at time of inspection: No ☒ Yes ☐ . If YES: A copy of the contract is attached.

_____                    _____
(Organisms treated)                    (Pesticide used)

(6) This company has treated the structure(s) No ☒ Yes ☐ . If YES: Date of treatment: _____

_____                    _____
(Common name of organisms)                    (Common name of pesticide)

(7) A notice of this inspection ☒ and/or treatment ☐ has been affixed to the structure(s)

_____
(Location of notice(s))

COMMENTS: _____

Neither the licensee nor the inspector has any financial interest in the property inspected or is associated in any way in the transaction with any party to the transaction other than for inspection purposes.

SEND REPORT TO PERSON WHO REQUESTED THIS INSPECTION AND TO:

Signature of Licensee or agent _Luke Gast_      Date _1/15/01_

**F I G U R E  12.3  ■  Area of Tropical Storms and Hurricanes that Cause Insurance Delays**

1 ■ all required repairs and maintenance have been completed; and
2 ■ the property has been maintained in the condition as it existed at the time of
3    contract, ordinary wear and tear excepted.

4 The sales associate should not conduct such an inspection because of the liability involved.
5 When the inspection has been completed to the buyer's satisfaction, the sales associate should
6 ask the buyer to sign a preclosing clearance form such as the one shown in the Forms-To-Go
7 Appendix, Preclosing Walk-Through Inspection Results.

8 **Closing Papers Reviewed with the Buyer and Seller One Day before Closing.** A sales associate
9 should attempt to work with lenders and title-closing agents who understand the sales associ-
10 ate's need to provide the highest level of service to his customers. Those lenders and title
11 agents work diligently to provide all documents for the closing one day in advance. The sales
12 associate must monitor all phases of the closing, including a careful review of the closing state-
13 ments. Many buyers and sellers attend their closings—at which large sums of money are dis-
14 bursed—without having seen any of the documents beforehand. They are expected to sign all
15 documents after a cursory review at the closing table. This is not fair to the participants and
16 can lead to embarrassment for their sales associates. Often a sales associate gets little more than
17 the dollar amount that the buyer must bring in the form of a certified or cashier's check. This is
18 simply not satisfactory to the sales associate who wishes to handle the closing professionally.

19    Upon receiving the documents, the sales associate should arrange an appointment to visit
20 the buyer or seller and deliver copies of all documents that the person will sign. The sales
21 associate should review the closing statement carefully to ensure that all items are correct and
22 should explain each item to the buyer or seller at the appointment. The sales associate work-
23 ing with the buyer should compare the closing statement with the lender's good-faith esti-
24 mate. The sales associate working with the seller should compare the figures to those given to
25 the seller on the approximate Seller's Net Proceeds Form. The closing will go more quickly
26 and pleasantly for the person who has reviewed all documents the evening before.

27    Closing statements are covered later in this chapter.

**Buyer Given Figure for Certified Check for Closing.**  This should be provided to the buyer as soon as possible to allow him time to get a **certified check** for the proper amount from his bank.

**Binder Check Prepared to Take to Closing.**  At least one day before closing, the sales associate should get the binder check from the broker and clip it to the file folder that will be taken to the closing. Also included in the folder will be the contract and other related material, as well as copies of the inspection reports.

## THE CLOSING STATEMENT

Buyers and sellers expect their sales associates to coordinate and monitor every step of the closing process. The last step is the closing itself. A sales associate must be familiar with the documents that will be presented to the parties at the closing table. One of the most important documents, the HUD-1 Settlement Statement, relates to the financial side of the transaction.

A closing statement is, in effect, the purchase and sales agreement reduced to numbers. The sales associate must understand each number in the statement and be able to explain it clearly to the buyer or seller. The material in this chapter is designed to make the process easier.

## PRORATIONS AND PREPAYMENTS

In every closing, property income and expenses should be prorated between the buyer and the seller. Usually, the 365-day method is used for prorations of annual expenses. The annual cost is divided by 365 days to get a daily rate. That rate is then multiplied by the number of days involved to get the amount due. When calculating prorations using the 30-day month method, the annual cost is divided by 12 months, then by 30 days to get the daily rate. That rate is then multiplied by the number of days involved to get the amount due.

Proration calculations should be based on the last day of seller ownership. The day of closing is charged to the buyer, although it is possible that, by negotiation or custom in an area, the day of closing would be charged to the seller.

The most common items prorated on a closing statement are rents and security deposits collected in advance by the seller, property taxes, and interest on assumed mortgages. While insurance can be prorated between the parties, it is not recommended and usually is not allowed by the insurer. The buyer should purchase a new policy, and the seller should cancel the existing policy.

### Prorating Rent

If the property is an income property, the seller should pay the buyer any rent that applies for the period after closing. The first step is to see the problem graphically by drawing a timeline. The rental period is shown, as is the day of closing. The following example illustrates the various aspects of prorations and prepayments. In the example, if the seller had collected the rent in advance, the seller would owe the buyer 16 days of the rent.

Closing date—April 15

Rent collected for April—$450

| Beginning 4/1 | | Closing date 4/15 | | End 4/30 |
|---|---|---|---|---|
| | Seller | | Buyer | |
| | 14 days | | 16 days | |

1   Daily rate—$450 ÷ 30 days = $15
2   Proration—$15 × 16 days = $240

3      ■ Debit the seller, credit the buyer.

---

### RENT PRORATION EXERCISE 12.1

Calculate the following rent prorations:

| Closing Date | Rent Received | Debit | Credit | Amount |
|---|---|---|---|---|
| July 12 | $760 | | | $ |
| November 12 | $900 | | | $ |
| January 6 | $425 | | | $ |

---

4 ## Prorating Property Taxes

5   The buyer normally pays property taxes in arrears, so they would be a debit to the seller and
6   credit to the buyer. If the closing occurs in November or December, it is possible that the
7   seller has paid the tax bill already, resulting in a credit to the seller and a debit to the buyer.

8   Closing date—April 15
9   Property taxes—$2,275

| Beginning 1/1 | | Closing date 4/15 | | End 12/31 |
|---|---|---|---|---|
| | Seller | | Buyer | |
| | 104 days | | 261 days | |

10      Number of days from January 1 through April 15:

| | |
|---|---|
| January | 31 |
| February | 28 |
| March | 31 |
| April | 14 |
| **Total** | **104** |

11   Daily rate—$2,275 ÷ 365 days = $6.23288 per day
12   Proration—$6.23288 × 104 days = $648.22

13      ■ Debit the seller, credit the buyer.

---

### PROPERTY TAX PRORATION EXERCISE 12.2

Do the following property tax prorations:

| Closing Date | Taxes | Debit | Credit | Amount |
|---|---|---|---|---|
| September 12 | $2,567.00 | | | $ |
| November 18 | $4,260.00 (Paid 11/3) | | | $ |
| April 24 | $1,892.56 | | | $ |

## Prorating Interest

Interest is prorated between the parties when a loan is to be assumed or when seller financing is involved. Interest usually is paid in arrears. For example, when the mortgage payment is made on May 1, it pays the principal due on May 1 and the interest for the month of April.

Closing date—April 15
Mortgage balance on April 1 is $67,125.
The interest rate is 8 percent.
Interest for April is $447.50 ($67,125 × .08 ÷ 12 months)
Daily rate—$447.50 ÷ 30 days = $14.91667 per day
Proration—$14.91667 × 14 days = $208.83

■ Debit the seller, credit the buyer.

| Beginning<br>4/1 | Closing date<br>4/15 | End<br>4/30 |
|---|---|---|
| Seller | Buyer | |
| 14 days | 16 days | |

### INTEREST PRORATION EXERCISE 12.3

Do the following interest prorations on these assumed mortgages:

| Closing | Mortgage Bal. | Int. Rate | Debit | Credit | Amount |
|---|---|---|---|---|---|
| 10/12 | $137,500.00 | 9.0% | | | $ |
| 11/18 | 246,532.50 | 8.5% | | | $ |
| 4/24 | 91,892.56 | 10.0% | | | $ |

With seller financing, the first payment usually is set up so that the buyer pays on the first of the month following closing. Because that first payment includes the interest due for the entire previous month, the buyer should receive a credit for the portion of that month the property was still owned by the seller. The proration would be handled the same way.

## Prepayments for New Loan

When an institutional lender makes a new loan, and if the loan-to-value ratio is greater than 80 percent, the lender likely will require that an escrow fund for taxes, hazard insurance, and mortgage insurance be maintained. The borrower must deposit a sum into a lender's escrow account so that adequate funds will be available to make the payments when required. The amount of the specific charges varies with the time of the year at which the loan is closed. Once the escrow account is established, a monthly amount for taxes, insurance, and any required mortgage insurance is added to the monthly principal and interest payment. These funds, placed in a trust account, become the responsibility of the financial institution, which must pay such items when they are due. Some of those prepaid items are discussed below.

## Prepaid Taxes

The lender normally collects taxes by adding the months of the year through closing, then adding two or three more months. For instance, if the closing is in April, the lender takes four months plus another three. In effect, the proration credit for three-plus months that the buyer receives from the seller offsets the effect of the lender's charge.

1      Closing date—April 15

2      Taxes—estimated at $2,275 for the year

3      Monthly taxes—$2,275 ÷ 12 = $189.58

4      The first payment will be on June 1. The lender will escrow seven months, so that when

5 November comes the lender will have sufficient funds to pay the property tax bill.

6                  Monthly taxes $189.58 × 7 months = $1,327.06

7      ■ Debit the buyer for the amount of prepaid taxes.

8      The buyer has received a proration credit of $648.22 from the seller, so the net from the

9 buyer to set up the account is $678.84.

---

### PREPAID TAX CALCULATION EXERCISE 12.4

Assuming the lender wants three extra months, calculate the amount of taxes to be escrowed.

| Closing Date | Taxes for the Year | Prepaid Amount |
|---|---|---|
| January 18 | $2,400.00 | $ |
| July 3 | $4,842.30 | $ |
| September 30 | $1,453.89 | $ |

---

10 ## Prepaid Insurance

11 The buyer must pay the first year's policy in advance, plus two months. For example, if the

12 insurance policy is $1,160, the monthly payment is $96.67 ($1,160 ÷ 12). Often the state-

13 ment shows 14 months prepayment. In other cases, if the buyer has paid the premium outside

14 closing (POC), the statement shows only two months.

15      ■ Debit the buyer for one year plus two months prepaid insurance.

---

### PREPAID INSURANCE CALCULATION EXERCISE 12.5

Calculate the amount of insurance to be escrowed in the following example. The lender wants it paid in advance plus two extra months.

| Closing | Insurance for the Year | Prepaid Amount |
|---|---|---|
| January 18 | $2,400 | $ |
| July 3 | $ 900 | $ |
| September 30 | $2,200 (POC) | $ |

---

16 ## Prepaid Interest

17 Because the first payment covers the interest for the previous month, interest is collected at

18 closing for the days remaining in the closing month. There are two methods of calculating the

19 daily rate of interest. One is to divide the annual interest by 12 months, then get a daily figure

20 by dividing the actual number of days in the month into the monthly figure. This method is

21 used for assumed loans. The other method (365-day method) divides the annual interest by

22 365 days to get the daily rate (most title-closing agents and lenders use this method). This

23 book uses the 365-day method.

1   Closing date—April 15
2   First payment on the mortgage—June 1

3   The first payment covers May interest. Interest must be collected on the day of closing
4   from April 15 through April 30 (16 days).

| Closing date 4/15 | | 1st Payment 6/1 |
|---|---|---|
| 4/15–4/30 to be prepaid | 1st pmt. pays interest for May | |

5   $112,500 × .09 = $10,125 per year
6   $10,125 per year ÷ 365 days per year = $27.73973 per day
7   $27.73973 per day × 16 days = $443.84

8   ■  Debit the buyer $443.84 for prepaid interest.

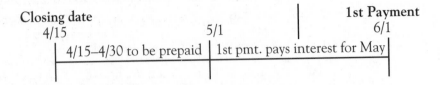

**PREPAID INTEREST CALCULATION EXERCISE 12.6**

Calculate the interest prepayment for the new loans as follows:

| Closing Date | Mortgage Loan Amount | Interest Rate | Prepaid Amount |
|---|---|---|---|
| September 12 | $245,000 | 8.875% | $ |
| January 17 | $ 92,500 | 8.75% | $ |
| December 29 | $127,000 | 9.0% | $ |

## 9  Prepaid Mortgage Insurance

10   If mortgage insurance is required as part of an FHA or conventional mortgage loan, the bor-
11   rower is charged for the coverage required.

12   The FHA requires homebuyers to pay two types of **mortgage insurance premiums**
13   **(MIPs)**:

14   1.  Up-front MIP (UFMIP), which is a percentage of the mortgage amount
15   2.  Annual premium, which is calculated on the unpaid principal balance

16   The VA does not charge for guaranteeing a loan; however, it imposes a **funding fee** based on
17   the mortgage amount. This funding fee may be included as part of the amount borrowed or
18   paid in one lump sum at closing. A lender also may require an amount in cash adequate to
19   open an escrow account, plus 1 percent of the loan amount as a maximum placement fee.
20   Under VA loan rules, the closing costs and placement fees cannot be included in the loan
21   amount.

22   Conventional lenders require **private mortgage insurance (PMI)** when a loan-to-value
23   (LTV) ratio is more than 80 percent. Premiums fall into two general categories. In the first
24   case, a single premium covers a lender's risk for a ten-year period. In the second case, a
25   lender imposes a lower initial fee on the borrower and charges an insurance premium each
26   year after that until the unpaid principal is reduced to a designated amount, normally
27   80 percent of appraised value. The first plan's one-time, single-premium charge or the sec-
28   ond plan's lower initial cost is payable by the borrower at the time the loan closes. It should
29   be noted that a PMI rate card must be used because of the different types of loans available
30   and the different coverages required. The rates given in the following example do *not* apply
31   to all loan types.

Assume a $112,500 (90 percent LTV) conventional mortgage has a first-year factor of 0.8 percent, with an annual factor in years two through ten of 0.34 percent. The up-front PMI would be $900 ($112,500 × 0.008), with a monthly PMI of $31.87 ($112,500 × 0.0034 ÷ 12).

Probably the best alternative is *not* to make a large up-front payment but instead make a higher monthly payment. In case of an early loan payoff, the premium is not refunded. The same PMI company has a factor of 0.54 percent for the monthly plan on this loan. The monthly payment using the alternate method would be $50.625 ($112,500 × 0.0054 ÷ 12).

■  Debit the buyer $101.24 ($50.62 × 2 months) for prepaid mortgage insurance.

### PREPAID PMI EXERCISE 12.7

Calculate the required prepayment for PMI on the following loans:

| Mortgage Amount | Factor/Year | 2 Months Prepaid |
|---|---|---|
| $350,000 | 0.54% | $ |
| $125,000 | 0.62% | $ |
| $ 90,000 | 0.73% | $ |

## DOCUMENTARY STAMP TAXES AND INTANGIBLE TAXES

**Documentary stamp taxes** are collected on the deed and the note. The seller normally pays for stamps on the deed, and the buyer pays for note stamps. The deed stamps are based on the sales price and are $.070 per $100 or fraction thereof. For example, if a property sells for $140,000, the documentary stamp taxes would be calculated as follows:

$$\$140,000 \div \$100 = 1,400 \text{ increments}$$
$$1,400 \times \$0.70 = \$980$$

### DEED STAMPS CALCULATION EXERCISE 12.8

Calculate the documentary stamp taxes on the deed for the following sales prices:

| Sales Price | Document Stamp Amount |
|---|---|
| $325,000 | $ |
| $127,415 | $ |
| $ 93,000 | $ |

Documentary stamp taxes on the new note are based on the amount of the new or the assumed mortgage and are $0.35 per $100 or fraction thereof. No stamps are charged on notes taken subject to the mortgage because the buyer has not assumed any of the debt obligations. For example, if the note amount on a new mortgage were $112,500, the documentary stamp tax would be calculated on the note amount as follows:

$$\$112,500 \div \$100 = 1,125 \text{ increments}$$
$$1,125 \times \$0.35 = \$393.75$$

**Intangible tax** on the new mortgage is calculated by multiplying the mortgage amount by 0.002. No tax is charged on existing recorded mortgages. The buyer normally pays this charge. For example, the intangible taxes on a new mortgage of $112,500 would be calculated as follows:

$$\$112,500 \times 0.002 = \$225. \text{ There is no rounding.}$$

## NOTE STAMPS AND INTANGIBLE TAX CALCULATION EXERCISE 12.9

Calculate the documentary stamp taxes on the following note amounts:   Intangible?

| Note Amount | Documentary Stamp Amount | Interest Tax Amount |
|---|---|---|
| $125,000 | $ | $ |
| $157,415 | $ | $ |
| $ 53,000 | $ | $ |

# RESPA SETTLEMENT STATEMENT (HUD-1)

The HUD-1 Settlement Statement provides an itemized listing of the funds payable at closing (See Figure 12.4). Closing agents must prepare the HUD-1 for the parties in a federally related mortgage loan. The HUD-1 is now used in nearly all residential closings, whether or not the form is legally required. Each item in the statement is assigned a separate number within a standardized numbering system. The totals at the bottom of page 1 of the HUD-1 statement show the seller's net proceeds and the amount due from the buyer at closing. A blank HUD-1 statement is included in the Forms-To-Go Appendix.

The HUD-1 statement has two pages. Page 1 shows the parties, the property description, the lender, the settlement agent, and a summary of the borrower's and seller's transactions. Page 2 (Section L) itemizes the settlement charges for each party, such as the broker's commission, loan closing costs, prepaid items, escrow account setup, title charges, and recording charges. The totals for each party on page 2 are transferred to the summary page on the front. When explaining the statement to the buyer and seller, the closing agents start at page 2, then go to page 1. A discussion of the lines on the statement follows.

## Page 2

**700. Sales/Broker's Commission.** This section shows the total dollar amount of sales commission, usually paid by the seller. If more than one broker is involved, the split is shown on the next lines.

**701–702. Division of Commission.** Cooperating brokers normally split commissions. This is only a disclosure item, and no actual charge is shown. The charge is listed on line 703.

**703. Commission Paid at Settlement.** This is the total commission to be paid; it is charged to the buyer, the seller, or both.

**800. Items Payable in Connection with Loan.** In this section, the fees the lender charges to process, approve, and make the mortgage loan are itemized.

**801. Loan Origination.** The lender charges this fee for processing. It is often expressed as a percentage of the loan and varies among lenders and from locality to locality. Generally, the borrower pays the loan origination fee.

**802. Loan Discount.** The loan discount is a one-time charge used to adjust the yield on the loan to what market conditions demand. It usually is expressed as points. Each point equals 1 percent of the mortgage amount. For example, if a lender charges two points on a $100,000 loan, this amounts to a fee of $2,000. On a 30-year loan, this fee increases the lender's yield by approximately one-fourth of 1 percent.

**803. Appraisal Fee.** This fee is paid to a state-certified appraiser who prepares an estimate of value of the property that will be mortgaged. The borrower usually pays the appraisal fee, but either party may pay it as agreed in the sales contract.

**F I G U R E  12.4  ■  HUD-1 Settlement Statement**

## A. Settlement Statement

**B. Type of Loan**

U.S. Department of Housing
and Urban Development

OMB No. 2502-0265

| 1. ☐FHA | 2. ☐FmHA | 3. ☐Conv. Unins. | 6. File Number | 7. Loan Number | 8. Mortgage Insurance Case Number |
|---|---|---|---|---|---|
| 4. ☐VA | 5. ☒Conv. Ins. | | EDODONNELL8LBM | 12345678 | |

**C. Note:** This form is furnished to give you a statement of actual settlement costs. Amounts paid to and by the settlement agent are shown. Items marked "(p.o.c.)" were paid outside the closing; they are shown here for information purposes and are not included in the totals. WARNING: It is a crime to knowingly make false statements to the United States on this or any other similar form. Penalties upon conviction can include a fine and imprisonment. For details see: Title 18 U. S. Code Section 1001 and Section 1010.

**D. NAME OF BORROWER:**  KYLE BYERS and KARI BYERS
   **ADDRESS:**  1460 LIME DRIVE, TALLAHASSEE, FLORIDA 32301

**E. NAME OF SELLER:**  JOHN SELLARS and SUSAN SELLARS
   **ADDRESS:**

**F. NAME OF LENDER:**  FIRST SOUTH BANK, A FEDERAL SAVINGS BANK
   **ADDRESS:**  3020 HARTLEY ROAD, SUITE 330, JACKSONVILLE, FLORIDA 32257

**G. PROPERTY ADDRESS:**  1460 LIME DRIVE, TALLAHASSEE, FLORIDA 32301
   LOT 8, ORANGE PARK SUBDIVISION

**H. SETTLEMENT AGENT:**  SMITH, JONES AND ADAMS, P.A.
   **PLACE OF SETTLEMENT:**  7889 Thomasville Rd, Tallahassee, Fl. 32308

**I. SETTLEMENT DATE:**  05/15/05

| J. SUMMARY OF BORROWER'S TRANSACTION: | | K. SUMMARY OF SELLER'S TRANSACTION: | |
|---|---|---|---|
| **100. GROSS AMOUNT DUE FROM BORROWER** | | **400. GROSS AMOUNT DUE TO SELLER:** | |
| 101. Contract sales price | 120,000.00 | 401. Contract sales price | 120,000.00 |
| 102. Personal Property | | 402. Personal Property | |
| 103. Settlement charges to borrower (line 1400) | 7,313.76 | 403. | |
| 104. | | 404. | |
| 105. | | 405. | |
| **Adjustments for items paid by seller in advance** | | **Adjustments for items paid by seller in advance** | |
| 106. City/town taxes | | 406. City/town taxes | |
| 107. County taxes  05/15/05 to 12/31/05 | 1,329.04 | 407. County taxes  05/15/05 to 12/31/05 | 1,329.04 |
| 108. Assessments | | 408. Assessments | |
| 109. | | 409. | |
| 110. | | 410. | |
| 111. | | 411. | |
| 112. | | 412. | |
| **120. GROSS AMOUNT DUE FROM BORROWER** | 128,642.80 | **420. GROSS AMOUNT DUE TO SELLER:** | 121,329.04 |
| **200. AMOUNTS PAID BY OR ON BEHALF OF BORROWER** | | **500. REDUCTIONS IN AMOUNT DUE TO SELLER** | |
| 201. Deposit or earnest money | 4,000.00 | 501. Excess Deposit (see instructions) | |
| 202. Principal Amount of new loans | 108,000.00 | 502. Settlement charges to seller (line 1400) | 9,315.50 |
| 203. Existing loan(s) taken subject to | | 503. Existing loan(s) taken subject to | |
| 204. | | 504. Payoff of First Mortgage Loan | 45,452.65 |
| | | BARNETT BANK | |
| 205. | | 505. Payoff of Second Mortgage Loan | |
| 206. | | 506. | |
| 207. | | 507. | |
| 208. | | 508. | |
| 209. | | 509. | |
| **Adjustments for items unpaid by seller** | | **Adjustments for items unpaid by seller** | |
| 210. City/town taxes | | 510. City/town taxes | |
| 211. County taxes | | 511. County taxes | |
| 212. Assessments | | 512. Assessments | |
| 213. | | 513. | |
| 214. | | 514. | |
| 215. | | 515. | |
| 216. | | 516. | |
| 217. | | 517. | |
| 218. | | 518. | |
| 219. | | 519. | |
| **220. TOTAL PAID BY/FOR BORROWER** | 112,000.00 | **520. TOTAL REDUCTION AMOUNT DUE SELLER** | 54,768.15 |
| **300. CASH AT SETTLEMENT FROM OR TO BORROWER** | | **600. CASH AT SETTLEMENT TO OR FROM SELLER** | |
| 301. Gross amount due from borrower (line 120) | 128,642.80 | 601. Gross amount due to seller (line 420) | 121,329.04 |
| 302. Less amounts paid by/for borrower (line 220) | 112,000.00 | 602. Less reduction amount due seller (line 520) | 54,768.15 |
| **303. CASH FROM BORROWER** | 16,642.80 | **603. CASH TO SELLER** | 66,560.89 |

**F I G U R E   12.4  ■  HUD-1 Settlement Statement (continued)**

U.S. DEPARTMENT OF HOUSING AND URBAN DEVELOPMENT
**SETTLEMENT STATEMENT**

File Number: EDODONNELL8
PAGE 2

| | PAID FROM BORROWER'S FUNDS AT SETTLEMENT | PAID FROM SELLER'S FUNDS AT SETTLEMENT |
|---|---|---|
| **L.   SETTLEMENT CHARGES** | | |
| 700. **TOTAL SALES/BROKER'S COMMISSION** based on price $ 120,000.00 @ 7.000 = 8,400.00 | | |
| Division of commission (line 700) as follows: | | |
| 701. $      8,400.00   to  BIG BEND REALTY | | |
| 702. $            to | | 8,400.00 |
| 703. Commission paid at Settlement | | |
| 800. **ITEMS PAYABLE IN CONNECTION WITH LOAN** | | |
| 801. Loan Origination Fee     1.000 % FIRST SOUTH BANK | 1,200.00 | |
| 802. Loan Discount     1.000 % FIRST SOUTH BANK | 1,200.00 | |
| 803. Appraisal Fee     to TALLAHASSEE APPRAISAL COMPANY     (P.O.C.) 300.00 Buyer | | |
| 804. Credit Report     to CREDCO | 55.00 | |
| 805. Lender's Inspection Fee | | |
| 806. Mortgage Application Fee | | |
| 807. Assumption Fee | | |
| 808. AMORITIZATION SCHEDULE     to FIRST SOUTH BANK | 25.00 | |
| 809. | | |
| 810. | | |
| 811. | | |
| 900. **ITEMS REQUIRED BY LENDER TO BE PAID IN ADVANCE** | | |
| 901. Interest From     05/15/05 to 06/01/05     @$   22.1917 /day     17 Days | 377.26 | |
| 902. Mortgage Insurance Premium for     to | | |
| 903. Hazard Insurance Premium for     12     to STATE FARM | 840.00 | |
| 904. | | |
| 905. | | |
| 1000. **RESERVES DEPOSITED WITH LENDER FOR** | | |
| 1001. Hazard Insurance     2 mo. @ $    70.00 /mo | 140.00 | |
| 1002. Mortgage Insurance     2 mo. @ $    45.00 /mo | 90.00 | |
| 1003. City Property Taxes     mo. @ $    /mo | | |
| 1004. County Property Taxes     8 mo. @ $    175.00 /mo | 1,400.00 | |
| 1005. Annual Assessments     mo. @ $    /mo | | |
| 1009. Aggregate Analysis Adjustment | | |
| 1100. **TITLE CHARGES** | | |
| 1101. Settlement or closing fee     to SMITH, JONES AND ADAMS, P.A. | 100.00 | |
| 1102. Abstract or title search     to SMITH, JONES AND ADAMS, P.A. | 100.00 | |
| 1103. Title examination     to SMITH, JONES AND ADAMS, P.A. | 75.00 | |
| 1104. Title insurance binder | | |
| 1105. Document Preparation | | |
| 1106. Notary Fees | | |
| 1107. Attorney's fees | | |
| (includes above items No:                    ) | | |
| 1108. Title Insurance     to SMITH, JONES AND ADAMS, P.A. | 700.00 | |
| (includes above items No:                    ) | | |
| 1109. Lender's Coverage $     108,000.00   - 25.00 | | |
| 1110. Owner's Coverage $     120,000.00   - 675.00 | | |
| 1111. FL 9     to SMITH, JONES AND ADAMS, P.A. | 70.00 | |
| 1112. ALTA 8.1     to SMITH, JONES AND ADAMS, P.A. | 25.00 | |
| 1113. COURIER FEE     to SMITH, JONES AND ADAMS, P.A. | 20.00 | 20.00 |
| 1200. **GOVERNMENT RECORDING AND TRANSFER CHARGES** | | |
| 1201. Recording Fees     Deed $ 10.50   ; Mortgage $ 42.00   ; Release $ 10.50 | 52.50 | 10.50 |
| 1202. City/County tax/stamps     Deed $ 840.00   ; Mortgage $ 378.00 | 378.00 | 840.00 |
| 1203. State Tax/stamps     Deed $   ; Mortgage $ 216.00 | 216.00 | |
| 1204. | | |
| 1205. | | |
| 1300. **ADDITIONAL SETTLEMENT CHARGES** | | |
| 1301. Survey     to ALL CORNERS SURVEYOR | 250.00 | |
| 1302. Pest Inspection     to NO REQUIRED PER CONTRACT AND LENDER | | |
| 1303. MISC REPAIRS     to FIX IT ALL, INC. | | 245.00 |
| 1304. | | |
| 1305. | | |
| 1306. | | |
| 1307. | | |
| 1308. | | |
| 1400. **TOTAL SETTLEMENT CHARGES**     (enter on lines 103, Section J and 502, Section K) | 7,313.76 | 9,515.50 |

**804. Credit Report Fee.** This fee covers the cost of the credit report, which shows the lender the borrower's attitude and willingness to pay debt on time.

**805. Lender's Inspection Fee.** This charge covers inspections, often of newly constructed housing, made by personnel of the lending institution or an outside inspector.

**806. Mortgage Insurance Application Fee.** This fee covers processing of the application for private mortgage insurance, which may be required on certain loans.

**807. Assumption Fee.** The assumption fee is charged for processing when the buyer takes over the seller's mortgage obligations.

**900. Items Required by Lender to be Paid in Advance.** This section lists prepaid items such as interest, mortgage insurance premium, and hazard insurance premium at the time of settlement.

**901. Interest.** Lenders usually require that borrowers pay at settlement the interest on the mortgage from the date of closing to the beginning of the period covered by the first monthly payment. For example, if a closing takes place on August 12 and the first regular monthly payment is due October 1, the lender collects enough for interest from August 12 through August 31. September's interest is included in the October 1 payment.

**902. Mortgage Insurance Premium.** Mortgage insurance protects the lender from loss if the borrower defaults. The premium may cover a specific number of months, a year in advance or the total amount. This type of insurance should not be confused with mortgage life, credit life, or disability insurance designed to pay off a mortgage in case of the borrower's disability or death.

**903. Hazard Insurance Premium.** This prepayment is for insurance protection against loss due to fire, windstorm, and natural hazards. Lenders usually require payment of the first year's premium at closing.

**904. Flood Insurance Premium.** If the property is located within a flood hazard area identified by Federal Emergency Management Agency (FEMA), the borrower may be required to carry flood insurance. The first year's premium must be paid in advance.

**1000. Reserves Deposited with Lenders.** Lenders normally require *reserves* if the loan-to-value ratio is more than 80 percent. Reserves are escrow accounts the lender holds to ensure future payment for such recurring costs as real estate taxes, mortgage insurance, and hazard insurance. An initial amount for each of these items is collected to start the reserve account. Then part of each monthly payment is added to the reserve account.

**1001. Hazard Insurance.** The lender determines how much money must be placed in the reserve to pay the next insurance premium when due. Normally, two months' premiums are collected.

**1002. Mortgage Insurance.** The lender may require that part of the total annual premium be placed in the reserve account at settlement. Normally, two months' premiums are collected.

**1003–1004. City/County Property Taxes.** The lender may require a regular monthly payment to the reserve account for property taxes. The lender pays the taxes in November, so a full year's taxes should be available in October. The lender collects an amount each month equal to one-twelfth of the estimated taxes.

**1005. Annual Assessments.** This reserve item covers assessments that may be imposed by subdivisions or municipalities for special improvements (such as sidewalks, sewers, or paving) or fees (such as homeowners' association fees).

**1009. Aggregate Analysis Adjustment.** This adjustment ensures that the lender has set up enough, but not too much, in reserves.

**1100. Title Charges.** Title charges may cover a variety of services the closing agent performs.

**1101. Settlement or Closing Fee.** The person who has agreed to pay for title insurance normally pays this fee to the closing agent.

**1102–1104. Abstract of Title Search, Title Examination, Title Insurance Binder.** These charges cover the costs of the search and examination of the public records to learn whether the seller can convey clear title to the property.

**1105. Document Preparation.** This document fee covers preparation of final legal papers, such as a mortgage, deed of trust, note, or deed.

**1106. Notary Fee.** If the notary charges for affixing her name and seal to various documents authenticating the parties' execution of these documents, the fee is shown here.

**1107. Attorney's Fees.** The buyer and seller are advised to retain attorneys to check the various documents and to represent them at all stages of the transaction, including closing. If this service is not required and is paid for outside closing, the person conducting settlement is not obligated to record the fee on the settlement form.

**1108. Title Insurance.** The total cost of the owner's and lender's title insurance is shown here. The borrower may pay all, a part, or none of this cost, depending on the terms of the sales contract or local custom.

**1109. Lender's Title Insurance.** A one-time premium may be charged at closing for a lender's title policy that protects the lender against loss due to problems or defects concerning the title. The insurance usually is written for the amount of the mortgage loan and covers losses due to defects or problems not identified by title search and examination.

**1110. Owner's Title Insurance.** This charge protects the buyer against losses due to title defects.

**1200. Government Recording and Transfer Charges.** The seller usually pays the documentary stamp taxes on the deed. The borrower usually pays the recording fees for the new deed and mortgage (line 1201) and the documentary stamp and intangible taxes on the note and mortgage.

**1300. Additional Settlement Charges.**

**1301. Survey.** Usually, the borrower pays the surveyor's fee, but sometimes the seller pays it, if agreed to in the contract.

**1302. Pest and Other Inspections.** This fee covers wood-destroying organisms inspections. Fees for other inspections, such as for structural soundness, are entered on line 1303.

**1400. Total Settlement Charges.** All the fees in the borrower's column entitled "Paid from Borrower's Funds at Settlement" are totaled here and transferred to line 103 of Section J, "Settlement charges to borrower," in the "Summary of Borrower's Transaction" on page 1 of the HUD-1 settlement statement. All the settlement fees the seller pays are transferred to line 502 of Section K, "Summary of Seller's Transaction," on page 1 of the HUD-1.

## Page 1

Section J summarizes the borrower's transaction.

**100. Gross Amount Due from Borrower.**

**101. Contract Sales Price.** This ultimate closing cost is taken directly from the sales contract.

**102. Personal Property.** The total price of items of personal property being sold to the buyer is entered on this line.

**103. Settlement Charges to Borrower.** This total closing cost is carried forward from page 2.

**107. County Taxes.** This line is used only if the seller paid the annual taxes before closing.

**108. Assessments.** This line is used if a seller prepaid a county or homeowners' association assessment.

**120. Gross Amounts Due from Borrower.** This is a subtotal of the above items.

**200. Amounts Paid by or in Behalf of Borrower.**

**201. Deposit or Earnest Money.** The buyer gets a credit for the binder deposit given at the time the contract was signed.

**202. Principal Amount of New Loan.** The buyer is credited with the loan amount, which the lender gives to the closing agent.

**203. Existing Loan(s) Taken Subject To.** If the buyer assumes or buys subject to a mortgage, the current principal balance is entered on this line.

**211. County Taxes.** The amount due from the borrower is reduced by the amount of the seller's share of annual ad valorem taxes.

**212. Assessments.** This line is used for amounts due to the buyer for assessments the seller has not paid.

**220. Total Paid by/for Borrower.** This is the subtotal of lines 200 through 218.

**300. Cash at Settlement to/from Borrower.** This section summarizes the transaction.

**301. Gross Amount Due from Borrower (line 120).**

**302. Less Amounts Paid by/for Borrower (line 220).**

**303. Cash ❏ from ❏ to Borrower.** This is the grand total of the borrower's transaction.

Section K summarizes the seller's transaction. Lines 400 through 420 are the seller's credits, which increase the amount due to the seller; lines 500 through 520 reduce the amount due to the seller; and lines 600 through 602 show the check due to the seller at closing.

**400. Gross Amount Due to Seller.**

**401. Contract Sales Price.** The sum is taken directly from the sales contract.

**402. Personal Property.** The total price of items of personal property being sold to the buyer is entered on this line.

**407. County Taxes.** This line would be used only in the case where the seller had paid the annual taxes before closing.

**408. Assessments.** This line would be used if a seller had prepaid a county or homeowners' association assessment.

**420. Gross Amount Due to Seller.** This is a subtotal of the above items.

**500. Reductions in Amount Due to Seller.**

**501. Excess Deposit.** If the buyer pays the earnest money deposit directly to the seller, not to the broker or title-closing agent, it is shown on this line.

**502. Settlement Charges to Seller.** This is the seller's total closing costs carried forward from page 2.

**503. Existing Loan(s) Taken Subject To.** If the buyer assumes or buys subject to a mortgage, the current principal balance is entered on this line.

**504–505. Payoff of Mortgage Loan.** This is the balance due on the seller's mortgage that the closing agent must pay off.

**511. County Taxes.** The amount due from the borrower is reduced by the amount of the seller's share of annual ad valorem taxes.

**512. Assessments.** This line is used for amounts due to the buyer for assessments the seller has not paid.

**520. Total Reductions in Amount Due Seller.** This is the subtotal of lines 500 through 519.

**600. Cash at Settlement to/from Seller.** This section summarizes the transaction.

**601. Gross Amount Due to Seller (Line 420).**

**602. Less Reductions in Amount Due Seller (Line 520).**

**603. Cash ❑ to ❑ from Seller.** This is the grand total of the seller's transaction.

## CLOSING STATEMENT EXAMPLE

Anita Wilson purchases a home from Wendy Stratton. Closing date is April 15, with the day of closing charged to the buyer. The price of the property is $125,000, and Anita is financing the purchase with a new 7.5 percent loan for 90 percent of the purchase price. She gives the broker a $5,000 binder check. The seller will pay off the existing first mortgage. The payoff amount, including interest, is $74,298.60. The seller has agreed to give the buyer a $2,000 allowance for new carpeting. The lender has approved the allowance. Annual property tax, estimated at $1,750, is the only item to be prorated.

The lender requires that a hazard insurance policy be purchased and the premium paid for one year ($545). An escrow account is collected at closing for three months of taxes, two months of hazard insurance, and two months of private mortgage insurance. The first payment on the mortgage is due on June 1.

The buyer paid for the appraisal ($300) at the time of loan application. Other expenses to be entered on each line item are discussed below.

The seller pays a commission of 7 percent, an attorney's fee of $225, documentary stamp taxes on the deed, and other items as discussed below.

Based on the following information, complete the blank HUD-1 statement in the Forms-To-Go Appendix. Start on page 2 with the buyer's side.

### Page 2

PAID FROM BORROWER'S FUNDS AT SETTLEMENT

ITEMS PAYABLE IN CONNECTION WITH LOAN

| | | | |
|---|---|---|---|
| 801 | Origination fee—1% of the loan amount | | ? |
| | **(Loan amount times the percentage: $112,500 × 0.01 = $?)** | | |
| 802 | Loan discount—1 point | | ? |
| | **(Loan amount times points: $112,500 × 0.01 = $?)** | | |
| 803 | Appraisal fee POC* $300.00 buyer | | |
| 804 | Credit report fee | | $ 55.00 |

| 807 | Tax service fee | $ 59.00 |
| 808 | Underwriting fee | $100.00 |
| 809 | Document preparation fee | $ 75.00 |
| 810 | Courier fee | $ 13.00 |

*POC on the statement means "paid outside closing."

## ITEMS REQUIRED BY LENDER TO BE PAID IN ADVANCE

901     Interest from 4/15/ to 4/30/     ?

**(Loan amount times interest rate divided by 365 times number of days remaining in month of closing, counting the day of closing:**

**$112,500 × 0.075 = $8,437.48**
**$8,437.48 ÷ 365 = $23.1164 per day:**
**$23.1164 × 16 days = $369.86)**

903     Hazard insurance premium for 12 months to State Farm     $ 545.00

## RESERVES DEPOSITED WITH LENDER

1001     Hazard insurance 2 mo. @ $?/mo     ?

**(Annual insurance divided by 12 months times number of months required by lender: $545.00 ÷ 12 = $? per month; $? × 2 months = $?)**

1002     Mortgage Insurance 2 months @ $?/mo.     ?

**($300 per yr. divided by 12 months = $? per month:**
**$? per month × 2 months = $50.00)**

1004     County property taxes ($1,750) 7 mo. @ $?/mo.     $1,020.81

**(Annual taxes divided by 12 months times number of month's reserve required by lender: $1,750.00 ÷ 12 = $? per month; $? × 7 months = $?)**

## TITLE CHARGES

| 1101 | Settlement or closing fee to Jones & Smith law firm | $  100.00 |
| 1102 | Abstract or title search to Jones & Smith law firm | $  100.00 |
| 1103 | Title examination to Jones & Smith law firm | $   75.00 |
| 1107 | Attorney's fee to Jones & Smith law firm | $  300.00 |
| 1108 | Title insurance to Jones & Smith law firm | $  725.00 |
| 1111 | Florida 9 endorsement to Jones & Smith law firm | $   72.50 |
| 1112 | ALTA 8.1 endorsement to Jones & Smith law firm | $   25.00 |

## GOVERNMENT RECORDING AND TRANSFER CHARGES

| 1201 | Recording fee—deed $6.00; mortgage $60.00 | $ 66.00 |
|------|-------------------------------------------|---------|
| 1202 | Documentary stamp tax on note | ? |
| | **(Loan amount divided by 100, round up to next whole number, multiply by $0.35)** | |
| 1203 | Intangible taxes on mortgage | $ 225.00 |
| | **(Loan amount times 0.002)** | |
| 1301 | Survey to All Corners Surveyor | $ 250.00 |
| 1302 | Pest inspection to All Pest Control | $ 50.00 |
| 1400 | Total settlement charges (total, then enter on page one, line 103) | ? |

## PAID FROM SELLER'S FUNDS AT SETTLEMENT

| 700, 701 | Commission paid to Tillie Evans Realty | ? |
|----------|----------------------------------------|---|
| 703 | **(Sales price times commission rate of 7%)** | |
| 1107 | Attorney's fees to Jones & Smith law firm | ? |
| 1113 | Courier fee for mortgage payoff to Jones & Smith law firm | $ 20.00 |
| 1201 | Satisfaction (release) recording fee | $ 6.00 |
| 1202 | Documentary stamp tax on deed | $ 875.00 |
| | **(Sales price divided by 100, rounded to next higher whole number, times $0.70)** | |
| 1400 | Total settlement charges (total, then enter on page one, line 502) | ? |

## Page 1

## SUMMARY OF BORROWER'S TRANSACTION

| 101 | Purchase price | 125,000.00 |
|-----|----------------|------------|
| 103 | Settlement charges to borrower (from page two, line 1400) | ? |
| 120 | Gross amount due from borrower | ? |
| 201 | Deposit or earnest money | 5,000.00 |
| 202 | Principal amount of new loans | 112,500.00 |
| | **(Price times loan-to-value ratio: $125,000 × 0.90 = $112,500)** | |
| 207 | Carpet allowance to buyer | 2,000.00 |
| 211, 511 | Property taxes for the year (paid in arrears)—$1,750 | ? |
| | **(Annual taxes divided by 365 days times number of seller days)** | |
| 220 | TOTAL PAID BY/FOR BORROWER **(Sum of lines 201–219)** | ? |
| 301 | GROSS AMOUNT DUE FROM BORROWER (Line 120) | ? |

| 302 | LESS AMOUNTS PAID BY/FOR BORROWER (Line 220) | ? |
|---|---|---|
| 303 | CASH FROM BORROWER | ? |

SUMMARY OF SELLER'S TRANSACTION

| 401 | Purchase price | $125,000.00 |
|---|---|---|
| 420 | GROSS AMOUNT DUE TO SELLER | ? |
| 502 | Settlement charges to seller (from page 2, line 1400) | ? |
| 504 | Payoff of existing first mortgage (given) | $ 74,298.60 |
| 507 | Carpet allowance to buyer | $ 2,000.00 |
| 511 | Property taxes for the year (paid in arrears)—$1,750 | ? |
| | **(See calculation for line 211)** | |
| **TOTAL REDUCTION AMOUNT DUE SELLER (Sum of lines 501–519)** | | ? |
| **601** | **GROSS AMOUNT DUE TO SELLER (Line 420)** | ? |
| **602** | **LESS REDUCTION AMOUNT DUE SELLER (Line 520)** | ? |
| **603** | **CASH TO SELLER** | ? |

## AT THE CLOSING TABLE

The closing normally includes the buyers, the sellers, and their respective licensees, if any. Sometimes attorneys of the parties attend, and occasionally a lender's representative. The title-closing agent conducts the closing.

### Separate Closings

Many licensees prefer that the buyers and sellers close separately, rather than at the same closing table. This reduces confusion and allows the title-closing agent to focus completely on each party as they close. It is appropriate if the parties have had a dispute over some issue. Sometimes separate closings occur when there is a mail-away closing package, or when the buyers or sellers live out of town.

### Closing Disputes

The title closer is not an advocate for any of the parties. It is the title closer's job to close the transaction based on the contract and the lender's closing instructions. If there is a problem between the buyer and the lender, the closer gets them together on the phone. If there is a dispute between the buyer and the seller, the closer will often step out of the room until the dispute is settled and the parties are ready to close.

## Truth-in-Lending Disclosure

If there is an institutional loan, the first document to be reviewed must be the Truth-in-Lending (TIL) disclosure. If the buyers were informed by the lender or the licensee when they applied for the loan that the annual percentage rate (APR) shown on the TIL would be higher than the interest rate on their note, this will not be a problem. If they were not informed, however, some buyers, upon seeing a 7.875 percent APR on the disclosure form say, "Wait a minute! I was supposed to be getting a 7½ percent loan!" The closer must explain that origination fees and discount points are included to calculate the APR, but the loan rate remains the same.

## Loan Application

Usually the lender will want a typed loan application signed at closing, verifying the information given to the lender at the time of application.

## Note

The closer presents the note for the buyer's signature. The note shows the principal balance, number of payments, and the dates and the amount of the payments. The amount will be for principal and interest only. The first payment date will normally be the first day of the second month after closing. The note is not witnessed or notarized. If a signature appears on the face of the note along with the borrower's signature, that person becomes a cosigner on the note.

## Mortgage

The mortgage is the security for the note. It is the document that may require that the borrower pay 1/12 of the ad valorem taxes and the hazard insurance and mortgage insurance premiums, along with the principal and interest. It requires that payments be made on time, that taxes be paid, and that the property be covered by insurance and describes prepayment options. It also probably states that a transfer of the property will make the loan due immediately.

## The Warranty Deed

The warranty deed is the most common deed, with the seller guaranteeing to the buyer that he has good title, without material defects or encumbrances, and will stand by the guarantee forever. Special attention should be given to the names and legal description and to any items in the "subject to" section, such as restrictive covenants and mortgages.

## Other Documents

Some of the other documents the buyer may sign include an anticoercion statement that says the lender did not require that the buyer choose a certain insurance company. The lender and title insurance company will want a compliance agreement that the parties will do anything necessary to give the lender an acceptable loan package, such as signing new documents, if required. If the loan is above 80 percent of a home's value, the lender will want an affidavit that the buyer will occupy the property. The seller will be required to sign an affidavit that (1) she owns the property, (2) she has the right to convey it, and (3) it is not encumbered by any lien or right to a lien, such as a construction lien.

## Disbursements at Closing

Everyone expects to be paid at closing. This is not always possible, and licensees should be prepared to explain the problem to the sellers. Perhaps an example using a broker's trust account is easier to understand. Many real estate brokers have hundreds of thousands of dollars in their escrow accounts. A broker who disburses from the escrow account before making a deposit into the account, even if the future deposit would be in certified funds, is guilty of a serious violation, because the broker would be using funds that belong to others.

Title insurance companies are faced with a similar problem. Some title insurance companies agree to disburse the proceeds at closing if the certified checks will be deposited by the close of business that day. (A real estate broker may never do this.) Many title insurance companies will not disburse if the closing takes place too late to make a same-day deposit or if the lender is holding the loan proceeds check until the loan package is delivered.

## Warehousing

Some companies are hesitant to insure title until the "gap" between the time of the title commitment and the time of recording is checked. Any documents filed against the property during the gap period may affect the title. A lot depends on whether the title insurance company has any reason to suspect problems.

After the closing, the title company makes all deposits, and the deeds and mortgages are copied for the lender's package before they are taken for recording. The closing package is prepared for the lender, awaiting only the recording information. The person who records the documents should ensure that the check amounts are correctly calculated, that the documents are put in the correct recording order (deed first, then mortgages), and that the "return to" address is properly entered. When the documents are recorded, the information, including the date and time and the book and page number, is entered into the final title insurance policy and the package is sent to the lender.

When the recorded instruments are returned, the closing agent will send the buyer the original deed with recording information, a copy of the mortgage (the lender gets the original), and the title insurance policy.

**Signed Closing Papers Received by Sales Associate.** The sales associate should be careful that the office file is fully documented. This includes any walk-through clearance papers the buyer signs for the seller and the closing statements all parties must sign. If disbursement is made at closing, the commission check also is received at this time.

## Postclosing Duties

**Commission Check to Broker.** Upon returning to the office, the sales associate should give the closing file as well as the commission check to the broker.

**Sign and Lockbox Picked up from Property.** The listing sales associate should ensure that the sign and lockbox are removed from the property and returned to the office. Often he does this just before closing. Many sales associates remove the lockbox for security reasons immediately after the contract has been signed.

**Letter of Thanks to Buyer or Seller.** The letter, which should include both the sales associate's and the broker's signatures, will be appreciated by the customer, will foster goodwill, and likely will result in future business. Many companies request that the buyer or seller complete a questionnaire about the level of service provided in the transaction.

**Follow-up Visit to Buyer or Seller.** The sales associate who calls on the customer after the closing demonstrates the careful attention needed to ensure that all details of the transaction have been completed satisfactorily.

**Notice of Closed Sale to MLS.** Most MLS systems require that listing status changes be submitted as soon as possible. This provides brokers and sales associates in the area with the most current information about listing availability and comparable sales information.

## SUMMARY

The sales associate's job really is just beginning when the parties sign the contract. Much work must be completed to ensure a successful closing. One of the first steps is to plan for each required task and enter it on a timeline. Each sales associate and broker involved should agree about who must do what, and when it must be done.

Licensees must complete tasks like attaching a "contract pending" sign, notifying the MLS, making the binder deposit, helping the buyer with the loan application and taking care of inspections and repairs. A major part of the sales associate's duties is reviewing the closing documents with the buyer or seller before closing.

## K E Y   T E R M S

certified check

contingency

documentary stamp taxes

funding fee

intangible tax

mortgage insurance
premium (MIP)

preclosing walk-through
inspection

private mortgage insurance

# PRACTICE EXAM

1.  When sales associate Phyllis sells her listing, she places a sign on the property. In this situation, which statement is correct?
    a.  Phyllis must put up a "contract pending" sign, by FREC rule.
    b.  Phyllis must put up a "sale pending" sign, by FREC rule.
    c.  Phyllis may not place the "sold" sign without the seller's approval.
    d.  Phyllis may place the "sold" sign without the seller's approval.

2.  The preclosing walk-through inspection is *NOT* intended to ensure that:
    a.  personal property the seller is required to leave remains on the property.
    b.  all required repairs have been completed.
    c.  the property has been maintained in the condition as it existed at the time of the contract, ordinary wear and tear excepted.
    d.  the roof is structurally sound.

3.  Sales associate Brian listed the Brantlys' home at 3217 Woodbrook Circle. Based on information the seller provided, Brian disclosed to the buyers, Jack and Helen Maxwell, that the pool liner was defective and needed replacement. The contract was written reflecting that the Maxwells would be responsible for the charges related to replacing the liner. After the sellers signed the contract, Brian contacted Pretty Pools Company and authorized the liner replacement at a cost of $1,750. The Maxwells were subsequently turned down for the required financing, and the sale did not close. Based on this information, Brian:
    a.  is not liable to the pool company; the Maxwells are.
    b.  is not liable to the pool company; the Brantlys are.
    c.  might have to pay for the pool liner.
    d.  may sue the Maxwells, because they defaulted.

4.  The best way for a buyer to determine that the seller has moved out and the property is ready for occupancy is by:
    a.  requiring a home inspection company to provide a report.
    b.  reading a termite report.
    c.  doing a preclosing walk-through inspection.
    d.  asking the sales associate.

5.  To expedite a closing, catch errors made in documents, and make the buyers feel more comfortable about documents they must sign, what should a sales associate do?
    a.  Obtain a hold-harmless agreement from the title insurance company
    b.  Limit the time for actually doing the closing
    c.  Get the papers to the parties at least 24 hours in advance of the closing
    d.  Have the lender sign an estoppel letter

6.  When the title closing agent gave the buyer the Truth-in-Lending Disclosure showing the annual percentage rate was 7.62 percent, the buyer declared, "Wait, I was told the interest rate was going to be 7.25 percent. This is wrong!" What is the most likely reason for the discrepancy?
    a.  Rates have gone up since the date of application.
    b.  The lender is trying to make extra money, believing the borrower won't remember the original interest quote.
    c.  While the note rate is probably 7.25 percent, the inclusion of lender fees such as discount points and origination fees has increased the annual percentage rate.
    d.  The Federal Reserve Board mandates a $3/8$ percent interest differential in mortgage loans.

7. A sales associate must give the earnest money deposit to the broker no later than the end of:
   a. the next business day.
   b. the second business day.
   c. the third business day.
   d. 15 days.

8. Contract contingencies should be cleared:
   a. within five days before closing.
   b. within five days after loan approval.
   c. within three days of contract.
   d. as soon as possible after the contract has been signed.

9. Jill listed a property for Sam, and he accepted an offer made on the property. The contract called for an additional binder to be deposited within ten days of the contract date. If the buyer failed to meet the contract's terms concerning the additional binder, the:
   a. contract is null and void.
   b. contract works like an option contract; the only remedy is the loss of the original binder.
   c. buyer has defaulted.
   d. contract should not have been accepted as written.

10. What would NOT be given to the title-closing agent when the order is given?
    a. A signed and dated listing agreement.
    b. The seller's and buyer's marital status.
    c. A complete legal description.
    d. Property address, including zip code.

## PRACTICE HUD-1 CLOSING STATEMENT

Questions 11–15 relate to the following information.

You recently listed and sold a home. The closing is scheduled for May 15. You have just received the HUD-1 settlement statement from Jillian Winkle at Smith, Jones, and Adams, P.A. (See Figure 12.5.) Using the listing agreement, the sales contract, and the good-faith estimate of settlement costs given by the lender at the time of application, you begin the review. You intend to visit both the sellers and the buyers to go over the closing information before the closing.

As you review the sales contract, you trace certain items to the HUD-1 statement and check off each as you do so. Names of the buyers (Kyle and Kari Byers) are as listed on the contract. The sellers' legal names, John and Susan Sellars, were taken from their deed when you first took the listing. They are shown correctly. The property address on the contract is 1462 Lime Drive. The contract sales price is $120,000. The Byers gave a $4,000 earnest money deposit. The new mortgage is for $108,000 at 7.5 percent interest.

You know the lender charges 1 percent for discount points and 1 percent for the loan origination fee. The Byers paid an appraisal fee of $300 at the time of loan application (POC). The good-faith estimate of settlement costs given by the lender at the time of application shows a $55 credit report fee, $25 for an amortization schedule, $1,070 for title insurance, and $20 for courier services. The estimate also shows recording fees of $10.50 for the deed and $42 for the mortgage, the documentary stamp tax on the note, and intangible tax on the mortgage. The survey was estimated at $250.

**F I G U R E   12.5  ■  HUD-1 Settlement Statement**

## A. Settlement Statement

U.S. Department of Housing and Urban Development

OMB No. 2502-0265

**B. Type of Loan**

| 1. ☐ FHA  2. ☐ FmHA  3. ☐ Conv. Unins. | 6. File Number | 7. Loan Number | 8. Mortgage Insurance Case Number |
|---|---|---|---|
| 4. ☐ VA  5. ☒ Conv. Ins. | EDODONNELL8LBM | 12345678 | |

**C. Note:** This form is furnished to give you a statement of actual settlement costs. Amounts paid to and by the settlement agent are shown. Items marked "(p.o.c.)" were paid outside the closing; they are shown here for information purposes and are not included in the totals. WARNING: It is a crime to knowingly make false statements to the United States on this or any other similar form. Penalties upon conviction can include a fine and imprisonment. For details see: Title 18 U. S. Code Section 1001 and Section 1010.

**D. NAME OF BORROWER:** KYLE BYERS and KARI BYERS
    ADDRESS: 1460 LIME DRIVE, TALLAHASSEE, FLORIDA 32301

**E. NAME OF SELLER:** JOHN SELLARS and SUSAN SELLARS
    ADDRESS:

**F. NAME OF LENDER:** FIRST SOUTH BANK, A FEDERAL SAVINGS BANK
    ADDRESS: 3020 HARTLEY ROAD, SUITE 330, JACKSONVILLE, FLORIDA 32257

**G. PROPERTY ADDRESS:** 1460 LIME DRIVE, TALLAHASSEE, FLORIDA 32301
    LOT 8, ORANGE PARK SUBDIVISION

**H. SETTLEMENT AGENT:** SMITH, JONES AND ADAMS, P.A.
    PLACE OF SETTLEMENT: 7889 Thomasville Rd, Tallahassee, Fl. 32308

**I. SETTLEMENT DATE:** 05/15/05

| J. SUMMARY OF BORROWER'S TRANSACTION: | | K. SUMMARY OF SELLER'S TRANSACTION: | |
|---|---|---|---|
| **100. GROSS AMOUNT DUE FROM BORROWER** | | **400. GROSS AMOUNT DUE TO SELLER:** | |
| 101. Contract sales price | 120,000.00 | 401. Contract sales price | 120,000.00 |
| 102. Personal Property | | 402. Personal Property | |
| 103. Settlement charges to borrower (line 1400) | 7,313.76 | 403. | |
| 104. | | 404. | |
| 105. | | 405. | |
| **Adjustments for items paid by seller in advance** | | **Adjustments for items paid by seller in advance** | |
| 106. City/town taxes | | 406. City/town taxes | |
| 107. County taxes  05/15/05 to 12/31/05 | 1,329.04 | 407. County taxes  05/15/05 to 12/31/05 | 1,329.04 |
| 108. Assessments | | 408. Assessments | |
| 109. | | 409. | |
| 110. | | 410. | |
| 111. | | 411. | |
| 112. | | 412. | |
| **120. GROSS AMOUNT DUE FROM BORROWER** | 128,642.80 | **420. GROSS AMOUNT DUE TO SELLER:** | 121,329.04 |
| **200. AMOUNTS PAID BY OR ON BEHALF OF BORROWER** | | **500. REDUCTIONS IN AMOUNT DUE TO SELLER** | |
| 201. Deposit or earnest money | 4,000.00 | 501. Excess Deposit (see instructions) | |
| 202. Principal Amount of new loans | 108,000.00 | 502. Settlement charges to seller (line 1400) | 9,315.50 |
| 203. Existing loan(s) taken subject to | | 503. Existing loan(s) taken subject to | |
| 204. | | 504. Payoff of First Mortgage Loan | 45,452.65 |
| | | BARNETT BANK | |
| 205. | | 505. Payoff of Second Mortgage Loan | |
| 206. | | 506. | |
| 207. | | 507. | |
| 208. | | 508. | |
| 209. | | 509. | |
| **Adjustments for items unpaid by seller** | | **Adjustments for items unpaid by seller** | |
| 210. City/town taxes | | 510. City/town taxes | |
| 211. County taxes | | 511. County taxes | |
| 212. Assessments | | 512. Assessments | |
| 213. | | 513. | |
| 214. | | 514. | |
| 215. | | 515. | |
| 216. | | 516. | |
| 217. | | 517. | |
| 218. | | 518. | |
| 219. | | 519. | |
| **220. TOTAL PAID BY/FOR BORROWER** | 112,000.00 | **520. TOTAL REDUCTION AMOUNT DUE SELLER** | 54,768.15 |
| **300. CASH AT SETTLEMENT FROM OR TO BORROWER** | | **600. CASH AT SETTLEMENT TO OR FROM SELLER** | |
| 301. Gross amount due from borrower (line 120) | 128,642.80 | 601. Gross amount due to seller (line 420) | 121,329.04 |
| 302. Less amounts paid by/for borrower (line 220) | 112,000.00 | 602. Less reduction amount due seller (line 520) | 54,768.15 |
| **303. CASH FROM BORROWER** | 16,642.80 | **603. CASH TO SELLER** | 66,560.89 |

# FIGURE 12.5 ■ HUD-1 Settlement Statement (continued)

U.S. DEPARTMENT OF HOUSING AND URBAN DEVELOPMENT

**SETTLEMENT STATEMENT**

File Number: EDODONNELL8

PAGE 2

| L. SETTLEMENT CHARGES | | PAID FROM BORROWER'S FUNDS AT SETTLEMENT | PAID FROM SELLER'S FUNDS AT SETTLEMENT |
|---|---|---|---|
| 700. TOTAL SALES/BROKER'S COMMISSION based on price $ 120,000.00 @ 7.000 = 8,400.00 | | | |
| Division of commission (line 700) as follows: | | | |
| 701. $ 8,400.00 to BIG BEND REALTY | | | |
| 702. $ to | | | |
| 703. Commission paid at Settlement | | | 8,400.00 |
| **800. ITEMS PAYABLE IN CONNECTION WITH LOAN** | | | |
| 801. Loan Origination Fee 1.000 % FIRST SOUTH BANK | | 1,200.00 | |
| 802. Loan Discount 1.000 % FIRST SOUTH BANK | | 1,200.00 | |
| 803. Appraisal Fee to TALLAHASSEE APPRAISAL COMPANY (P.O.C.) 300.00 Buyer | | | |
| 804. Credit Report to CREDCO | | 55.00 | |
| 805. Lender's Inspection Fee | | | |
| 806. Mortgage Application Fee | | | |
| 807. Assumption Fee | | | |
| 808. AMORITIZATION SCHEDULE to FIRST SOUTH BANK | | 25.00 | |
| 809. | | | |
| 810. | | | |
| 811. | | | |
| **900. ITEMS REQUIRED BY LENDER TO BE PAID IN ADVANCE** | | | |
| 901. Interest From 05/15/05 to 06/01/05 @$ 22.1917 /day 17 Days | | 377.26 | |
| 902. Mortgage Insurance Premium for to | | | |
| 903. Hazard Insurance Premium for 12 to STATE FARM | | 840.00 | |
| 904. | | | |
| 905. | | | |
| **1000. RESERVES DEPOSITED WITH LENDER FOR** | | | |
| 1001. Hazard Insurance 2 mo. @ $ 70.00 /mo | | 140.00 | |
| 1002. Mortgage Insurance 2 mo. @ $ 45.00 /mo | | 90.00 | |
| 1003. City Property Taxes mo. @ $ /mo | | | |
| 1004. County Property Taxes 8 mo. @ $ 175.00 /mo | | 1,400.00 | |
| 1005. Annual Assessments mo. @ $ /mo | | | |
| 1009. Aggregate Analysis Adjustment | | | |
| **1100. TITLE CHARGES** | | | |
| 1101. Settlement or closing fee to SMITH, JONES AND ADAMS, P.A. | | 100.00 | |
| 1102. Abstract or title search to SMITH, JONES AND ADAMS, P.A. | | 100.00 | |
| 1103. Title examination to SMITH, JONES AND ADAMS, P.A. | | 75.00 | |
| 1104. Title insurance binder | | | |
| 1105. Document Preparation | | | |
| 1106. Notary Fees | | | |
| 1107. Attorney's fees | | | |
| (includes above items No: ) | | | |
| 1108. Title Insurance to SMITH, JONES AND ADAMS, P.A. | | 700.00 | |
| (includes above items No: ) | | | |
| 1109. Lender's Coverage $ 108,000.00 - 25.00 | | | |
| 1110. Owner's Coverage $ 120,000.00 - 675.00 | | | |
| 1111. FL 9 to SMITH, JONES AND ADAMS, P.A. | | 70.00 | |
| 1112. ALTA 8.1 to SMITH, JONES AND ADAMS, P.A. | | 25.00 | |
| 1113. COURIER FEE to SMITH, JONES AND ADAMS, P.A. | | 20.00 | 20.00 |
| **1200. GOVERNMENT RECORDING AND TRANSFER CHARGES** | | | |
| 1201. Recording Fees Deed $ 10.50 ; Mortgage $ 42.00 ; Release $ 10.50 | | 52.50 | 10.50 |
| 1202. City/County tax/stamps Deed $ 840.00 ; Mortgage $ 378.00 | | 378.00 | 840.00 |
| 1203. State Tax/stamps Deed $ ; Mortgage $ 216.00 | | 216.00 | |
| 1204. | | | |
| 1205. | | | |
| **1300. ADDITIONAL SETTLEMENT CHARGES** | | | |
| 1301. Survey to ALL CORNERS SURVEYOR | | 250.00 | |
| 1302. Pest Inspection to NO REQUIRED PER CONTRACT AND LENDER | | | |
| 1303. MISC REPAIRS to FIX IT ALL, INC. | | | 245.00 |
| 1304. | | | |
| 1305. | | | |
| 1306. | | | |
| 1307. | | | |
| 1308. | | | |
| **1400. TOTAL SETTLEMENT CHARGES** (enter on lines 103, Section J and 502, Section K) | | 7,313.76 | 9,515.50 |

The Byers must prepay interest on the loan from May 15 through May 31 because the first payment on the new mortgage is not due until July 1. The Byers also need to buy a one-year hazard insurance policy. They have chosen a State Farm policy with an annual premium of $840.

The lender requires that an escrow account be set up with two months' advance hazard insurance deposit, two months' advance mortgage insurance ($540 annual premium), and eight months' advance property taxes based on an estimate of $2,100 annually.

The payoff letter for the existing first mortgage requires $45,452.65, including interest. The Sellars have agreed to pay for recording the satisfaction of mortgage, and the $10.50 charge looks about right. The $20 courier fee to send the payoff check also seems OK. They have agreed to pay a bill from Fix It All, Inc., for $245 for miscellaneous repairs to the property. You calculate the documentary stamps on the deed and check your figures against the closing agent's figures. The Sellars' hazard insurance policy will be canceled. You review the listing agreement to see that the commission is 7 percent. It is not to be split with any cooperating brokerage firm.

If you find any errors on the statement, circle them and replace them with the correct figures. Totals on the statement may need to be changed. Once you have completed the review, answer questions 11 through 15.

11. What incorrect entries, if any, are in the Byers' expenses in Section L?
    a. None
    b. The title insurance charges are wrong.
    c. The discount points and origination fees are incorrect.
    d. The documentary stamp taxes on the note are wrong.

12. What incorrect entries, if any, are in the Sellars' expenses in Section L?
    a. None
    b. The commission is calculated incorrectly.
    c. The documentary stamp taxes on the deed are calculated incorrectly.
    d. The total at the bottom of the page is wrong.

13. What incorrect entries, if any, were made in the general information section of the statement?
    a. None
    b. The Sellars' names are spelled incorrectly.
    c. The Byers' names are incorrectly spelled.
    d. The address is incorrect.

14. Is the tax proration correct?
    a. Yes
    b. No, line 107 should be $1,329.04 and line 407 should show the difference, $770.96.
    c. No, the amount shown on lines 107 and 407 should be calculated from 1/1/05 through 5/15/05 ($770.96).
    d. No, the amount shown on line 107 should be calculated from 1/1/05 through 5/15/05 ($770.96) and be transferred to lines 211 and 511.

15. Are there any other problems on the statement?
    a. No
    b. There are at least eight more mistakes.
    c. The expenses on line 502 are incorrect.
    d. The purchase price on line 101 is incorrect.

# A C T I O N ✓ L I S T

## APPLY WHAT YOU'VE LEARNED!

The authors suggest the following actions to reinforce the material in *Section IV—Financing and Closing Real Estate Transactions:*

❑ Select a three-bedroom home that is currently for sale that you would like to own. Calculate the PITI payment, assuming you pay the listed price and make a 10 percent down payment. Use current interest rates.

❑ Based on the previous action, divide the PITI payment by the mortgage amount. This will give you the mortgage payment factor *including taxes, insurance, and PMI.* It will probably be just under 1 percent.

❑ Using the factor calculated above, quickly figure the payment for a $165,000 mortgage (1% × $165,000 = $1,650, quote just under that and estimate $1,634). Now quickly estimate the PITI payments for the following mortgage amounts

| Loan Amount | Payment (PITI) |
| --- | --- |
| $89,000 | $_____ |
| $138,000 | $_____ |
| $198,500 | $_____ |
| $212,000 | $_____ |

❑ Ask a title-closing officer to show you the entire closing process (usually the end of the month is a bad time for this). Ask to watch a title search to see what the title company looks for. Examine the closing officer's checklist for closings. See what an instruction package from the lender looks like. Watch as the closing officer enters information into the computer for the HUD-1 settlement statement.

❑ With your broker's approval, randomly select five file folders for closed transactions. Thoroughly review each file, and list every document in the file. Do some files seem more complete to you? Are there any that you believe are *not* complete? Note what documents you want in all *your* closed files.

❑ Start again at the first file folder. Inspect the contract, the good-faith buyer's estimate of settlement costs and payment amounts, and the HUD-1 form. Check to see whether the amount the sales associate estimated for the seller or buyer matched the actual amount on the HUD-1 form. Can you account for any material differences?

❑ Next, check every entry on the HUD-1 form for accuracy. If you have not yet had a closing, arrange with an associate to attend one of his closings. Remember, you should listen, not talk, at the closing.

# COMMERCIAL AND RESIDENTIAL INVESTMENT PROPERTY

CHAPTER 13.     ANALYZING REAL ESTATE INVESTMENTS

CHAPTER 14.     PROFESSIONAL PROPERTY MANAGEMENT

A substantial part of our country's wealth has been generated by investments in real property. Chapter 13 shows some of the advantages and disadvantages of investing in income property, the pros and cons of different property types, and methods of evaluating the investment.

Because of the substantial amounts of capital required for real estate investments, most owners want the property managed professionally. Chapter 14 describes the relationship between owners and property managers, the employment of resident managers, and the marketing and maintenance of property. ■

# CHAPTER
# 13

# ANALYZING REAL ESTATE INVESTMENTS

## LEARNING OBJECTIVES

Upon completion of this chapter, *you should be able to*

1.  list the three basic categories of changes and trends in the economy;

2.  itemize the four phases of an economic cycle;

3.  name four advantages of investing in real estate;

4.  list at least four disadvantages of investing in real estate;

5.  itemize five types of investment properties;

6.  enter the major headings of an income property financial statement;

7.  list and calculate four important income property ratios; and

8.  itemize the three basic types of income tax deductions for investment property.

## OVERVIEW

Investment in real estate has produced a substantial portion of the wealth of our country and its citizens. Real estate licensees should be prepared to assist buyers and sellers of investment real estate. Consumers expect their sales associates to have a basic understanding of the fundamentals of investment. An investment study includes analysis of the national and local economies, specifically as they relate to real estate.

Investing in real estate has advantages and disadvantages, and each investor must determine if an investment is suitable. This chapter focuses primarily on investment opportunities in smaller income properties such as raw land and residential, office, and commercial properties.

Basic investment ratios help buyers analyze properties to help reduce risk. Several methods presented may help an investor use these ratios to determine the appropriate amount to offer for a property.

While federal income taxes are an important consideration when weighing an investment in real estate, the property's operating economics are more important. ■

# THE GENERAL BUSINESS ECONOMY

Timing is important in real estate investment. A good property purchased at the wrong time may result in substantial losses to the investor. Many investors also understand that a rapidly appreciating real estate market can make even marginal properties show acceptable returns. Before deciding which type of real estate is right, the investor must try to understand the current economic trends.

Trends in the business economy may either originate from or result in changes in the real estate market. The condition of one directly affects the condition of the other. Changes and trends in the general economy fall into three basic categories: seasonal variations, **cyclic fluctuations,** and random changes.

## Seasonal Variations

Changes that recur at regular intervals at least once a year are called **seasonal variations.** Such changes arise from both nature and custom. In the northern United States, for example, construction stops during the winter months; this seasonal change affects both the general economy and the real estate economy. Customs such as the nine-month school year have a seasonal effect on residential sales. Each year, retired persons fleeing cold weather swell Florida's winter population.

## Cyclic Fluctuations

Business cycles usually are defined as wavelike movements of increasing and decreasing economic prosperity. A **cycle** consists of four phases: expansion, recession, contraction, and recovery. (See Figure 13.1.)

Production increases during **expansion** periods. High employment levels, wages, and consumer purchasing power increase demand for goods and services. Prices rise because of greater demand, and credit is easy, making more money available for purchasing.

**Recession** normally is defined as two successive quarterly declines in the **gross domestic product (GDP).** GDP is the sum total of goods and services produced by the United States. The four major components of GDP are: consumption, investment, government purchases, and net exports.

**Contraction** begins immediately after recession. Confidence in the economy is shaken, and consumers reduce spending in anticipation of lower earnings. Slower sales cause reduced

**F I G U R E   13.1  ■  General Business Cycle**

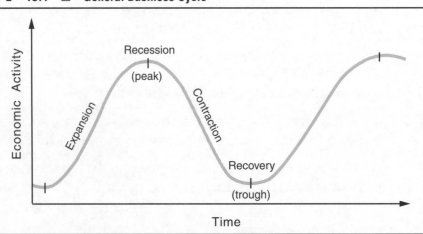

Source: Adapted by permission from Robert C. Kyle and Floyd M. Baird, *Property Management,* 6th edition (Dearborn™ Real Estate Education, 1997), 25.

production, worker layoffs, and unemployment. Prices are reduced to clear out inventories of unsold goods.

**Recovery,** defined as two successive quarterly increases in the GDP, begins when consumers, lured by lower prices, venture back into the market. As business activity increases, confidence begins to return. Slowly, production facilities gear up to meet the new consumer demand, capital begins to flow back into business enterprises, and additional employees are hired. Finally, as the gradual use in employment generates more spendable income and an increasing demand for more goods, the business cycle again enters the expansion phase.

Although business cycles technically consist of the four phases defined above, most discussions deal simply with expansion and contraction, measuring expansion from trough to peak and contraction from peak to trough. Business cycles are recurrent, but not periodic; that is, they vary in duration and timing. Economists have observed that a complete cycle in the general economy may vary from 1 to 12 years in length.

## Specific Cycles

**Specific cycles** are wavelike movements similar to business cycles. They occur in specific sectors of the general economy, such as the real estate economy, and in individual sectors of the real estate economy, such as housing starts and real estate sales. Specific cycles do not always coincide with cycles of the general business economy, as the business cycle actually is a weighted average of all specific cycles.

Regardless of the state of the national economy, certain areas boom in recessions and stagnate in prosperous times because local demand runs counter to current broad economic trends. Northeastern manufacturing towns were in trouble in the early 1980s, for example, while an influx of new residents and industries into central Florida kept that area building and growing.

---

### DISCUSSION EXERCISE 13.1

Review the following "Selected Headlines" from a major business newspaper. Then break into small groups to discuss what the likely effects will be on real estate investment properties, real estate brokerage firms, and other investment possibilities. Discuss which businesses will suffer in the near term and which will prosper.

#### SELECTED HEADLINES IN AN INFLATIONARY ECONOMY

"Strong business expansion under way, may lead to inflationary
pressures on the economy"
"General Motors reports quarterly sales increase
of 22%. Stock price surges!"
"Current rate of inflation is _____ %, expected to be
at 9% within six months"
"Retail sales increase dramatically, paced by
JC Penney, Wal-Mart, and The Limited"
"Federal Reserve Board raises discount rate $1/2$%.
Economists foresee higher interest rates soon"
"Travel industry sees bumpy road ahead if
oil prices increase substantially"
"'Mortgage interest rates anticipated to rise to the 12–14% rate
in six months,' warns Citibank economist Wilton Smathers"
"Inflation will continue for at least two years, according
to Congressional Budget Office"
"Oil prices in the $35 price range within two months,
according to industry sources"

## Random Changes

**Random changes** are irregular fluctuations of the economy that may be caused by legislative and judicial decisions or by strikes, revolutions, wars, fires, storms, floods, and other catastrophes. These changes, impossible to predict or analyze, may affect one or more sectors of the aggregate economy. They may influence all industries in an area or one industry nationwide. Real estate activity, especially construction, is very vulnerable to labor strikes, political changes, and natural disasters. One example of a random change in regard to real estate is a zoning ordinance change allowing undeveloped land to be used for industrial purposes that would stimulate construction activity locally. Government policy changes and changes in tax laws also can cause random changes in real estate activity on a nationwide scale. Investors must be aware of what is happening on both the national and local levels and have contingency plans to cope with events as they occur.

## THE REAL ESTATE ECONOMY

The real estate economy is an important component of the general business economy, subject to the same four types of fluctuations. Specific cycles are the most pronounced and important trends that appear in the real estate sector. They can be observed in all phases of real estate: land development, building, sales, finance, investment, rental, and redevelopment.

Most sectors of the real estate economy are subject to both long and short cycles. Long-term cycles last from 15 to 22 years, and short-term cycles take about 3 years.

A controlling factor in the building cycle is the availability of money and credit in the mortgage and construction markets. In general, when the economy is strong and prices are rising, the Federal Reserve tightens the money supply to control inflation. The resulting higher interest rates make real estate investment less attractive because builders must either pass the higher costs on to consumers or accept lower profits. Either situation slows the rate of construction. Conversely, interest rates decline during a recession, making construction of new projects more feasible.

An extremely important indicator for forecasting the economy is the monthly report of Housing Starts, published by the Census Department between the 16th and the 20th of each month. Housing starts, along with auto sales, are the first to rise in an economic recovery and the first to drop in a recession. Not only does new housing have a direct effect on the market but housing-related purchases such as furniture and appliances also fuel a rebounding economy.

Building permit data are released with the housing starts report. Because permits are secured about a month ahead of construction starts, reviewing the increase or decrease in building permits gives a pretty good idea of what housing starts will do next month.

Once investors have satisfied themselves that the general economic situation is sound, it may be time to review the advantages and disadvantages of investment in real estate.

## SPECULATION IN REAL ESTATE MARKETS

In recent years, low interest rates have been a driving factor in changing Florida's real estate market from a buyers' market to a strong sellers' market. In many areas of the state, particularly in coastal areas, property appreciation has been nothing short of amazing. Many investors feel that trend will continue into the foreseeable future.

Recently, those expectations have fueled a boom in preconstruction contracts, where speculators agree to purchase a single-family home or a condominium before it is built with the intent to "flip" the property for a substantial profit before it is completed. Usually, the buyer is required to put up a good-faith deposit of 20 percent at the time the contract is signed. Some properties are flipped several times in rapid succession before completion. Many of these buyers have accumulated substantial profits, attracting even more speculators.

Some builders and lenders have become concerned that the speculation has resulted in a false view of the market, and the sales do not represent real needs of buyers. They remember too well the speculative buying binges of the late 1980s that resulted in rapid price declines when the market weakened. Buyers who had the contracts at higher prices did not close on the contracts. That resulted in a glut of unsold homes and condominiums and bankrupted many builders.

Several large builders and developers have recently begun requiring that buyers commit to live for at least one year in the homes they have purchased. Other builders require that buyers present a list of homes for which they have contracted that have not been completed.

While high profits in preconstruction contracts have been wonderful for investors to date, some experts suggest, "Don't stay too long at the party."

# REAL ESTATE INVESTMENT ANALYSIS

Most of the wealthy people in this country amassed their great fortunes from real estate investments. The most significant asset of most families is the equity in their homes. Real estate may not be the right investment for everyone, however. Advantages and disadvantages exist, and should be evaluated by each individual.

## Advantages of Investing in Real Estate

The advantages of investing in real estate include high leverage, good return, shelter from federal income taxes, and personal control of the asset.

**Leverage.** **Leverage** is the use of other people's money to increase the investor's return. Few other investments offer the high leverage real estate does. Stocks and bonds typically require at least a 50 percent down payment; mutual funds want 100 percent invested. Yet real estate investments can be made with 25 percent down payments, and less in many cases. The following example shows the benefits of leverage.

---

### PRACTICE EXERCISE—LEVERAGE

Jack Gormley is considering the purchase of a duplex in an attractive neighborhood. He has reviewed the rental records for the previous four years that the property manager provided. The property's net income has increased about 4 percent annually. Property values have increased at about the same rate. The property value is $100,000, with a $20,000 down payment. Based on the new financing, Jack anticipates before-tax cash flows of about $1,500 per year. He wants to compare this investment with a mutual fund that has averaged a 10 percent return over the previous five years. Assuming a holding period of five years and an annual property appreciation of 4 percent, how does the simple arithmetic look?

| | |
|---|---|
| Property value at a 4% annual compound rate | $121,665 |
| Less mortgage balance at year five | $ 73,800 |
| Equals increase in equity | $ 47,865 |
| Plus $1,500 per year for five years | $ 7,500 |
| Equals total cash from investment | $ 55,365 |

The final figure averages $11,073 for each year. Divided by the original investment of $20,000, the average annual return is about 55 percent. The return from annual cash flows was only 7.5 percent ($1,500 ÷ $20,000); the balance came from the increase in equity.

This type of analysis would be more accurate using the discounted cash flow approach, but the mutual fund returns would come in about the same pattern, making the comparison valid. Because of leverage, Jack's clear choice is the real estate.

**Good Returns.** Many careful and astute investors achieve excellent returns, often exceeding 20 percent.

**Income Tax Shelter.** Most investment opportunities such as savings accounts, bonds, stocks, and mutual funds require that the investor pay taxes on all current income (dividends). Real estate investments often provide tax-deferred cash flows, primarily because of cost recovery deductions (depreciation). This allows the investor to avoid paying taxes on the cash flows until she sells the property.

Exchanging and installment basis reporting are other ways to defer paying taxes. They will be discussed later in this section.

**More Personal Control.** Many investors are uncomfortable with the notion of entrusting their assets to other persons or companies with little or no control over the use of those assets. The purchase of real estate gives an investor much more control over the investment's operation and management. This is true even if the investor employs a property manager, as the manager is under the investor's control.

## Disadvantages of Investing in Real Estate

Disadvantages of investing in real estate include management time, high capital requirements, poor liquidity, personal stress, and high risk.

**Management Time.** Along with the advantage of personal control comes the disadvantage of the amount of time required to manage the property. Continuing review and management of an income property's operations is absolutely essential. A prudent investor takes an active role in overseeing management. The investor must seek a higher return on the investment to compensate for the time requirements.

**High Capital Requirements.** Real estate requires a substantial capital investment. Not only does the investor need funds to acquire the property, he also must have reserve funds available to make major renovations when required or to cover unexpected events. If vacancy rates are high, the investor will find it difficult to sell the property and may need to inject more money into the real estate to pay its operating costs and debt service to carry him through the hard times.

**Poor Liquidity.** Investment real estate is a complicated purchase, even in the best markets. Land-use requirements, environmental audits, maintenance inspections, lease reviews, and new financing all take a substantial amount of time. A seller must understand that it could be a year or more after putting the property on the market before a sale is closed. In bad markets, however, it can be close to impossible to sell property at a fair price because so many other properties are available. This is a significant disadvantage of investment real estate.

**Personal Stress.** Many first-time real estate investors suffer rude awakenings when they discover that property management isn't just about cash flow projections and planning, but also about personal interaction with tenants. Because an owner's first few properties usually are not large or profitable enough to justify hiring a manager, an owner is left with the task. When the mortgage payment is due, slow-paying tenants can become an irritation. Tenant complaints take time and interpersonal skills to resolve. Tenants sometimes leave a property in poor condition when they move, requiring a large contribution of time and money to restore the premises for the next tenant. Eviction is sometimes necessary and is usually distressing to both landlord and tenant.

**High Risk.**  It is said that the longer an asset is held, the greater the chance of catastrophe. Many examples exist of seemingly good real estate investments gone bad. It could result from over-building in the market, causing high competition and lower rents. Environmental laws also may require expensive retrofitting. Or a major employer may relocate to another area, causing wide-spread unemployment. Insurance does not cover this **dynamic risk.** To overcome dynamic risk, the investor must analyze a property carefully before purchasing, then manage it effectively.

**Static risk** is risk that can be insured. Examples include fire, windstorm, accident liability, floods, appliance contracts, and worker's compensation.

## TYPES OF INVESTMENT PROPERTY

A wide range of property is available for investment, and the type of property suitable for an investor often depends on the investor's age, assets, and risk profile. Young investors usually are willing to take greater risks. This may be due partly to optimism that has not been dimmed by hard knocks and partly to higher energy levels. Older investors want to keep what they have because they don't have a lot of time to get it back if it is lost. They avoid high risk and are more likely to look for attractive current cash flows as opposed to speculative appreciation.

Persons with very few assets have little to lose and are often risk-takers in their efforts to strike it rich. Persons who are financially comfortable usually are more conservative in their investment decisions.

Risk-averse investors ordinarily are not comfortable with industrial property, speculative land, or new construction of income property. They are more likely to want established income property with a proven record of income.

Types of investment property discussed below are raw land, residential income properties, office buildings, commercial properties, and industrial properties.

**Raw Land.**  Investment in raw land can be extremely profitable if good research skills, good instincts, and good luck come together in one transaction. This type of property investment also can be extremely risky for the novice investor. Cities and counties in Florida, when trying to get a handle on growth guidelines, often change land uses in an area, which may have either wonderful or disastrous consequences for the investor. Income tax laws can change the feasibility of many projects. Raw land usually does not offer a cash flow to the investor and requires continuing infusions of funds to pay property taxes and interest on mortgages. Timing is important because the longer the property is held, the lower the rate of return tends to be.

The most important determinant of value for a vacant site is location. If land is planned for commercial use, it must have access and visibility from a major arterial road. Shopping centers should have easy access to expressways. Topography is important because it can affect building costs to correct for heavily sloping land.

**Residential Income Properties.**  A single-family home usually is the investor's initial purchase. A single-family rental home provides the investor with a breakeven cash flow or a little income if the investor combines good management with good luck. It also has some limited tax advantages from depreciation. Because the margins are so slim, however, a vacancy for even a month can wipe out all the profit for the year.

As the investor's assets and borrowing power grow, her next investment may be a multi-family property. Larger properties benefit from the efficiencies of land use and management. Where single-family homes usually are breakeven propositions for the investors, larger properties can bring substantially higher yields. Because of the much larger investment required, a buyer should make a complete and detailed investment analysis.

**Office Buildings.** In the 1980s, office building construction was spurred on by the tax code and by infusion of capital into the market through limited partnerships. As a result, the office market became overbuilt in almost every major city, and vacancy rates of 25 percent were common. Many of the buildings were economically unsound, and there were many foreclosure sales. The market finally began to recover in the late 1990s, and developers are building again. Lenders, however, still are cautious and demand strong financial statements and tenant commitment to ensure reasonable occupancy rates when the buildings are complete.

Small investors must analyze the office building market carefully before committing their funds. What is the competition? How many new buildings are permitted? What's happening in the area economy? It is not enough to look at the overall occupancy rate. An investor should segment the market by age, location, and amenities. It is possible that vacancies are high in the older downtown buildings, while newer suburban office parks are nearly full. Prestige office buildings can be unprofitable for the investor. They're really pretty but often have low yields.

When analyzing the rent rates for competitive properties, the investor should pay careful attention to the services and tenant improvements included. Many buildings pay for utilities and janitorial service and give each tenant an initial allowance for partitioning.

Many investors prefer office buildings to residential apartments because tenants tend to occupy the properties longer, tenant complaints usually are made during business hours, and fewer collection problems occur. Smaller office buildings tend to have somewhat higher tenant turnover than buildings rented by national tenants.

**Commercial Properties.** Many opportunities exist for small investors as well as shopping center developers to invest in commercial properties. Small strip shopping centers, because of their rectangular shape, lend themselves well to a variety of uses. They can be converted from storefronts to offices to restaurants with relatively little expense. A typical strip center consists of a 100' by 60' building with four 25' or five 20' wide bays. The market in many areas became very soft during the last economic downturn, making new construction loans difficult to obtain for some years. The market has improved in recent years, becoming attractive again to small investors.

Larger neighborhood shopping centers usually include a grocery store or a drugstore as the anchor, along with some personal service stores such as dry cleaners, laundromats, or restaurants.

Community shopping centers may include a Home Depot, K-Mart, or Stein Mart as the anchor, along with a supermarket and other retailers, restaurants, and service companies. Management should try to arrange the mix of tenants so that each complements the others in the center and the overall effect is to generate additional traffic. Lease terms in these centers run longer than in strip centers. Professional property managers usually manage centers of this kind.

Regional shopping centers usually have three or more major department stores as anchors. They generally are located near expressways to draw more distant shoppers to the sites. The centers often have large numbers of general merchandise retailers. A professional manager is essential to enhance the value of this very large investment.

**Industrial Properties.** Industrial properties usually are located near expressways, airports, seaports, or railroad lines. Investment in industrial property requires substantial research and carries significant risk. Most small investors should be wary about investment in this market.

Many industrial properties serve special purposes and are subject to long periods of vacancy in market downturns. However, with a successful company as a tenant, an industrial property can achieve reasonable returns.

## MARKET ANALYSIS

Once the investor is satisfied that the economy is sound and begins to target the type of property for investment, a market study is the next necessary step. A regional market analysis should include demographic and economic information such as population statistics and trends, a list of major employers in the area, and income and employment data. It should explore the economic base of the city and prospects for the future in that locale. A neighborhood market analysis should assess five major factors:

1. **Boundaries and land usage.** Rivers, lakes, railroad tracks, parks, or major highways may help define the neighborhood's boundaries.
2. **Transportation and utilities.** Transportation and utilities are crucial to the success of income property. The investor should analyze the effect of major traffic artery changes, as well as proposed or scheduled widening of streets, opening or closing of bridges, or new highway construction, all of which may enhance or hurt a location.
3. **Economy.** The investor also should review the neighborhood's economic health. Rental rates in the neighborhood are a sound indicator of the real estate market's economic strength. The investor can obtain the most reliable current rental rate information by shopping the competition.
4. **Supply and demand.** A high occupancy rate indicates a shortage of space and the possibility of rental increases. A low rate, as evidenced by many "for rent" signs posted in the area, results in tenant demands for lower rents and other owner concessions.
5. **Neighborhood amenities and facilities.** The neighborhood's social, recreational, and cultural amenities can be important. Parks, theaters, restaurants, schools, and shopping centers attract potential tenants.

## FINANCIAL ANALYSIS

After analyzing the market, the investor must examine the property's financial performance. This provides the basis for estimating the property's value, based on return criteria the investor establishes. Assembling the data is the most time-consuming part of the analysis process. The investor must review the property's financial history, as well as rent data, financial results, and amenities for competing properties. The first step after assembling the data is to prepare a one-year financial statement for the property.

**Estimate Potential Gross Income.**  By multiplying the amount of space in the building by the base rental rate for that type of space, the investor can estimate rental income for each type of space found in the building. For example, the residential investor multiplies the number of studio, one-bedroom, and two-bedroom apartments by the rent for each type. The total of the estimated rent amounts from each type of space is the **potential gross income (PGI)** for the entire property.

**Estimate Effective Gross Income.**  Effective gross income **(EGI)** is potential gross income minus vacancy and collection losses plus other income. Vacancy and collection losses are forecast from the experience of the subject property and of competing properties in the market, assuming typical, competent management. A good balance of supply and demand is a 95 percent occupancy rate. Occupancy rates change based on changing economic conditions, such as rising unemployment rates or overbuilding. Other income from sources such as vending machines and laundry areas is added to potential gross income *after* subtracting vacancy and collection losses.

**Estimate Operating Expenses.** The next step is to calculate the property's **operating expenses (OE).** Operating expenses are divided into three categories: fixed expenses, variable expenses, and reserves for replacement (see below). Ad valorem taxes and property insurance are examples of fixed operating expenses. Their amounts normally do not vary with the level of the property's operation. Variable expenses include such items as utilities, maintenance, trash removal, supplies, janitorial services, and management. These expenses move in direct relationship with the level of occupancy. Regional norms for these expenses are available through trade journals and professional property management associations.

**Establish Necessary Reserves for Replacement.** If the level of expenses fluctuates widely from year to year, based on major maintenance and replacements of property components, it is difficult for the analyst to get a clear picture of typical expenses. To be meaningful, the expense figure must be stabilized. This is accomplished by establishing a **"reserves for replacement"** category of expenses. It is not a current cash outlay but an annual charge that should account for future expenses. The most accurate way to establish reserves is to divide the cost of each item and piece of equipment by its expected useful life in years.

**Estimate Net Operating Income.** The **net operating income (NOI)** is obtained by deducting operating expenses (fixed, variable, and reserves) from effective gross income.

**Determine Before-Tax Cash Flow.** Income properties normally are purchased with mortgage financing, so owners must make mortgage payments from the NOI. When an annual mortgage payment is subtracted from NOI, the remaining amount is called **before-tax cash flow (BTCF),** sometimes called *cash throwoff*.

## Constructing a Financial Statement for a Residential Investment

The following example describes the process of analyzing a residential investment. Sigrid Fleming is considering an investment in an apartment property located in southeast Tallahassee. The property, which is about seven years old and well maintained, is located near some office buildings and shopping. Many of the tenants are employed in clerical and secretarial positions. The rental rates are very competitive in the area. Sigrid's broker has given her the bookkeeper's statements for the previous two years. Based on those statements and information from competing properties, she has constructed the operating statement shown in Figure 13.2.

**Ratio Analysis.** Sigrid's next step is to prepare a ratio analysis that helps her evaluate different investment opportunities. Some of the important ratios include capitalization rate, equity dividend rate, cash breakeven ratio, and debt coverage ratio. Use the statement on the Tallahassee Villas Apartments in Figure 13.2 to compute these ratios.

***The Capitalization Rate.*** Capitalizing net operating income is a basic approach to estimating value. While an appraiser uses a rate determined by verified sales in the marketplace, an investor sets the rate that provides an acceptable return using subjective criteria the investor establishes. The capitalization rate is the one-year before-tax operating return on a real property investment without considering debt service on the property. If an investor pays all cash for a $300,000 investment and the net operating income is $30,000, the rate of return is 10 percent. This is calculated by dividing the net operating income by the value ($30,000 ÷ $300,000).

---

**DISCUSSION EXERCISE 13.2**

What is the capitalization rate for the Tallahassee Villas Apartments?
If Sigrid desires a return of 14 percent, what will she pay for the property?

**F I G U R E   13.2  ■  Operating Statement for Residential Property**

**Tallahassee Villas Apartments**
**Operating Statement**
Purchase Price: $1,000,000/Mortgage $800,000

| | |
|---|---:|
| **Potential Gross Income** | |
| 25 units @ $425/mo. | $127,500 |
| 12 units @ $500/mo. | 72,000 |
| | $199,500 |
| Less vacancy and collection losses @ 5% | 9,975 |
| **Effective Gross Income** | $189,525 |
| Operating Expenses: | |
| Property taxes | $8,700 |
| Garbage collection | 2,800 |
| Pest control | 4,500 |
| Insurance | 3,500 |
| Maintenance | 9,600 |
| Management @ 5% | 9,476 |
| Resident manager's apartment | 4,200 |
| Reserves for replacements | $ 30,000 |
| **Total Operating Expenses** | $ 72,776 |
| **Net Operating Income** | $116,749 |
| Mortgage payment ($800,000 @ 10% for 25 years) | $ 87,235 |
| **Before-Tax Cash Flow** (cash throw-off) | $ 29,514 |

Assume, however, that the investor would not purchase the property unless it yielded 12 percent. By dividing the net operating income by the rate desired ($30,000 ÷ .12), the investor would agree to pay only $250,000.

***Equity Dividend Rate.*** The equity dividend rate differs from the capitalization rate when a mortgage is considered in the analysis. If no mortgage exists, the capitalization rate is the same as the equity dividend rate. To calculate the equity dividend rate, divide the before-tax cash flow by the equity (value minus the mortgage).

Therefore, a property returning $14,000 after the owner makes the mortgage payment and having equity of $102,000 returns 13.7 percent on the equity ($14,000 ÷ $102,000). This percentage sometimes is called the *cash-on-cash return*.

Many investors believe that the equity should return 50 percent more than current mortgage rates. If mortgages are currently 8 percent, for example, the investor should look for at least a 12 percent return.

Assume that the above investor will purchase only if the property returns 16 percent on the equity. In that case, the investor would want to reduce the down payment from $102,000 to $87,500, determined by dividing the cash flow by the desired return ($14,000 ÷ .16). The price is determined by adding the down payment to the mortgage calculated originally.

---

**DISCUSSION EXERCISE 13.3**

What is the equity dividend rate for the Tallahassee Villas Apartments?
If Sigrid desires a return of 16 percent, what down payment would she be willing to pay?
What price would she pay (add the down payment to the mortgage)?

---

***Differences Between the Capitalization Rate and the Equity Dividend Rate.*** If the equity dividend rate is higher than the capitalization rate, the investor has achieved positive leverage. If the equity dividend rate is lower than the capitalization rate, negative leverage exists. Investors want positive leverage.

In the Tallahassee Villas Apartments, positive leverage exists. The capitalization rate is 11.67 percent, and the equity dividend rate is 14.75 percent. The investor increased her return by borrowing money with a favorable repayment rate. The repayment rate is called the **annual mortgage constant,** with a symbol of **k.** The annual constant is calculated by dividing the annual debt service by the original mortgage balance. In the Tallahassee Villas, the annual debt service is $87,235, and the mortgage is $800,000; $k$ is 10.9 percent (the interest rate is 10 percent, and principal amortization accounts for the balance.) The rule then becomes simple: *To achieve positive leverage,* k *must be lower than the capitalization rate.*

***Cash Breakeven Ratio.*** This ratio is extremely important to the investor because it shows levels of occupancy required to generate enough revenue to make the required payments for expenses and debt service. It is calculated by dividing the cash outflows (expenses and debt service) by the potential gross income. The operating expenses should show only those expenses required to be paid in cash. Reserves for replacements usually are not a cash expense.

Assume that a small retail strip center has potential gross income of $100,000, annual expenses of $40,000, including $4,000 in reserves for replacements, and annual debt service of $47,000. What is the breakeven ratio? Divide the total cash expenses ($40,000 − $4,000 = $36,000) plus the debt service by the potential gross income.

$$\$36,000 + \$47,000 \div \$100,000 = .83, \text{ or } 83\%$$

If all bays in the center rent for the same amount, the developer knows that the occupancy rate must be greater than 83 percent or the developer will have to use his own funds to make up the shortfall.

---

### DISCUSSION EXERCISE 13.4

What is the cash breakeven ratio for the Tallahassee Villas Apartments? What will be the impact on the owner if the vacancy rate is 20 percent?

---

***Debt Service Coverage Ratio.*** A lender is concerned if a property has net operating income that is too low to allow the owner to make mortgage payments easily. The lender wants a cushion so that even if vacancies or expenses increase, enough income will remain to make the mortgage payment. The debt coverage ratio demonstrates the amount of cushion. It is calculated by dividing the net operating income by the annual debt service.

Assume the strip center discussed above has a 5 percent vacancy rate, the net operating income is $55,000, and the annual debt service is $47,000. The debt service coverage ratio is 1.17. That means the net operating income is 117 percent of the amount needed to cover the mortgage payment (a 17 percent cushion). A lender feels more comfortable with a coverage ratio of at least 1.3.

---

### DISCUSSION EXERCISE 13.5

What is the debt service coverage ratio for the Tallahassee Villas Apartments? Does it appear to be adequate?

---

The ratios discussed above should not be used solely to report on a property's status. Astute investors use the ratios to help them determine the prices they would be willing to pay based on income and cash flows. For instance, assume the seller's broker provided the statement on the Tallahassee Villas Apartments. After Sigrid Fleming verifies the statement for accuracy and prepares the ratio analysis as described above, she may be prepared to make an offer on the property. The following format uses two calculations to assist in that process. The first calculation estimates the amount of mortgage loan that would be available; the second determines how much down payment the investor is willing to make. When the two figures are added, the result is the purchase price.

**Estimating the Amount of Available Financing Based on Lender Standards.** To determine the financing, the investor needs to know the lender's requirements for the debt service coverage ratio, and she needs to calculate the mortgage **loan constant** (k) based on current lending rates. Dividing the NOI by the required debt coverage ratio generates the allowed annual debt service. Dividing that figure by the loan constant results in the available loan amount.

Assume that the mortgage market will allow a commercial building a 25-year loan at a rate of 8 percent. The monthly payment factor is .00772 and the annual factor is .09261. The second factor is k. With a net operating income of $55,000, a required debt coverage ratio of 1.3, and an annual loan constant of .09261, the annual debt service can be $42,308, as shown below:

1. Net operating income ÷ Debt coverage ratio = Annual debt service

$$\$55,000 \div 1.3 = \$42,308$$

2. Annual debt service ÷ Mortgage loan constant = Mortgage loan amount

$$\$42,308 \div .09261 = \$456,840$$

**Calculating the Down Payment Based on Investor Return Standards.** The next step is to calculate the maximum down payment. Once the mortgage amount is determined, the investor subtracts the annual debt service from the net operating income to get before-tax cash flow. If the investor divides that figure by the required equity dividend rate, the result is the down payment the investor is willing to make.

In the example above, we estimated that the debt service allowed by the lender is $42,308. The net operating income is $55,000. Deducting the debt service of $42,308 results in a $12,692 cash flow. If the investor's required return is 15 percent, the down payment would be $84,613, as shown below

1. Net operating income − Debt service = Before-tax cash flow

$$\$55,000 - \$42,308 = \$12,692$$

2. Before-tax cash flow ÷ Required rate of return = Down payment

$$\$12,692 \div .15 = \$84,613$$

**Calculating the Purchase Price.** Once the above two steps are complete, the purchase price is simply the addition of each figure. Continuing the above example, the calculation is as follows

| | |
|---|---|
| Mortgage amount available from lender | $456,840 |
| Plus down payment from buyer | 84,613 |
| Equals purchase price offered | $541,453 |

This technique for valuing income property is superior to simply capitalizing net income.

**Other Financial Analysis Techniques.** More sophisticated discounted cash flow techniques require the use of financial tables or a financial calculator and include the *net present value*, the *internal rate of return*, and the *financial management rate of return*. In general, after-tax cash flows for future periods, including sales proceeds, are discounted back to the present value so that the pattern of receipts does not distort the analysis. While these techniques are important tools, they are beyond the scope of this text. The material is covered more fully in the broker's course and in commercial and investment real estate classes.

# FEDERAL INCOME TAXES AND REAL ESTATE INVESTING

Real estate investors should not purchase property solely because of tax considerations. Many remember the large losses suffered by those who did so and were ruined financially by the 1986 Tax Reform Act. However, careful tax planning may help to maximize an investor's return on certain investments and should be considered when weighing alternative investments.

Income property owners enjoy certain tax advantages other investors do not. An owner is allowed three types of deductions from gross income when calculating taxable income from investment property: operating expenses, financing expenses, and depreciation.

Operating expenses include those cash outlays necessary for operating and maintaining the property. Financing expenses include interest on indebtedness, as well as amortization of the costs of borrowing money, such as discount points.

Depreciation expense is not related to the depreciation used in appraising, which is based on realistic improvement lives. This is an arbitrary method of allowing the investor to recover the cost of improvements over a specified period. Costs of residential income property may be recovered over a life of $27\frac{1}{2}$ years, and nonresidential income property may be written off over 39 years. For example, if a person bought a duplex three years ago for $125,000, paid closing costs of $5,000, and obtained an appraisal showing that the building was worth 80 percent of the total, what is the depreciation deduction?

To determine the deduction, first allocate the acquisition costs to the building and the land, then divide the building's acquisition costs by the applicable depreciable life. The $125,000 purchase price plus the $5,000 in closing costs equals the acquisition cost of $130,000. Because the building is worth 80 percent of value, the building's depreciable basis is $104,000. Residential property is depreciated over 27.5 years, so $104,000 divided by 27.5 years equals a deduction for this year of $3,781.81.

> ### DISCUSSION EXERCISE 13.6
>
> If closing costs on Tallahassee Villas Apartments are $12,000 and the improvements are estimated to represent 75 percent of the total value, what is the depreciation deduction?

The tax laws concerning capital gains taxes are covered in Chapter 1.

## Tax-Deferred Exchange

While the new capital gains rates are attractive, most investors attempt to defer (not eliminate) paying any taxes by exchanging the property for "like" investment property. "Like" investment property includes real estate such as vacant land, residential income property, commercial income property or industrial income property.

1   The rules do not require a "barter" of property. A person may sell investment property,
2   escrow the proceeds out of his personal control, then identify another property to buy within
3   45 days, closing within 180 days.

### Installment Basis Reporting

5   Taxes on the gain from the sale of a property need not be paid at once if the seller does not
6   receive her proceeds in the year of sale. The law allows the taxpayer to pay taxes on the gain
7   as the seller receives the proceeds. No minimum or maximum down payment is required. A
8   loss on sale may not be reported using installment basis reporting.

## SUMMARY

Real estate licensees are quite active in marketing investment properties. Most small investors concentrate initially on small residential properties but later may investigate the opportunities in the office and commercial markets.

An understanding of the general business economy is helpful in timing investment decisions. If the market is at the top of the cycle, buyers should be wary, but sellers might wish to market their properties aggressively. Specific cycles are the most important cycles that affect the real estate market. Low interest rates are a critical component to a strong real estate market.

Real estate investing offers many advantages, such as leverage, good returns, tax shelters, and personal control. However, those advantages are tempered by problems with stress, management time, risk, and poor liquidity.

After analyzing the market, an investor must prepare a careful financial statement, together with meaningful ratios. The investor can use the ratios to help her determine what price to offer for the property.

Licensees have an opportunity to help their customers take one of the most important steps of their lives—beginning a program of real estate investment.

## K E Y   T E R M S

| | | |
|---|---|---|
| annual mortgage constant | expansion | potential gross income (PGI) |
| before-tax cash flow (BTCF) | gross domestic product (GDP) | random changes |
| contraction | $k$ | recession |
| cycle | leverage | recovery |
| cyclic fluctuation | loan constant | reserves for replacements |
| dynamic risk | net operating income (NOI) | seasonal variation |
| effective gross income (EGI) | operating expenses (OE) | specific cycles |
| | | static risk |

# PRACTICE EXAM

1. Funds set aside to prepare for the eventual replacement of worn-out appliances, carpeting and drapes are called:
   a. contingency funds.
   b. reserves for expenses.
   c. reserves for replacements.
   d. operating expenses.

2. Changes and trends in the general business economy fall into three categories—seasonal, random, and:
   a. expansion.
   b. recovery.
   c. periodic.
   d. cyclic.

3. Wavelike movements of increasing and decreasing economic prosperity in the general economy usually are called:
   a. random changes.
   b. cyclic fluctuations.
   c. seasonal variations.
   d. long-term movements.

4. The most pronounced and important economic changes and trends appearing in the real estate sector are the:
   a. seasonal fluctuations.
   b. specific cycles.
   c. expansion phases.
   d. random changes.

5. In general, when the economy is strong and prices are rising, the Federal Reserve Board tends to:
   a. loosen the money supply, causing interest rates to rise.
   b. loosen the money supply, causing interest rates to fall.
   c. tighten the money supply, causing interest rates to rise.
   d. tighten the money supply, causing interest rates to fall.

6. You are the property manager for a new, 60-unit garden apartment complex. The annual potential gross income is $291,000, other income is $480 per month, and vacancy and collection losses are 5 percent. What is the property's effective gross income?
   a. $276,450
   b. $276,930
   c. $281,922
   d. $282,210

7. Which of the following describes the debt service coverage ratio?
   a. Shows the level of occupancy necessary to pay all bills
   b. Important to lenders in showing how much net income exceeds the mortgage payment
   c. Indicates the length of time required to repay the mortgage based on current income rates
   d. Shows the amount of down payment the investor is willing to make

8. Changes that recur annually are called:
   a. familiar changes.
   b. long-term cyclic changes.
   c. random changes.
   d. seasonal variations.

9. An apartment property has potential gross income of $155,000, effective gross income of $150,000, operating expenses of $58,000, including reserves for replacement of $2,400, and debt service of $40,800. What is the property's net operating income?
   a. $48,800
   b. $51,200
   c. $92,000
   d. $94,600

10. Nonresidential income property may be depreciated over how many years?
    a. 15, with a 175% declining balance
    b. 27.5
    c. 31
    d. 39

11. An investor obtains the best and most reliable information about rental rates in a neighborhood by checking:
    a. the Bureau of Labor Statistics' survey of sample cities.
    b. competing properties.
    c. classified ads in local newspapers that cover the past 18 to 24 months.
    d. current classified ads in local newspapers for advertisements of comparable space.

12. Total operating expenses include variable expenses, fixed expenses, and:
    a. debt-service expenses.
    b. management expenses.
    c. reserves for replacement.
    d. property taxes.

13. A problem many investors have with industrial properties is that:
    a. land boundaries are unstable.
    b. many properties serve special purposes and are difficult to rent once they are vacant.
    c. they rarely need proximity to airports.
    d. rates of return are always low.

14. A property has annual net operating income of $145,000. A lender has agreed to a loan at 7 percent interest and requires a debt coverage ratio of exactly 1.5. The loan will have what monthly mortgage payment?
    a. $217,500
    b. $96,667
    c. $10,800
    d. $8,056

**Use the following information to answer questions 15 through 20.**

Patti Jansen is considering an investment in an office building priced at $560,000. She can secure a mortgage on the property as long as the net operating income is 1.3 times the new mortgage payment. She can get a new 8.5 percent 25-year mortgage, but has decided that she

276

will not purchase unless her equity dividend rate is 12 percent. Patti prepares an abbreviated financial statement that shows the following:

| | |
|---|---|
| Potential gross income | $100,000 |
| Less vacancy of 10% | 10,000 |
| Equals effective gross income | $ 90,000 |
| Less operating expenses | 36,000 |
| Equals net operating income | $ 54,000 |
| Annual debt service | |
| Before-tax cash flow | |

15. What maximum annual debt service will the lender accept?
   a. $41,538
   b. $44,378
   c. $46,800
   d. $70,222

16. What maximum amount will the lender loan to Patti, based on an annual constant of 0.096627?
   a. $429,880
   b. $440,345
   c. $475,000
   d. $503,000

17. What is the before-tax cash flow?
   a. $11,687
   b. $12,462
   c. $14,901
   d. $22,789

18. What would Patti be willing to pay as a down payment based on the figures?
   a. $86,587
   b. $91,345
   c. $93,451
   d. $103,850

19. What total price would Patti be willing to pay based on the figures?
   a. $425,987
   b. $469,091
   c. $533,730
   d. $541,890

20. Is the leverage positive or negative?
   a. Positive
   b. Negative
   c. Neutral
   d. Not enough information to calculate

# CHAPTER

# 14 PROFESSIONAL PROPERTY MANAGEMENT

## LEARNING OBJECTIVES

Upon completion of this chapter, *you should be able to*

1. describe the general duties of professional property managers;

2. list the four major classifications of rental properties;

3. list at least six important elements of a management contract;

4. list the four major property maintenance categories;

5. describe the requirements that determine the need for an on-site maintenance staff, contract services, or a resident manager;

6. describe the differences between a property manager and a resident manager;

7. list at least three different advertising media that help to market rental property;

8. describe the uses and benefits of a show list;

9. identify at least five of the essential elements of a valid lease;

10. identify and explain the purpose of three of the financial reports an apartment building owner needs; and

11. identify those property managers who are exempt from the provisions of F.S. 475.

## OVERVIEW

Investors generally agree that professional property management is the key to maximizing their returns. The professional property manager must have a comprehensive understanding of the economic forces at work in the real estate market. He must be able to evaluate the property in terms of operating income, forecast its potential for the future, and construct a management plan that reflects the owner's objectives. The property manager must become a specialist skilled in space marketing, tenant psychology, the legal aspects of the landlord-tenant relationship, maintenance procedures, and accounting. This chapter examines these topics. ∎

# INTRODUCTION TO PROPERTY MANAGEMENT

A professional property manager may be an individual licensee, a member of a real estate firm specializing in property management, or a member of the property management department of a large full-service real estate company. She also may work within the trust department of a financial institution or within the real estate department of a large corporation or public institution. Regardless of their employment status, property managers pursue similar objectives and handle a wide variety of duties, including planning, merchandising, maintenance, and accounting. Although management duties vary according to the specific situation and particular property, a successful manager is competent in all of these areas.

The **Institute of Real Estate Management (IREM)** was created in 1933 by a group of property management firms as a subsidiary group of the National Association of REALTORS®. Currently, individuals wishing to join the institute must satisfy education and experience requirements, pass examinations given or approved by the institute, and adhere to a specific code of ethics. They are then awarded the prestigious designation **Certified Property Manager (CPM)** in recognition of their professional status as property managers.

# CLASSIFICATION OF REAL PROPERTY

Real estate property managers manage four major classifications of real property: residential, commercial, industrial, and special-purpose. Each classification can be further subdivided and requires a different combination of property management knowledge and skills. This chapter introduces the field; it is not intended to be a complete discussion of property management. Residential property is emphasized in this introduction.

---

**DISCUSSION EXERCISE 14.1**

Relate a personal experience in renting or leasing residential property as a landlord or tenant.

---

## Residential Property

Residential real estate is the largest source of demand for the services of professional property managers. Two principal categories of residential real estate exist: single-family homes and multifamily residences.

**Single-Family Homes.**  Freestanding, single-family homes are the most popular form of housing in the United States. According to the Census Bureau, more than 60 percent of housing in this country is owner-occupied and does not require professional management. Although homes that are rented to other parties often are managed directly by the owners, there is a growing trend toward professional management of such properties, particularly condominiums and vacation homes. Many large corporations and their relocation companies hire property managers for homes vacated by employees who have been transferred.

Rising construction costs and a decrease in the availability of usable land have resulted in the growing popularity of town houses, condominiums, and cooperatives. Although each unit is a single-family residence, the individual owners of the units share certain responsibilities, such as maintenance of the roof, common walls, grounds, and common facilities, for the development as a whole. They usually employ professional managers to handle these jobs and maintain accounting records.

**Multifamily Residences.**  The economy of design and land usage inherent in multifamily housing allows for a lower per-family cost of construction. Thus, multifamily residences are a rapidly growing segment of the national residential real estate market.

Multifamily residences can be held under various forms of ownership. Small properties of two to six units often are owner-occupied and owner-managed, whereas most large highrise apartment communities are professionally managed for their owners. Cooperative and condominium apartments usually are owner-occupied buildings governed by boards of directors the owners elect. These boards generally hire professional managers for their properties.

Multifamily residences can be classified as garden apartments, walkup buildings, or highrise apartments. Each type is unique in its location, design, construction, services, and amenities.

### Owner-Broker Relationship

Three basic relationships can exist between the individual or corporate owner of a building and the property manager: owner-broker, employer-employee, and trustor-trustee. Property managers in all categories are considered professionals, and their responsibilities are very similar. Because this section focuses on residential property management, only the principal-agent relationship is covered here.

Usually, when an owner engages a broker to be the property manager, the broker acts as a single agent for the owner. The principal-agent relationship is created by a written contract signed by both parties that empowers the property manager, as agent, to act on behalf of the owner, or principal, in certain situations. Specifically, the agent acts for the principal to bring her into legal relations with third parties. Implicit in this fiduciary relationship are the legal and ethical considerations that any agent must accord her principal. The property manager has the duties of skill, care and diligence, obedience, loyalty, accounting, disclosure, and confidentiality.

## THE MANAGEMENT CONTRACT

Once the property manager and the owner have agreed on principles, objectives, and a viable management plan, it is in both parties' best interests to formalize their accord. The manager and the owner must work out the structure of their relationship, their specific responsibilities and liabilities, the scope of the manager's authority, management fees, and the duration of the management agreement. In addition, the owner must turn over management records and other information to the manager to facilitate the property's operation.

Whether the property involved is a duplex or a highrise complex, the responsibilities the manager assumes are of enough importance to warrant a written statement of intent. An agreement signed by both the manager and the owner defines the relationship between the parties, serves as a guide for the property's operation, and helps prevent misunderstandings. The terms of management contracts are as varied, but most share the following essential elements:

- Identification of the parties and the property
- The term of the contract
- Responsibilities of the manager
- Responsibilities of the owner
- Fees and leasing/sales commissions;
- Signatures of the parties

## PROPERTY MAINTENANCE

Maintenance is a continual process of balancing services and costs in an attempt to please the tenants, preserve the physical condition of the property, and improve the owner's long-term margin of profit. Efficient property maintenance demands careful assessment of the status of the building's condition. Staffing and scheduling requirements vary with the type, size, and regional location of the property, so owner and manager usually agree in advance on maintenance objectives for the property. In some cases, the owner instructs the manager to reduce rental rates and expenditures for services and maintenance. Under this shortsighted policy, the manager may encounter management problems and the manager's reputation may be affected adversely. Properties can command premium rental rates if they are kept in top condition and operated with all possible tenant services.

## Types of Maintenance

The successful property manager must be able to function effectively at four different levels of maintenance operations:

1. Preventive maintenance
2. Corrective maintenance
3. Routine maintenance
4. New construction maintenance

**Preventive maintenance** is aimed at preserving the physical integrity of the premises and eliminating corrective maintenance costs. Regular maintenance activities and routine inspections of the building and its equipment disclose structural and mechanical problems before major repairs become necessary.

**Corrective maintenance** involves the actual repairs that keep the building's equipment, utilities, and amenities functioning as contracted for by the tenants. Fixing a leaky faucet and replacing a broken air-conditioning unit are corrective maintenance activities.

**Routine maintenance** is the most frequently recurring type of maintenance activity. Common areas and grounds must be cleaned and patrolled daily. Also, cleaning and housekeeping chores should be scheduled and controlled carefully because such costs easily can become excessive.

**New construction maintenance,** linked closely with leasing and tenant relations, is designed to increase the property's marketability. This may be as elementary as new wallpaper, light fixtures, and carpeting. If the new construction is extensive, it might include new entryways, the addition of a swimming pool, conversion of space to a meeting room, or renovation of a previously occupied space. New construction often is performed at a tenant's request and expense. Sometimes a landlord redecorates or rehabilitates a space for a tenant as a condition of lease renewal.

**Deferred maintenance** is necessary maintenance that cannot or will not be performed. Deferred maintenance results in physical deterioration, unhappy tenants, and reduced rent collections.

## On-Site Maintenance Staff

The manager's hiring policy for on-site maintenance personnel usually is based on the cost differential between maintaining a permanent building staff and contracting for the needed services. For example, the amount of construction activity stemming from alterations tenants require determines the hiring policy. It makes sense to hire outside contractors for major construction jobs or for small buildings that cannot support permanent staffs.

The Building Owners and Managers Institute (BOMI) sponsors instruction that leads to professional designations for maintenance personnel and supervisors. These courses are particularly instructive for on-site maintenance personnel. Property managers who wish to learn more about the technical and mechanical aspects of their properties will find these courses a good source of information.

### Contract Services

Services performed by outside persons on a regular basis for specified fees are known as **contract services.** For the protection of both the manager and the owner, a service contract always should be in writing and contain a termination provision. The latter stipulation becomes important if service is not satisfactory or if the property is sold.

Before entering into any service contract, the manager should solicit competitive bids on the job from several local contractors. He can then compare the cost of contracting with the expense of using on-site personnel. The management agreement terms often set a ceiling on the service contracts the manager can execute without owner approval. Window cleaning, refuse removal, pest control, and security are services that usually can be performed more efficiently and inexpensively by outside contractors. The manager should check a contracting firm's references and work history before he employs them. The manager should determine whether the firm's employees are bonded and whether it has the necessary licenses or permits.

## RESIDENT MANAGER—PROPERTY MANAGER RELATIONSHIP

Most properties of 20 units or more have a manager on the premises at all times. This **resident manager** is a salaried employee who usually coordinates rent collection, tenant relations, and maintenance work on the property. Obviously, these responsibilities increase with the building's size. The resident manager reports to the property manager. With this system, a single property manager can stay current with the operations of several large apartment properties without becoming consumed by the details. In addition to reviewing the reports submitted by resident managers, the property manager should visit each building regularly to gather information on necessary maintenance and repairs. Periodic inspections show the property manager how occupancy rates may be increased, indicate where operating costs can be cut, help improve tenant relations, and provide training and feedback reviews to the on-site manager.

In the past, building superintendents not only collected rents but also served as the maintenance staff. As the property management field grows more sophisticated and building equipment becomes more complicated, managers who perform all four maintenance functions have become the exception rather than the rule. Property managers are expected to recognize when maintenance is necessary and know where to turn for help with specific maintenance problems. While a property manager need not be a jack-of-all-trades, she should understand the basic operation of mechanical and electrical systems well enough to make intelligent decisions about their care and operation. The manager also must understand the economics, staffing, and scheduling involved in the smooth performance of maintenance tasks.

The hiring and firing of employees should be under the control of the property manager, not the resident manager. When screening a potential employee or making a decision to terminate an employee, the property manager should ask for the resident manager's opinion of the person's integrity, industry, and skills.

## MARKETING THE SPACE

Two basic principles of marketing are "Know your product" and "Your best source of new business is your present customer base." Thorough preparation is required to give a suitable presentation of the premises as well as to determine such items as rental rates and advertising methods necessary to attract tenants. Maximum use of referrals from satisfied tenants is the best and least expensive method of renting property and is essential to any marketing effort.

It is the property manager's responsibility to generate the maximum beautification and functional utility per dollar spent. Items such as an attractive lobby, well-landscaped grounds, and the use of pleasant colors inside and outside the building may not create greater functional utility, but they may increase marketability and profitability.

Rental space is a consumer good that can be marketed with promotional techniques like those used to sell cars or homes. Because most apartment renter prospects come to the property as a result of a neighborhood search, attractive signage and strong curb appeal is essential. Each residential property should display a tasteful sign on the premises identifying the community, the management firm, the type of apartment, the person to call for further information, and a telephone number. However, walk-ins alone will not supply all the prospects needed. Other types of advertising also are necessary to attract qualified tenants.

## Advertising and Display

Even if the property is priced at the appropriate market level, the premises are clean and attractive, and the property has a good location, the building still may experience an unacceptable vacancy rate if prospective tenants are not attracted to inspect the premises. The most common advertising is newspaper classified and display ads and apartment guides. The Florida Real Estate Commission (FREC) mandates that a broker's advertising must describe the property fairly and must not mislead. It also requires that the brokerage name appear in all advertising. Other agencies also impose restrictions on ads, particularly with respect to fair housing laws.

**Classified Ads.**  Newspaper classified advertising is the most important advertising medium for renting apartments. The property manager must keep the prospective tenant's needs in mind when composing the ad. For example, in a neighborhood where three-bedroom apartments are difficult to rent, an ad may appeal to a broader segment of the market if it offers a two-bedroom apartment with den. The classified advertisement should include the amount of rent, apartment size, property address, and manager's phone number. A brief summary of the property's major amenities also is very effective.

**Display Ads.**  More prestigious residential projects, especially when newly built, find it advantageous to use display advertisements. These larger ads attract immediate attention, appeal to potential tenants' desire for attractive living space, and demonstrate the many amenities a building offers. The specific rental rates often are omitted, with reference to a general range.

---

### DISCUSSION EXERCISE 14.2

Bring to class a copy of the entire classified ad section of your local newspaper. Examine the sections dealing with display ads for large residential properties and compare various ads' effectiveness. Also, examine the help wanted sections for property and resident managers.

---

**Apartment Guides.**  Just as homes magazines are one of the most effective ways to market residential homes for sale, apartment guides appeal to potential tenants. Color photos make the property's presentation attractive and interesting. Many management firms report that the excellent response to ads in the guides is beginning to rival the effectiveness of newspaper classified advertising.

## Broker Cooperation

While all selling activities have as their ultimate objective the closing of a sale or lease with the ultimate user, the property manager will want to take advantage of all opportunities for reaching customers. This means that sales efforts should be directed not only toward prospective buyers and tenants but also toward brokers and agents who can reach rental prospects.

Broker cooperation can be especially helpful when renting or leasing a new or very large development. Managers secure that cooperation by sending to key brokers brochures or newsletters describing available properties. Compensation usually is a split commission or referral fee. A manager also can make brokers aware of a property by making a personal presentation or by sponsoring an open house.

## Rental Rate Strategy

Even when the space itself is clean, attractively decorated, and in good condition, market conditions may be such that some units cannot be leased. An alert manager quickly realizes which units are renting rapidly or are not moving fast enough and either adjusts the price or changes the method of advertising and display.

The goal in establishing a rental fee schedule is to realize the maximum market price for each unit. If each apartment type is priced correctly, all types will have the same rate of demand; that is, demand for studio, one-bedroom, and two-bedroom units will be equal, and the manager will be able to achieve a balanced occupancy rate for all three types. However, this level of demand is the exception in the real market. More often than not, the manager will have to raise the base rent on the unit types that are fully occupied and decrease the rate for those units less in demand. An optimal price structure assures the manager of a 95 percent occupancy level for all units. For this strategy to be economically sound, the revenue from the new 95 percent schedule must exceed the income that was collected when some types of units were fully occupied and others had tenant levels of less than 95 percent. The optimum rental rates in a local market are best determined by market analysis.

## Show List

To establish a reasonable rental price schedule like the one outlined above, the manager must follow certain organizational procedures, such as compiling a **show list.** This show list should designate a few specific apartments in the building that are available currently for inspection by prospects. No more than three apartments of each type and size should be on the list at any one time; when a unit is rented, it should be replaced by another vacated apartment that is ready for rental.

The manager should use the show list both as a control guide for the marketing program and as a source of feedback on its success or failure. The features of particular units are itemized on the list so that the manager can do a better and more informed selling job. The maintenance staff will have no problem keeping a small number of vacant units on the list in top-notch condition. The limited number of show units also suggests that space is at a premium and that the prospective tenant must make her decision quickly.

The show list and traffic count should be reviewed weekly to determine which units are not moving. Particular units may not rent even after several showings to prospects. The manager then should inspect these units personally to find out why they are hard to rent. All curable flaws (for example, worn carpeting or obsolete fixtures) should be corrected. If poor curb appeal is the problem, painting or cleaning up entranceways, planting new landscaping, cutting grass, and trimming shrubs often works wonders.

It is important that fair housing laws be observed carefully. The limited show list must never be used as a method of illegal steering within the property.

## Selling the Customer

The best advertising programs, landscaping, decorating, and maintenance may be wasted if the rental agent is unresponsive or unprofessional or does not properly show the property. Probably the most important ingredient of achieving occupancy targets is well-trained rental staff members who are personable, enthusiastic, and professional. Many large management organizations spend substantial time and money to ensure that rental agents have the technical knowledge and sales skills to best represent the property owner. The property manager should maintain records carefully, including guest books to record visitors' names. The rental agent should describe the result of each visit and record subsequent follow-up calls.

# LEASES AND TENANT RELATIONS

Potential conflicts between property managers and tenants usually can be avoided when sound property management practices are employed. Sound management begins with negotiation between the property manager and the prospective tenant, the results of which should be in written form (the lease).

## Essentials of a Valid Lease

The general requirements for a valid lease are similar to those for any legally enforceable contract:

- Complete and legal names of both parties (lessor and lessee)
- Legal description of the property
- Contractual capacity of the parties and legal purpose of the agreement
- Consideration or amount of rent
- Term of occupancy
- Use of the premises
- Rights and obligations of the lessor and lessee
- In writing and signed (if for more than one year)

Licensees may fill in the blanks on only the lease forms specifically approved by the Florida Supreme Court. Changing or adding to the terms of the approved forms or completing the blanks on any other lease form is considered unauthorized practice of law. Currently, there are two leases approved by the Supreme Court: the *Residential Lease for Single-Family Home and Duplex*, and a form developed by the Florida Bar.

The manager should explain the key points in the lease agreement. Rent collection policies should be covered. Tenants will usually pay rent promptly if the collection policy is efficient, effective, and reasonable. The manager should itemize other regulations that control the property and discuss the methods of enforcing them. The manager must be certain that the tenant understands maintenance policies and how responsibilities are divided between landlord and tenant. These policies and procedures are often outlined in a tenant brochure.

Most tenant-management problems center on maintenance service requests. When such a request is made, the tenant should be told immediately whether it will be granted. The tenant is the customer, not an adversary, and the staff should be reminded of that fact continually. Happy tenants remain in residence, eliminate expensive turnover, protect the owner's property (which lowers maintenance costs), and promote the property's reputation (which reduces vacancy losses and promotional expenses).

A tenant request for service should be entered on a standardized request form. The top copy and a copy to be left in the unit on completion of the work are assigned to the maintenance person answering the request. The manager keeps the third copy until the job is completed. An estimated completion date should be entered on the manager's copy for follow-up. The resident manager should contact the tenant to ensure that the work was completed properly.

## Landlord and Tenant Act

Chapter 83, F.S., the Florida Residential Landlord and Tenant Act, outlines the rights and duties of landlords and tenants, as well as the legal remedies available to both parties in case of noncompliance with lease terms. The intent was to create a reasonable balance between the two parties in their legal relationship. The law includes, among its many requirements, very specific rules for handling security deposits and advance rent. Florida licensees acting as residential managers must comply with the act. Those real estate licensees desiring to know more about this subject should obtain a current copy of this Florida law.

## OPERATING REPORTS

Owners of residential rental apartments need current operating reports to measure the profitability of their investments. The annual operating budget, cash flow statement, and profit and loss statement give an owner the data necessary to evaluate his property and its management.

## Operating Budget

The property manager must prepare a meaningful annual operating budget that includes all anticipated income and expense items for the property. The starting point for this year's budget most often is based on the actual data from the previous year. The annual budget is helpful as a guide for overall profitability. It must, however, be broken down into monthly budgets if it is to be useful for controlling operations. There, the manager should produce monthly statements that compare actual and budgeted amounts and should be able to explain any significant variations.

## Cash Flow Statement

Probably the most important operating record is the manager's monthly **cash flow report** on receipts and disbursements. This report includes all operating income, such as the income from parking, washing machines, dryers, and vending machines, and all operating expenses as well as debt service. The reports show the owner how the property is doing on a cash basis. The report also can include the annual budget as well as the previous year's results, providing a budgetary control as well as a cash control. A sample cash flow statement is shown in the Forms-To-Go Appendix.

## Profit and Loss Statement

A **profit and loss statement** is a financial report of a property's actual net profit, which may differ from the cash flow. The full mortgage payment is not shown; only the interest payment is an expense. The manager usually prepares a profit and loss statement quarterly, semiannually, and yearly. Monthly income and expense reports provide the raw data for these statements. The more detail provided in the report, the better the opportunities for meaningful analysis.

### Additional Reports

Managers must be completely familiar with all phases of a property's operation. Other reports, such as vacancy ratios, bad-debt ratios, showings-to-rent ratios, and changes in tenant profiles, illustrate important trends that may require corrective action. Scrutiny of the budgets and actual expenditures per account from month to month and year to year can indicate the relative performance of management personnel.

## LICENSING REQUIREMENTS IN FLORIDA

Property managers must be certain that the requirements of Chapter 475 of the Florida Statutes are followed carefully. The law requires that any person who rents or leases real property for another party for compensation have a current, active license. Two exemptions exist:

1. Salaried employees of an owner, or of a registered broker working for an owner or for the properly licensed property manager of an apartment complex, who work in an on-site rental office of the apartment community in a leasing capacity
2. Salaried persons employed as managers of condominiums or cooperative apartment complexes who rent individual units, if the rentals arranged by the employees are for periods not exceeding one year

These exemptions are granted under the law to unlicensed, salaried employees. They may not be paid a commission or any form of compensation on a transactional basis.

### Community Association Management

Property managers of certain community associations must obtain community association manager licenses from the Department of Business and Professional Regulation. This law does not affect apartment properties and commercial property.

## SUMMARY

When an owner hires a manager, the parties enter into one of three relationships: principal-agent, employer-employee, or trustor-trustee. Most management contracts share six basic characteristics and specify the duties and details of management operations that must be decided before responsibility for the property is transferred to the manager.

To handle the property's maintenance demands, the manager must know the building's needs and the number and type of personnel required to perform the maintenance functions. Staff and scheduling requirements vary with a property's type, size, and regional location.

Four types of maintenance operations exist: preventive maintenance, corrective maintenance, routine housekeeping, and new construction. Deferred maintenance is the term applied to accumulated postponed maintenance.

The hiring policy for on-site maintenance staff depends on the cost differential between maintaining a permanent building staff and contracting for needed services. A particular property's circumstances dictate which alternative is more efficient and economical.

Multifamily dwellings differ from one another in size, structure, location, and number of amenities provided. These differences exert a direct influence on the advertising techniques used to market each type of space. A show list of units available for inspection also is important to a property manager's marketing program, as is newspaper advertising, the most widely used medium for renting space because it reaches a large audience.

In addition to leasing, supervising the resident manager, and inspecting the maintenance of the premises, the property manager must provide the owner with regular financial reports. Various financial statements provide the owner with the data necessary to evaluate the performance of the manager and the property itself.

Property managers in Florida must meet the requirements of Chapters 83 and 475 of the Florida Statutes, unless specifically exempted.

# K E Y   T E R M S

| | | |
|---|---|---|
| cash flow report | deferred maintenance | preventive maintenance |
| Certified Property Manager (CPM) | Institute of Real Estate Management (IREM) | profit and loss statement |
| contract service | new construction | resident manager |
| corrective maintenance | maintenance | routine maintenance |
| | | show list |

# PRACTICE EXAM

1. A salaried, unlicensed manager of a resort condominium in Florida legally may rent individual condominium units if the rental periods do not exceed:
   a. one month.
   b. 90 days.
   c. six months.
   d. one year.

2. A person who provides services that require licensing under the Community Association Management Act must be licensed by the:
   a. Florida Real Estate Commission.
   b. Department of Administration.
   c. Department of Business and Professional Regulation.
   d. Department of Community Affairs.

3. Maintenance on a building that cannot or will not be performed when necessary is which of the following types of maintenance?
   a. Elective
   b. Deferred
   c. Corrective
   d. Routine

4. Maintenance services performed by a person or company outside the management company are called:
   a. service contracts.
   b. contract services.
   c. in-house maintenance.
   d. preventive maintenance.

5. The fastest-growing advertising medium for real estate residential rentals is:
   a. display advertising.
   b. apartment guides.
   c. homes magazines.
   d. classified advertising.

6. The major form of advertising used to rent apartments is:
   a. outdoor signs.
   b. television spot commercials.
   c. display ads.
   d. classified ads.

7. Apartments that are vacant and available for immediate rental are placed on the:
   a. floor list.
   b. up list.
   c. show list.
   d. cleared list.

8. According to the text, most tenant-management problems are related to:
   a. late or unpaid rent.
   b. maintenance service requests.
   c. conduct of tenants and their guests.
   d. handling of security deposits and advance rent.

9. The most important operating record for the property manager is probably the:
   a. vacancy and bad-debt report.
   b. after-tax cash flow analysis.
   c. annual profit and loss statement.
   d. monthly cash flow report.

10. Which of the following is NOT a category of property maintenance?
    a. Elective
    b. Preventive
    c. Routine
    d. Corrective

11. The individual responsible for the fiscal, physical, and administrative management functions for an investment property owner is the:
    a. resident manager.
    b. property manager.
    c. maintenance manager.
    d. residential property consultant.

12. What is NOT a requirement for a valid lease?
    a. Contractual capacity of the parties
    b. Amount of leasing commissions
    c. Term of occupancy
    d. Consideration

13. The starting point for most annual budgets is:
    a. what the manager thinks will happen.
    b. last year's actual results.
    c. this year's actual results.
    d. last year's budget.

14. Howard is an employee of a property management firm. He shows prospective tenants many of the duplexes the company manages around the city and writes up leases on the court-approved forms. Howard is paid $700 per month plus $50 per signed lease. Howard:
    a. must have a community association manager's license.
    b. must have a community association manager's license *and* a real estate license.
    c. must have a real estate license.
    d. need not be licensed because he is not paid a commission.

15. Wendy is the property manager for a new apartment community. She cannot seem to get occupancy up to budgeted levels, even with additional advertising. What else might be helpful?
    a. Additional training for the rental agents
    b. Soliciting broker cooperation
    c. Sprucing up the property's curb appeal
    d. All the above

16. What prestigious designation is awarded to property managers who complete rigorous education and experience requirements?
    a. GRI
    b. CPM
    c. CRS
    d. CRB

17. What would *NOT* normally be included in a management contract?
    a. Term
    b. Compensation
    c. Financing clause
    d. Signatures of the parties

18. The type of maintenance aimed at preserving the physical integrity of the premises is:
    a. deferred.
    b. preventive.
    c. corrective.
    d. routine.

19. How many apartments should be on the show list?
    a. At least five of each type
    b. No more than one
    c. No more than three of each type
    d. All available units

20. Probably the most important ingredient of achieving occupancy targets is:
    a. classified advertising.
    b. good curb appeal.
    c. excellent maintenance.
    d. well-trained rental staff who are personable, enthusiastic, and professional.

## APPLY WHAT YOU'VE LEARNED!

The authors suggest the following actions to reinforce the material in *Section V—Commercial and Residential Investment Property:*

❑ Select an apartment property in your area that has at least 30 units and learn the rental rate. Find out the typical vacancy rates in the area, then prepare a financial statement. Use an operating expense ratio of 40 percent.

❑ When you have completed the financial statement, capitalize the income at 10 percent to estimate a "ride-by" opinion of value.

❑ Call a lender and ask for information about what loans are available for properties of this type. Discuss loan-to-value ratios, debt coverage ratios, and interest rates.

❑ Based on this information, calculate the before-tax cash flow. Make sure the debt coverage ratio is at least what the lender requires. Using the before-tax cash flow, determine what an investor would be willing to pay in a down payment if she requires a 14 percent equity dividend rate.

❑ Travel on a thoroughfare, and visit at least three vacant commercial buildings. Make notes on the structures, and try to decide the highest and best uses. List three potential tenants for each site. Call the listing agent and get information on each property.

❑ Assume a potential buyer from out of town asks you to describe the local economy and estimate about what it will do in the next three years. Write your response as completely as possible. Get information from the local chamber of commerce, and compare your description with your classmates' descriptions.

❑ If you work in residential real estate, you often may encounter potential commercial customers. Ask your broker which commercial broker he recommends for referrals. Check with a licensee in that firm to see whether the referrals could go in both directions, with you getting her residential referrals.

❑ Visit several apartment properties in your area. List the ones you would recommend to a friend looking for an apartment.

# RESOURCES

The following sources are selective and not exhaustive. Each is listed by section in the book and in the order recommended by the author for further study. Numerous other available resources exist, including books, journals (e.g., FAR's Florida REALTOR® magazine), periodicals, newsletters, articles, legal cases, research studies, video programs, and seminars. Consult your broker, instructor, or local board librarian for further assistance.

## SECTION I. LAYING THE FOUNDATION FOR A SUCCESSFUL CAREER

1. Reilly, John W. *Agency Relationships in Real Estate*. 1997 or later edition. Chicago: Dearborn Real Estate Education®.
2. Crawford, Linda L., and Edward J. O'Donnell. *Florida Real Estate Broker's Guide*. 1st edition. Chicago: Dearborn Real Estate Education®, 2003.
3. Gaines, George, Jr., David S. Coleman, and Linda Crawford. *Florida Real Estate Principles, Practices & Law*. 27th edition. Chicago: Dearborn Real Estate Education®.
4. Lyons, Gail G., and Donald L. Harlan. *Buyer Agency: Your Competitive Edge in Real Estate*. 3rd or later edition. Chicago: Dearborn Real Estate Education®.
5. O'Donnell, Edward J. *Continuing Education for Florida Real Estate Professionals*. 2004 edition. Chicago: Dearborn Real Estate Education®, 2003.
6. O'Donnell, Edward J. *30-Day Track to Success*. Tallahassee: O'Donnell Publishing, 2003.
7. Zeller, Dirk. *Your 1st Year in Real Estate*. New York: Three Rivers Press, 2001.
8. Ferry, Mike. *How to Develop a Six Figure Income in Real Estate*. Chicago: Dearborn Real Estate Education®, 1993.

## SECTION II. OBTAINING LISTINGS THAT SELL

1. Keller, Gary. *The Millionaire Real Estate Agent*. New York: McGraw-Hill, 2004.
2. Lyons, Gail G. *Real Estate Sales Handbook*. Chicago: Dearborn Real Estate Education®, 1994.
3. Davis, Darryl. *How to Become a Power Agent in Real Estate*. New York: McGraw-Hill, 2003.
4. Edwards, Kenneth W. *Your Successful Real Estate Career*. 4th edition. New York: Amacom, 2003.

## SECTION III.  SELLING REAL PROPERTY

1. Galaty, Fillmore W., et al. *Modern Real Estate Practice*. 14th or later edition. Chicago: Dearborn Real Estate Education®.

2. Reilly, John W. *The Language of Real Estate*. 4th or later edition. Chicago: Dearborn Real Estate Education®.

3. Keane, Gerald B. *Florida Law: A Layman's Guide*. Englewood, Fla.: Pineapple Press, Inc., 1987.

4. Gibson, Frank, et al. *Real Estate Law*. 4th or later edition. Chicago: Dearborn Real Estate Education®.

5. Ventolo, William L., Jr., and Martha R. Williams. *Fundamentals of Real Estate Appraisal*. 7th or later edition. Chicago: Dearborn Real Estate Education®.

6. Crawford, Linda L., and Edward J. O'Donnell. *Florida Real Estate Broker's Guide*. 1st edition. Chicago: Dearborn Real Estate Education®, 1999.

7. Smith, Halbert C. *Real Estate Appraisal*. 2nd or later edition. Worthington, Ohio: Century VII Publishing Company.

8. Ring, Alfred A., and James H. Boykin. *The Valuation of Real Estate*. 1986 or later edition. Englewood Cliffs, N.J.: Prentice-Hall, Inc.

## SECTION IV.  FINANCING AND CLOSING REAL ESTATE TRANSACTIONS

1. Sirota, David. *Essentials of Real Estate Finance*. 9th or later edition. Chicago: Dearborn Real Estate Education®.

2. Crawford, Linda L., and Edward J. O'Donnell. *Florida Real Estate Broker's Guide*. 2nd edition. Chicago: Dearborn Real Estate Education®, 1999.

3. Steinmetz, Thomas C. *The Mortgage Kit*. 4th or later edition. Chicago: Dearborn Real Estate Education®.

4. Mettling, Stephen R., and Gerald R. Cortesi. *Modern Residential Financing Methods*. 2nd or later edition. Chicago: Dearborn Real Estate Education®.

5. Turner, R. J. *The Mortgage Maze*. 1982 or later edition. Arlington, Va.: Alexandria House Books.

6. Gaines, George, Jr., David S. Coleman, and Linda Crawford. *Florida Real Estate Principles, Practices & Law*. 25th or later edition. Chicago: Dearborn Real Estate Education®.

7. O'Donnell, Edward J. *Continuing Education for Florida Real Estate Professionals*. 2004 edition. Chicago: Dearborn Real Estate Education®.

8. Koogler, Karen E. *Closing Concepts—A Title Training Manual for Settlement Escrow Professionals*. 3rd edition. Largo, Fla.: The Koogler Group, 1996.

# SECTION V.  COMMERCIAL AND RESIDENTIAL INVESTMENT PROPERTY

1. Sirota, David. *Essentials of Real Estate Investment.* 6th or later edition. Chicago: Dearborn Real Estate Education®.

2. Kyle, Robert C., and Floyd M. Baird. *Property Management.* 5th or later edition. Chicago: Dearborn Real Estate Education®.

3. Crawford, Linda L., and Edward J. O'Donnell. *Florida Real Estate Broker's Guide.* 1st edition. Chicago: Dearborn Real Estate Education®, 1999.

4. Downs, James C., Jr. *Principles of Real Estate Management.* 12th or later edition. Chicago: Institute of Real Estate Management.

# FORMS-TO-GO

This appendix is intended as a resource for real estate professionals. The forms included here have been carefully prepared and may be freely copied and used in your practice. While we believe the forms to be complete and accurate, we make no representations as to their legality. Before using these forms, licensees are cautioned to seek legal and other professional advice.

| No Brokerage Relationship Notice |
| --- |

IMPORTANT NOTICE

FLORIDA LAW REQUIRES THAT REAL ESTATE LICENSEES PROVIDE THIS
NOTICE TO POTENTIAL SELLERS AND BUYERS OF REAL ESTATE.

You should not assume that any real estate broker or sales associate represents you unless you agree to engage in a real estate licensee in an authorized brokerage relationship, either as a single agent or as a transaction broker. You are advised not to disclose any information you want to be held in confidence until you decide on representation.

NO BROKERAGE RELATIONSHIP NOTICE

FLORIDA LAW REQUIRES THAT REAL ESTATE LICENSEES WHO HAVE NO BROKERAGE
RELATIONSHIP WITH A POTENTIAL SELLER OR BUYER DISCLOSE THEIR DUTIES TO SELLERS
AND BUYERS.

As a real estate licensee who has no brokerage relationship with you,
_____ (insert name of real estate entity) and its Associates owe to
you the following duties:

1.  Dealing honestly and fairly.
2.  Disclosing all known facts that materially affect the value of residential real property which are not readily observable to the buyer.
3.  Accounting for all funds entrusted to the licensee.

_____          _____
Date                              Signature

_____          _____
Date                              Signature

## Single Agent Notice

IMPORTANT NOTICE

FLORIDA LAW REQUIRES THAT REAL ESTATE LICENSEES PROVIDE
THIS NOTICE TO POTENTIAL SELLERS AND BUYERS OF REAL ESTATE.

You should not assume that any real estate broker or sales associate represents you unless you agree to engage a real estate licensee in an authorized brokerage relationship, either as a single agent or as a transaction broker. You are advised not to disclose any information you want to be held in confidence until you make a decision on representation.

SINGLE AGENT NOTICE

FLORIDA LAW REQUIRES THAT REAL ESTATE LICENSEES OPERATING
AS SINGLE AGENTS DISCLOSE TO BUYERS AND SELLERS THEIR DUTIES.

As a single agent, _____, *(insert name of real estate entity)* and its associates owe to you the following duties:

1. Dealing honestly and fairly;

2. Loyalty;

3. Confidentiality;

4. Obedience;

5. Full disclosure;

6. Accounting for all funds;

7. Skill, care, and diligence in the transaction;

8. Presenting all offers and counteroffers in a timely manner, unless a party has previously directed the licensee otherwise in writing; and

9. Disclosing all known facts that materially affect the value of residential real property and are not readily observable.

_____          _____
Date                                      Signature

_____          _____
Date                                      Signature

## Transaction Broker Notice

IMPORTANT NOTICE

FLORIDA LAW REQUIRES THAT REAL ESTATE LICENSEES PROVIDE
THIS NOTICE TO POTENTIAL SELLERS AND BUYERS OF REAL ESTATE.

You should not assume that any real estate broker or sales associate represents you unless you agree to engage a real estate licensee in an authorized brokerage relationship, either as a single agent or as a transaction broker. You are advised not to disclose any information you want to be held in confidence until you make a decision on representation.

TRANSACTION BROKER NOTICE

FLORIDA LAW REQUIRES THAT REAL ESTATE LICENSEES OPERATING AS
TRANSACTION BROKERS DISCLOSE TO BUYERS AND SELLERS THEIR ROLE AND
DUTIES IN PROVIDING A LIMITED FORM OF REPRESENTATION.

As a transaction broker, _____ *(insert name of real estate entity)* and its Associates, provides to you a limited form of representation that includes the following duties:

1. Dealing honestly and fairly;
2. Accounting for all funds;
3. Using skill, care, and diligence in the transaction;
4. Disclosing all known facts that materially affect the value of residential real property and are not readily observable to the buyer;
5. Presenting all offers and counteroffers in a timely manner, unless a party has previously directed the licensee otherwise in writing;
6. Limited confidentiality, unless waived in writing by a party. This limited confidentiality will prevent disclosure that the seller will accept a price less than the asking or listed price, that the buyer will pay a price greater than the price submitted in a written offer, of the motivation of any party for selling or buying property, that a seller or buyer will agree to financing terms other than those offered, or of any other information requested by a party to remain confidential; and
7. Any additional duties that are entered into by this or by separate written agreement.

Limited representation means that a buyer or seller is not responsible for the acts of the licensee. Additionally, parties are giving up their rights to the undivided loyalty of the licensee. This aspect of limited representation allows a licensee to facilitate a real estate transaction by assisting both the buyer and the seller, but a licensee will not work to represent one party to the detriment of the other party when acting as a transaction broker to both parties.

_____          _____
Date                                                        Signature

_____          _____
Date                                                        Signature

| Consent to Transition to Transaction Broker Notice |
|---|

## CONSENT TO TRANSITION TO
## TRANSACTION BROKER

FLORIDA LAW ALLOWS REAL ESTATE LICENSEES WHO REPRESENT A BUYER OR SELLER AS A SINGLE AGENT TO CHANGE FROM A SINGLE AGENT RELATIONSHIP TO A TRANSACTION BROKERAGE RELATIONSHIP IN ORDER FOR THE LICENSEE TO ASSIST BOTH PARTIES IN A REAL ESTATE TRANSACTION BY PROVIDING A LIMITED FORM OF REPRESENTATION TO BOTH THE BUYER AND THE SELLER. THIS CHANGE IN RELATIONSHIP CANNOT OCCUR WITHOUT YOUR PRIOR WRITTEN CONSENT.

As a transaction broker,_____, *(insert name of real estate entity and its associates)* provides to you a limited form of representation that includes the following duties:

1. Dealing honestly and fairly;
2. Accounting for all funds;
3. Using skill, care and diligence in the transaction;
4. Disclosing all known facts that materially affect the value of residential real property and are not readily observable to the buyer;
5. Presenting all offers and counteroffers in a timely manner, unless a party has previously directed the licensee otherwise in writing;
6. Limited confidentiality, unless waived in writing by a party. This limited confidentiality will prevent disclosure that the seller will accept a price less than the asking or listed price, that the buyer will pay a price greater than the price submitted in a written offer, of the motivation of any party for selling or buying property, that a seller or buyer will agree to financing terms other than those offered, or of any other information requested by a party to remain confidential; and
7. Any additional duties that are entered into by this or by separate written agreement.

Limited representation means that a buyer or seller is not responsible for the acts of the licensee. Additionally, parties are giving up their rights to the undivided loyalty of the licensee. This aspect of limited representation allows a licensee to facilitate a real estate transaction by assisting both the buyer and the seller, but a licensee will not work to represent one party to the detriment of the other party when acting as a transaction broker to both parties.

I agree that my agent may assume the role and duties of a transaction broker.
[Must be initialed or signed]

_____    _____
Date                                           Signature

_____    _____
Date                                           Signature

## Designated Sales Associate Notice

### DESIGNATED SALES ASSOCIATE

I have assets of one million dollars or more. I request that _____ use the
(Name of broker)
designated sales associate form or representation.


Signature:_____ (circle one)  Seller / Buyer


### SINGLE AGENT NOTICE

#### FIORIDA LAW REQUIRES THAT REAL ESTATE LICENSEES OPERATING AS SINGLE AGENTS DISCLOSE TO BUYERS AND SELLERS THEIR DUTIES

As a single agent, _____ owe to you the following
duties:       *(insert name of Real Estate Entity)* and its Associates
1. Dealing honestly and fairly;
2. Loyalty;
3. Confidentiality;
4. Obedience;
5. Full disclosure;
6. Accounting for all funds;
7. Skill, care, and diligence in the transaction;
8. Presenting all offers and counteroffers in a timely manner, unless a party has previously directed the licensee otherwise in writing; and
9. Disclosing all known facts that materially affect the value of residential real property and are not readily observable.


_____  _____     _____

Date      Signature                     Signature

_____

### Designated Sales Associate Notice

Florida law prohibits a designated sales associate from disclosing, except to the broker or persons specified by the broker, information made confidential by request or at the instruction of the customer the designated sales associate is representing. However, Florida law allows a designated sales associate to disclose information allowed to be disclosed or required to be disclosed by law and also allows a designated sales associate to disclose to his or her broker, or persons specified by the broker, confidential information of a customer for the purpose of seeking advice or assistance for the benefit of the customer in regard to a transaction. Florida law requires that the broker must hold this information confidential and may not use such information to the detriment of the other party.


_____  _____     _____

Date      Signature optional            Signature optional

**Goals Worksheet**

# GOALS WORKSHEET

1. During the next 12 months, I want to earn $ _____

2. That works out to be monthly earnings of $ _____
   (Line 1 ÷ 12)

3. Approximately 60% of my earnings should come from listings sold $ _____
   (Line 2 × .60)

4. Approximately 40% of my earnings should come from sales made $ _____
   (Line 2 × .40)

**Achieving my listing income:**

5. In my market area, the average listing commission amount is $ _____
   (Get this amount from your broker.)

6. So I must have the following number of listings sold _____
   (Line 3 ÷ Line 5)

7. If only 75% of my listings sell, I have to get this many listings: _____
   (Line 6 ÷ .75)

8. It may take this many listing appointments to get a listing: _____
   (Get this number from your broker.)

9. So I need to go on this many listing appointments _____
   (Line 7 × Line 8)

10. It may take this many calls to get an appointment _____
    (Get this number from your broker.)

11. So I have to make this many calls per month: _____
    (Line 9 × Line 10)

12. Which means this many calls per week _____
    (Line 11 ÷ 4.3 weeks per month)

**Achieving my sales income:**

13. In my market area, the average sales commission is $ _____
    (Get this amount from your broker.)

14. So I've got to make this many sales per month: _____
    (Line 4 ÷ Line 13)

15. It takes about this many showings to make a sale: _____
    (Get this number from your broker.)

16. So I must show this many properties per month: _____
    (Line 14 × Line 15)

# SELLER'S PROPERTY DISCLOSURE
(IT IS SUGGESTED THAT COPIES OF THIS DISCLOSURE BE AVAILABLE AT THE PROPERTY)
## STATEMENT

SELLER: _____

Property Address: _____

Date Property Purchased _____ If improved, year built_____

**NOTICE TO SELLER**: Every SELLER is obligated to disclose to a BUYER all known facts that materially and/or adversely affect the value of the property being sold. This disclosure statement is intended to assist SELLER in complying with disclosure requirements and to assist BUYER in evaluating the property being considered. The listing broker, the selling broker and their respective salespersons will also rely upon this information when they evaluate, market and present SELLER'S property to prospective BUYERS.

**NOTICE TO BUYER**: This is a disclosure of SELLER'S knowledge of the condition of the property as of the date signed by the SELLER and is not a substitute for any inspections that BUYER may wish to obtain. It is not a warranty of any kind by SELLER or a warranty or representation by the listing broker, the selling broker, or their salespersons.

• If this property is unimproved, complete sections 15 to 19 only.
• When explanations are needed please give details such as location, extent, date, and name of repair persons. Use extra sheets if necessary.

## 1. OCCUPANCY
(a) Does SELLER currently occupy this property? ❑ Yes ❑ No
(b) If not, when did SELLER vacate property?_____
(c) If property is vacant, provide date it was vacated. _____
(d) Is the property tenant occupied? ❑ Yes ❑ No
(e) If "Yes," is there a written lease? ❑ Yes ❑ No
(f) Length of lease_____ Date lease ends: _____
(g) Payment due under lease_____

## 2. STRUCTURAL ITEMS
(a) Name of Contractor or Builder who built home, if known_____
(b) Are you aware of any past or present movement, shifting, deterioration, structural damage or other problems with walls or foundations? ❑ Yes ❑ No
(c) Are you aware of any past or present cracks or flaws in the walls, foundation or other parts of property? ❑ Yes ❑ No
(d) Are you aware of any past or present water leakage or intrusion in the property? ❑ Yes ❑ No
(e) Are you aware of any past or present problems with driveways, walkways, patios, or retaining walls? ❑ Yes ❑ No
(f) Have there been any repairs or other efforts to control the cause or effect of any problem described above? ❑ Yes ❑ No
(g) Has there ever been a fire in this property? ❑ Yes ❑ No ❑ Unknown
(h) Are you aware of any problems with the fireplace? ❑ Yes ❑ No
If any of your answers are "Yes," explain in detail: _____
_____
_____

## 3. ADDITIONS / REMODELING
(a) Have you made any additions, structural changes, or other alterations to the property? ❑ Yes ❑ No
(b) If "Yes," explain: _____
(c) If "Yes," did you obtain all necessary permits? ❑ Yes ❑ No    Was all the work in compliance with building codes? ❑ Yes ❑ No
If your answer is "No," explain: _____
(d) Did the previous owners make any additions, structural changes, or other alterations to the property that you are aware of?
❑ Yes ❑ No ❑ Unknown
(e) If "Yes," explain: _____
(f) Please provide the name of any Contractor or individual who did any additions, structural changes or other alterations to the property, if known._____

## 4. ROOF
(a) Year roof put on_____
(b) Has the roof ever leaked during your ownership? ❑ Yes ❑ No
(c) Has the roof been replaced or repaired during your ownership? ❑ Yes ❑ No
If "Yes," provide name of Contractor or individual who did the work and details of replacement/repair_____
_____
(d) Do you know of any problems with the roof or gutters? ❑ Yes ❑ No
If any of your answers are "Yes," explain in detail: _____
_____
_____

## Seller's Property Disclosure Statement (continued)

### 5. SIDING

(a) Exterior siding material(s)

☐ Brick     ☐ Wood     ☐ Vinyl     ☐ Stucco     ☐ Synthetic Stucco     ☐ Manufactured Siding

☐ Other_____     ☐ Unknown

(b) If manufactured siding, provide name of manufacturer, if known_____

(c) Do you know of any problems/defects with the siding? ☐ Yes     ☐ No

(d) Have you filed any claims with manufacturers in regards to the siding? ☐ Yes     ☐ No

If any of your answers are "Yes," explain in detail: _____

_____

_____

### 6. WINDOWS

(a) Are the windows insulated glass? ☐ Yes     ☐ No

(b) If "Yes," are there any fogged windows? ☐ Yes     ☐ No     ☐ Unknown

If "Yes," which ones_____

(c) Are any windows broken or cracked? ☐ Yes     ☐ No     ☐ Unknown

(d) Do all operable windows open, stay open, close and lock properly? ☐ Yes     ☐ No     ☐ Unknown

(e) Are any screens missing or damaged? ☐ Yes     ☐ No     ☐ Unknown

If "Yes," which ones_____

Page 1 of 3          Initials  _____  _____

### 7. HEATING AND AIR CONDITIONING

(a) Air Conditioning: ☐ Central Electric  ☐ Natural Gas     ☐ Window Units   Number units included in sale_____

(b) Heating:          ☐ Central Electric  ☐ Central Electric Heat Pump  ☐ Fuel Oil  ☐ Natural Gas  ☐ Other_____

Are you aware of any problems regarding these items? ☐ Yes     ☐ No

If "Yes," explain in detail: _____

_____

_____

### 8. ELECTRICAL SYSTEM

(a) Are you aware of any problems with the electrical system? ☐ Yes     ☐ No

(b) Who supplies electrical service: ☐ City of Tallahassee     ☐ Talquin

(c) Average utility bill? $_____ month

(d) Number of people living in property_____

Comments:_____

_____

### 9. PLUMBING

(a) Are you aware of any problems with the plumbing system? ☐ Yes     ☐ No

(b) Are you aware of any leaks, back-ups, water, and sewer/septic tank problems? ☐ Yes     ☐ No

(c) What is your water supply source: ☐ Public     ☐ Community Well     ☐ Well on Property

(d) If your water is from a well, have there ever been repairs/replacements to the well or pump? ☐ Yes     ☐ No     ☐ Unknown

(e) Has the well water ever been tested? ☐ Yes     ☐ No     ☐ Unknown   Test Results:_____

(f) Do you have a water softener? ☐ Yes     ☐ No     If "Yes," is the system ☐ Owned     ☐ Leased

(g) What is the type of sewage system do you have? ☐ Public  ☐ Community Sewer  ☐ Septic Tank(s) How Many_____

Location(s) _____   When was septic tank last pumped?_____

(h) Type of water heater?  ☐ Gas  ☐ Electric  ☐ Solar  ☐ Number of gallons?_____  Is it on a timer? ☐ Yes  ☐ No

If any of your answers are "Yes," explain in detail: _____

_____

### 10. OTHER EQUIPMENT AND APPLIANCES INCLUDED IN SALE

Mark the items included in the sale of your property:

☐ Electric Garage Door Opener     Number of transmitters?_____

☐ Smoke Detector(s)     How many?_____

☐ Refrigerator          ☐ Refrigerator w/ice maker     ☐ Ice Maker

☐ Microwave Oven        ☐ Dishwasher                   ☐ Garbage Disposal

☐ Trash Compactor       ☐ Intercom                     ☐ Washer          ☐ Dryer

☐ Ceiling Fan(s) Number of fans?_____              ☐ Central Vacuum

☐ Fireplace insert      ☐ Sprinkler system

☐ Oil/Propane Tanks     ☐ Owned  ☐ Leased, If leased, from whom _____ Cost _____

☐ Security System       ☐ Owned  ☐ Leased, If leased, from whom _____ Cost _____

☐ Other:_____

If any of these items have any defects, explain in detail: _____

_____

## Seller's Property Disclosure Statement (continued)

11. <u>POOL / SPA / HOT TUB</u> **(Complete if applicable)**
   (a) ❑ **POOL** year installed_____
      ❑ In ground:   ❑ gunnite   ❑ fiberglass   ❑ vinyl   age of liner _____
      ❑ Above ground
   (b) Pool heater:   ❑ none   ❑ gas   ❑ electric   ❑ solar
   (c) Pool pump: year installed_____   Filter type:_____ year installed_____
   (d) Is pool equipment included? ❑ Yes   ❑ No
      If "Yes," itemize: _____
   (e) ❑ **SPA/HOT TUB**   year installed_____
   (f) Spa heater:   ❑ none   ❑ gas   ❑ electric   ❑ solar
   (g) Is Spa equipment included? ❑ Yes   ❑ No
      If "Yes," itemize: _____
   If you are aware of any problems with any of the items above, please explain in detail:_____
   _____
   _____

12. <u>EXCLUSIONS/LEASED SYSTEMS</u>
   (a) Is there anything on or about the property excluded from the sale? ❑ Yes   ❑ No
      If "Yes," itemize_____
      _____
   (b) Are there any other leased systems that are not addressed elsewhere in the disclosure? ❑ Yes   ❑ No
      If "Yes," itemize:_____
      _____

13. <u>CRAWL SPACES AND BASEMENTS</u> **(Complete if applicable)**
   (a) Has there ever been any water leakage, accumulation of water or dampness in the basement or crawl space? ❑ Yes   ❑ No
   (b) Have there been any repairs or other attempts to control any water or dampness problems in the basement or crawlspace? ❑ Yes   ❑ No
   If any of your answers are "Yes," explain in detail:_____
   _____

14. <u>WOOD DESTROYING ORGANISMS</u>
   (a) Have termites, wood destroying insects, or wood rot affected the property during your ownership? ❑ Yes   ❑ No
   (b) Has there ever been any damage to the property caused by termites, wood destroying insects or wood rot during your ownership? ❑ Yes   ❑ No
   (c) Is the property currently under bond for a wood destroying insect from a licensed pest control company? ❑ Yes   ❑ No
      What type of bond?_____What company?_____
   (d) Do you know of any wood destroying organisms reports on the property in the last five years? ❑ Yes   ❑ No
   If any of your answers are "Yes," explain in detail:_____
   _____
   _____

Page 2 of 3     Initials _____  _____
                         _____  _____

15. <u>SOIL / DRAINAGE / BOUNDARIES</u>
   (a) Is there any fill or pipe clay on the property?   ❑ Yes   ❑ No   ❑ Unknown
   (b) Has there been any settling or earth movement on the property or in the immediate neighborhood?   ❑ Yes   ❑ No   ❑ Unknown
   (c) Is the property located in a flood hazard area?   ❑ Yes   ❑ No   ❑ Unknown
      Flood zone, if known_____
   (d) Is flood insurance required by your lender?   ❑ Yes   ❑ No
   (e) Have there been any past or present drainage or flood problems affecting the property or adjacent properties?   ❑ Yes   ❑ No   ❑ Unknown
   (f) Are there any encroachments, excroachments, boundary line disputes, or easements affecting the property?   ❑ Yes   ❑ No   ❑ Unknown
   (g) Are there any shared driveways, fences or joint use agreements?   ❑ Yes   ❑ No
   (h) Who owns any fences? _____
   If any answers are "Yes," explain in detail:_____
   _____

16. <u>TOXIC SUBSTANCES</u>
   (a) Are you aware of any hazardous materials in, on or about the property? (Hazardous Materials may include but shall not be limited to: lead-based paint, asbestos materials, asbestos siding, and buried oil, fuel or other storage tanks)   ❑ Yes   ❑ No
   (b) Are you aware of the property ever being tested for radon or any other toxic substances?   ❑ Yes   ❑ No
   If any answers are "Yes," explain in detail:_____

## Seller's Property Disclosure Statement (continued)

### 17. NEIGHBORHOOD

(a)  Are you aware of any proposed change or condition in your neighborhood that could affect the value or desirability of the property?
❏ Yes   ❏ No

(b)  If "Yes," explain in detail:_____

_____

### 18. ASSOCIATIONS

(a)  Is the property part of a  ❏ homeowner's association   ❏ condominium association   ❏ other type of association._____

(b)  Is the property subject to covenants, conditions and restrictions of the association?  ❏ Yes   ❏ No

(c)  Are you aware if the property has any violations of the restrictive covenants?  ❏ Yes   ❏ No

(d)  If "Yes," explain in detail:_____

_____

If the property is part of an association, complete the following:

(e)  What is the annual fee? $_____   How is it paid?_____  ❏ monthly   ❏ yearly   ❏ other_____

(f)  What does the annual fee cover?_____

(g)  Are fees current?  ❏ Yes   ❏ No

(h)  Who is the contact person for the association?_____   Phone #_____

(i)  Are there any defects, damages, legal actions, conditions or assessments that may affect the association or its fees?  ❏ Yes   ❏ No

(j)  If "Yes," explain in detail:_____

_____

### 19. OTHER MATTERS

(a)  Does anyone have a first right of refusal to buy or an option to buy to this property?  ❏ Yes   ❏ No

(b)  Is there any existing or threatened legal action affecting the property?  ❏ Yes   ❏ No

(c)  Are you aware of any zoning violation, non-conforming use, set back violations, or proposed zoning or road changes?  ❏ Yes   ❏ No

(d)  Are you aware of any violations of local, state, or federal laws or regulations relating to this property?  ❏ Yes   ❏ No

(d)  Is there anything else you feel you should disclose to a prospective buyer that may materially and/or adversely affect the value or desirability of the property?  ❏ Yes   ❏ No

(e)  If "Yes," explain in detail:_____

_____

_____

_____

The undersigned SELLER represents that the information set forth in the foregoing property disclosure statement is accurate and complete to the best of the SELLER'S knowledge. SELLER does not intend this property disclosure statement to be a warranty or guaranty of any kind. SELLER hereby authorizes Listing Broker to provide this information to prospective BUYERS and to other real estate brokers and other agents.

SELLER understands and agrees that SELLER will immediately notify Listing Broker in writing if any information set forth in this property disclosure changes.

Seller:_____   Date:_____

Seller:_____   Date:_____

### RECEIPT AND ACKNOWLEDGMENT BY BUYER

BUYER hereby acknowledges receipt of a copy of this property disclosure. BUYER furthermore acknowledges BUYER has been in and upon subject property. BUYER is strongly advised to obtain property inspection(s) as provided for in the Deposit Receipt and Contract for Sale and Purchase. BUYER should select professionals with appropriate qualifications to conduct inspections. BUYER is advised that some properties may have siding materials (such as, but not limited to, Louisiana Pacific and Synthetic Stucco) that have failed the manufacturer's warranties and/or have been known to have defects, and that inspection is one way to identify this and determine what conditions these materials may be in. BUYER is aware that this property disclosure is not intended as a warranty or guaranty of any kind by SELLER. The Brokers and their salespersons do not warrant or guarantee the condition of the property and are in no way responsible for the condition of the property. BUYER understands that the property is being sold in its present condition unless otherwise agreed upon in the Deposit Receipt and Contract for Sale and Purchase. BUYER acknowledges no representations concerning the condition of the property are being relied upon by BUYER except as disclosed herein or in the Deposit Receipt and Contract for Sale and Purchase.

Buyer:_____   Date:_____

Buyer:_____   Date:_____

## Disclosure of Lead-Based Paint and Lead-Based Paint Hazards

### LEAD-BASED PAINT OR LEAD-BASED PAINT HAZARD ADDENDUM

It is a condition of this contract that, until midnight of _____ , Buyer shall have the right to obtain a risk assessment or inspection of the Property for the presence of lead-based paint and/or lead-based paint hazards* at Buyer's expense. This contingency will terminate at that time unless Buyer or Buyer's agent delivers to the Seller or Seller's agent a written inspection and/or risk assessment report listing the specific existing deficiencies and corrections needed, if any. If any corrections are necessary, Seller shall have the option of (i) completing them, (ii) providing for their completion, or (iii) refusing to complete them. If Seller elects not to complete or provide for completion of the corrections, then Buyer shall have the option of (iv) accepting the Property in its present condition, or (v) terminating this contract, in which case all earnest monies shall be refunded to Buyer. Buyer may waive the right to obtain a risk assessment or inspection of the Property for the presence of lead-based paint and/or lead based paint hazards at any time without cause.

*Intact lead-based paint that is in good condition is not necessarily a hazard. See EPA pamphlet "Protect Your Family From Lead in Your Home" for more information.

### Disclosure of Information on Lead-Based Paint and Lead-Based Paint Hazards

**Lead Warning Statement**

Every Buyer of any interest in residential real property on which a residential dwelling was built prior to 1978 is notified that such property may present exposure to lead from lead-based paint that may place young children at risk of developing lead poisoning. Lead poisoning in young children may produce permanent neurological damage, including learning disabilities, reduced intelligence quotient, behavioral problems, and impaired memory. Lead poisoning also poses a particular risk to pregnant women. The Seller of any interest in residential real property is required to provide the Buyer with any information on lead-based paint hazards from risk assessments or inspections in the Seller's possession and notify the Buyer of any known lead-based paint hazards. A risk assessment or inspection for possible lead-based paint hazards is recommended prior to purchase.

**Seller's Disclosure (initial)**

_____ (a) Presence of lead-based paint and/or lead-based paint hazards (check one below):
   ❏ Known lead-based paint and/or lead-based paint hazards are present in the housing (explain).

   _____

   _____

   ❏ Seller has no knowledge of lead-based paint and/or lead-based paint hazards in the housing.
_____ (b) Records and reports available to the Seller (check one below):
   ❏ Seller has provided the Buyer with all available records and reports pertaining to lead-based paint and/or lead-based paint hazards in the housing (list documents below).

   _____

   ❏ Seller has no reports or records pertaining to lead-based paint and/or lead-based paint hazards in the housing.

**Buyer's Acknowledgment (initial)**

_____ (c) Buyer has received copies of all information listed above.
_____ (d) Buyer has received the pamphlet Protect Your Family from Lead in Your Home.
_____ (e) Buyer has (check one below):
   ❏ Received a 10-day opportunity (or mutually agreed upon period) to conduct a risk assessment or inspection for the presence of lead-based paint and/or lead-based paint hazards; or
   ❏ Waived the opportunity to conduct a risk assessment or inspection for the presence of lead-based paint and/or lead-based paint hazards.

**Agent's Acknowledgment (initial)**

_____ (f) Agent has informed the Seller of the Seller's obligations under 42 U.S.C. 4582(d) and is aware of his/her responsibility to ensure compliance.

**Certification of Accuracy**

The following parties have reviewed the information above and certify, to the best of their knowledge, that the information provided by the signatory is true and accurate.

Buyer: _____ (SEAL) Date

Buyer: _____ (SEAL) Date

Agent: _____ Date

Seller: _____ (SEAL) Date

Seller: _____ (SEAL) Date

Agent: _____ Date

SOURCE: *Modern Real Estate Practice*, 15th Edition, by Galaty, Allaway and Kyle. Dearborn™ Real Estate Education, Chicago, 2000.

## Comparative Market Analysis

### Comparative Market Analysis

Prepared by: _____

Date: _____

Prepared for: _____
Property Address: _____
Features: _____

**Properties sold within the previous 12 months**

| Property Address | Sales Price | List Price | Days on Mkt. | Living Area | Features | Estimated Adjustment | Adjusted Sales Price | Comments |
|---|---|---|---|---|---|---|---|---|
| | | | | | | | | |
| | | | | | | | | |
| | | | | | | | | |
| | | | | | | | | |

Percent sales price/list price _____ %          Median $ _____

**Properties currently on the market**

| Property Address | List Price | Days on Mkt. | Living Area | Features | Estimated Adjustment | As Adjusted | Comments |
|---|---|---|---|---|---|---|---|
| | | | | | | | |
| | | | | | | | |
| | | | | | | | |

Median $ _____

**Properties which were listed but failed to sell during the previous 12 months**

| Property Address | List Price | Days on Mkt. | Living Area | Features | Estimated Adjustment | As Adjusted | Comments |
|---|---|---|---|---|---|---|---|
| | | | | | | | |
| | | | | | | | |
| | | | | | | | |

Median $ _____

The suggested marketing range is $ _____ to $ _____

This information is believed to be accurate, but is not warranted.
This is an opinion of value and should not be considered an appraisal.

## Mortgage Loan Application Checklist

| Place personal and company information/logo here | Mortgage Lender: _____<br>Address: _____<br>Loan Officer: _____ Phone: _____<br>Date of Application: _____ Time: _____ |
| --- | --- |

Thanks for using our real estate firm to find your home. To assist you in making your mortgage loan application, we have prepared the list of items that may be needed by the lender. Additional information may be requested.

**The Transaction:**
- ❏ Copy of the signed purchase contract.
- ❏ If you have sold your present home, a copy of the HUD-1 closing statement. If the sale is not complete, a copy of the signed purchase contract.

**Your Income:**
- ❏ Original pay stubs for the latest 30-day period.
- ❏ Original W-2 forms for the previous two years.
- ❏ If you are self-employed or have commission income: a year-to-date profit and loss statement and balance sheet; copies of your last two years' personal and business signed federal tax returns.
- ❏ If you are using child support payments to qualify for mortgage: proof of receipt.

**Your Assets:**
- ❏ Original bank statements for all checking and savings accounts for the past three months. You should be able to explain all deposits not from payroll.
- ❏ Original statements from investment or brokerage firms for the last three months (if applicable).
- ❏ Original IRA or 401(k) statements (if applicable).
- ❏ List of real estate owned: address, market value, mortgage balance, name and address of mortgage company.
- ❏ List of life insurance policies with company name, face value, beneficiaries, and cash surrender value.
- ❏ List of automobiles, with make, model, value, amount owed, lender name, address and account number.
- ❏ Estimate of replacement value of household furniture and appliances.
- ❏ Value of other assets (collections, art, etc.).
- ❏ If you have sold a home in the past two years, a copy of the closing statement and a copy of the deed given.

**Your Liabilties:**
- ❏ Credit cards: name, address, account number, monthly payment; and present balance.
- ❏ Other liabilities: name, address, account number, monthly payment and present balance.

**Payments for Housing:**
- ❏ List of addresses for previous two years, along with names, addresses and phone numbers of landlords and/or mortgage companies where housing payments were made.
- ❏ Last 12 month's cancelled checks for housing payments (landlord or mortgage company).

**If you are divorced:**
- ❏ Copies of all divorce decrees, including any modifications or stipulations.
- ❏ Child support or alimony payments: amount, duration, and proof of payment for 12 months.

**If you are applying for an FHA loan:**
- ❏ Photocopy of driver's license or other acceptable photo ID.
- ❏ Photocopy of Social Security Card.

**If you are applying for a VA loan:**
- ❏ VA Certificate of Eligibilty.
- ❏ Form DD-214.

For in-service veterans or those discharged within the past two years.
- ❏ Statement of Service.
- ❏ Most recent Leave and Earnings Statement.

**Other items:**
- ❏ If you have graduated from high school or college within the previous two years, a copy of your diploma or transcripts.
- ❏ If you have a gap in employment for 30 days or more, include a letter explaining the reason.
- ❏ If part of your down payment is a gift, the lender will give you a gift letter for signature when you apply.
- ❏ If you have filed bankruptcy in the last seven years, give a letter explaining the reasons, a copy of the Petition Decree, a Schedule of Creditors, and the Discharge document.
- ❏ If you have rental property, a copy of the current lease and two year's signed income tax returns.

**Your Check:**
- ❏ Your check for the appraisal and application fee.

## Authorization for Sales Associate to Order Work and Customer's Agreement to Pay

Re: Property Address: _____

**Responsible Person:** _____ as   ❑ Owner   ❑ Buyer

Address: _____

Phone Number: _____

I hereby authorize _____ of

_____ to order on my behalf the item specified below and agree to pay for said item upon demand as required by supplier regardless of the outcome of this property transaction. I understand that these arrangements are being made by the sales associate as a courtesy to me. I shall look to the supplier only for performance and workmanship and absolve sales associate and the brokerage firm for the performance and workmanship of the supplier.

Item to be ordered by sales associate:

_____

_____

Supplier: _____ Price Quoted: _____

Signature: _____ Date: _____

### SUPPLIER AGREEMENT TO PROVIDE SERVICE AND TO LOOK ONLY TO RESPONSIBLE PARTY FOR PAYMENT

Re: Property Address: _____

City: _____

**Supplier:** _____

Phone Number: _____

I agree to provide the item/service specified below and agree to seek compensation from "responsible party" shown above. I understand that these arrangements are being made by the sales associate in this transaction as a courtesy to me. I agree to look to the "responsible party" only for compensation and absolve sales associate and brokerage firm for the cost of the item/service.

Item to be ordered by sales associate:

_____

_____

Supplier: _____ Price Quoted: _____

Signature: _____ Date: _____

## Sample Letter to a For-Sale-By-Owner

Dear Mr. Hendricks:

I heard recently that you were hoping to sell your house. Obviously, you have made the decision not to be assisted by a brokerage firm, and I understand and respect your decision. During the time you are working to sell your house, I hope you won't be offended if I "touch base" with you from time to time. I have enclosed some materials that may be helpful in your efforts:

- A sample sales contract;
- A buyers' statement that may show you what some of the buyers' costs may be; and
- Information on some currently available financing programs for your buyer.

I'll be happy to visit with you and perhaps suggest some ideas for the transaction specifically tailored to your situation.

I've assisted many sellers in this way, and have retained their confidence because I do not pressure them to "list." Often, sellers become weary of trying to sell on their own and have asked me to help. I only ask that if you change your plans that you consider me. In the meantime, if you have any questions, please don't hesitate to call.

Sincerely,


Alice Newby
Sales Associate

## Preclosing Walk-Through Inspection Results

Property Address: _____ . Date of Inspection: _____

Seller: _____ Buyer: _____

I have made a walk-through inspection of the property. I acknowledge that the sales associate has accompanied me to the property to make it available, and not to conduct the inspection. I take complete responsibility for the inspection and agree to hold harmless the sales associate and the brokerage firm from any liability in connection with the inspection.

My inspection shows that:

1. personal property items required by the contract to
be left are present in the property ❏ Yes ❏ No

2. required repairs, if any, have been completed ❏ Yes ❏ No

3. the property has been maintained in the condition as it
existed at the time of the contract, reasonable wear and
tear excepted. ❏ Yes ❏ No

Comments _____

_____

I accept the property as inspected and release the sellers, sales associates and brokers in this transaction of any further responsibilty for warranting the property. I have been notified of the benefits of having the property covered by a homeowner's warranty. If the seller has not provided such a warranty, I ❏ accept ❏ decline to purchase coverage at a cost of $ _____.

Buyer: _____ Date: _____

Buyer: _____ Date: _____

## Property Sale Information Sheet

Property Address: _____

Seller: _____ Buyer: _____

Contract Date: _____ Closing Date (Est.): _____

| Seller | Buyer |
|---|---|
| **Listing Broker:** _____ | **Selling Broker:** _____ |
| Phone:      Fax: | Phone: _____     Fax: _____ |
| Listing sales associate: _____ | Selling sales associate: _____ |
| Home Ph.: _____    Office Ph.: _____ | Home Ph.: _____    Office Ph.: _____ |
| Mobile Ph.: _____ | Mobile Ph.: _____ |

| | |
|---|---|
| **Seller:** _____ | **Buyer:** _____ |
| Old address: _____ | Present address: _____ |
| New address: _____ | City, State, Zip _____ |
| City, State, Zip _____ | Current Home Ph.: _____   Ofc.: _____ |
| Current Home Ph.: _____   Ofc.: _____ | Will buyer occupy new home? _____ |

| | |
|---|---|
| Existing mortgage for Payoff (P) | New Mortgage Lender: _____ |
| Assumption (A) | Type (Fixed; ARM: FHA, VA, Conv.): _____ |
| 1st Mortgage holder: _____ | LTV Ratio: ___% Interest Rate: ___% Yrs: ___ |
| 2nd Mortgage holder: _____ | |

| | |
|---|---|
| Seller's Attorney:_____ | Buyer's Attorney: _____ |
| Ph.: _____ | Ph.: _____ |

**Lender:** _____     **Loan Officer:** _____

**Title Company:**_____     **Closing Agent:**_____

**Appraiser:** _____

**Date Scheduled to Close:** _____

**Service Providers:**

   Pest inspection: _____     Ph.: _____

   Home inspection: _____     Ph.: _____

   Roof inspection: _____     Ph.: _____

   Contractor: _____     Ph.: _____

   Surveyor: _____     Ph.: _____

**Buyer's Insurance Company:**

_____

Agent: _____     Phone: _____

**Property status:**   ❏ Occupied by seller     ❏ Occupied by tenant     ❏ Vacant

**Key to property for inspection:** ❏ At listing office  ❏ In lockbox at property  ❏ Call seller for appointment

| Closing Progress Chart | | | | | | | | |
|---|---|---|---|---|---|---|---|---|
| Listing Sales Associate | | | | Closing Progress Chart | | | | |
| # | Sched Date | Actual Date | X | Closing Duties | Done | X | Sched Date | Actual Date |
| 1 | | | | "Sale pending" sign on listing | | | | |
| 2 | | | | Notice of under contract to MLS | | | | |
| 3 | | | | Binder deposited in bank $_____ | | | | |
| 4 | | | | Additional binder received, if required. $ _____ | | | | |
| 5 | | | | Loan application made by buyer | | | | |
| 6 | | | | Contingencies cleared in writing: | | | | |
| 7 | | | | Home inspection  By: _____ | | | | |
| 8 | | | | Soil test from: _____ | | | | |
| 9 | | | | Roof inspection  By: _____ | | | | |
| 10 | | | | Other (describe): _____ | | | | |
| 11 | | | | Appraisal  By: _____ | | | | |
| 12 | | | | Loan approval  From: _____ | | | | |
| 13 | | | | Title insurance ordered from: _____ | | | | |
| 14 | | | | Pest inspection ordered (after loan approval) from: | | | | |
| 15 | | | | Report received and delivered to buyer | | | | |
| 16 | | | | Report received and delivered to lender | | | | |
| 17 | | | | Treatment ordered, if required | | | | |
| 18 | | | | Structure inspection ordered, if necessary | | | | |
| 19 | | | | Work completed and approved | | | | |
| 20 | | | | Required repairs ordered | | | | |
| 21 | | | | Required repairs completed | | | | |
| 22 | | | | Survey ordered (After loan approval) | | | | |
| 23 | | | | Survey completed. Results. . . | | | | |
| 24 | | | | Encroachments, survey problems cleared | | | | |
| 25 | | | | Buyer to get hazard insurance | | | | |
| 26 | | | | Insurance policy to title closing agent | | | | |
| 27 | | | | Buyer/seller contacted for closing appointment | | | | |
| 28 | | | | Pre-closing inspection | | | | |
| 29 | | | | Closing papers reviewed with buyer/seller 1 day prior | | | | |
| 30 | | | | Buyer given figure for certified check for closing | | | | |
| 31 | | | | Binder check prepared to take to closing | | | | |
| 32 | | | | Closing date | | | | |
| 33 | | | | Signed closing papers received by sales associate | | | | |
| 34 | | | | Post-closing duties: | | | | |
| 35 | | | | Commission check to broker | | | | |
| 36 | | | | Sign/lockbox picked up from property | | | | |
| 37 | | | | Buyer/seller letter of thanks | | | | |
| 38 | | | | Follow-up visit to buyer/seller | | | | |
| 39 | | | | Notice of closed sale to MLS | | | | |

## HUD-1 Closing Statement

### A. Settlement Statement

**U.S. Department of Housing and Urban Development**

OMB Approval No. 2502-0265

**B. Type of Loan**

| | | | |
|---|---|---|---|
| 1. ☐ FHA | 2. ☐ FmHA | 3. ☐ Conv. Unins. | 6. File Number: |
| 4. ☐ VA | 5. ☐ Conv. Ins. | | 7. Loan Number: |
| | | | 8. Mortgage Insurance Case Number: |

**C. Note:** This form is furnished to give you a statement of actual settlement costs. Amounts paid to and by the settlement agent are shown. Items marked "(p.o.c.)" were paid outside the closing; they are shown here for informational purposes and are not included in the totals.

| D. Name & Address of Borrower: | E. Name & Address of Seller: | F. Name & Address of Lender: |
|---|---|---|
| | | |

| G. Property Location: | H. Settlement Agent: | |
|---|---|---|
| | Place of Settlement: | I. Settlement Date: |

| **J. Summary of Borrower's Transaction** | | **K. Summary of Seller's Transaction** | |
|---|---|---|---|
| **100. Gross Amount Due From Borrower** | | **400. Gross Amount Due To Seller** | |
| 101. Contract sales price | | 401. Contract sales price | |
| 102. Personal property | | 402. Personal property | |
| 103. Settlement charges to borrower (line 1400) | | 403. | |
| 104. | | 404. | |
| 105. | | 405. | |
| **Adjustments for items paid by seller in advance** | | **Adjustments for items paid by seller in advance** | |
| 106. City/town taxes        to | | 406. City/town taxes        to | |
| 107. County taxes        to | | 407. County taxes        to | |
| 108. Assessments        to | | 408. Assessments        to | |
| 109. | | 409. | |
| 110. | | 410. | |
| 111. | | 411. | |
| 112. | | 412. | |
| **120. Gross Amount Due From Borrower** | | **420. Gross Amount Due To Seller** | |
| **200. Amounts Paid By Or In Behalf Of Borrower** | | **500. Reductions In Amount Due To Seller** | |
| 201. Deposit or earnest money | | 501. Excess deposit (see instructions) | |
| 202. Principal amount of new loan(s) | | 502. Settlement charges to seller (line 1400) | |
| 203. Existing loan(s) taken subject to | | 503. Existing loan(s) taken subject to | |
| 204. | | 504. Payoff of first mortgage loan | |
| 205. | | 505. Payoff of second mortgage loan | |
| 206. | | 506. | |
| 207. | | 507. | |
| 208. | | 508. | |
| 209. | | 509. | |
| **Adjustments for items unpaid by seller** | | **Adjustments for items unpaid by seller** | |
| 210. City/town taxes        to | | 510. City/town taxes        to | |
| 211. County taxes        to | | 511. County taxes        to | |
| 212. Assessments        to | | 512. Assessments        to | |
| 213. | | 513. | |
| 214. | | 514. | |
| 215. | | 515. | |
| 216. | | 516. | |
| 217. | | 517. | |
| 218. | | 518. | |
| 219. | | 519. | |
| **220. Total Paid By/For Borrower** | | **520. Total Reduction Amount Due Seller** | |
| **300. Cash At Settlement From/To Borrower** | | **600. Cash At Settlement To/From Seller** | |
| 301. Gross Amount due from borrower (line 120) | | 601. Gross amount due to seller (line 420) | |
| 302. Less amounts paid by/for borrower (line 220) | ( ) | 602. Less reductions in amt. due seller (line 520) | ( ) |
| **303. Cash** ☐ From ☐ To Borrower | | **603. Cash** ☐ To ☐ From Seller | |

## HUD-1 Closing Statement (continued)

**L. Settlement Charges**

| 700. | Total Sales/Broker's Commission based on price $            @            % = | Paid From Borrowers Funds at Settlement | Paid From Seller's Funds at Settlement |
|------|---|---|---|
| | Division of Commission (line 700) as follows: | | |
| 701. | $                                             to | | |
| 702. | $                                             to | | |
| 703. | Commission paid at Settlement | | |
| 704. | | | |

| 800. | Items Payable In Connection With Loan | | |
|------|---|---|---|
| 801. | Loan Origination Fee                     % | | |
| 802. | Loan Discount                            % | | |
| 803. | Appraisal Fee                            to | | |
| 804. | Credit Report                            to | | |
| 805. | Lender's Inspection Fee | | |
| 806. | Mortgage Insurance Application Fee to | | |
| 807. | Assumption Fee | | |
| 808. | | | |
| 809. | | | |
| 810. | | | |
| 811. | | | |

| 900. | Items Required By Lender To Be Paid In Advance | | |
|------|---|---|---|
| 901. | Interest from            to            @$            /day | | |
| 902. | Mortgage Insurance Premium for            months to | | |
| 903. | Hazard Insurance Premium for            years to | | |
| 904. |            years to | | |
| 905. | | | |

| 1000. | Reserves Deposited With Lender | | |
|-------|---|---|---|
| 1001. | Hazard insurance            months@$            per month | | |
| 1002. | Mortgage insurance          months@$            per month | | |
| 1003. | City property taxes         months@$            per month | | |
| 1004. | County property taxes       months@$            per month | | |
| 1005. | Annual assessments          months@$            per month | | |
| 1006. |                             months@$            per month | | |
| 1007. |                             months@$            per month | | |
| 1008. |                             months@$            per month | | |

| 1100. | Title Charges | | |
|-------|---|---|---|
| 1101. | Settlement or closing fee            to | | |
| 1102. | Abstract or title search            to | | |
| 1103. | Title examination            to | | |
| 1104. | Title insurance binder            to | | |
| 1105. | Document preparation            to | | |
| 1106. | Notary fees            to | | |
| 1107. | Attorney's fees            to | | |
| | (includes above items numbers:                              ) | | |
| 1108. | Title insurance            to | | |
| | (includes above items numbers:                              ) | | |
| 1109. | Lender's coverage            $ | | |
| 1110. | Owner's coverage            $ | | |
| 1111. | | | |
| 1112. | | | |
| 1113. | | | |

| 1200. | Government Recording and Transfer Charges | | |
|-------|---|---|---|
| 1201. | Recording fees: Deed $            ; Mortgage $            ; Releases $ | | |
| 1202. | City/county tax/stamps: Deed $            ; Mortgage $ | | |
| 1203. | State tax/stamps: Deed $            ; Mortgage $ | | |
| 1204. | | | |
| 1205. | | | |

| 1300. | Additional Settlement Charges | | |
|-------|---|---|---|
| 1301. | Survey            to | | |
| 1302. | Pest inspection to | | |
| 1303. | | | |
| 1304. | | | |
| 1305. | | | |

| 1400. | Total Settlement Charges (enter on lines 103, Section J and 502, Section K) | | |
|-------|---|---|---|

## HUD-1 Closing Statement

**A. Settlement Statement**

U.S. Department of Housing
and Urban Development

OMB Approval No. 2502-0265

**B. Type of Loan**

| 1. ☐ FHA | 2. ☐ FmHA | 3. ☐ Conv. Unins. | 6. File Number: | 7. Loan Number: | 8. Mortgage Insurance Case Number: |
|---|---|---|---|---|---|
| 4. ☐ VA | 5. ☐ Conv. Ins. | | | | |

**C. Note:** This form is furnished to give you a statement of actual settlement costs. Amounts paid to and by the settlement agent are shown. Items marked "(p.o.c.)" were paid outside the closing; they are shown here for informational purposes and are not included in the totals.

| D. Name & Address of Borrower: | E. Name & Address of Seller: | F. Name & Address of Lender: |
|---|---|---|
| | | |

| G. Property Location: | H. Settlement Agent: |
|---|---|
| | Place of Settlement: |
| | I. Settlement Date: |

| J. Summary of Borrower's Transaction | | K. Summary of Seller's Transaction | |
|---|---|---|---|
| **100. Gross Amount Due From Borrower** | | **400. Gross Amount Due To Seller** | |
| 101. Contract sales price | | 401. Contract sales price | |
| 102. Personal property | | 402. Personal property | |
| 103. Settlement charges to borrower (line 1400) | | 403. | |
| 104. | | 404. | |
| 105. | | 405. | |
| **Adjustments for items paid by seller in advance** | | **Adjustments for items paid by seller in advance** | |
| 106. City/town taxes          to | | 406. City/town taxes          to | |
| 107. County taxes          to | | 407. County taxes          to | |
| 108. Assessments          to | | 408. Assessments          to | |
| 109. | | 409. | |
| 110. | | 410. | |
| 111. | | 411. | |
| 112. | | 412. | |
| **120. Gross Amount Due From Borrower** | | **420. Gross Amount Due To Seller** | |
| **200. Amounts Paid By Or In Behalf Of Borrower** | | **500. Reductions In Amount Due To Seller** | |
| 201. Deposit or earnest money | | 501. Excess deposit (see instructions) | |
| 202. Principal amount of new loan(s) | | 502. Settlement charges to seller (line 1400) | |
| 203. Existing loan(s) taken subject to | | 503. Existing loan(s) taken subject to | |
| 204. | | 504. Payoff of first mortgage loan | |
| 205. | | 505. Payoff of second mortgage loan | |
| 206. | | 506. | |
| 207. | | 507. | |
| 208. | | 508. | |
| 209. | | 509. | |
| **Adjustments for items unpaid by seller** | | **Adjustments for items unpaid by seller** | |
| 210. City/town taxes          to | | 510. City/town taxes          to | |
| 211. County taxes          to | | 511. County taxes          to | |
| 212. Assessments          to | | 512. Assessments          to | |
| 213. | | 513. | |
| 214. | | 514. | |
| 215. | | 515. | |
| 216. | | 516. | |
| 217. | | 517. | |
| 218. | | 518. | |
| 219. | | 519. | |
| **220. Total Paid By/For Borrower** | | **520. Total Reduction Amount Due Seller** | |
| **300. Cash At Settlement From/To Borrower** | | **600. Cash At Settlement To/From Seller** | |
| 301. Gross Amount due from borrower (line 120) | | 601. Gross amount due to seller (line 420) | |
| 302. Less amounts paid by/for borrower (line 220) | ( ) | 602. Less reductions in amt. due seller (line 520) | ( ) |
| **303. Cash** ☐ From ☐ To Borrower | | **603. Cash** ☐ To ☐ From Seller | |

## HUD-1 Closing Statement (continued)

**L. Settlement Charges**

| | | | Paid From Borrowers Funds at Settlement | Paid From Seller's Funds at Settlement |
|---|---|---|---|---|
| **700. Total Sales/Broker's Commission based on price $** | | @      % = | | |
| Division of Commission (line 700) as follows: | | | | |
| 701. $ | to | | | |
| 702. $ | to | | | |
| 703. Commission paid at Settlement | | | | |
| 704. | | | | |
| **800. Items Payable In Connection With Loan** | | | | |
| 801. Loan Origination Fee | % | | | |
| 802. Loan Discount | % | | | |
| 803. Appraisal Fee | to | | | |
| 804. Credit Report | to | | | |
| 805. Lender's Inspection Fee | | | | |
| 806. Mortgage Insurance Application Fee to | | | | |
| 807. Assumption Fee | | | | |
| 808. | | | | |
| 809. | | | | |
| 810. | | | | |
| 811. | | | | |
| **900. Items Required By Lender To Be Paid In Advance** | | | | |
| 901. Interest from      to | @$ | /day | | |
| 902. Mortgage Insurance Premium for | | months to | | |
| 903. Hazard Insurance Premium for | | years to | | |
| 904. | | years to | | |
| 905. | | | | |
| **1000. Reserves Deposited With Lender** | | | | |
| 1001. Hazard insurance | months@$ | per month | | |
| 1002. Mortgage insurance | months@$ | per month | | |
| 1003. City property taxes | months@$ | per month | | |
| 1004. County property taxes | months@$ | per month | | |
| 1005. Annual assessments | months@$ | per month | | |
| 1006. | months@$ | per month | | |
| 1007. | months@$ | per month | | |
| 1008. | months@$ | per month | | |
| **1100. Title Charges** | | | | |
| 1101. Settlement or closing fee | to | | | |
| 1102. Abstract or title search | to | | | |
| 1103. Title examination | to | | | |
| 1104. Title insurance binder | to | | | |
| 1105. Document preparation | to | | | |
| 1106. Notary fees | to | | | |
| 1107. Attorney's fees | to | | | |
| (includes above items numbers: | | ) | | |
| 1108. Title insurance | to | | | |
| (includes above items numbers: | | ) | | |
| 1109. Lender's coverage | $ | | | |
| 1110. Owner's coverage | $ | | | |
| 1111. | | | | |
| 1112. | | | | |
| 1113. | | | | |
| **1200. Government Recording and Transfer Charges** | | | | |
| 1201. Recording fees: Deed $ | ; Mortgage $ | ; Releases $ | | |
| 1202. City/county tax/stamps: Deed $ | ; Mortgage $ | | | |
| 1203. State tax/stamps: Deed $ | ; Mortgage $ | | | |
| 1204. | | | | |
| 1205. | | | | |
| **1300. Additional Settlement Charges** | | | | |
| 1301. Survey      to | | | | |
| 1302. Pest inspection to | | | | |
| 1303. | | | | |
| 1304. | | | | |
| 1305. | | | | |
| **1400. Total Settlement Charges (enter on lines 103, Section J and 502, Section K)** | | | | |

## Real Property Sales Disclosure

PURCHASER: _____     PROPERTY ADDRESS: _____

Date of Contract: _____     Sales Price $ _____          $ _____
Mortgage Lender: _____      1st Mortgage $ _____ + _____   $ _____
Prepared by: _____      2nd Mortgage $ _____ FHA MIP OR FUNDNG   TOTAL LOAN AMOUNT
                                                                                         $ _____

                                       **Estimated Down Payment**      **(1)**  $ _____

**Estimated closing costs:**

1.  Title Insurance: ❑ owner's ❑ mortgagee's        _____
2.  Title Insurance Endorsements                    _____
3.  Origination fee ____%                           _____
4.  Discount points estimated _____%                _____
5.  Intangible Tax ($.002/$1) on new mortgage       _____
6.  Documentary Stamps ($.35/$100) on all notes     _____
7.  Recording Fees . . . . . . . . . . . . . . . .  _____
8.  Credit Report . . . . . . . . . . . . . . . . . _____
9.  Appraisal Fee                                   _____
10. Survey                                          _____
11. Document Preparation Fee                        _____
12. Tax Service Fee                                 _____
13. Underwriting Fee                                _____
14. Express Mail Fee(s)                             _____
15. VA Funding Fee at _____%                       _____
16. Assumption Fee on Existing Mortgage             _____
17. Purchase of Escrow Account                      _____
18. Home Inspection Fee                             _____
19. Homeowner's Warranty _____                  _____
20. Attorney's Fee (if any)                         _____
21. _____                          _____
22. _____                          _____

                                       **Total Estimated Closing Costs**     **(2)**  $ _____

**Estimated escrow/prepaid items:**

1. Taxes _____ months                              _____
2. Hazard Insurance, 1 year                         _____
3. Hazard Insurance, 2 months                       _____
4. First Year Mortgage Insurance                    _____
5. Mortgage Insurance, 2 months                     _____
6. Flood Insurance, 14 months                       _____
7. Prepaid Interest                                 _____
8. Homeowner's Assn. Dues                           _____

                                       **Total Estimated escrow/prepaid items**   **(3)**  $ _____

| ESTIMATED MONTHLY PAYMENTS | |
|---|---|
| ❑ Fixed    ❑ ARM    ___% Interest Rate    ___Years | **Total Lines 1, 2 and 3**          $ _____ |
| Principal & Interest $_____ | **Less: Deposit money**          $ _____ |
| Property Taxes • _____ | |
| Hazard Insurance_____ | |
| Mortgage Insurance_____ | |
| Other _____ | Estimated Total due at Closing          $ _____ |
| TOTAL $_____ | (Must be tendered in cash or certified funds) |
| Other Association fees may be due monthly | |

Source: Tallahasee Board of REALTORS®, used with permision.

## Residential Sale and Purchase Contract

**Residential Sale and Purchase Contract**
FLORIDA ASSOCIATION OF REALTORS®

1. **SALE AND PURCHASE:** _____ ("Seller")

3      and _____ ("Buyer")

3      agree to sell and buy on the terms and conditions specified below the property described as:
4*     Address: _____
5*     _____ County: _____
6*     Legal Description: _____
7*     _____ Tax ID No: _____
8      together with all improvements and attached items, including fixtures, built-in furnishings, built-in appliances, ceiling fans, light
9      fixtures, attached wall-to-wall carpeting, rods, draperies and other window coverings. The only other items included in the
10*    purchase are: _____
11*    _____
12*
13*    The following attached items are excluded from the purchase: _____
14*
15     The real and personal property described above as included in the purchase is referred to as the "Property." Personal property listed
16     in this Contract is included in the purchase price, has no contributory value and is being left for **Seller's** convenience.

17                                        **PRICE AND FINANCING**
18*    2. **PURCHASE PRICE:**        $_____ payable by **Buyer** in U.S. currency as follows:
19*       (a) $_____    Deposit received (checks are subject to clearance) _____, _____ by
20*                             _____ for _____ ("Escrow Agent")
21                                        *Signature*                    *Name of Company*
22*       (b) $_____    Additional deposit to be delivered to Escrow Agent by _____,
23*                             _____ or _____ days from Effective Date. (10 days if left blank)
24*       (c)  _____    Total financing (see Paragraph 3 below) (express as a dollar amount or percentage)
25*       (d) $_____    Other: _____
26*       (e) $_____    Balance to close (not including **Buyer's** closing costs, prepaid items and prorations). All funds paid
27                             at closing must be paid by locally drawn cashier's check, official bank check, or wired funds.
28*    3. **FINANCING:** (Check as applicable) ❏ **(a) Buyer** will pay cash for the Property with no financing contingency.
29*    ❏ **(b) Buyer** will apply for the financing specified in paragraph 2(c) at the prevailing interest rate and loan costs based on
30*    **Buyer's** creditworthiness (the "Financing") within _____ days from Effective Date (5 days if left blank) and provide **Seller** with a
31*    written Financing commitment or approval letter ("Commitment") within _____ days from Effective Date (30 days if left blank)
32     ("Commitment Period"). **Buyer** will keep **Seller** and Broker fully informed about loan application status, progress and
33     Commitment issues and authorizes the mortgage broker and lender to disclose all such information to **Seller** and **Broker**. Once
34     **Buyer** provides the Commitment to **Seller**, the financing contingency is waived and **Seller** will be entitled to retain the deposits
35     if the transaction does not close by the Closing Date unless (1) the Property appraises below the purchase price and either the
36     parties cannot agree on a new purchase price or **Buyer** elects not to proceed, or (2) another provision of this Contract requires
37     the deposits to be returned. If **Buyer**, using diligence and good faith, cannot provide the Commitment within the Commitment
38     Period, this Contract will be terminated and **Buyer's** deposits refunded.

39                                              **CLOSING**
40     4. **CLOSING DATE; OCCUPANCY:** Unless extended by other provisions of this Contract, this Contract will be closed on
41*    _____ ("Closing Date") at the time established by the closing agent, by which time **Seller** will (a) have removed all
42     personal items and trash from the Property and swept the Property clean and (b) deliver the deed, occupancy and possession, along with
43     all keys, garage door openers and access codes, to **Buyer**. If on Closing Date insurance underwriting is suspended, **Buyer** may
44     postpone closing up to 5 days after the insurance suspension is lifted. If this transaction does not close for any reason, **Buyer** will
45     immediately return all **Seller**-provided title evidence, surveys, association documents and other items.

46     5. **CLOSING PROCEDURE; COSTS:** Closing will take place in the county where the Property is located and may be conducted by
47     mail or electronic means. If title insurance insures **Buyer** for title defects arising between the title binder effective date and recording
48     of **Buyer's** deed, closing agent will disburse at closing the net sale proceeds to **Seller** and brokerage fees to Broker as per
49     Paragraph **19**. In addition to other expenses provided in this Contract, **Seller** and **Buyer** will pay the costs indicated below.
50     **(a) Seller Costs: Seller** will pay taxes and surtaxes on the deed and recording fees for documents needed to cure title; up to
51*    $_____ or _____% (1.5% if left blank) of the purchase price for repairs to warranted items (**"Repair Limit"**);

52*    **Buyer** (____) (____) and **Seller** (____) (____) acknowledge receipt of a copy of this page, which is Page 1 of 7 Pages.
53     FAR-8   Rev. 10/04   © 2004   Florida Association of REALTORS®   All Rights Reserved

## Residential Sale and Purchase Contract (continued)

54* and up to $_____ or _____% (1.5% if left blank) of the purchase price for wood-destroying organism
55* treatment and repairs **("WDO Repair Limit")**; Other: _____
56 **(b) Buyer Costs: Buyer** will pay taxes and recording fees on notes and mortgages; recording fees on the deed and financing
57* statements; loan expenses; lender's title policy; inspections; survey; flood insurance; Other: _____
58 **(c) Title Evidence and Insurance: Check (1) or (2):**
59* ❑ **(1)** The title evidence will be a Paragraph 10(a)(1) owner's title insurance commitment. ❑ **Seller** ❑ **Buyer** will select the title
60* agent. ❑ **Seller** ❑ **Buyer** will pay for the owner's title policy, search, examination and related charges. Each party will
61 pay its own closing fees.
62* ❑ **(2) Seller** will provide an abstract as specified in Paragraph 10(a)(2) as title evidence. ❑ **Seller** ❑ **Buyer** will pay for
63 the owner's title policy and select the title agent. **Seller** will pay fees for title searches prior to closing, including tax
64 search and lien search fees, and **Buyer** will pay fees for title searches after closing (if any), title examination fees and
65 closing fees.
66 **(d) Prorations:** The following items will be made current (if applicable) and prorated as of the day before Closing Date: real
67 estate taxes, interest, bonds, assessments, association fees, insurance, rents and other current expenses and revenues of
68 the Property. If taxes and assessments for the current year cannot be determined, the previous year's rates will be used with
69 adjustment for exemptions and improvements. **Buyer** is responsible for property tax increases due to change in ownership.
70 **(e) Special Assessment by Public Body:** Regarding special assessments imposed by a public body, **Seller** will pay (i) the full
71 amount of liens that are certified, confirmed and ratified before closing and (ii) the amount of the last estimate of the assessment if
72 an improvement is substantially completed as of Effective Date but has not resulted in a lien before closing, and **Buyer** will pay all
73 other amounts.
74 **(f) Tax Withholding: Buyer** and **Seller** will comply with the Foreign Investment in Real Property Tax Act, which may require
75 **Seller** to provide additional cash at closing if **Seller** is a "foreign person" as defined by federal law.
76* **(g) Home Warranty:** ❑ **Buyer** ❑ **Seller** ❑ **N/A** will pay for a home warranty plan issued by _____ at a
77* cost not to exceed $_____. A home warranty plan provides for repair or replacement of many of a home's mechanical
78 systems and major built-in appliances in the event of breakdown due to normal wear and tear during the agreement period.

79 **PROPERTY CONDITION**
80* **6. INSPECTION PERIODS: Buyer** will complete the inspections referenced in Paragraphs **7** and **8(a)(2)** by _____,
81* _____ (within 10 days from Effective Date if left blank) ("Inspection Period"); the wood-destroying organism inspection
82* by _____, _____ (at least 5 days prior to closing if left blank); and the walk-through inspection on the
83 day before Closing Date or any other time agreeable to the parties; and the survey referenced in Paragraph 10(c) by
84* _____, _____ (at least 5 days prior to closing if left blank).

85 **7. REAL PROPERTY DISCLOSURES: Seller** represents that **Seller** does not know of any facts that materially affect the value
86 of the Property, including but not limited to violations of governmental laws, rules and regulations, other than those that **Buyer**
87 can readily observe or that are known by or have been disclosed to **Buyer**. **Seller** will have all open permits (if any) closed out,
88 with final inspections completed, no later than 5 days prior to closing.
89 **(a) Energy Efficiency: Buyer** acknowledges receipt of the energy-efficiency information brochure required by Section 553.996,
90 *Florida Statutes*.
91 **(b) Radon Gas:** Radon is a naturally occurring radioactive gas that, when it has accumulated in a building in sufficient
92 quantities, may present health risks to persons who are exposed to it over time. Levels of radon that exceed federal and
93 state guidelines have been found in buildings in Florida. Additional information regarding radon and radon testing may be
94 obtained from your county public health unit. **Buyer** may, within the Inspection Period, have an appropriately licensed person
95 test the Property for radon. If the radon level exceeds acceptable EPA standards, **Seller** may choose to reduce the radon
96 level to an acceptable EPA level, failing which either party may cancel this Contract.
97 **(c) Flood Zone: Buyer** is advised to verify by survey, with the lender and with appropriate government agencies which flood
98 zone the Property is in, whether flood insurance is required and what restrictions apply to improving the Property and rebuilding
99 in the event of casualty. If the Property is in a Special Flood Hazard Area or Coastal High Hazard Area **and** the buildings are built
100 below the minimum flood elevation, **Buyer** may cancel this Contract by delivering written notice to **Seller** within 20 days from
101 Effective Date, failing which **Buyer** accepts the existing elevation of the buildings and zone designation of the Property.
102 **(d) Homeowners' Association:** If membership in a homeowners' association is mandatory, an association disclosure
103 summary is attached and incorporated into this Contract. **BUYER SHOULD NOT SIGN THIS CONTRACT UNTIL**
104 **BUYER HAS RECEIVED AND READ THE DISCLOSURE SUMMARY.**
105 **(e) PROPERTY TAX DISCLOSURE SUMMARY: BUYER** SHOULD NOT RELY ON THE **SELLER'S** CURRENT PROPERTY
106 TAXES AS THE AMOUNT OF PROPERTY TAXES THAT **BUYER** MAY BE OBLIGATED TO PAY IN THE YEAR SUBSEQUENT
107 TO PURCHASE. A CHANGE OF OWNERSHIP OR PROPERTY IMPROVEMENTS TRIGGERS REASSESSMENTS OF THE
108 PROPERTY THAT COULD RESULT IN HIGHER PROPERTY TAXES. IF YOU HAVE ANY QUESTIONS CONCERNING
109 VALUATION, CONTACT THE COUNTY PROPERTY APPRAISER'S OFFICE FOR FURTHER INFORMATION.
110 **(f) Mold:** Mold is part of the natural environment that, when accumulated in sufficient quantities, may present health risks to
111 susceptible persons. For more information, contact the county indoor air quality specialist or other appropriate professional.

112* **Buyer** (_____)(_____) and **Seller** (_____)(_____) acknowledge receipt of a copy of this page, which is Page 2 of 7 Pages.
FAR-8   Rev. 10/04   © 2004   Florida Association of REALTORS®   All Rights Reserved

## Residential Sale and Purchase Contract (continued)

113 **8. MAINTENANCE, INSPECTIONS AND REPAIR: Seller** will keep the Property in the same condition from Effective Date until
114 closing, except for normal wear and tear ("maintenance requirement") and repairs required by this Contract. **Seller** will provide
115 access and utilities for **Buyer's** inspections. **Buyer** will repair all damages to the Property resulting from the inspections,
116 return the Property to its pre-inspection condition and provide **Seller** with paid receipts for all work done on Property upon its
117 completion. If **Seller**, using best efforts, is unable to complete required repairs or treatments prior to closing, **Seller** will give
118 **Buyer** a credit at closing for the cost of the repairs **Seller** was obligated to make. At closing, **Seller** will assign all assignable repair
119 and treatment contracts to **Buyer** and provide **Buyer** with paid receipts for all work done on the Property pursuant to the
120 terms of this Contract.
121    **(a) Warranty, Inspections and Repair:**
122      **(1) Warranty: Seller** warrants that non-leased major appliances and heating, cooling, mechanical, electrical, security,
123      sprinkler, septic and plumbing systems, seawall, dock and pool equipment, if any, are and will be maintained in working
124      condition until closing; that the structures (including roofs) and pool, if any, are structurally sound and watertight; and
125      that torn or missing pool cage and screen room screens and missing roof tiles will be replaced. **Seller** does not warrant
126      and is not required to repair cosmetic conditions, unless the cosmetic condition resulted from a defect in a warranted
127      item. **Seller** is not obligated to bring any item into compliance with existing building code regulations unless necessary
128      to repair a warranted item. "Working condition" means operating in the manner in which the item was designed to
129      operate and "cosmetic conditions" means aesthetic imperfections that do not affect the working condition of the item,
130      including pitted marcite; missing or torn window screens; fogged windows; tears, worn spots and discoloration of floor
131      coverings/wallpapers/window treatments; nail holes, scratches, dents, scrapes, chips and caulking in bathroom
132      ceiling/walls/flooring/tile/fixtures/mirrors; cracked roof tiles; curling or worn shingles; and minor cracks in floor
133      tiles/windows/driveways/sidewalks/pool decks/garage and patio floors.
134      **(2) Professional Inspection: Buyer** may, at **Buyer's** expense, have warranted items inspected by a person who
135      specializes in and holds an occupational license (if required by law) to conduct home inspections or who holds a Florida
136      license to repair and maintain the items inspected ("professional inspector"). **Buyer** must, within 5 days from the end of the
137      Inspection Period, deliver written notice of any items that are not in the condition warranted and a copy of the inspector's
138      written report, if any, to **Seller**. If **Buyer** fails to deliver timely written notice, **Buyer** waives **Seller's** warranty and accepts
139      the items listed in subparagraph (a) in their "as is" conditions, except that **Seller** must meet the maintenance requirement.
140      **(3) Repair: Seller** will obtain repair estimates and is obligated only to make repairs necessary to bring warranted items
141      into the condition warranted, up to the Repair Limit. **Seller** may, within 5 days from receipt of **Buyer's** notice of items
142      that are not in the condition warranted, have a second inspection made by a professional inspector and will report
143      repair estimates to **Buyer.** If the first and second inspection reports differ and the parties cannot resolve the differences,
144      **Buyer** and **Seller** together will choose, and equally split the cost of, a third inspector, whose written report will be
145      binding on the parties. If the cost to repair warranted items equals or is less than the Repair Limit, **Seller** will have the
146      repairs made in a workmanlike manner by an appropriately licensed person. If the cost to repair warranted items
147      exceeds the Repair Limit, either party may cancel this Contract unless either party pays the excess or **Buyer**
148      designates which repairs to make at a total cost to **Seller** not exceeding the Repair Limit and accepts the balance of
149      the Property in its "as is" condition.
150    **(b) Wood-Destroying Organisms:** "Wood-destroying organism" means arthropod or plant life, including termites, powder-post
151 beetles, oldhouse borers and wood-decaying fungi, that damages or infests seasoned wood in a structure, excluding fences.
152 **Buyer** may, at **Buyer's** expense and prior to closing, have the Property inspected by a Florida-licensed pest control business to
153 determine the existence of past or present wood-destroying organism infestation and damage caused by infestation. If the
154 inspector finds evidence of infestation or damage, **Buyer** will deliver a copy of the inspector's written report to **Seller** within 5
155 days from the date of the inspection. If **Seller** previously treated the Property for wood-destroying organisms, **Seller** does not
156 have to treat the Property again if (i) there is no visible live infestation, and (ii) **Seller** transfers a current full treatment warranty to
157 **Buyer** at closing. Otherwise, **Seller** will have 5 days from receipt of the inspector's report to have reported damage estimated by
158 a licensed building or general contractor and corrective treatment estimated by a licensed pest control business. **Seller** will have
159 treatments and repairs made by an appropriately licensed person at **Seller's** expense up to the WDO Repair Limit. If the cost to
160 treat and repair the Property exceeds the WDO Repair Limit, either party may pay the excess, failing which either party may
161 cancel this Contract by written notice to the other. If **Buyer** fails to timely deliver the inspector's written report, **Buyer** accepts the
162 Property "as is" with regard to wood-destroying organism infestation and damage, subject to the maintenance requirement.
163    **(c) Walk-through Inspection: Buyer** may walk through the Property solely to verify that **Seller** has made repairs required
164 by this Contract and has met contractual obligations. No other issues may be raised as a result of the walk-through
165 inspection. If **Buyer** fails to conduct this inspection, **Seller's** repair and maintenance obligations will be deemed fulfilled.

166 **9. RISK OF LOSS:** If any portion of the Property is damaged by fire or other casualty before closing and can be restored within
167 45 days from the Closing Date to substantially the same condition as it was on Effective Date, **Seller** will, at **Seller's** expense,
168 restore the Property and the Closing Date will be extended accordingly. **Seller** will not be obligated to replace trees. If the
169 restoration cannot be completed in time, **Buyer** may accept the Property "as is", in which case with **Seller** will credit the
170 deductible and assign the insurance proceeds, if any, to **Buyer** at closing in such amounts as are (i) attributable to the Property
171 and (ii) not yet expended in making repairs, failing which either party may cancel this Contract. If the Property is a
172 condominium, this paragraph applies only to the unit and limited common elements appurtenant to the unit; if the Property is in
173 a homeowners' association, this paragraph will not apply to common elements or recreation or other facilities.

174* **Buyer** (____) (____) and **Seller** (____) (____) acknowledge receipt of a copy of this page, which is Page 3 of 7 Pages.
    FAR-8   Rev. 10/04   © 2004   Florida Association of REALTORS®   All Rights Reserved

## Residential Sale and Purchase Contract (continued)

### TITLE

175

176 **10. TITLE: Seller** will convey marketable title to the Property by statutory warranty deed or trustee, personal representative or
177 guardian deed as appropriate to **Seller's** status.

178     **(a) Title Evidence:** Title evidence will show legal access to the Property and marketable title of record in **Seller** in accordance with
179     current title standards adopted by the Florida Bar, subject only to the following title exceptions, none of which prevent residential
180     use of the Property: covenants, easements and restrictions of record; matters of plat; existing zoning and government regulations;
181     oil, gas and mineral rights of record if there is no right of entry; current taxes; mortgages that **Buyer** will assume; and
182     encumbrances that **Seller** will discharge at or before closing. **Seller** will, at least 2 days prior to closing, deliver to **Buyer Seller's**
183     choice of one of the following types of title evidence, which must be generally accepted in the county where the Property is located
184     (specify in Paragraph **5(c)** the selected type). **Seller** will use option (1) in Palm Beach County and option (2) in Miami-Dade County.
185         **(1) A title insurance commitment** issued by a Florida-licensed title insurer in the amount of the purchase price and
186         subject only to title exceptions set forth in this Contract.
187         **(2) An existing abstract of title** from a reputable and existing abstract firm (if firm is not existing, then abstract must be
188         certified as correct by an existing firm) purporting to be an accurate synopsis of the instruments affecting title to the
189         Property recorded in the public records of the county where the Property is located and certified to Effective Date.
190         However, if such an abstract is not available to **Seller,** then a **prior owner's title policy** acceptable to the proposed
191         insurer as a base for reissuance of coverage. **Seller** will pay for copies of all policy exceptions and an update in a format
192         acceptable to **Buyer's** closing agent from the policy effective date and certified to **Buyer** or **Buyer's** closing agent,
193         together with copies of all documents recited in the prior policy and in the update. If a prior policy is not available to
194         **Seller** then (1) above will be the title evidence. Title evidence will be delivered no later than 10 days before Closing Date.
195     **(b) Title Examination: Buyer** will examine the title evidence and deliver written notice to **Seller,** within 5 days from receipt of
196     title evidence but no later than closing, of any defects that make the title unmarketable. **Seller** will have 30 days from
197     receipt of **Buyer's** notice of defects ("Curative Period") to cure the defects at **Seller's** expense. If **Seller** cures the defects
198     within the Curative Period, **Seller** will deliver written notice to **Buyer** and the parties will close the transaction on Closing
199     Date or within 10 days from **Buyer's** receipt of **Seller's** notice if Closing Date has passed. If **Seller** is unable to cure the
200     defects within the Curative Period, **Seller** will deliver written notice to **Buyer** and **Buyer** will, within 10 days from receipt of
201     **Seller's** notice, either cancel this Contract or accept title with existing defects and close the transaction.
202     **(c) Survey: Buyer** may, at **Buyer's** expense, have the Property surveyed and deliver written notice to **Seller,** within 5 days from
203     receipt of survey but no later than closing, of any encroachments on the Property, encroachments by the Property's improvements
204     on other lands or deed restriction or zoning violations. Any such encroachment or violation will be treated in the same manner as a
205     title defect and **Buyer's** and **Seller's** obligations will be determined in accordance with subparagraph **(b)** above. If any part of the
206     Property lies seaward of the coastal construction control line, **Seller** will provide **Buyer** with an affidavit or survey as required by law
207     delineating the line's location on the property, unless **Buyer** waives this requirement in writing.

### MISCELLANEOUS

208

209 **11. EFFECTIVE DATE; TIME:** The "Effective Date" of this Contract is the date on which the last of the parties initials or signs the
210 latest offer. **Time is of the essence for all provisions of this Contract.** All time periods will be computed in business days (a
211 "business day" is every calendar day except Saturday, Sunday and national legal holidays). If any deadline falls on a Saturday,
212 Sunday or national legal holiday, performance will be due the next business day. All time periods will end at 5:00 p.m. local
213 time (meaning in the county where the Property is located) of the appropriate day.

214 **12. NOTICES:** All notices will be made to the parties and Broker by mail, personal delivery or electronic media. **Buyer's failure**
215 **to deliver timely written notice to Seller, when such notice is required by this Contract, regarding any contingencies will**
216 **render that contingency null and void and the Contract will be construed as if the contingency did not exist.** Any notice,
217 document or item given to or received by an attorney or Broker (including a transaction broker) representing a party will
218 be as effective as if given to or by that party.

219 **13. COMPLETE AGREEMENT:** This Contract is the entire agreement between **Buyer** and **Seller.** Except for brokerage
220 **agreements, no prior or present agreements will bind Buyer, Seller or Broker unless incorporated into this Contract.**
221 Modifications of this Contract will not be binding unless in writing, signed or initialed and delivered by the party to be bound.
222 Signatures, initials, documents referenced in this Contract, counterparts and written modifications communicated electronically
223 or on paper will be acceptable for all purposes, including delivery, and will be binding. Handwritten or typewritten terms
224 inserted in or attached to this Contract prevail over preprinted terms. If any provision of this Contract is or becomes invalid or
225 unenforceable, all remaining provisions will continue to be fully effective. **Buyer** and **Seller** will use diligence and good faith in
226 performing all obligations under this Agreement. This Contract will not be recorded in any public records.

227 **14. ASSIGNABILITY; PERSONS BOUND: Buyer** may **not** assign this Contract without **Seller's** written consent. The terms
228 **"Buyer," "Seller,"** and **"Broker"** may be singular or plural. This Contract is binding on the heirs, administrators, executors,
229 personal representatives and assigns (if permitted) of **Buyer, Seller** and Broker.

### DEFAULT AND DISPUTE RESOLUTION

230

231 **15. DEFAULT: (a) Seller Default:** If for any reason other than failure of **Seller** to make **Seller's** title marketable after diligent effort, **Seller**
232 fails, refuses or neglects to perform this Contract, **Buyer** may choose to receive a return of **Buyer's** deposit without waiving the right to
233 seek damages or to seek specific performance as per Paragraph **16. Seller** will also be liable to Broker for the full amount of the

234* **Buyer** (____) (____) and **Seller** (____) (____) acknowledge receipt of a copy of this page, which is Page 4 of 7 Pages.
    FAR-8   Rev. 10/04   © 2004   Florida Association of REALTORS®   All Rights Reserved

## Residential Sale and Purchase Contract (continued)

235 brokerage fee. **(b) Buyer Default:** If **Buyer** fails to perform this Contract within the time specified, including timely payment of all deposits,
236 **Seller** may choose to retain and collect all deposits paid and agreed to be paid as liquidated damages or to seek specific performance as
237 per Paragraph **16**; and Broker will, upon demand, receive 50% of all deposits paid and agreed to be paid (to be split equally among
238 cooperating brokers except when closing does not occur due to **Buyer** not being able to secure Financing after providing a Commitment,
239 in which case Broker's portion of the deposits will go solely to the listing broker) up to the full amount of the brokerage fee.

240 **16. DISPUTE RESOLUTION:** This Contract will be construed under Florida law. All controversies, claims and other matters in
241 question arising out of or relating to this transaction or this Contract or its breach will be settled as follows:
242     **(a) Disputes concerning entitlement to deposits made and agreed to be made: Buyer** and **Seller** will have 30 days from the
243     date conflicting demands are made to attempt to resolve the dispute through **mediation**. If that fails, Escrow Agent will
244     submit the dispute, if so required by Florida law, to Escrow Agent's choice of arbitration, a Florida court or the Florida Real
245     Estate Commission. **Buyer** and **Seller** will be bound by any resulting award, judgment or order.
246     **(b) All other disputes: Buyer** and **Seller** will have 30 days from the date a dispute arises between them to attempt to
247     resolve the matter through mediation, failing which the parties will resolve the dispute through neutral binding **arbitration**
248     in the county where the Property is located. The arbitrator may not alter the Contract terms or award any remedy not
249     provided for in this Contract. The award will be based on the greater weight of the evidence and will state findings of fact
250     and the contractual authority on which it is based. If the parties agree to use discovery, it will be in accordance with the
251     Florida Rules of Civil Procedure and the arbitrator will resolve all discovery-related disputes. Any disputes with a real
252     estate licensee or firm named in Paragraph **19** will be submitted to arbitration only if the licensee's broker consents in
253     writing to become a party to the proceeding. This clause will survive closing.
254     **(c) Mediation and Arbitration; Expenses:** "Mediation" is a process in which parties attempt to resolve a dispute by
255     submitting it to an impartial mediator who facilitates the resolution of the dispute but who is not empowered to impose a
256     settlement on the parties. Mediation will be in accordance with the rules of the American Arbitration Association ("AAA") or
257     other mediator agreed on by the parties. The parties will equally divide the mediation fee, if any. "Arbitration" is a process in
258     which the parties resolve a dispute by a hearing before a neutral person who decides the matter and whose decision is
259     binding on the parties. Arbitration will be in accordance with the rules of the AAA or other arbitrator agreed on by the
260     parties. Each party to any arbitration will pay its own fees, costs and expenses, including attorneys' fees, and will equally
261     split the arbitrators' fees and administrative fees of arbitration.

262                                    **ESCROW AGENT AND BROKER**
263 **17. ESCROW AGENT**: **Buyer** and **Seller** authorize Escrow Agent to receive, deposit and hold funds and other items in escrow and,
264 subject to clearance, disburse them upon proper authorization and in accordance with Florida law and the terms of this Contract,
265 including disbursing brokerage fees. The parties agree that Escrow Agent will not be liable to any person for misdelivery of escrowed
266 items to **Buyer** or **Seller**, unless the misdelivery is due to Escrow Agent's willful breach of this Contract or gross negligence. If Escrow
267 Agent interpleads the subject matter of the escrow, Escrow Agent will pay the filing fees and costs from the deposit and will recover
268 reasonable attorneys' fees and costs to be paid from the escrowed funds or equivalent and charged and awarded as court costs in
269 favor of the prevailing party. All claims against Escrow Agent will be arbitrated, so long as Escrow Agent consents to arbitrate.

270 **18. PROFESSIONAL ADVICE; BROKER LIABILITY:** Broker advises **Buyer** and **Seller** to verify all facts and representations that are
271 important to them and to consult an appropriate professional for legal advice (for example, interpreting contracts, determining the
272 effect of laws on the Property and transaction, status of title, foreign investor reporting requirements, etc.) and for tax, property
273 condition, environmental and other specialized advice. **Buyer** acknowledges that Broker does not reside in the Property and that all
274 representations (oral, written or otherwise) by Broker are based on **Seller** representations or public records. **Buyer agrees to rely**
275 **solely on Seller, professional inspectors and governmental agencies for verification of the Property condition, square footage**
276 **and facts that materially affect Property value. Buyer** and **Seller** respectively will pay all costs and expenses, including reasonable
277 attorneys' fees at all levels, incurred by Broker and Broker's officers, directors, agents and employees in connection with or arising
278 from **Buyer's** or **Seller's** misstatement or failure to perform contractual obligations. **Buyer** and **Seller** hold harmless and release
279 Broker and Broker's officers, directors, agents and employees from all liability for loss or damage based on **(1)** **Buyer's** or **Seller's**
280 misstatement or failure to perform contractual obligations; **(2)** Broker's performance, at **Buyer's** and/or **Seller's** request, of any task
281 beyond the scope of services regulated by Chapter 475, F.S., as amended, including Broker's referral, recommendation or retention
282 of any vendor; **(3)** products or services provided by any vendor; and **(4)** expenses incurred by any vendor. **Buyer** and **Seller** each
283 assume full responsibility for selecting and compensating their respective vendors. This paragraph will not relieve Broker of statutory
284 obligations. For purposes of this paragraph, Broker will be treated as a party to this Contract. This paragraph will survive closing.

285 **19. BROKERS**: The licensee(s) and brokerage(s) named below are collectively referred to as "Broker." **Instruction to Closing**
286 **Agent:** Seller and **Buyer** direct closing agent to disburse at closing the full amount of the brokerage fees as specified in separate
287 brokerage agreements with the parties and cooperative agreements between the brokers, except to the extent Broker has
288 retained such fees from the escrowed funds. In the absence of such brokerage agreements, closing agent will disburse
289 brokerage fees as indicated below. This paragraph will not be used to modify any MLS or other offer of compensation made by
290 **Seller** or listing broker to cooperating brokers.

291* **Buyer** (_____) (_____) and **Seller** (_____) (_____) acknowledge receipt of a copy of this page, which is Page 5 of 7 Pages.
FAR-8   Rev. 10/04   © 2004   Florida Association of REALTORS®   All Rights Reserved

## Residential Sale and Purchase Contract (continued)

292* _____
293* *Selling Sales Associate/License No.* _____     *Selling Firm/Brokerage Fee: ($ or % of Purchase Price)* _____

294* _____
295* *Listing Sales Associate/License No.* _____     *Listing Firm/Brokerage fee: ($ or % of Purchase Price)* _____

296                              **ADDENDA AND ADDITIONAL TERMS**

297  **20. ADDENDA:** The following additional terms are included in addenda and incorporated into this Contract (check if applicable):

298* ❏ A. Condo. Assn.          ❏ H. As Is w/Right to Inspect    ❏ O. Interest-Bearing Account    ❏ V. Prop. Disclosure Stmt.
299* ❏ B. Homeowners' Assn.     ❏ I. Inspections                 ❏ P. Back-up Contract            ❏ W. FIRPTA
300* ❏ C. Seller Financing      ❏ J. Insulation Disclosure       ❏ Q. Broker - Pers. Int. in Prop. ❏ X. 1031 Exchange
301* ❏ D. Mort. Assumption      ❏ K. Pre-1978 Housing Stmt. (LBP) ❏ R. Rentals                    ❏ Y. Additional Clauses
302* ❏ E. FHA Financing         ❏ L. Insurance                   ❏ S. Sale/Lease of Buyer's Property ❏ Other_____
303* ❏ F. VA Financing          ❏ M. Housing Older Persons       ❏ T. Rezoning                    ❏ Other_____
304* ❏ G. New Mort. Rates       ❏ N. Unimproved/Ag. Prop.        ❏ U. Assignment                  ❏ Other_____

305* **21. ADDITIONAL TERMS:** _____
306* _____
307* _____
308* _____
309* _____
310* _____
311* _____
312* _____
313* _____
314* _____
315* _____
316* _____
317* _____
318* _____
319* _____
320* _____
321* _____
322* _____
323* _____
324* _____
325* _____
326* _____
327* _____
328* _____
329* _____
330* _____
331* _____
332* _____
333* _____
334* _____
335* _____
336* _____
337* _____
338* _____
339* _____
340* _____
341* _____
342* _____
343* _____
344* _____
345* _____
346* _____
347* _____

348* **Buyer** (____) (____) and **Seller** (____) (____) acknowledge receipt of a copy of this page, which is Page 6 of 7 Pages.
FAR-8   Rev. 10/04   © 2004   Florida Association of REALTORS®   All Rights Reserved

## Residential Sale and Purchase Contract (continued)

349    This is intended to be a legally binding contract. If not fully understood, seek the advice of an attorney prior to signing.

350    OFFER AND ACCEPTANCE

351* (**Check if applicable:** ❏ **Buyer** received a written real property disclosure statement from **Seller** before making this Offer.)

352    **Buyer** offers to purchase the Property on the above terms and conditions. Unless this Contract is signed by **Seller** and a copy

353* delivered to **Buyer** no later than _____ ❏ a.m. ❏ p.m. on _____, _____, this offer will be revoked

354    and **Buyer's** deposit refunded subject to clearance of funds.

355* Date: _____    **Buyer:** _____

356*    Print name: _____

357* Date: _____    **Buyer:** _____

358* Phone: _____    Print name: _____

359* Fax: _____    Address: _____

360* E-mail: _____    _____

361* Date: _____    **Seller:** _____

362*    Print name: _____

363* Date: _____    **Seller:** _____

364* Phone: _____    Print name: _____

365* Fax: _____    Address: _____

366* E-mail: _____    _____

367    COUNTER OFFER/REJECTION

368* ❏ **Seller** counters **Buyer's** offer (to accept the counter offer, **Buyer** must sign or initial the counter offered terms and deliver a copy

369* of the acceptance to **Seller** by 5:00 p.m. on _____, _____). ❏ **Seller** rejects **Buyer's** offer.

370*    **Effective Date:** _____ (The date on which the last party signed or initialed acceptance of the final offer.)

371* **Buyer** (____) (____) and **Seller** (____) (____) acknowledge receipt of a copy of this page, which is Page 7 of 7 Pages.

The Florida Association of REALTORS and local Board/Association of REALTORS make no representation as to the legal validity or adequacy of any provision of this form in any specific transaction. This standardized form should not be used in complex transactions or with extensive riders or additions. This form is available for use by the entire real estate industry and is not intended to identify the user as a REALTOR. REALTOR is a registered collective membership mark that may be used only by real estate licensees who are members of the National Association of REALTORS and who subscribe to its Code of Ethics.

The copyright laws of the United States (17 U.S. Code) forbid the unauthorized reproduction of blank forms by any means including facsimile or computerized forms.

FAR-8    Rev. 10/04    © 2004    Florida Association of REALTORS®    All Rights Reserved

## Property Management Cash Flow Statement

Your firm logo here

### PROPERTY CASH FLOW STATEMENT

Owner: _____    Report period: _____

Property location: _____    Prepared by: _____

| Item | % | Actual | Budget | Comments |
|---|---|---|---|---|
| Cash Receipts | | | | |
|    Gross rents collected | | | | |
|    Other: | | | | |
|    Other: | | | | |
|    Total cash collected | | $ | $ | |
| Cash Disbursements | | | | |
|    Accounting & Legal | | | | |
|    Advertising | | | | |
|    Insurance | | | | |
|    Management fee | | | | |
|    Payroll | | | | |
|    Property taxes | | | | |
|    Repairs and maintenance | | | | |
|    Services:   janitorial<br>lawn<br>pest control<br>trash | | | | |
|    Supplies | | | | |
|    Utilities:   electric<br>gas & oil<br>water & sewer | | | | |
|    Other: | | | | |
|    Other: | | | | |
|    Other: | | | | |
|    Other: | | | | |
| Monthly mortgage payment | | | | |
| Total cash disbursements | | $ | $ | |
| Cash flow (deficit) | | $ | $ | |

## Change of Status

**DBPR RE-2050-1 – Request for Change of Status**
REV 12/01

*Florida's Future...*
**Right Here.**
**Right Now.**

**STATE OF FLORIDA**
**DEPARTMENT OF BUSINESS AND PROFESSIONAL**
**REGULATION**
**1940 North Monroe Street**
**Tallahassee, FL 32399-0783**

### CHECK ACTION REQUESTED

**Transaction Type:**
- ❑ Become Active – no charge
- ❑ Become Inactive – no charge
- ❑ Add/Delete Trade Name – no charge
- ❑ Become Sole Proprietor – no charge
- ❑ Change Broker/Owner Employer – no charge
- ❑ Terminate Employee – no charge
- ❑ Add/Delete PA - $30.00 fee required
- ❑ Request for Multiple License - $95.00

### SALESPERSON INFORMATION

License Number

Applicant Name

### BROKER OR CORPORATION INFORMATION

| Broker License Number | Corporation/Partnership License Number |
|---|---|

Broker or Corporation Name

Trade Name (if applicable)

Are you now or with the issuance of this license an officer or director of any corporation or partnership which acts as a broker?  Yes ❑  No ❑

If yes, please list name of entity

### ATTEST STATEMENT
### REQUIRES SIGNATURE OF EMPLOYING BROKER
### (EXCEPT FOR ADD/DELETE PA - WHICH MAY BE SIGNED BY THE LICENSEE)

**I affirm that I have provided the above information completely and truthfully to the best of my knowledge.**

Sign Here:_____ Date: _____

**Mail this form to:**

**Division of Real Estate**
**Hurston North Tower**
**Suite N309**
**400 West Robinson Street**
**Orlando, FL 32801**

97. What is the difference between effective gross income and net operating income?
    a. Before-tax cash flow
    b. Vacancy
    c. Operating expenses
    d. Cash throwoff

98. The relationship between supply and demand for a particular type of multifamily property at its current rental level is reflected by the:
    a. rental market's equilibrium.
    b. turnover of tenants whose leases expire.
    c. area's location quotient.
    d. occupancy rate for that type of property.

99. The best and least expensive method of renting or leasing residential properties is the use of:
    a. referrals from satisfied tenants.
    b. newspaper classified ads.
    c. radio ads of 30 seconds or less.
    d. short, relatively inexpensive television commercials.

100. Marilyn is searching for a new apartment. When she drives through the entrance of The Fountains, she gets a wonderful impression and decides to rent if the price is right. Marilyn's first impression is called:
    a. market value.
    b. eye invitation.
    c. curb appeal.
    d. comparative market analysis.

# GLOSSARY

## A

**abstract.**  A history of a property shown by the public records used to give an opinion of title. Less frequently used today than title insurance.

**adjustable-rate mortgage (ARM).**  A loan that allows the borrower's interest rate to fluctuate based on some external index beyond the control of the lender.

**adjustments.**  The method used by brokers and appraisers to account for differences in comparable properties. If a subject property is superior, the appraiser makes a dollar adjustment increasing the sale price of the comparable. If the subject property is inferior to the comparable property, a negative adjustment is made.

**after-tax cash flow.**  The amount remaining to an owner of income property after all expenses, debt service, and income taxes have been paid.

**agency.**  The relationship of agents and their principals.

**agent.**  A person who represents another person in a fiduciary relationship.

**ambiguity.**  A statement that is unclear or may have several meanings.

**annual mortgage constant.**  The factor that, if multiplied by the original loan balance, will result in the annual mortgage payment; the mortgage payment's percentage of the original loan.

**annual percentage rate (APR).**  An expression of credit costs over the life of a loan, taking into account the contract interest rate plus lender fees for originating, processing, and closing a mortgage loan.

**antitrust.**  Federal law that prohibits monopolistic practices such as price fixing.

**appraisal.**  An unbiased estimate of a property's market value.

**appraising.**  The process of estimating the market value of property.

**arm's-length transaction.**  A business transaction in which the parties are dealing in their own self-interest, not being under the control of the other party. One of the requirements before a comparable sale should be used in an appraisal.

**assets.**  Things of value owned by a person or organization.

**automated underwriting.**  The evaluation of a mortgage loan application using predetermined formulas and credit scores. Fannie Mae's *Desktop Underwriter* performs automated underwriting.

**automated valuation.**  The use of computers and linear regression formulas to calculate the market value of property based on large numbers of comparable sales.

## B

**before-tax cash flow (BTCF).**  The amount of spendable income from an income property after paying operating expenses and debt service, but before the effect of income taxes.

**bilateral contract.**  A contract that requires both parties to perform, such as a sales contract.

**biweekly mortgage.**  A mortgage that requires that the borrower make payments every two weeks (26 payments per year). The payment is calculated by dividing the monthly mortgage payment by two. The effective result is that the borrower makes 13 monthly payments per year.

**blockbusting.**  The illegal act of a licensee who frightens homeowners into selling by raising fears that minority homeowners are moving into a neighborhood.

**body language.**  Nonverbal communication expressed by the position of the body, hands, arms, legs, or facial expressions.

**browser.**  A software program that makes access to Web pages possible. *Netscape* and *Internet Explorer* are examples.

**buyer agency.**  The fiduciary relationship between a buyer and the buyer's single-agent broker.

**buyer brokerage agreement.**  An agreement between a buyer and a broker for the broker to provide services to a buyer for compensation. The broker may be acting as a single agent, a transaction broker, or a nonrepresentative.

## C

**calculated interest rate.**  The interest rate in an adjustable-rate mortgage that is calculated by adding the margin to the index.

**canvassing.**  Prospecting for buyers or sellers by telephoning or walking door-to-door.

**cap.**  The maximum amount that an interest rate can increase per year, or during the life of a loan.

**capitalization rate.**   The net operating income divided by the property value. A percentage representing the return on the investment, assuming the property was purchased for cash.

**cash flow report.**   A property manager's monthly report to the owner, showing cash receipts and cash disbursements of an income property.

**certified check.**   A check issued by a bank guaranteeing payment. The buyer is usually required to bring a certified check to closing by most title closing agents to speed disbursement at closing.

**Certified Property Manager (CPM).**   A professional designation awarded by the Institute of Real Estate Management (IREM) to a property manager who has successfully completed required education and experience.

**closing statement.**   A detailed accounting of charges and credits for the buyer and the seller in a real estate transaction.

**Coastal Construction Control Line (CCCL).**   An imaginary line established by Florida counties a specified distance from the mean high water mark of the Atlantic Ocean or the Gulf of Mexico that prohibits construction seaward from the line.

**collateral.**   Something of value given as security for a debt. In real estate, the mortgage pledges the property as collateral for the repayment of the loan.

**commission.**   Compensation for professional services that is usually calculated as a percentage of the property's sales price.

**community association manager.**   An individual licensed by the Department of Business and Professional Regulation who is paid to perform certain functions for a residential homeowners' association.

**compact disc (CD) drive.**   A part of the computer that allows the user to access information or programs on a compact disc.

**comparable property.**   A similar property in the same market area that may be used to help estimate the value of the property being appraised.

**comparative market analysis (CMA).**   Similar to the comparable sales approach used by appraisers, but usually less detailed. Used by brokers and sales associates to estimate the most likely selling price of properties they are listing or selling.

**computer-assisted design (CAD).**   A software program that assists the user in making technical drawings.

**computer valuation.**   The use of computers and linear regression formulas to estimate the market value of property based on large numbers of comparable sales.

**concurrency.**   A state law requiring that infrastructure such as roads, sewers, schools, etc., be in place as development occurs.

**Consent to Transition to Transaction Broker Notice.**   A disclosure form that allows a single agent to become a transaction broker. The notice must be signed by the principal before the broker can make the change.

**contingency.**   A condition in a contract that, unless satisfied, may make the contract voidable by one of the parties.

**contract.**   An agreement between two or more parties to do or not do a specific act.

**contraction.**   The phase of a business cycle that begins after a recession when economic conditions worsen.

**contract service.**   A property maintenance service that is done by an individual or company not in the employ of the property manager.

**cooperative sale.**   Sale of a property by a broker who is not the listing broker. Normally, commissions are split between the two brokerage firms.

**corrective maintenance.**   The repairs to a building's structure and equipment following breakdown.

**counteroffer.**   A substitution for the original offer made by the offeree who changes the price or terms offered, sending it back to the offeror. The original offer is terminated. The original offeree becomes the offeror.

**crash.**   The termination of a software program on a computer so that all unsaved data in random access memory is lost. Usually, the computer must be restarted.

**credit scoring.**   A method of credit reporting using a numeric score. A higher score reflects a person with better credit history.

**cross-defaulting clause.**   A mortgage clause that results in a default of a junior mortgage in case a senior mortgage becomes delinquent.

**curb appeal.**   The impression, good or bad, that is made when a person first looks at a house from the street.

**customer.**   A person who works with a sales associate or a broker. While the person could be a principal, the usual definition is that the broker is either a transaction broker or has no brokerage relationship with the person.

**cycle.**   Periodic fluctuations of the overall economy, or any part of the economy, between good times and bad. The four parts of a general cycle are expansion, recession, contraction, and recovery.

**cyclic fluctuation.**   Part of an economic cycle.

## D

**database.**   A listing of information in a form that allows easy manipulation and reporting. It is also the name for a software program that makes the organization of information easier.

**deferred maintenance.**   Maintenance that needs to be done, but has not been done for some reason, usually economic.

**designated sales associate.**   A sales associate who is appointed by a broker to be a single agent for a buyer or seller in a nonresidential transaction when another sales associate in the firm has been appointed to be the single agent for the other party in the transaction. Both buyer and seller must have assets of at least $1 million and agree to the arrangement.

**digital camera.**   A camera that does not use conventional film, but instead stores images in a memory chip in the camera, ready to be loaded into a computer for display or printing.

**disclosure.**   The revelation of information important to a transaction.

**documentary stamp taxes.**   A tax on a real estate transaction that may be levied on the sales price of a property or on the amount of a mortgage note.

**dual agent.**   An illegal arrangement whereby the broker tries to represent both the buyer and the seller in the same transaction.

**dynamic risk.**   Uninsurable risk, such as that of an economic downturn.

## E

**effective gross income (EGI).**   The amount of rent and other income actually collected by the owner. When preparing an income statement, vacancy and collection losses are deducted from potential gross income, and other income such as vending machine collections is added.

**e-mail.**   Electronic mail that is sent over the Internet.

**equity.**   The amount of the owner's portion of the property value after deducting mortgages and other liens.

**ethical.**   The right thing to do. Usually a higher standard than legality.

**exclusive-agency listing.**   A listing that requires that the owner pay the listing broker if the property is sold by any broker, but allows the owner to personally sell the property without being liable for a commission.

**exclusive-right-of-sale listing.**   A listing that requires that the owner pay the listing broker no matter who sells the property. The broker is automatically the procuring cause of the sale.

**executed contract.**   A contract in which nothing else remains to be done. All requirements have been performed by the parties.

**executory contract.**   A contract in which part of the agreement remains to be done. It has not yet "closed."

**exercised.**   Used in connection with an option contract. An option contract is a unilateral contract until the optionee agrees to purchase and is then said to have "exercised" the option.

**expansion.**   The phase of a business cycle that begins after a recovery when economic conditions improve.

**express contract.**   An oral or written agreement where the words specifically describe the intent of the parties.

## F

**fact of execution.**   The acceptance of an offer. The offeree or his licensee must communicate the fact of execution to the offeror in order to make a valid contract.

**Fair Housing Act.**   The federal law that prohibits discrimination in housing based on race, color, religion, sex, national origin, familial status, and handicap.

**fallback list.**   A list of properties similar to the property being advertised that can be used by the licensee if the advertised property does not appeal to the person responding to the ad.

**false or misleading statement.**   In real estate, a statement made by a licensee or party in a real estate transaction that is not factual.

**FAR Residential Sale and Purchase Contract.**   The most widely used contract in Florida, prepared and updated regularly by the Florida Association of REALTORS® .

**farm.**   A geographic area selected for special prospecting attention by a real estate licensee.

**federally related transaction.**   A real estate transaction financed by a lender insured by the federal government or a loan insured or guaranteed by the federal government that requires the services of an appraiser.

**fee.**   Compensation, either as a fixed dollar amount or a percentage of the sale price.

**FICO score.**   A proprietary numeric credit score used to evaluate a prospective borrower, developed by Fair, Isaacs & Co.

**fiduciary relationship.**   A relationship of trust and confidence between an agent and principal.

**fixed-rate mortgage.**   A loan secured by real estate that has the same rate of interest for the life of the loan.

**Foreign Investment in Real Property Tax Act (FIRPTA).**   A federal law for aliens and alien corporations for U.S. income tax requiring that the buyer withhold a percentage of the sale price as taxes on the gain from the sale of a real property interest located in the United States.

**for-rent-by-owner**   An owner who attempts to rent his or her own property without using a broker.

**for-sale-by-owner** An owner who attempts to sell his or her own property without using a broker.

**funding fee.** A charge levied by the Department of Veteran's Affairs to veterans who use VA loans.

## G

**gross domestic product (GDP).** The sum total of goods and services produced by the United States. The four major components of GDP are consumption, investment, government purchases, and net exports.

## H

**hardware.** Tangible computer equipment that runs programs, called *software*.

**http.** A prefix for Web site addresses, meaning "hypertext transport protocol."

**hyperlink.** A link on a Web page that, when clicked, transports the user to another Web page.

**hypertext.** The text, usually colored blue and underlined, in a Web page that is the hyperlink to another Web page.

## I

**implied contract.** An agreement not spelled out in words, where the agreement of the parties is demonstrated by their acts and conduct.

**index.** An indicator beyond the control of a lender to which the interest rate on an adjustable-rate mortgage is tied.

**infrastructure.** The system of public works for a country, state, or region, such as roads, schools, sewers, water treatment facilities, etc.

**inkjet printer.** A printer that uses an ink spray for black and color printing.

**innocent purchaser status.** An amendment to the Comprehensive Environmental Response, Compensation, and Liability Act (CERCLA) that exempts from liability landowners who made reasonable inquiries about hazardous substances before purchasing the property.

**Institute of Real Estate Management (IREM).** A national organization of property managers affiliated with the National Association of REALTORS®.

**intangible tax.** A tax of 2 mills (.002) levied on the amount of new mortgage indebtedness.

**Internet.** The global network of computers connected by cable and phone lines.

**Internet service provider.** A company or organization that acts as the portal for a user to gain access to the Internet.

## J

**jargon.** A word or expression related to a specific vocation that a layperson may not understand.

## K

**k.** The symbol for the annual mortgage constant, calculated by dividing the annual payment of principal and interest by the original amount of the loan.

**keysafe.** A lockbox holding the key to the home, usually attached to a door handle allowing licensees who are members of the MLS easy access to the property.

## L

**laptop.** A small computer designed for travel that can run on battery power.

**laser printer.** A printer using a toner bonded to the paper by laser and heat.

**latent defects addenda.** A disclosure by the seller that informs the seller of a duty to disclose known property defects and to hold the licensee harmless for the seller's failure to disclose.

**leverage.** The use of borrowed money with the intent to increase the investor's return on the cash invested. If the return on the investment is greater than the interest rate paid by the borrower, the owner has positive leverage.

**liabilities.** Amounts owed by a person.

**listing agreement.** An agreement between a seller and a broker whereby the seller agrees to pay the broker a commission if the broker is successful in selling the property.

**loan constant.** Calculated by dividing the annual payment of principal and interest by the original amount of the loan.

**loan processing procedures.** Steps taken by a lender to ensure that underwriting and documentation of a mortgage loan are done in a manner that reduces the lender's exposure to loss.

**loan underwriting.** The evaluation of risk when a lender makes a mortgage loan to reduce the lender's exposure to loss.

**lockbox.** A secure box holding the key to the home, usually attached to a door handle allowing licensees who are members of the MLS easy access to the property by using a special access key to the box.

## M

**margin.** The additional percentage added to the index on an adjustable-rate mortgage, resulting in the calculated interest rate.

**marketing knowledge.** A licensee's knowledge of the sales process, including the psychology of selling, advertising, personal marketing, and prospecting.

**material fact.** An important fact that may affect a buyer's decision to buy or a seller's decision to sell. Licensees must disclose facts that materially affect the value of residential property.

**misrepresentation.**   A false or misleading statement made intentionally or unintentionally, or the failure to disclose a material fact.

**modem.**   A device allowing a computer to communicate with other computers by phone lines or cable.

**mortgage insurance premium (MIP).**   The amount paid by a borrower for insurance that protects the lender against loss in case of the borrower's default. FHA mortgage insurance is called *MIP*.

**mutual recognition.**   An agreement between states to recognize a licensee's education obtained in another state. Florida has mutual recognition agreements with several states that exempt licensees in those states from taking a Florida prelicense course if the licensee can pass a 40-question test on Florida real estate law.

### N

**negative amortization.**   A situation occurring, usually under a graduated payment mortgage, where the payment on the loan is less than the amount required to pay the accrued interest. The unpaid interest is added to the principal balance of the loan, and the loan balance gradually increases.

**net operating income (NOI).**   The income from an investment property remaining after operating expenses have been paid from the effective gross income.

**net worth.**   The amount remaining when liabilities are subtracted from assets.

**new construction maintenance.**   Work done on an income property designed to enhance the property's appeal to tenants. Includes adding new wallpaper, carpeting, and light fixtures.

**No Brokerage Relationship Notice.**   A disclosure that must be given by a licensee who does not represent a buyer or seller before entering into an agreement or showing a property.

**nonverbal communication.**   Unspoken communication expressed by the position of the body, hands, arms, legs, or facial expressions, commonly called *body language*.

### O

**open listing.**   A nonexclusive agreement in which a seller agrees to pay a broker if the broker sells the property. The broker is not paid if the seller or another broker sells the property.

**operating expenses (OE).**   Costs of operating an income property. Includes property taxes, maintenance, insurance, payrolls, and reserves for replacements.

**opinion of value.**   A broker's price opinion, usually based on a comparative market analysis.

**option contract.**   An agreement that allows one party to buy, sell, or lease real property for specified terms within a specified time limit.

### P

**paperless mortgage.**   A mortgage that is "signed" electronically, using digital signatures.

**passive prospecting**   A method of prospecting that does not include direct face-to-face or telephone conversations. Advertising and direct mail are examples of passive prospecting.

**performance.**   The completion of a contract's requirements.

**PITI payment.**   The payment required of a borrower that includes principal, interest, taxes, and insurance.

**planned unit development (PUD).**   A residential development designed to have mixed land uses and a high residential density.

**point.**   A lender's charge to the borrower that increases the lender's yield. One point is equal to 1 percent of the loan amount.

**potential gross income (PGI).**   The total annual income a property would produce if it were 100 percent occupied, with no vacancy or collection loss.

**power prospecting.**   A type of prospecting that seeks to make contact with many more buyers and sellers and that results in much higher income levels.

**preclosing walk-through inspection.**   An inspection of the house by the buyer, done sometime before the sale closes, to determine that the property is in the same condition as it was when the contract was signed and to ensure that all required repairs have been completed.

**prequalification.**   The preliminary process during which a prospective lender evaluates the buyer's ability to obtain a mortgage loan. Most licensees want a buyer to be prequalified or preapproved before showing properties.

**preventive maintenance.**   A work program designed to preserve the physical integrity of the premises and eliminate the more costly corrective maintenance.

**previewing properties.**   The activity a licensee uses to stay abreast of the market and to find specific properties to show to a prospective buyer.

**principal.**   (1) The person who enters into a fiduciary relationship with a single-agent licensee. (2) The amount of money remaining due on a mortgage loan.

**prioritize.**   To set up a list of activities in an order based on their importance.

**private mortgage insurance (PMI).** The amount paid by a borrower for insurance that protects the lender against loss in case of the borrower's default. Conventional lenders use the term *private mortgage insurance;* FHA mortgage insurance is called *MIP.*

**product knowledge.** A licensee's familiarity with the real estate market and specific properties available for sale.

**professional ethics.** A body of accepted codes of behavior for a specific industry.

**profile sheet.** A form designed to organize the gathering and input of property listing information into the multiple-listing service.

**profit and loss statement.** A detailed report of the income and expenses of an investment property over a stated period of time.

**property characteristics.** The features of a property that are used as a basis of comparison in an appraisal or comparative market analysis.

**property condition disclosure.** A form designed for disclosure to a buyer of any property defects. The form is normally signed by the seller, and the buyer signs a receipt that the buyer has received the disclosure.

## Q

**qualifying.** The process used by a licensee to determine whether to spend time working with a buyer or seller. For example, a buyer would first be qualified financially, then based on motivation to buy.

**quality of income.** A lender's analysis of factors that reveal the likelihood of the borrower's income continuing over a long period of time.

**quantity of income.** The total amount of a borrower's income from all sources.

**quasi-contract.** A contract that is imposed by law to prevent unjust enrichment. For example, if a person's bank made an error in the person's favor, the quasi-contract invented by the courts would require that the person repay the bank.

## R

**radon gas.** A colorless, odorless gas occurring from the natural breakdown of uranium in the soil. Many experts believe radon gas to be the second leading cause of lung cancer.

**random access memory (RAM).** Dynamic memory in a computer that disappears when the computer is turned off. Information in the RAM would be lost if it were not saved on the hard drive.

**random changes.** Irregular fluctuations of the economy that may be caused by legislative and judicial decisions, wars, weather, etc.

**Real Estate Settlement Procedures Act (RESPA).** A federal law requiring disclosure of loan closing costs in certain real estate financial transactions.

**recession.** Two successive quarterly declines in the Gross Domestic Product (GDP). This is the point at which economic activity has peaked and will be followed by a contraction.

**reconciliation.** The final step in the appraisal process before the report is prepared. The correlation of property values derived from each of the three appraisal approaches into a single estimate of value.

**recovery.** Two successive quarterly increases in the Gross Domestic Product (GDP). This is the point at which economic activity has bottomed and will be followed by expansion.

**redlining.** A lender's refusal to loan money in an area based on illegal discrimination.

**refinancing.** Placing a new mortgage on a property to replace another mortgage.

**Regulation Z.** The part of the Truth-in-Lending Act that requires that lenders calculate and disclose the effective annual percentage rate to the consumer.

**reserves for replacements.** A portion of an investment property's income that is set aside to pay the cost of replacing major building components when necessary.

**resident manager.** A salaried individual employed for specific management functions for a single investment property.

**rewritable CD drive (CD-RW).** A computer device that writes information, graphics, or music onto a compact disc.

**rider.** An attachment to a contract.

**routine maintenance.** The most common maintenance performed on an investment property, such as grounds care and housekeeping.

## S

**sales contract (contract for sale and purchase).** A bilateral agreement in which a buyer agrees to purchase a seller's property at a specified price and terms.

**scanner.** A computer device that allows the user to copy a document or picture and for use in a computer.

**search engine.** A Web site that has indexed millions of Web pages, allowing users to locate information by entering key words.

**seasonal variation.** Changes in the economy (for example, winter tourism in Florida) that recur at regular intervals at least once a year.

**seller agency.** The relationship of a single agent and his principal, the seller.

**Seller's Net Proceeds Form.**   A form used to show the seller's equity, expenses, and prorations, as well as the net amount the seller is estimated to receive as proceeds from the sale of the property.

**servicing the listing.**   The actions of a licensee who stays in touch with a seller regularly, getting feedback from licensees who have shown the property, sending the seller copies of advertisements, and generally keeping the seller informed of the marketing efforts.

**show list.**   A selected inventory of apartments that are available for inspection by prospective tenants.

**single agent.**   A broker who represents either the seller or the buyer in a real estate transaction, but not both.

**Single Agent Notice.**   A disclosure form informing the principal of the duties of his single agent.

**software.**   Computer programs designed specifically to perform specialized functions.

**specific cycles.**   Wavelike movements similar to business cycles that occur in specific sectors of the general economy, such as the real estate market.

**spreadsheet.**   A software program using columns and rows that allows the user to create formulas that act on the numbers stored in the spreadsheet. A change in one amount will change other numbers or totals in the spreadsheet, making "what-if" scenarios simple.

**static risk.**   Risk that is quantifiable and insurable. For example, the risk of fire is a static risk. Fire insurance will transfer the risk from the owner to the insurance company.

**statute of frauds.**   A body of law that requires certain contracts, such as those for the sale of real property, to be written.

**steering.**   The illegal, discriminatory act of a sales associate who brings buyers into an area based on the racial or ethnic makeup of the neighborhood.

**subject property.**   The property being appraised.

**surfing.**   The actions of a person using the Internet who visits many Web sites.

### T

**targeted strangers**   Persons not known to a licensee who are qualified as prospects by income, occupation, or residence address.

**technical knowledge.**   The knowledge needed by licensees to properly conduct their business that relates to filling out contracts, preparing seller's proceeds estimates, doing comparative market analyses, etc.

**thumbnail.**   A picture reduced in size to save loading time that, when clicked on in a Web page, is converted to full size.

**time is of the essence.**   A contract clause that requires strict compliance with all dates and times specified in the contract. If a party fails to perform some act by the time specified, the person may be in default.

**time management**   The organization of a person's day to maximize efficiency. It includes planning, scheduling, and prioritizing.

**title insurance.**   A guarantee to reimburse a loss arising from defects in title or liens against real property.

**"to-do" list.**   A daily list, usually designed in priority order, of tasks to be completed that day.

**transactional characteristics.**   The factors related to a real estate transaction itself, such as time of sale, and financing terms.

**transaction broker.**   A licensee who has limited representation to the buyer and/or the seller in a transaction. Instead of being an advocate for the buyer or the seller, the licensee is working for the contract.

**Transaction Broker Notice.**   A disclosure form disclosing the transaction broker's duties to buyers and sellers.

**Truth-in-Lending Act.**   A federal law that requires that lenders inform consumers of exact credit costs before they make their purchases.

### U

**unconscionable contract.**   An agreement that a court may declare unenforceable because it would be grossly unfair to one party if enforced.

**Uniform Resource Locator (URL).**   A specific Web site address, such as *http://www.dearborn-fla.com*.

**Uniform Standards of Professional Appraisal Practice (USPAP).**   Strict requirements for appraisers interpreted and amended by the Appraisal Standards Board. Florida appraisers and brokers who prepare appraisals must follow the guidelines.

**unilateral contract.**   A contract in which only one of the parties is required to perform, such as an option contract. The optionor must sell if the optionee exercises the option, but the optionee is not required to buy.

### V

**valid contract.**   An agreement that complies with all the essentials of a contract and is binding on all parties.

**verbal communications skills.**   The ability to speak effectively one-on-one or in a group presentation.

**voidable contract.**   An agreement that may be canceled by the party who would be damaged if the contract were enforced.

**void contract.**   An agreement that is not binding on either party.

**W**

**warranty of owner.**   A hold harmless clause in a listing agreement whereby the seller warrants that all information given to the broker is correct.

**World Wide Web.**   A collection of millions of documents on the Internet.

**written communication skills.**   The ability to communicate effectively in letters, e-mails, and other documents.

# I N D E X

# Post-Licensing Education for Real Estate Sales Associates
## Student Feedback Survey

Thank you for using this text to complete your post-licensing education requirement. We would appreciate your taking time to help make this a better course. We will use your comments to make this text current, relevant and useful.

Date:_____

A. At what school did you take this course? _____

B. When did you complete the course? Month: _____ Year:_____

C. Overall, I found the textbook to be:  ❑ excellent   ❑ good   ❑ fair   ❑ poor

D. What new subject areas do you think should be added to future editions of the book?

_____

E.  Is your license active or inactive?   ❑ active   ❑ inactive

F. Other comments concerning this text:

_____

_____

**Thank you for your comments.**
**We will give them careful consideration when planning the next edition.**

Post-Licensing Education for Real Estate Sales Associates
Sixth Edition

NOTE: This page, when folded over and taped, becomes a postage-free envelope that has been approved by the United States Postal Service. It has been provided for your convenience.

Important—Please Fold Over and Tape Before Mailing

- - - - - - - - - - - - - - - - - - - - - - - - - - - - - - - - - - - - - - - - - - - - - - - - - - - - - - - - - - - - - - - - - - - - - - - - - - - - - - - - - - - - - -

Important—Please Fold Over and Tape Before Mailing

- - - - - - - - - - - - - - - - - - - - - - - - - - - - - - - - - - - - - - - - - - - - - - - - - - - - - - - - - - - - - - - - - - - - - - - - - - - - - - - - -

Return Address:

_____

_____

_____

# BUSINESS REPLY MAIL

FIRST CLASS MAIL     PERMIT NO. 88176    CHICAGO, IL

POSTAGE WILL BE PAID BY ADDRESSEE:

Dearborn™
Real Estate Education
30 South Wacker Drive, Suite 2500
Chicago, Illinois 60606-7481

Attn: Editorial Department